HIDEYUKI FURUHASHI

At last, we're diving into the final big event. This has been a wonderful series that's already run for far longer than expected, but I want to see the story through and do it justice!

BETTEN COURT

I had to keep doing the serialized chapters in the middle of a move to a new house, so preparing the content for this volume was tougher than it's ever been…

D0167479

MY HERO ACADEMIA VIGILANTES

VOLUME 12
SHONEN JUMP Edition

STORY: HIDEYUKI FURUHASHI
ART: BETTEN COURT
ORIGINAL CONCEPT: KOHEI HORIKOSHI

Translation & English Adaptation/Caleb Cook
Touch-Up Art & Lettering/John Hunt
Designer/Julian [JR] Robinson
Editor/Mike Montesa

VIGILANTE -BOKU NO HERO ACADEMIA ILLEGALS-
© 2016 by Hideyuki Furuhashi, Betten Court, Kohei Horikoshi
All rights reserved.
First published in Japan in 2016 by SHUEISHA Inc., Tokyo.
English translation rights arranged by SHUEISHA Inc.

Printed in Canada

Published by VIZ Media, LLC
P.O. Box 77010
San Francisco, CA 94107

10 9 8 7 6 5 4 3 2 1
First printing, April 2022

MY HERO ACADEMIA
VIGILANTES

12

Writer / Letterer
Hideyuki Furuhashi

Penciller / Colorist
Betten Court

Original Concept
Kohei Horikoshi

【charisma】

noun | cha • ris • ma
: a superhuman power or talent;
or : the ability to inspire admiration and
devotion in others

CHARACTERS

[Vigilantes]

WANTED

POP☆STEP

(REAL NAME: KAZUHO HANEYAMA)

A self-styled freelance idol who gives impromptu live performances without the proper licensing or permits. Primary suspect in the Naruhata serial bombing case. Currently unconscious and receiving medical treatment for her grave condition.

WANTED

KNUCKLEDUSTER

(REAL NAME: UNKNOWN)

A middle-aged man of mystery who became the master Koichi never asked for. Though Quirkless, his fighting prowess is on par with pro heroes. Disappeared after the Sky Egg incident.

WANTED

THE CRAWLER

(REAL NAME: KOICHI HAIMAWARI)

A college senior and good-natured young man who started out his vigilante career under the moniker "Nice Guy," while making use of his Slide and Glide Quirk. Material witness in the Naruhata bombing case.

[Allies]

THE RAPPER

Brawler in the underground fighting club.

TIGER BUNNY

Mysterious bunny-eared high school girl.

SOGA KUGISAKI

Leader of a trio of ruffians in Naruhata.

MAKOTO TSUKAUCHI

Detective Tsukauchi's younger sister.

STORY

What is "justice" anyway? Get ready for a PLUS ULTRA spin-off set in the world of *My Hero Academia*!!

Heroes. The chosen ones who, with explicit government permission, use their natural talents, or Quirks, to aid society. However, not everyone can be chosen, and some take action of their own accord, becoming illegal heroes. What does justice mean to them? And can we really call them heroes? This story takes to the streets in order to follow the exploits of those known as *vigilantes*.

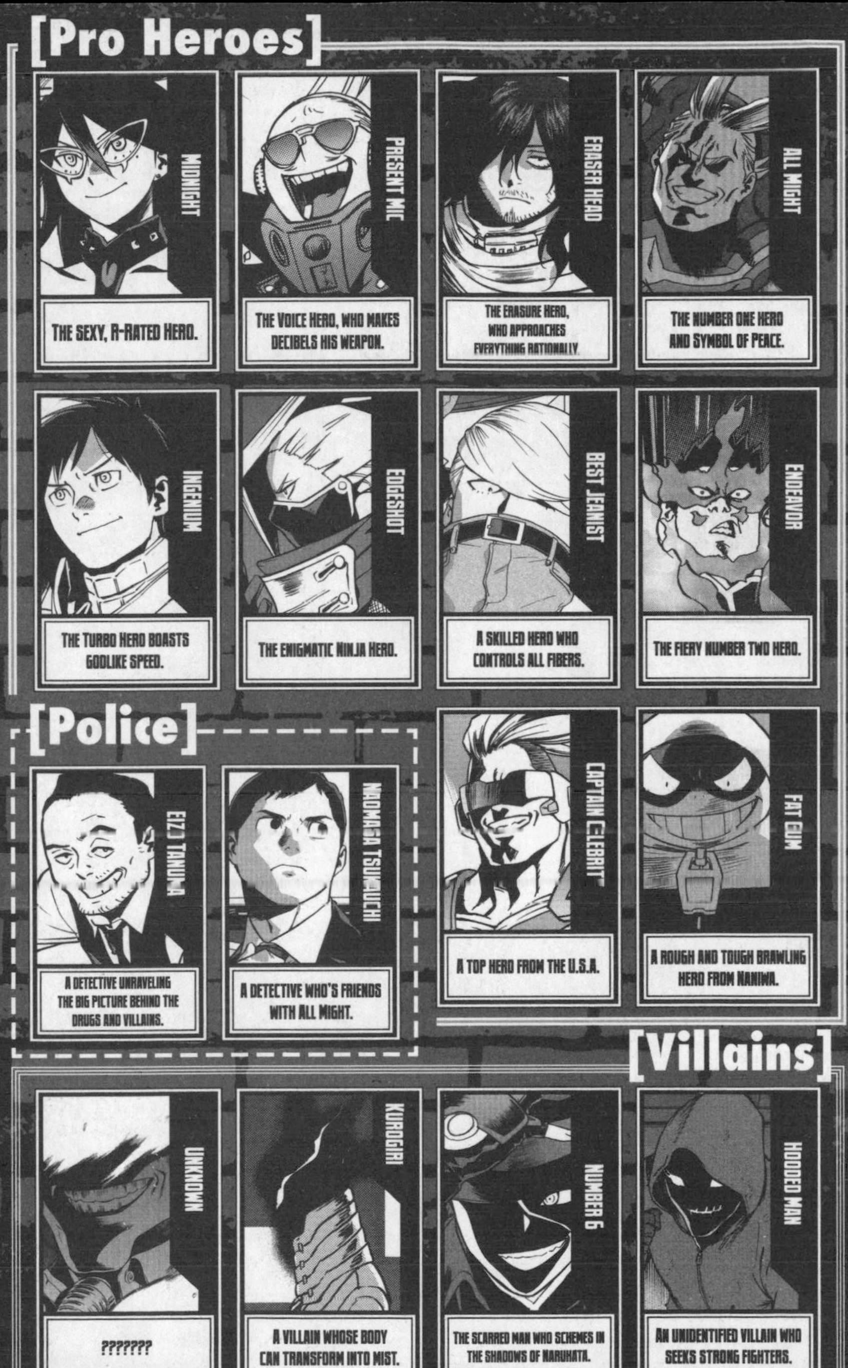
[Pro Heroes]
MIDNIGHT
THE SEXY, R-RATED HERO.
PRESENT MIC
THE VOICE HERO, WHO MAKES DECIBELS HIS WEAPON.
ERASER HEAD
THE ERASURE HERO, WHO APPROACHES EVERYTHING RATIONALLY.
ALL MIGHT
THE NUMBER ONE HERO AND SYMBOL OF PEACE.
INGENIUM
THE TURBO HERO BOASTS GODLIKE SPEED.
EDGESHOT
THE ENIGMATIC NINJA HERO.
BEST JEANIST
A SKILLED HERO WHO CONTROLS ALL FIBERS.
ENDEAVOR
THE FIERY NUMBER TWO HERO.
[Police]
EIZO TANUMA
A DETECTIVE UNRAVELING THE BIG PICTURE BEHIND THE DRUGS AND VILLAINS.
NAOMASA TSUKAUCHI
A DETECTIVE WHO'S FRIENDS WITH ALL MIGHT.
CAPTAIN CELEBRITY
A TOP HERO FROM THE U.S.A.
FAT GUM
A ROUGH AND TOUGH BRAWLING HERO FROM NANIWA.
[Villains]
UNKNOWN
???????
KUROGIRI
A VILLAIN WHOSE BODY CAN TRANSFORM INTO MIST.
NUMBER 6
THE SCARRED MAN WHO SCHEMES IN THE SHADOWS OF NARUHATA.
HOODED MAN
AN UNIDENTIFIED VILLAIN WHO SEEKS STRONG FIGHTERS.

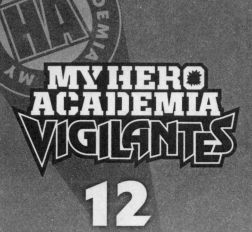

MY HERO ACADEMIA VIGILANTES

12

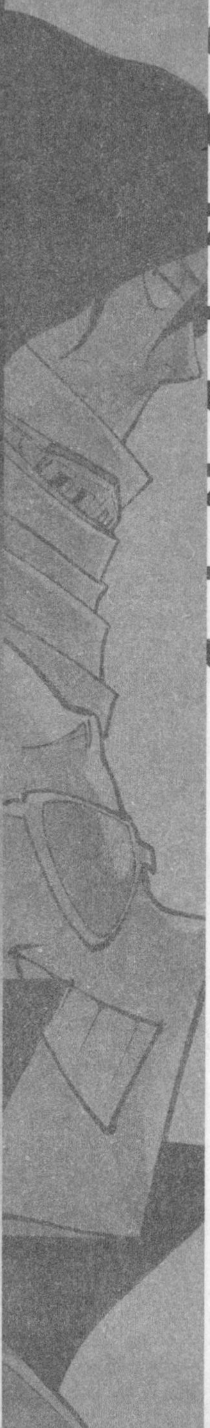

EP. 92 - MIGHT SIGNAL

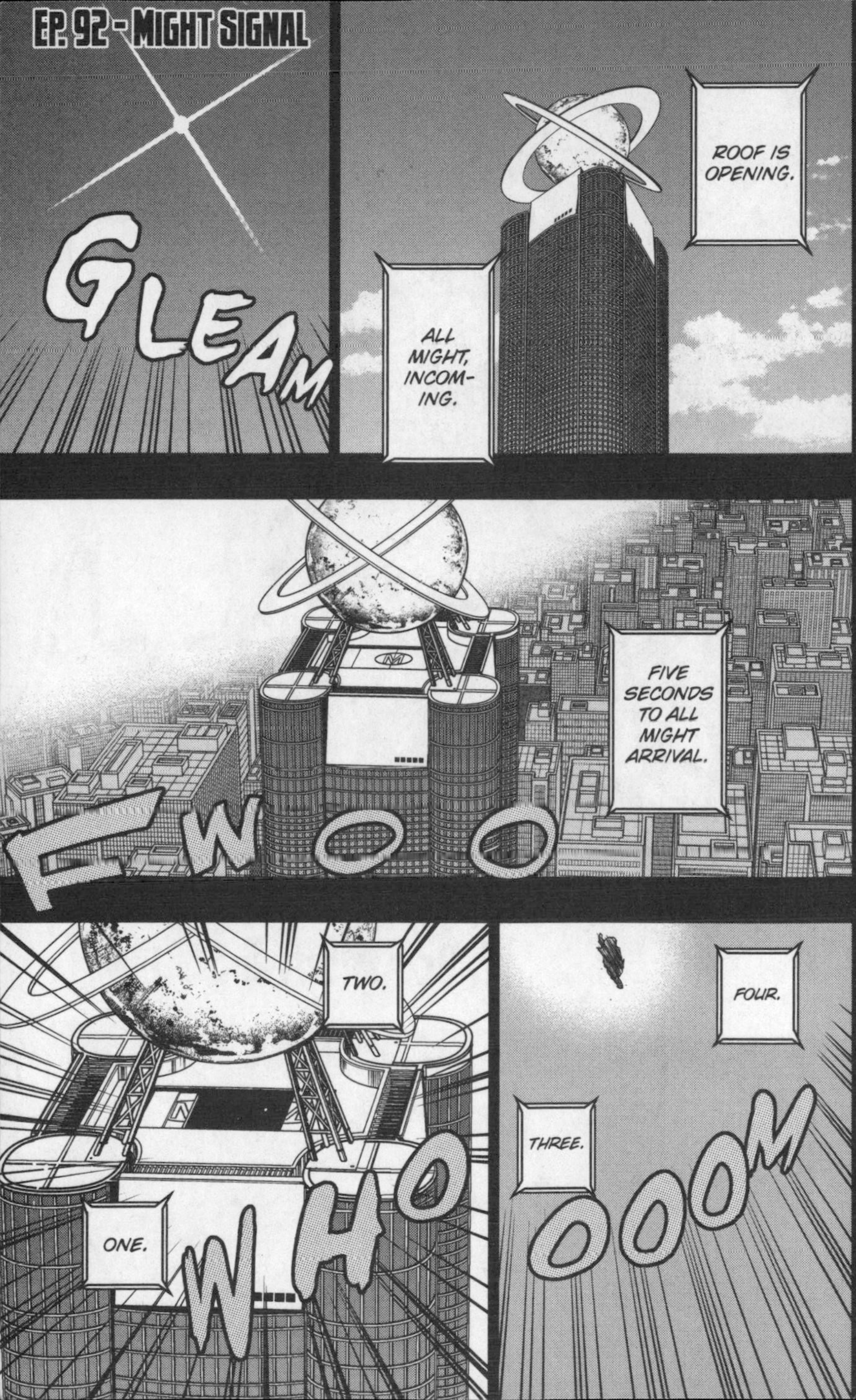
ROOF IS OPENING.
ALL MIGHT, INCOMING.
GLEAM
FIVE SECONDS TO ALL MIGHT ARRIVAL.
FWOOO
FOUR.
THREE.
TWO.
ONE.
WHOOOOM

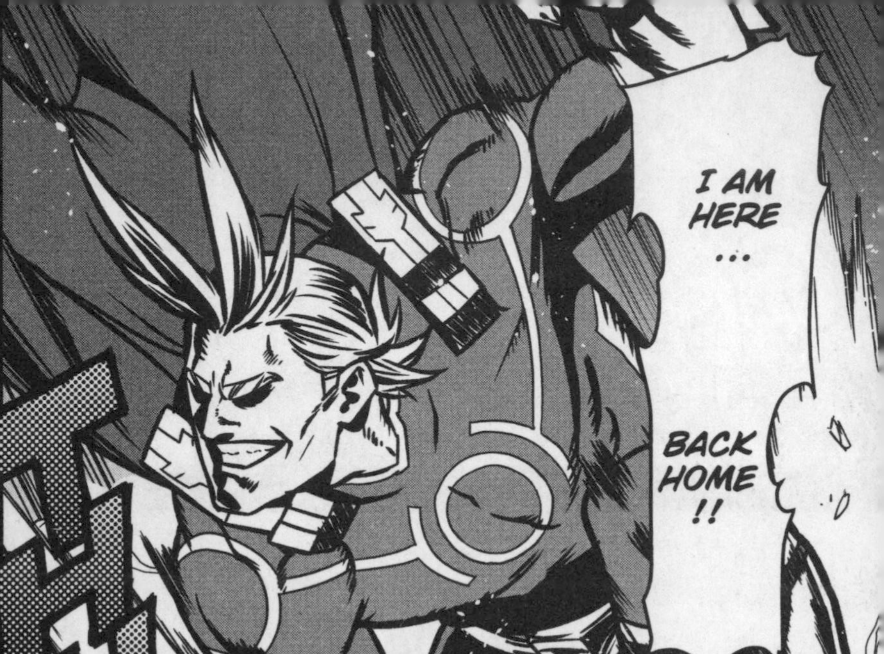
I AM HERE ...
BACK HOME !!
THUD!!

EP. 92 - MIGHT SIGNAL

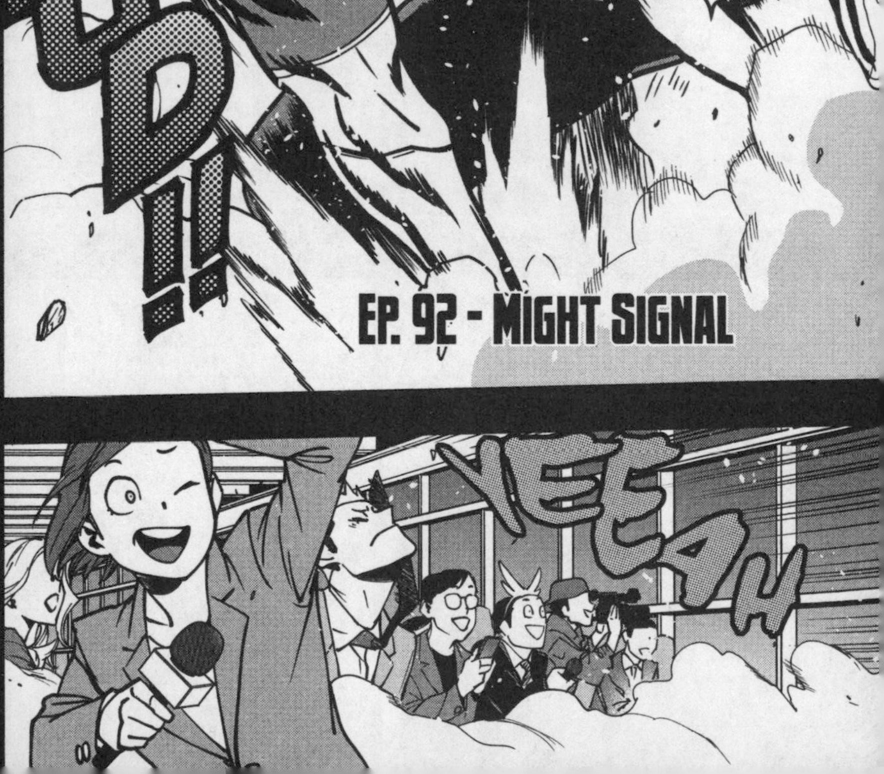
YEEEAH

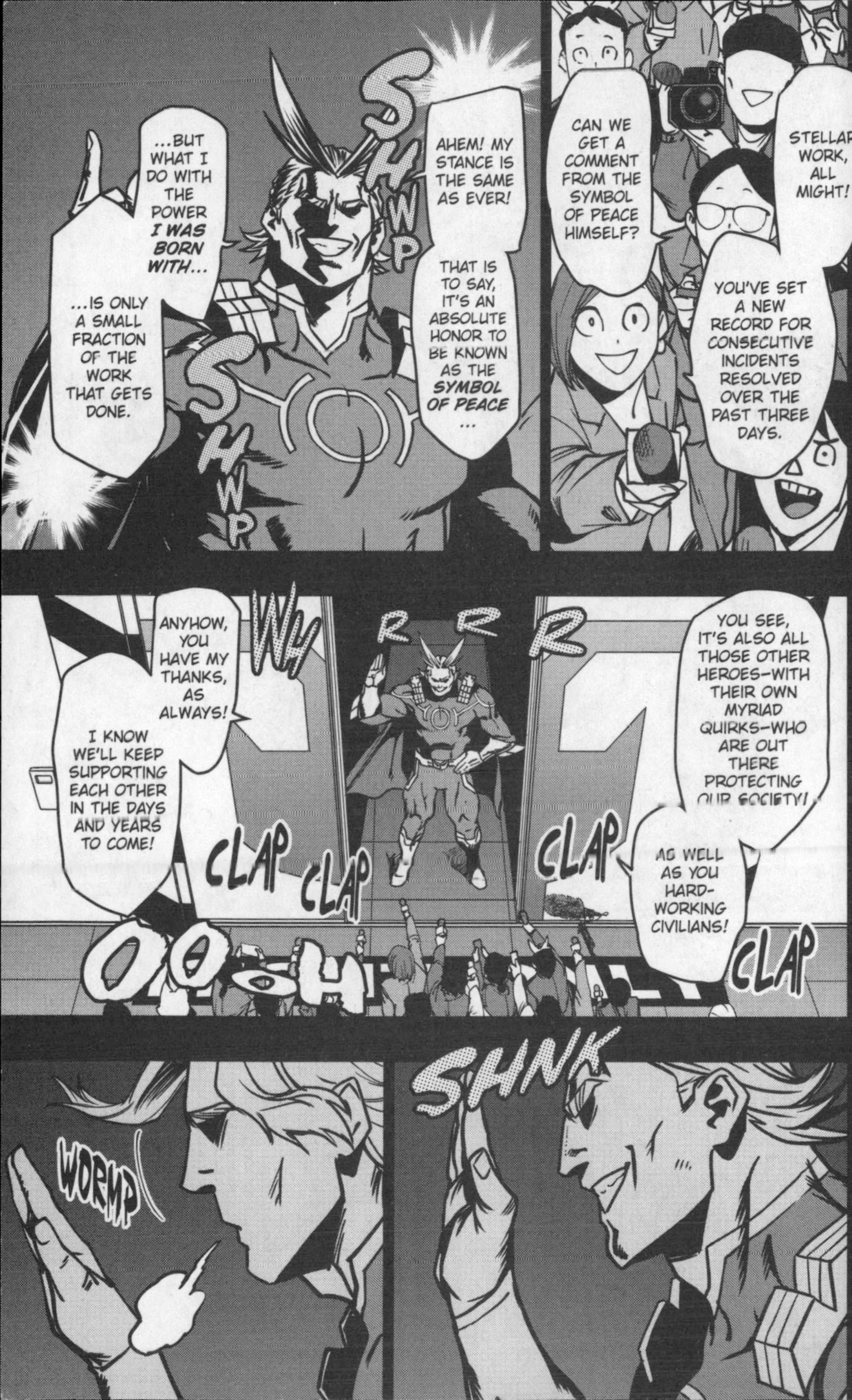
STELLAR WORK, ALL MIGHT!
CAN WE GET A COMMENT FROM THE SYMBOL OF PEACE HIMSELF?
YOU'VE SET A NEW RECORD FOR CONSECUTIVE INCIDENTS RESOLVED OVER THE PAST THREE DAYS.
AHEM! MY STANCE IS THE SAME AS EVER!
THAT IS TO SAY, IT'S AN ABSOLUTE HONOR TO BE KNOWN AS THE SYMBOL OF PEACE...
SHWP
...BUT WHAT I DO WITH THE POWER I WAS BORN WITH...
...IS ONLY A SMALL FRACTION OF THE WORK THAT GETS DONE.
SHWP
YOU SEE, IT'S ALSO ALL THOSE OTHER HEROES—WITH THEIR OWN MYRIAD QUIRKS—WHO ARE OUT THERE PROTECTING OUR SOCIETY!
AS WELL AS YOU HARD-WORKING CIVILIANS!
CLAP
CLAP
WHRRR
ANYHOW, YOU HAVE MY THANKS, AS ALWAYS!
I KNOW WE'LL KEEP SUPPORTING EACH OTHER IN THE DAYS AND YEARS TO COME!
CLAP
CLAP
OOOOH
SHNK
WORMP

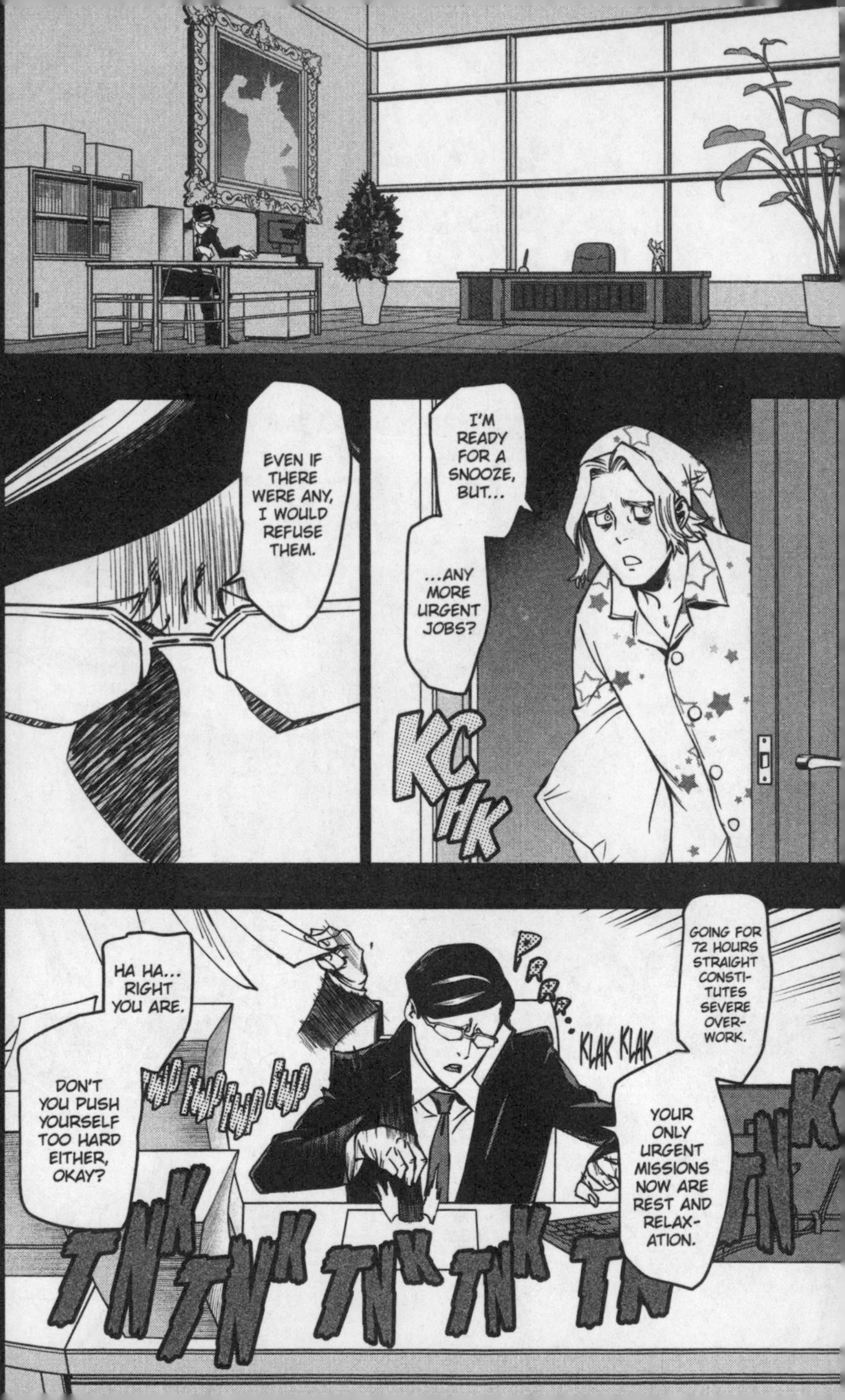
I'M READY FOR A SNOOZE, BUT...
...ANY MORE URGENT JOBS?
KCHK
EVEN IF THERE WERE ANY, I WOULD REFUSE THEM.
GOING FOR 72 HOURS STRAIGHT CONSTI-TUTES SEVERE OVER-WORK.
YOUR ONLY URGENT MISSIONS NOW ARE REST AND RELAX-ATION.
KLAK KLAK
HA HA... RIGHT YOU ARE.
DON'T YOU PUSH YOURSELF TOO HARD EITHER, OKAY?
TNK TNK TNK TNK TNK TNK

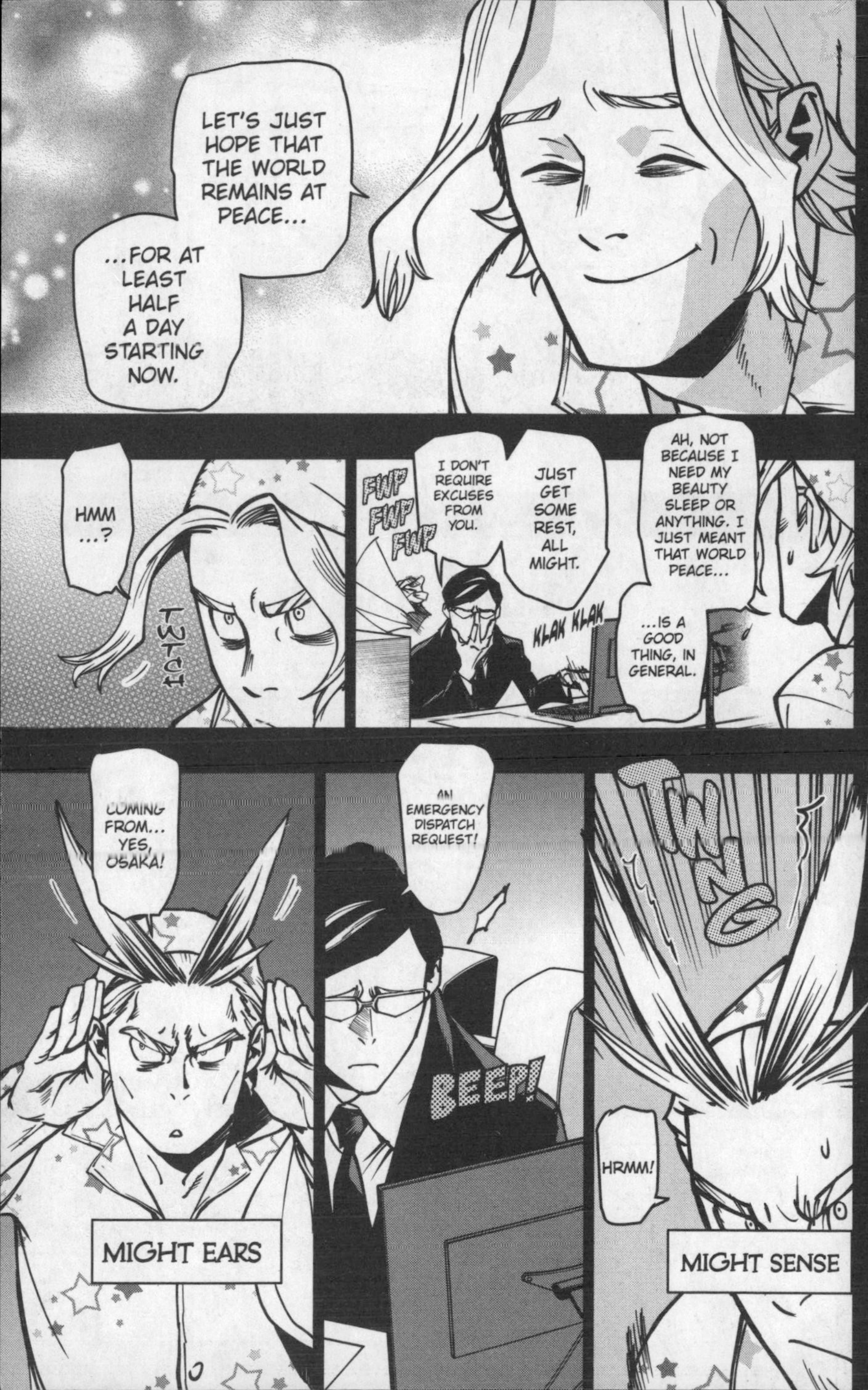
LET'S JUST HOPE THAT THE WORLD REMAINS AT PEACE...
...FOR AT LEAST HALF A DAY STARTING NOW.
AH, NOT BECAUSE I NEED MY BEAUTY SLEEP OR ANYTHING. I JUST MEANT THAT WORLD PEACE...
JUST GET SOME REST, ALL MIGHT.
I DON'T REQUIRE EXCUSES FROM YOU.
FWP FWP FWP
KLAK KLAK
...IS A GOOD THING, IN GENERAL.
HMM ...?
TWITCH
TWING
HRMM!
MIGHT SENSE
AN EMERGENCY DISPATCH REQUEST!
BEEP!
COMING FROM... YES, OSAKA!
MIGHT EARS

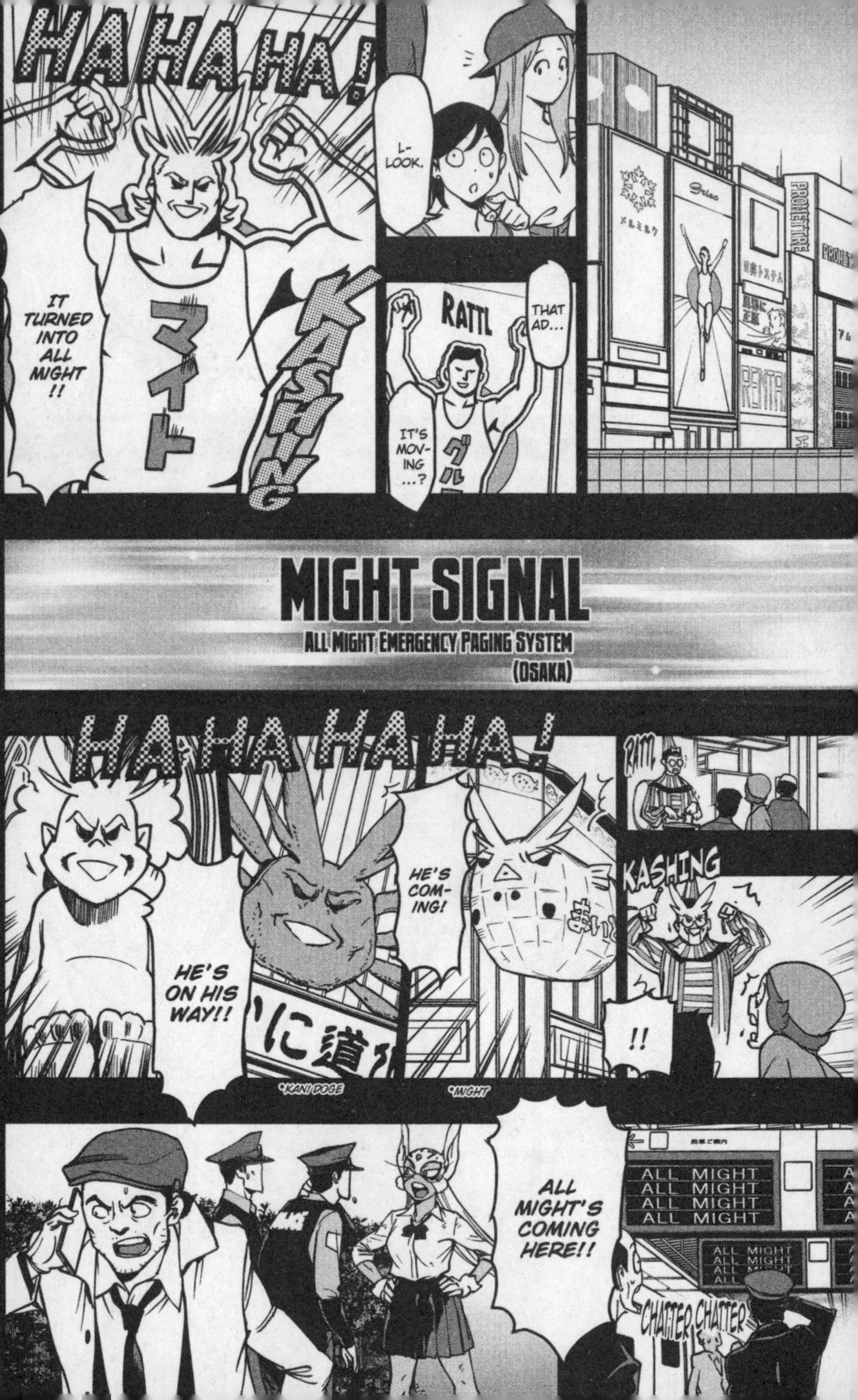
L-LOOK.
THAT AD...
RATTL
IT'S MOVING...?
HAHAHA!
IT TURNED INTO ALL MIGHT!!
KASHING
MIGHT SIGNAL
ALL MIGHT EMERGENCY PAGING SYSTEM
(OSAKA)
RATTL
KASHING
!!
HE'S COMING!
*MIGHT
HAHA HAHAHA!
HE'S ON HIS WAY!!
*KANI DOGE
ALL MIGHT
ALL MIGHT
ALL MIGHT
ALL MIGHT
ALL MIGHT'S COMING HERE!!
CHATTER CHATTER

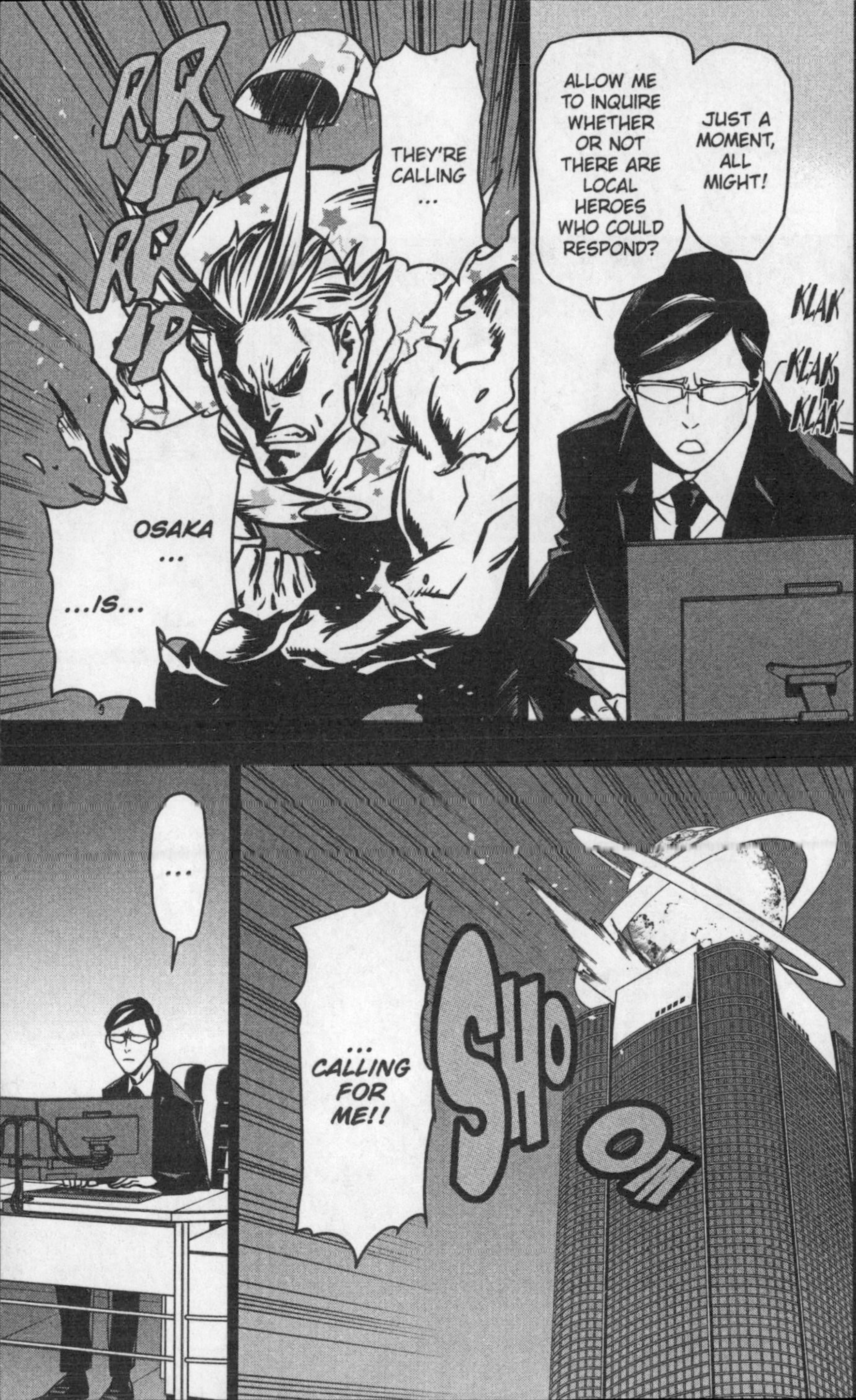

JUST A MOMENT, ALL MIGHT!
ALLOW ME TO INQUIRE WHETHER OR NOT THERE ARE LOCAL HEROES WHO COULD RESPOND?
KLAK
KLAK
KLAK
THEY'RE CALLING ...
RRIP
RRIP
OSAKA ...
...IS...
SHOOM
... CALLING FOR ME!!
...

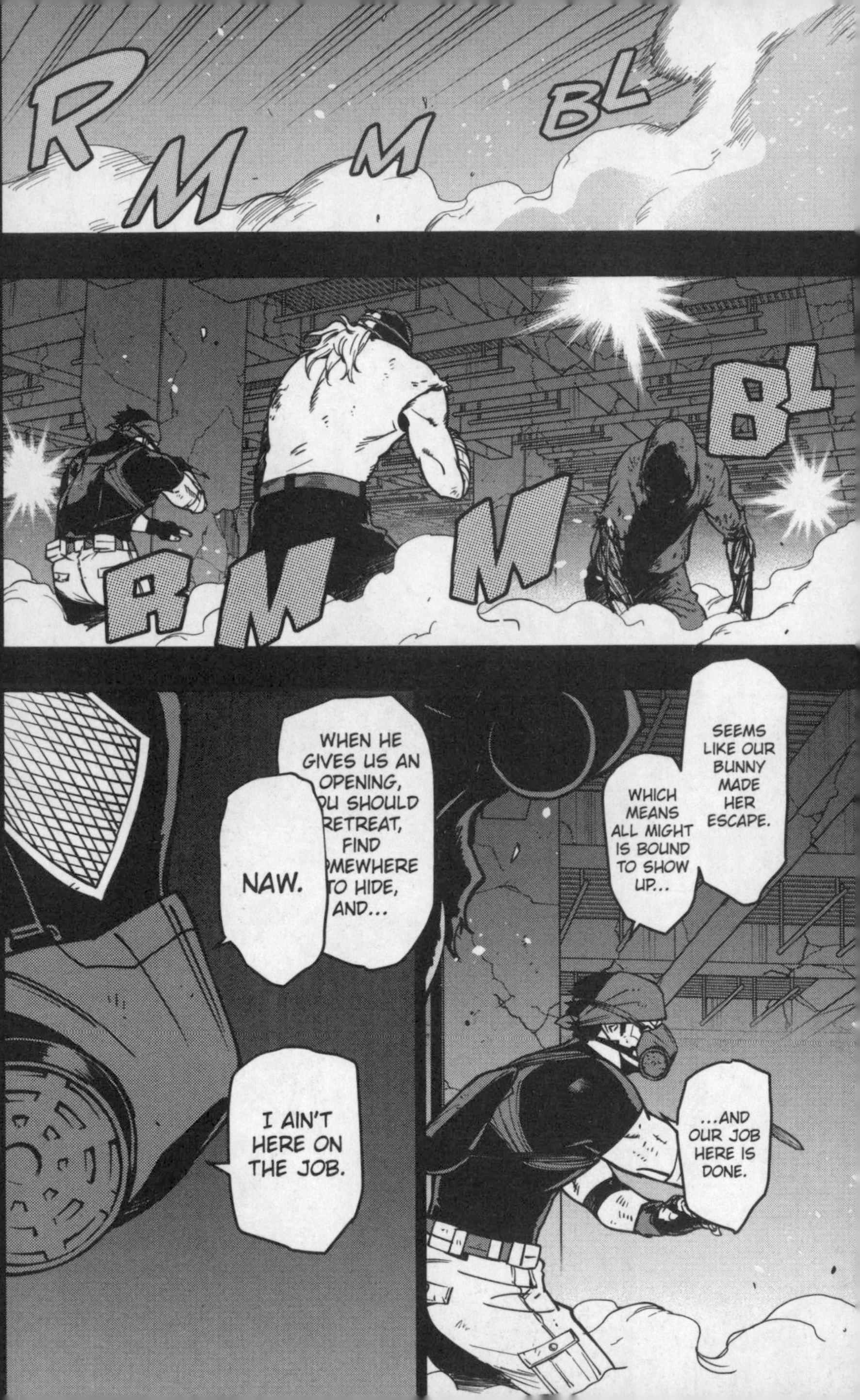
RMMMBL
RMMBL
SEEMS LIKE OUR BUNNY MADE HER ESCAPE.
WHICH MEANS ALL MIGHT IS BOUND TO SHOW UP...
...AND OUR JOB HERE IS DONE.
WHEN HE GIVES US AN OPENING, OU SHOULD RETREAT, FIND OMEWHERE TO HIDE, AND...
NAW.
I AIN'T HERE ON THE JOB.

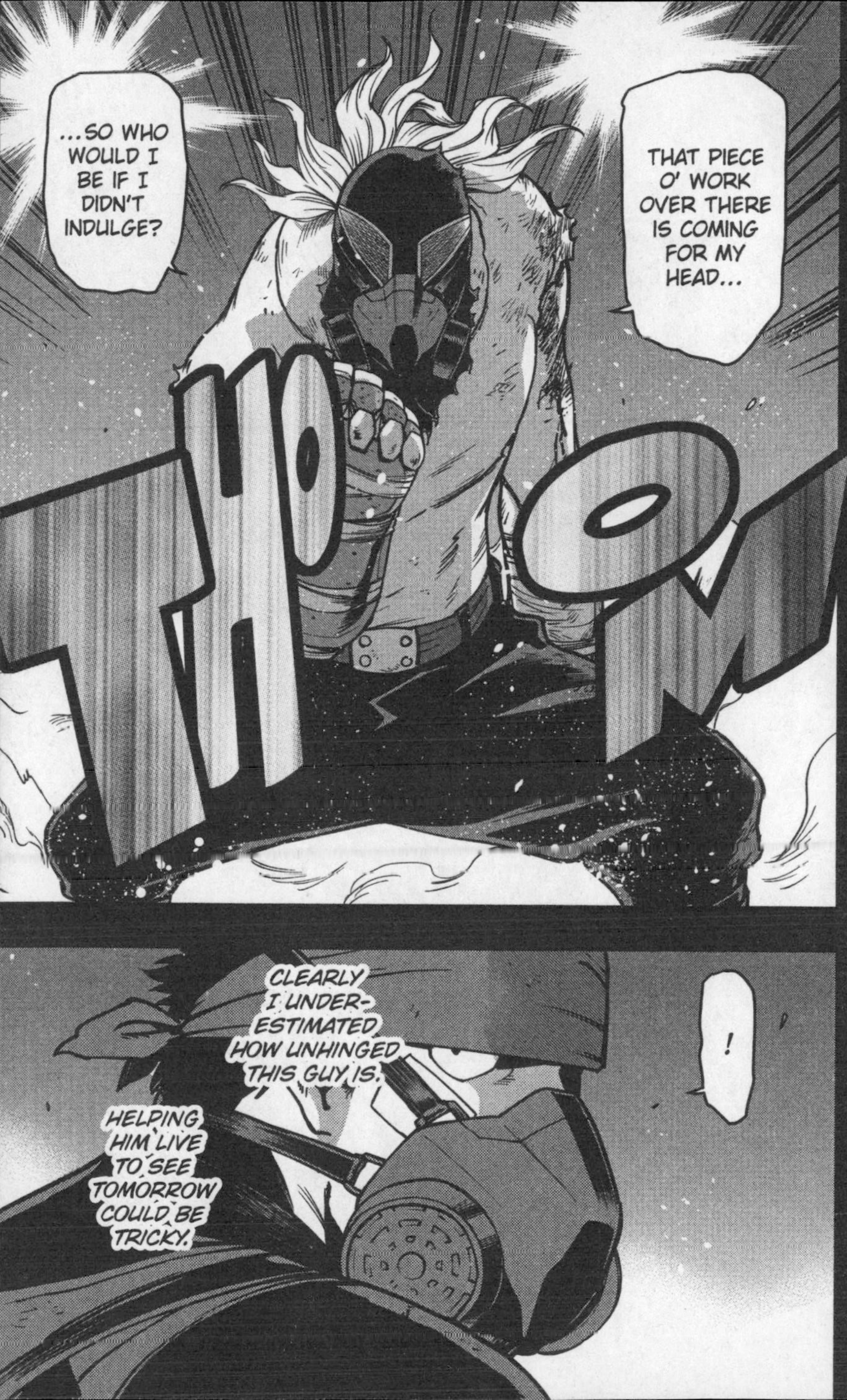
THAT PIECE O' WORK OVER THERE IS COMING FOR MY HEAD...
...SO WHO WOULD I BE IF I DIDN'T INDULGE?
THOOM
!
CLEARLY I UNDER-ESTIMATED HOW UNHINGED THIS GUY IS.
HELPING HIM LIVE TO SEE TOMORROW COULD BE TRICKY.

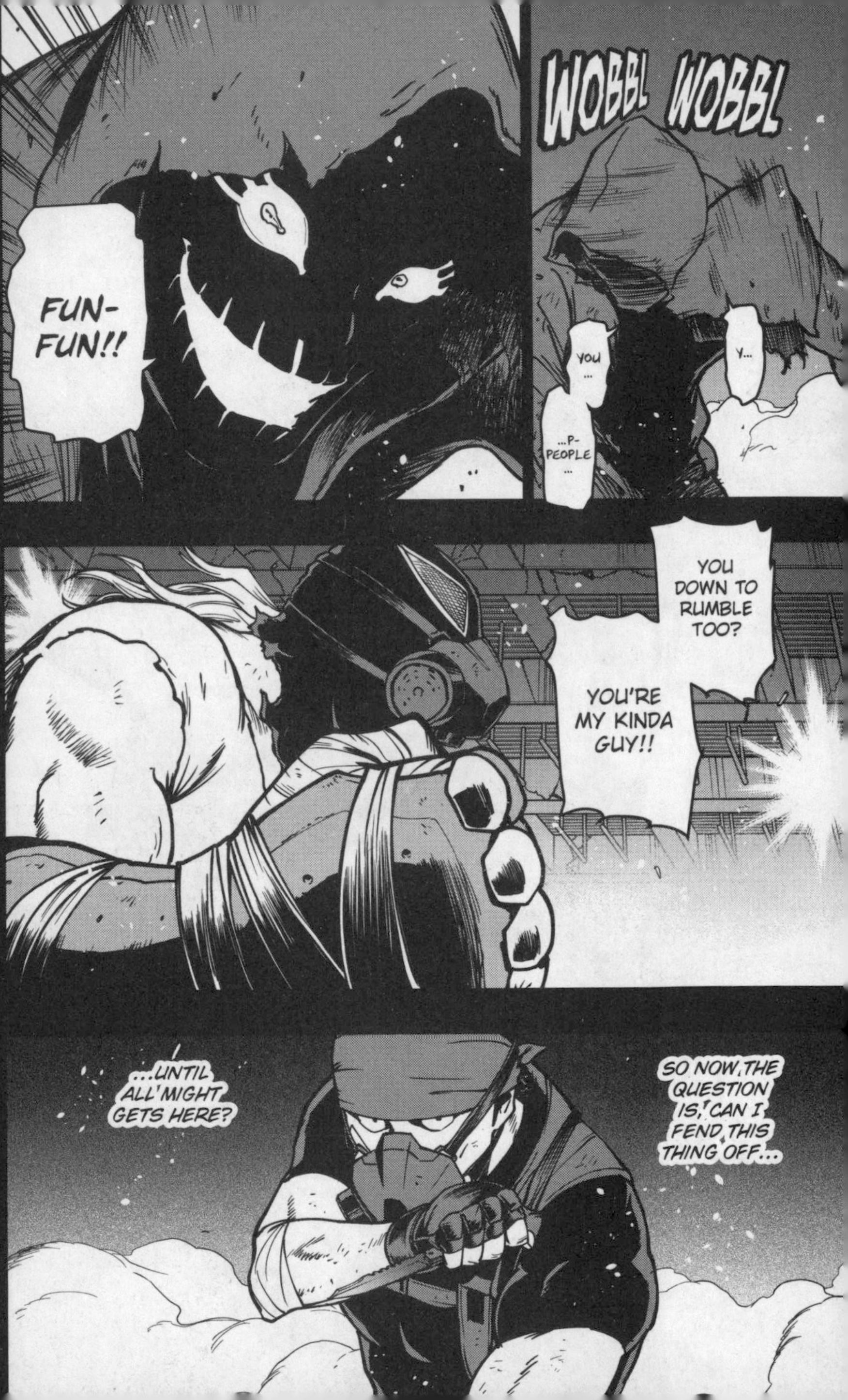
WOBBL WOBBL
Y...
YOU ...
...P-PEOPLE ...
FUN-FUN!!
YOU DOWN TO RUMBLE TOO?
YOU'RE MY KINDA GUY!!
SO NOW THE QUESTION IS, CAN I FEND THIS THING OFF...
...UNTIL ALL MIGHT GETS HERE?

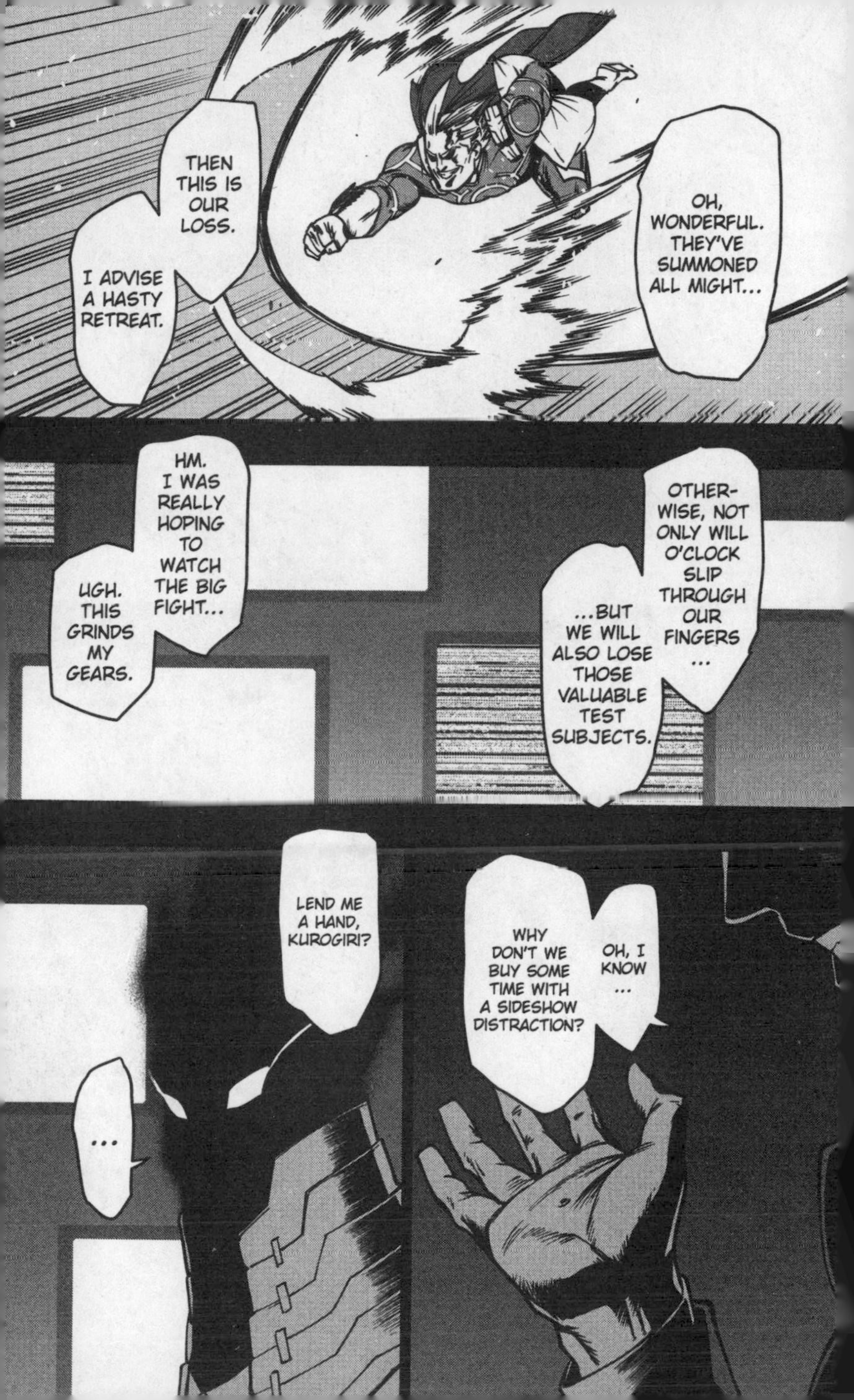
OH, WONDERFUL. THEY'VE SUMMONED ALL MIGHT...
THEN THIS IS OUR LOSS.
I ADVISE A HASTY RETREAT.
OTHER-WISE, NOT ONLY WILL O'CLOCK SLIP THROUGH OUR FINGERS...
...BUT WE WILL ALSO LOSE THOSE VALUABLE TEST SUBJECTS.
HM. I WAS REALLY HOPING TO WATCH THE BIG FIGHT...
UGH. THIS GRINDS MY GEARS.
OH, I KNOW...
WHY DON'T WE BUY SOME TIME WITH A SIDESHOW DISTRACTION?
LEND ME A HAND, KUROGIRI?
...

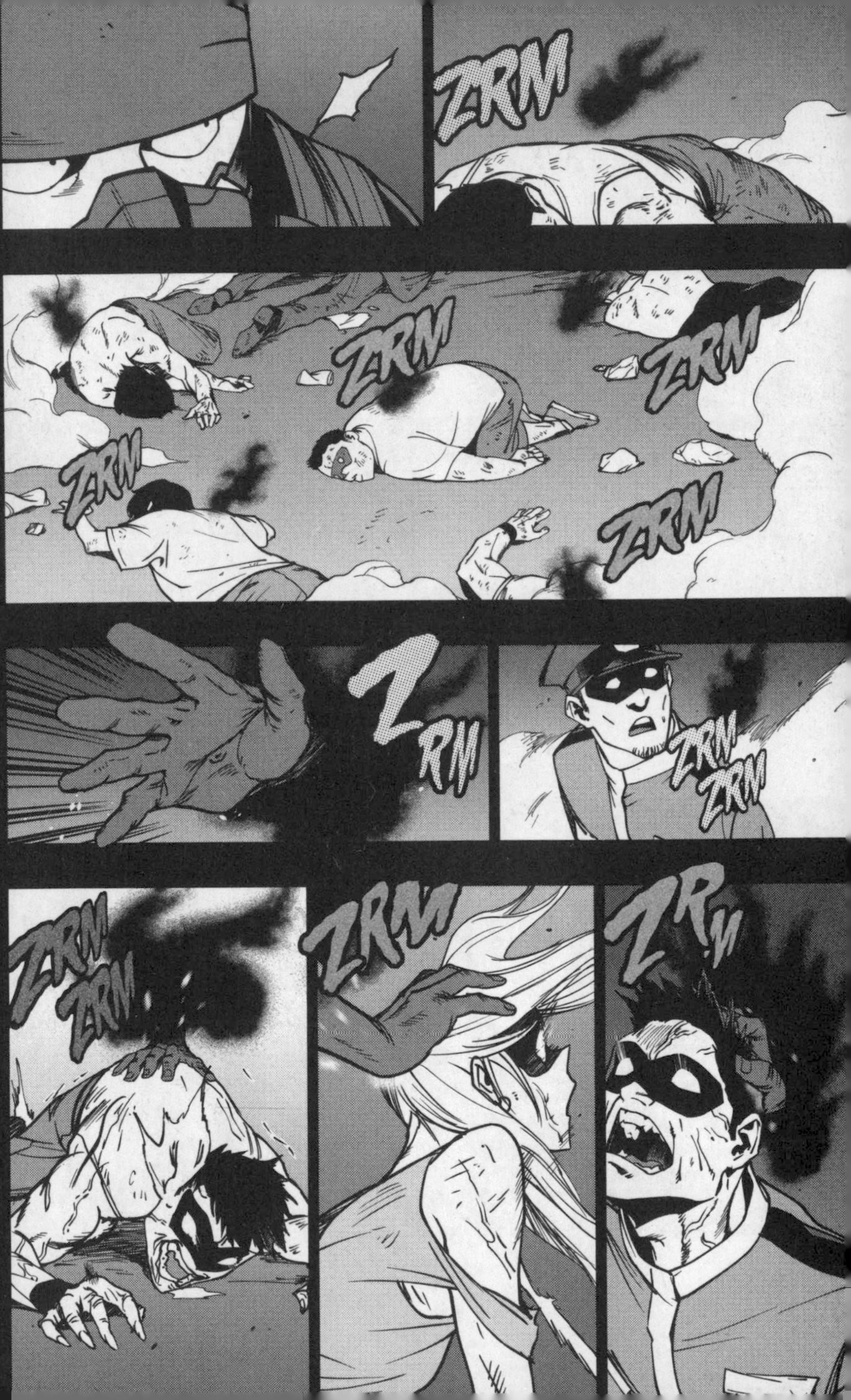
ZRM
ZRM
ZRM
ZRM
ZRM
ZRM ZRM
ZRM
ZRM
ZRM
ZRM ZRM

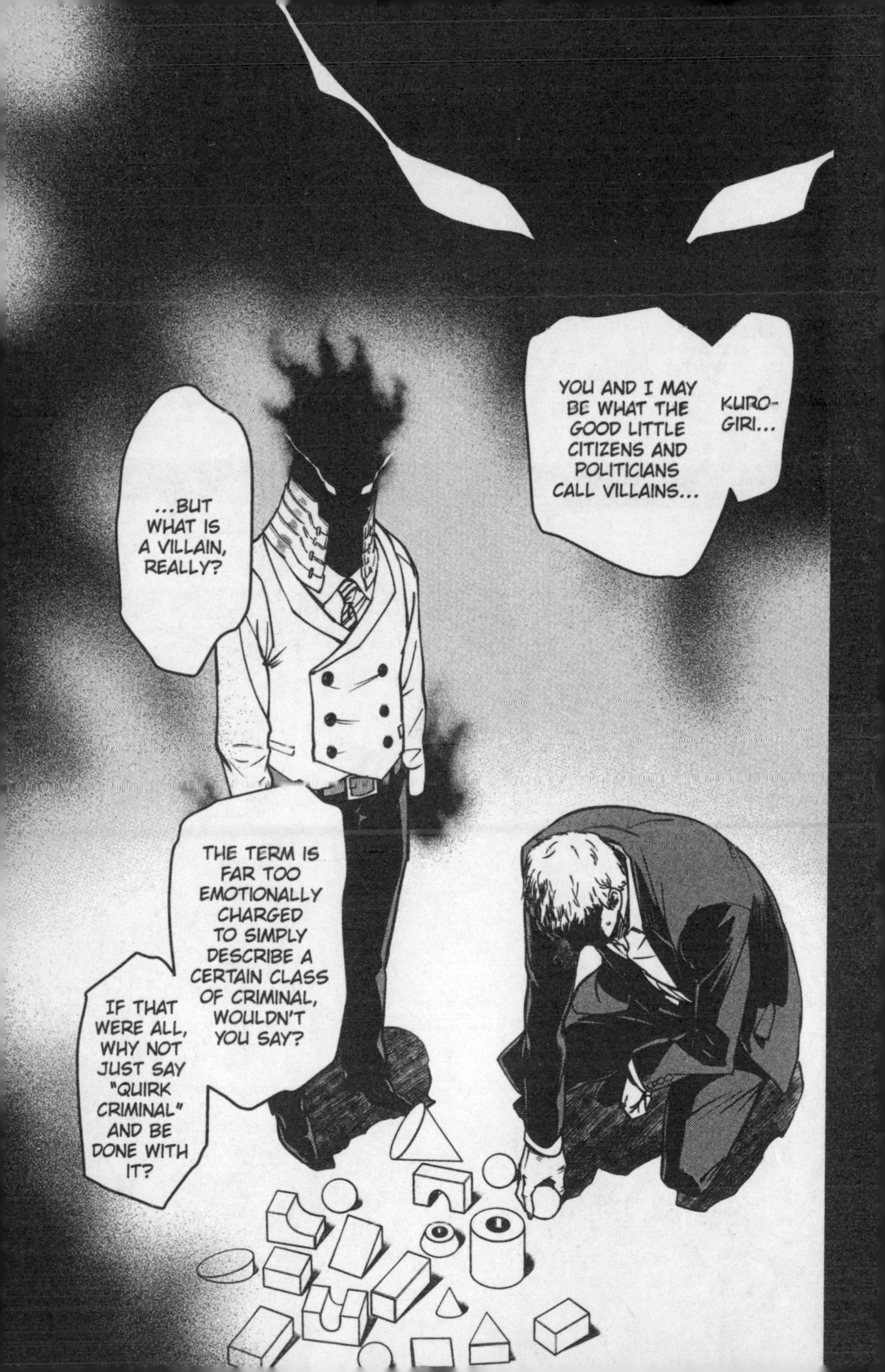
KURO-GIRI...
YOU AND I MAY BE WHAT THE GOOD LITTLE CITIZENS AND POLITICIANS CALL VILLAINS...
...BUT WHAT IS A VILLAIN, REALLY?
THE TERM IS FAR TOO EMOTIONALLY CHARGED TO SIMPLY DESCRIBE A CERTAIN CLASS OF CRIMINAL, WOULDN'T YOU SAY?
IF THAT WERE ALL, WHY NOT JUST SAY "QUIRK CRIMINAL" AND BE DONE WITH IT?

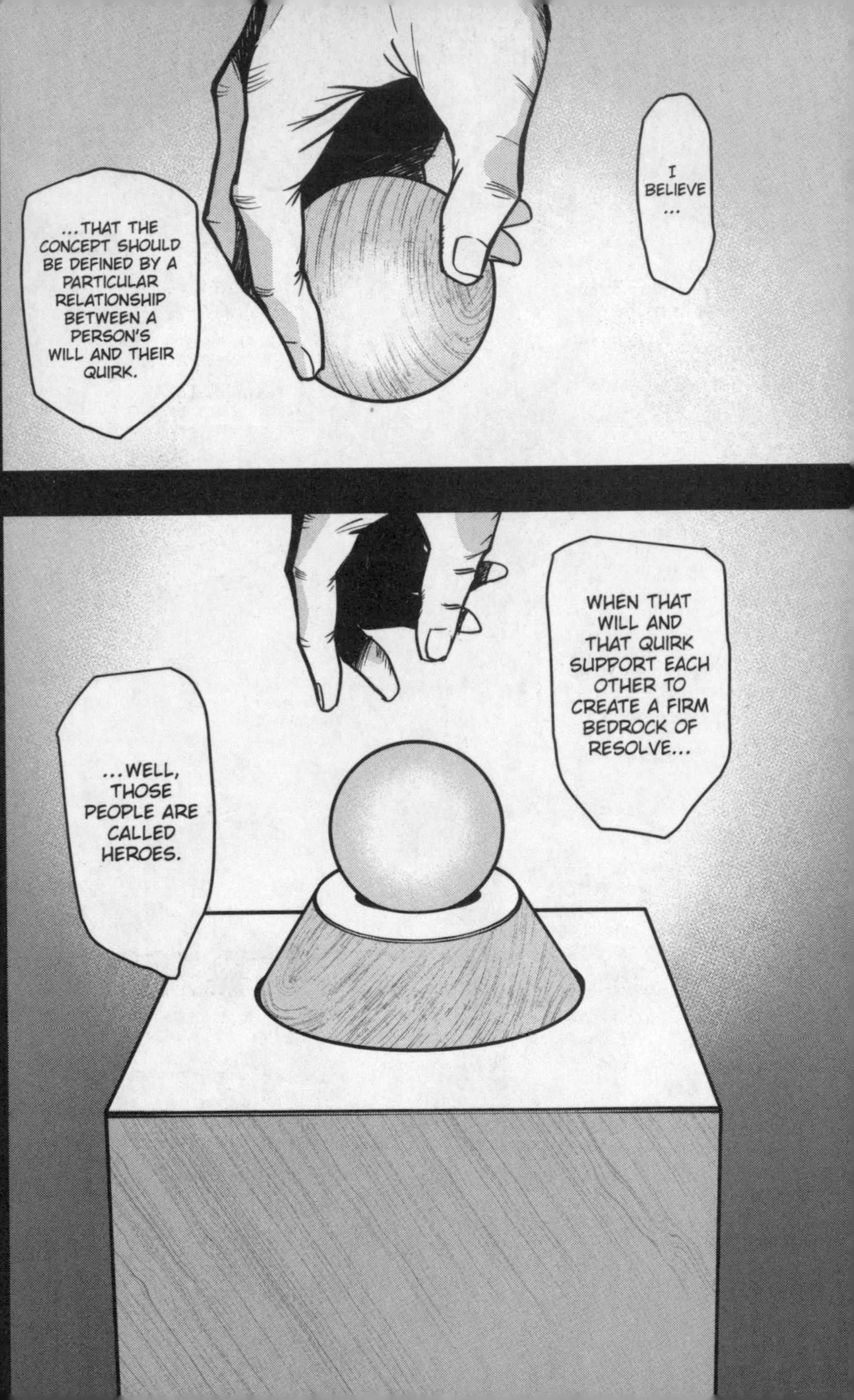
I BELIEVE...
...THAT THE CONCEPT SHOULD BE DEFINED BY A PARTICULAR RELATIONSHIP BETWEEN A PERSON'S WILL AND THEIR QUIRK.
WHEN THAT WILL AND THAT QUIRK SUPPORT EACH OTHER TO CREATE A FIRM BEDROCK OF RESOLVE...
...WELL, THOSE PEOPLE ARE CALLED HEROES.

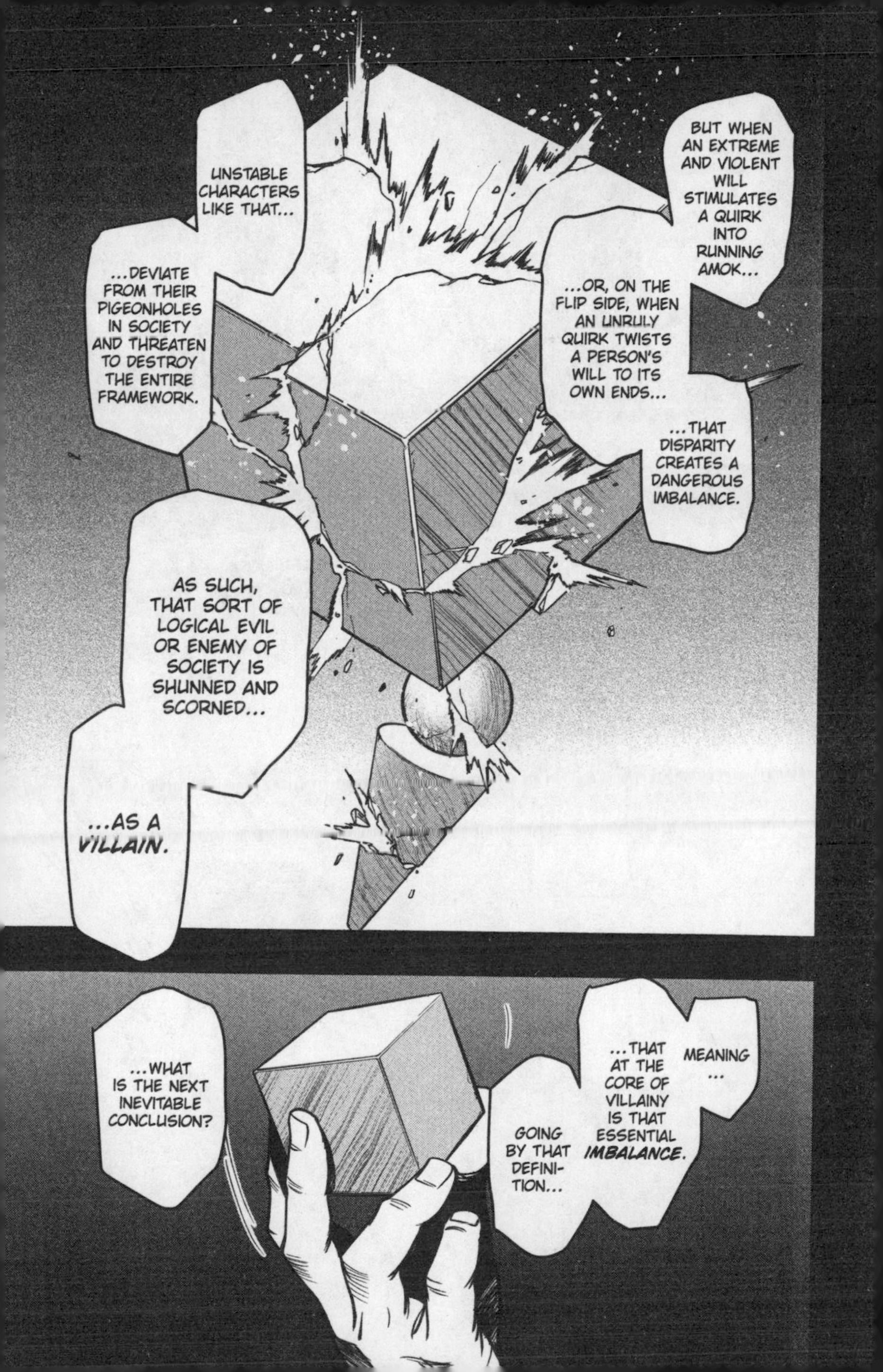
BUT WHEN AN EXTREME AND VIOLENT WILL STIMULATES A QUIRK INTO RUNNING AMOK...
...OR, ON THE FLIP SIDE, WHEN AN UNRULY QUIRK TWISTS A PERSON'S WILL TO ITS OWN ENDS...
...THAT DISPARITY CREATES A DANGEROUS IMBALANCE.
UNSTABLE CHARACTERS LIKE THAT...
...DEVIATE FROM THEIR PIGEONHOLES IN SOCIETY AND THREATEN TO DESTROY THE ENTIRE FRAMEWORK.
AS SUCH, THAT SORT OF LOGICAL EVIL OR ENEMY OF SOCIETY IS SHUNNED AND SCORNED...
...AS A *VILLAIN*.
MEANING...
...THAT AT THE CORE OF VILLAINY IS THAT ESSENTIAL *IMBALANCE*.
GOING BY THAT DEFINITION...
...WHAT IS THE NEXT INEVITABLE CONCLUSION?

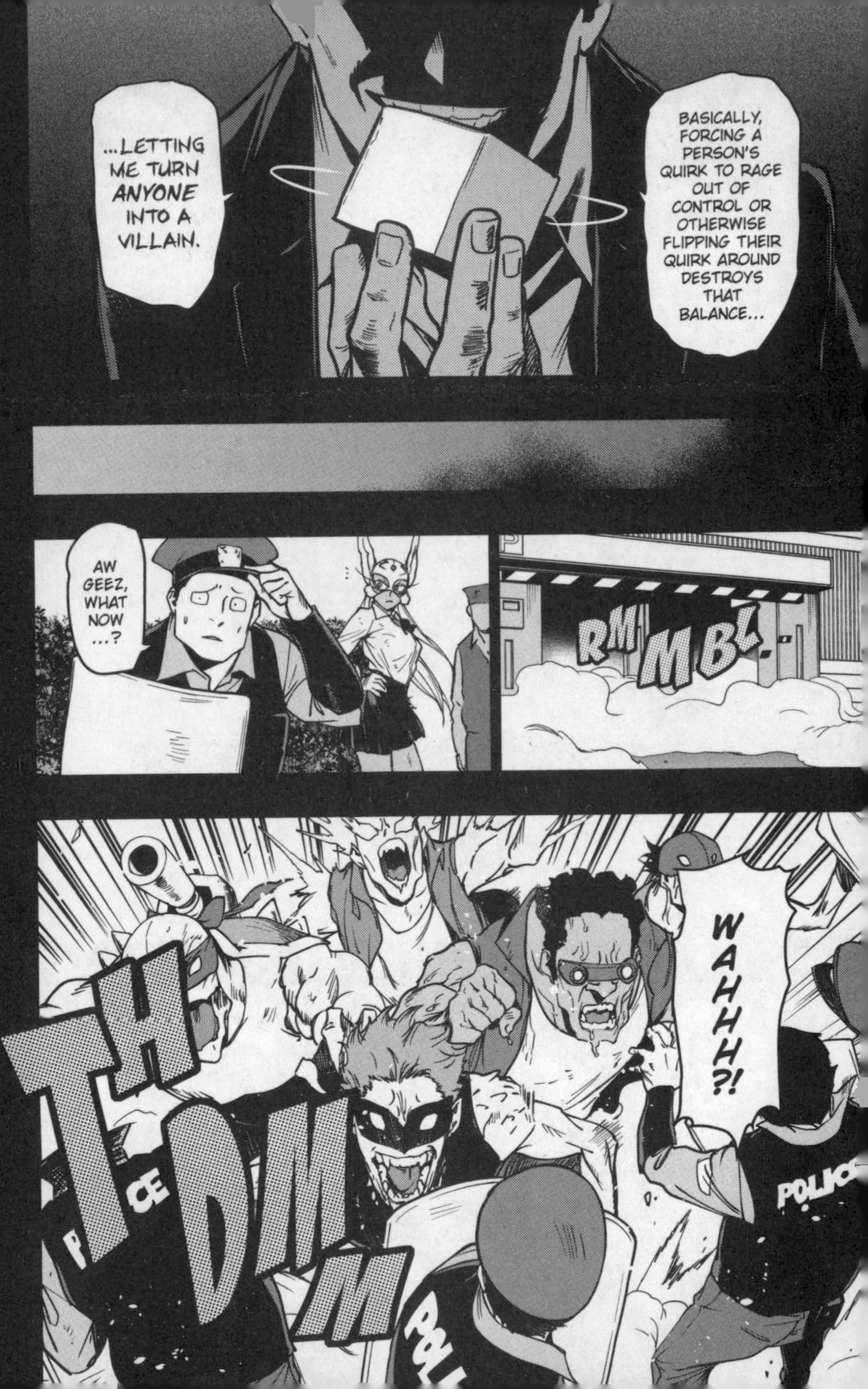
BASICALLY, FORCING A PERSON'S QUIRK TO RAGE OUT OF CONTROL OR OTHERWISE FLIPPING THEIR QUIRK AROUND DESTROYS THAT BALANCE...
...LETTING ME TURN ANYONE INTO A VILLAIN.
RMMBL
AW GEEZ, WHAT NOW ...?
WAHHHH?!
THDMM

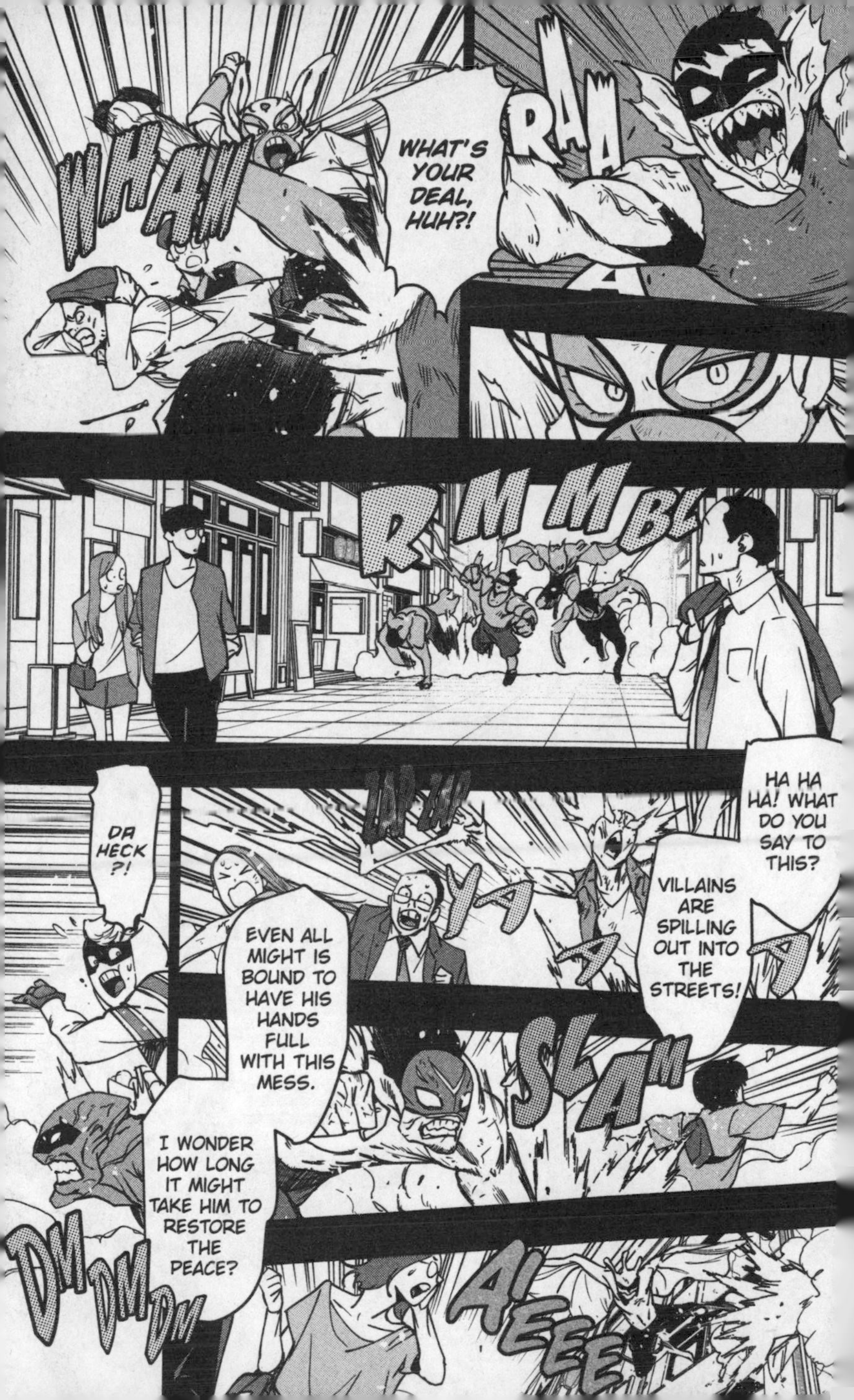
RAA
WHAT'S YOUR DEAL, HUH?!
WHAA
RMMBL
HA HA HA! WHAT DO YOU SAY TO THIS?
VILLAINS ARE SPILLING OUT INTO THE STREETS!
YAAA
EVEN ALL MIGHT IS BOUND TO HAVE HIS HANDS FULL WITH THIS MESS.
DA HECK?!
SLA
I WONDER HOW LONG IT MIGHT TAKE HIM TO RESTORE THE PEACE?
DM DM DM
AEEEE

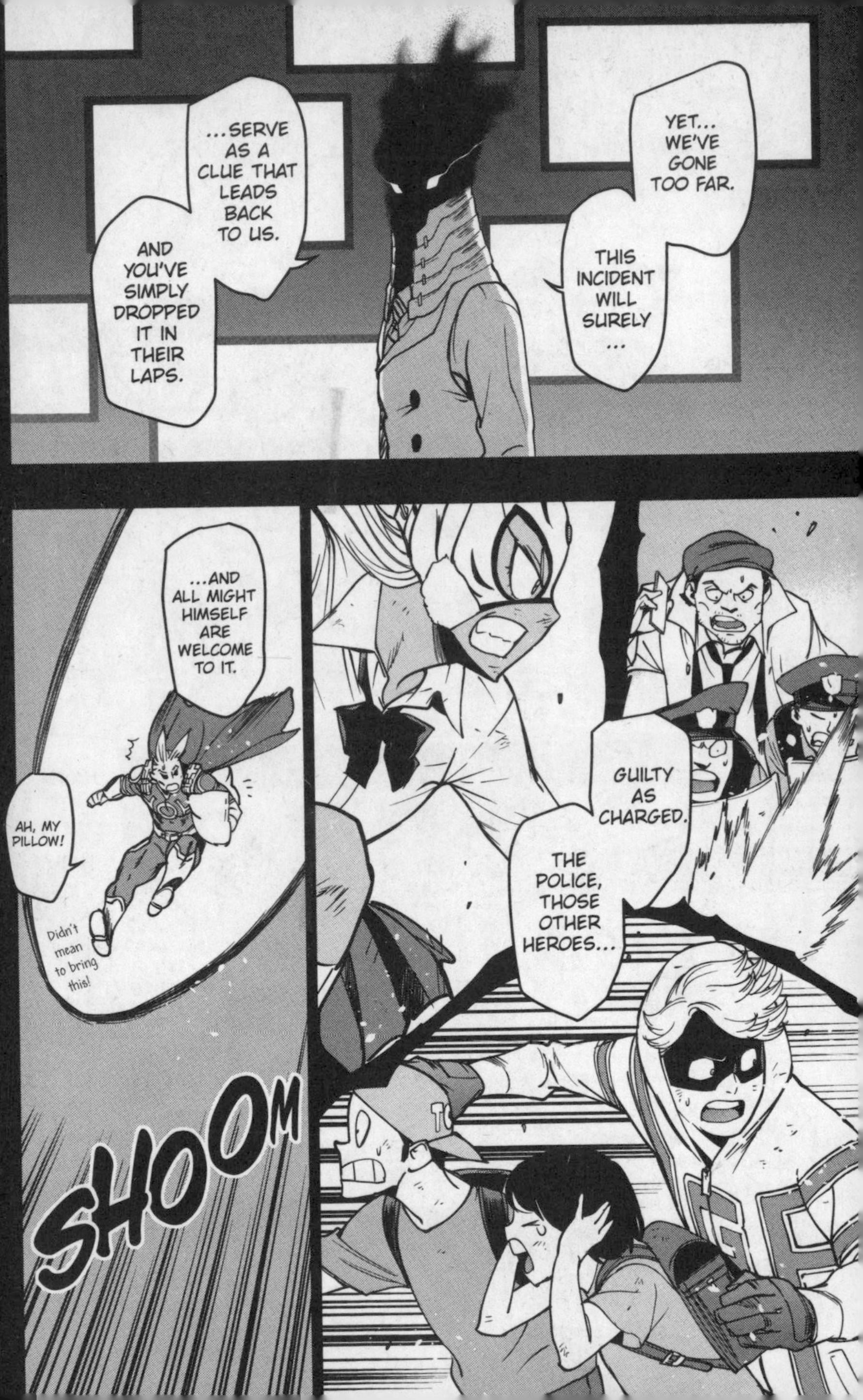
YET... WE'VE GONE TOO FAR.
THIS INCIDENT WILL SURELY...
...SERVE AS A CLUE THAT LEADS BACK TO US.
AND YOU'VE SIMPLY DROPPED IT IN THEIR LAPS.
GUILTY AS CHARGED.
THE POLICE, THOSE OTHER HEROES...
...AND ALL MIGHT HIMSELF ARE WELCOME TO IT.
AH, MY PILLOW!
Didn't mean to bring this!
SHOOOM

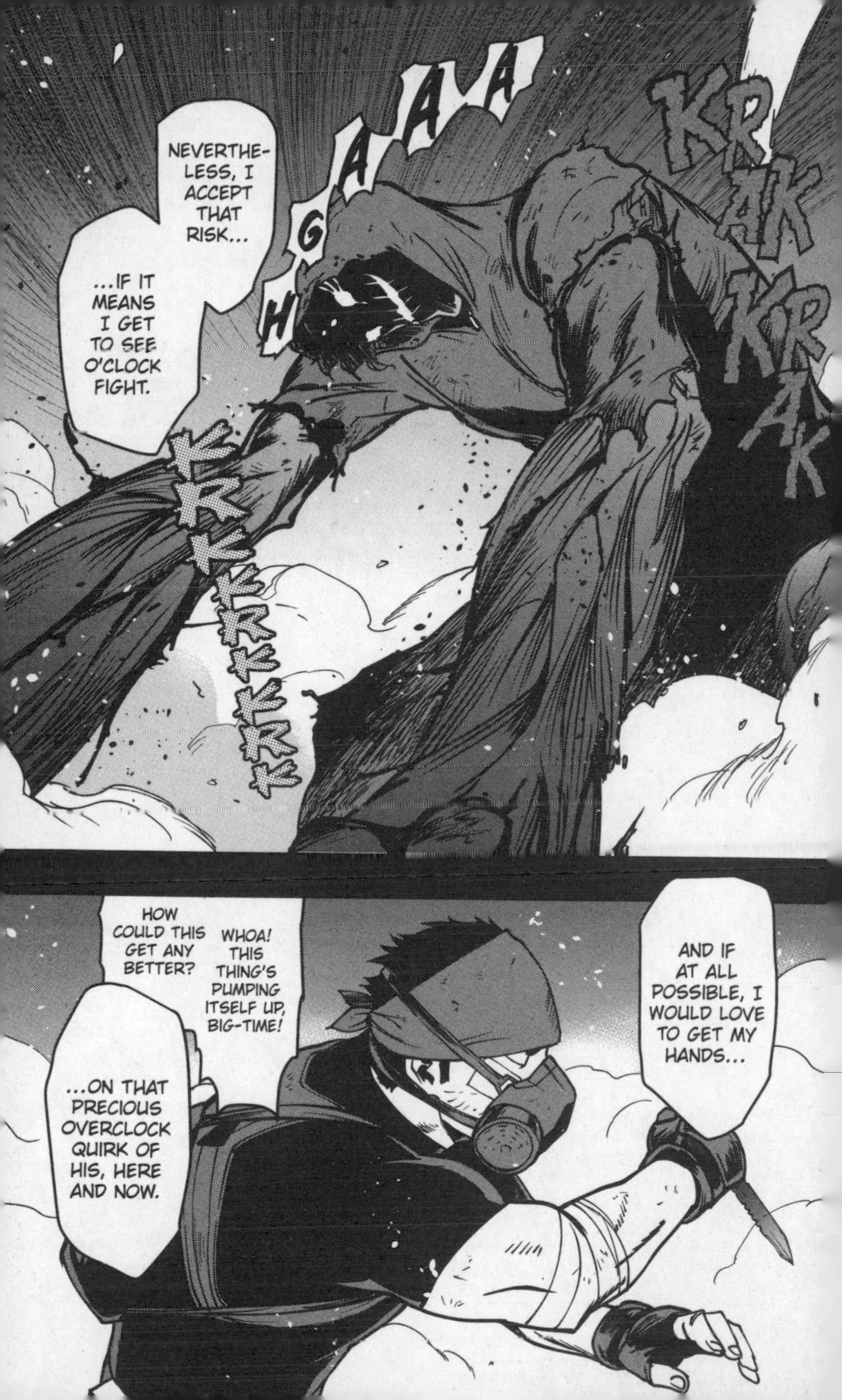
KRAK KRAK
HGAAAAA
NEVERTHELESS, I ACCEPT THAT RISK...
...IF IT MEANS I GET TO SEE O'CLOCK FIGHT.
KRKKRKKRKKRK
AND IF AT ALL POSSIBLE, I WOULD LOVE TO GET MY HANDS...
WHOA! THIS THING'S PUMPING ITSELF UP, BIG-TIME!
HOW COULD THIS GET ANY BETTER?
...ON THAT PRECIOUS OVERCLOCK QUIRK OF HIS, HERE AND NOW.

THE COLUMN

SIR AND ALL MIGHT

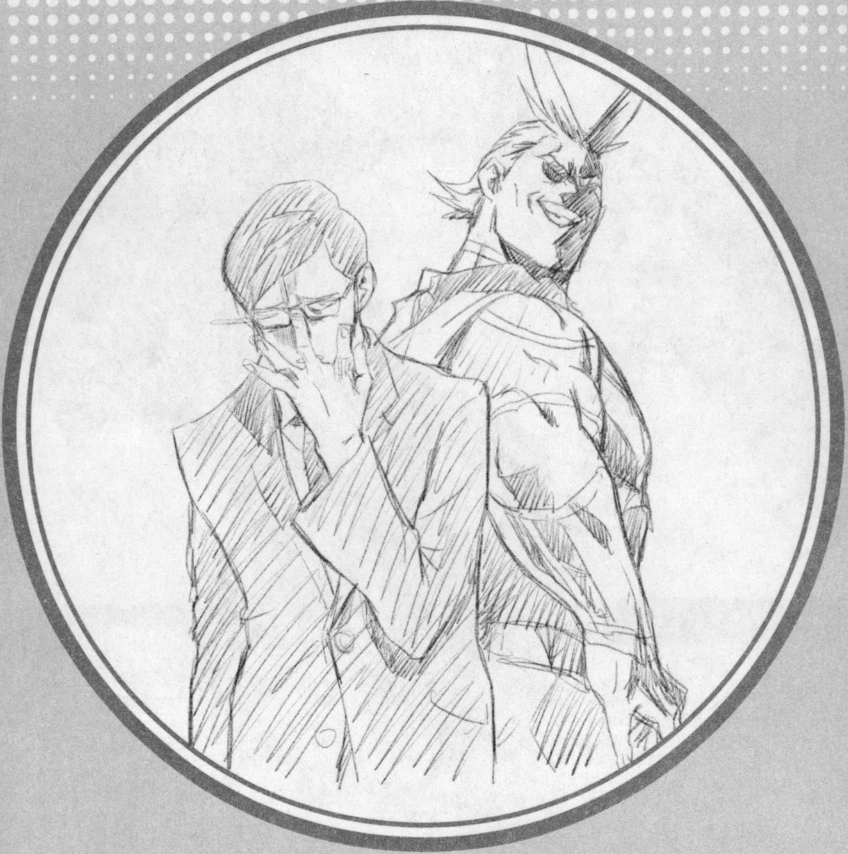

Based on his design alone, Sir looks like someone who'd be amazing at paperwork, but an unintended consequence of that is the implication that All Might sucks at it by comparison.

That theory is sort of supported by evidence in the main series though.

—Furuhashi

I never imagined I'd get to draw Sir in *Vigilantes*. He was wearing a black suit in the flashback in the main series, so that's what I went with here.

I didn't have a chance to show his eyes behind the reflective glasses in the chapter, so here you go! (LOL)

—Betten

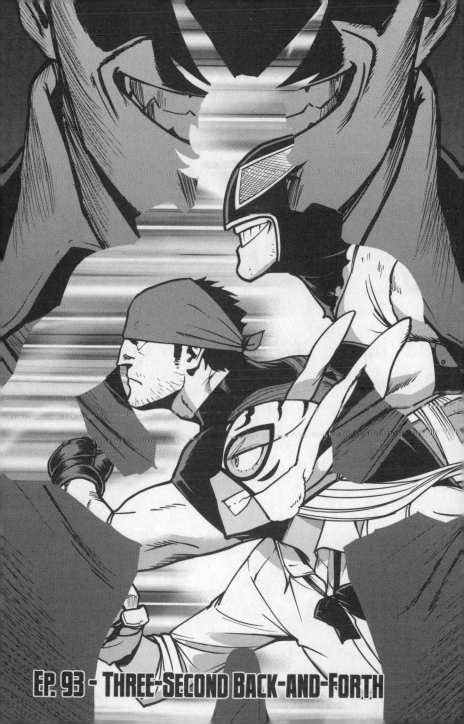

EP. 93 - THREE-SECOND BACK-AND-FORTH

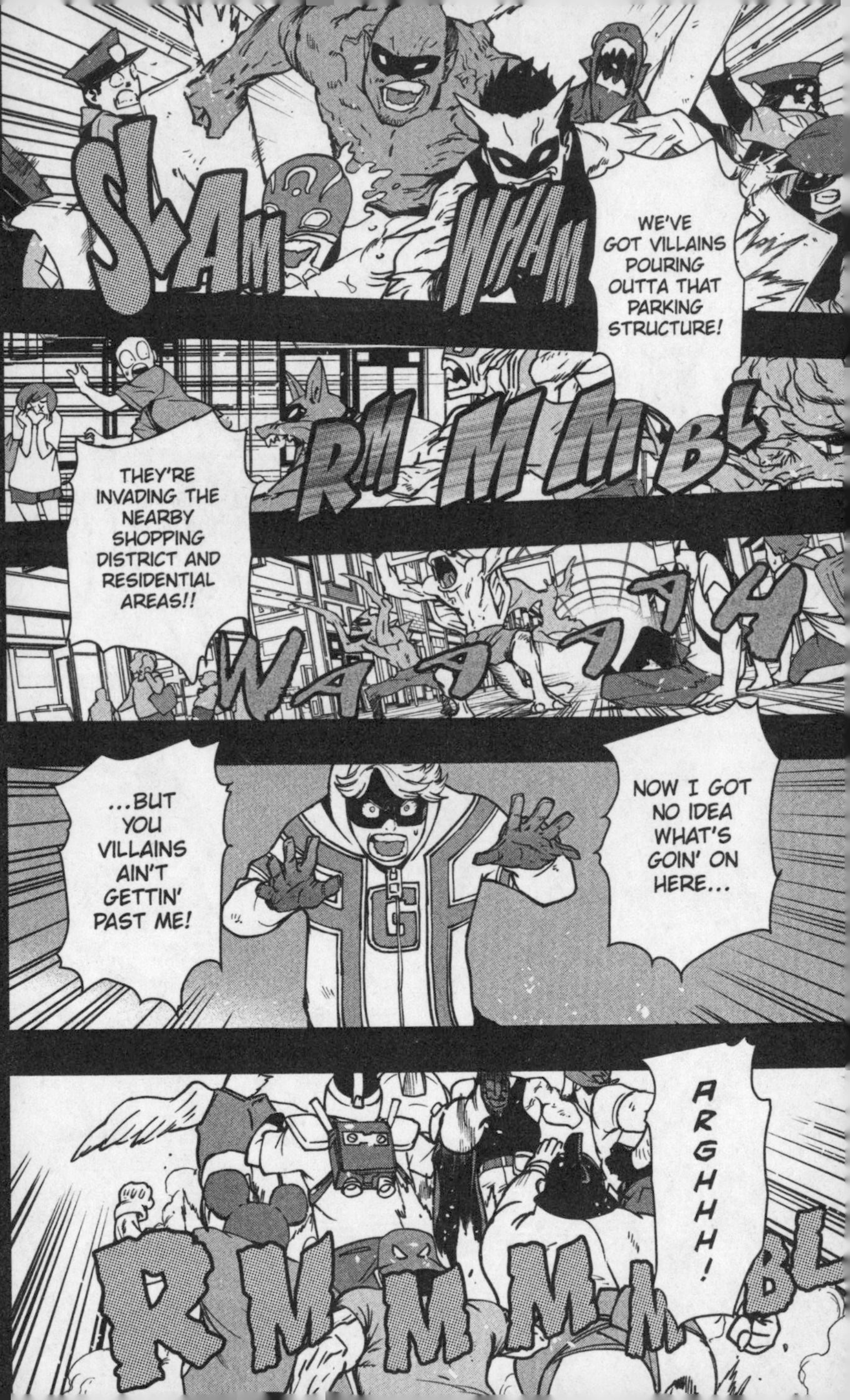
WE'VE GOT VILLAINS POURING OUTTA THAT PARKING STRUCTURE!
WHAM
SLAM
RMMMBL
THEY'RE INVADING THE NEARBY SHOPPING DISTRICT AND RESIDENTIAL AREAS!!
WAAAAH
NOW I GOT NO IDEA WHAT'S GOIN' ON HERE...
...BUT YOU VILLAINS AIN'T GETTIN' PAST ME!
ARGHHH!
RMMMMBL

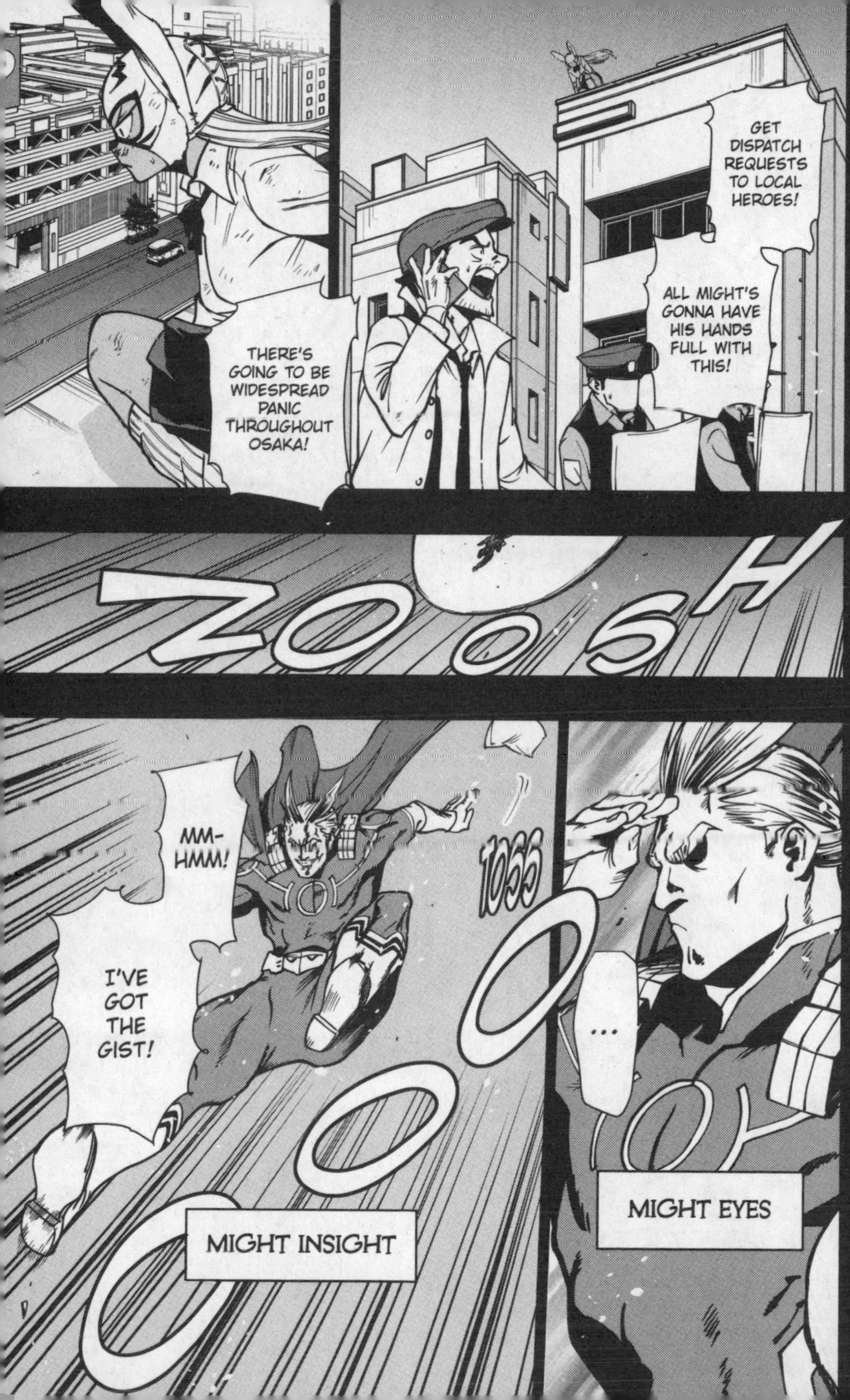
GET DISPATCH REQUESTS TO LOCAL HEROES!
ALL MIGHT'S GONNA HAVE HIS HANDS FULL WITH THIS!
THERE'S GOING TO BE WIDESPREAD PANIC THROUGHOUT OSAKA!
ZOOSH
...
MIGHT EYES
MM-HMM!
I'VE GOT THE GIST!
MIGHT INSIGHT

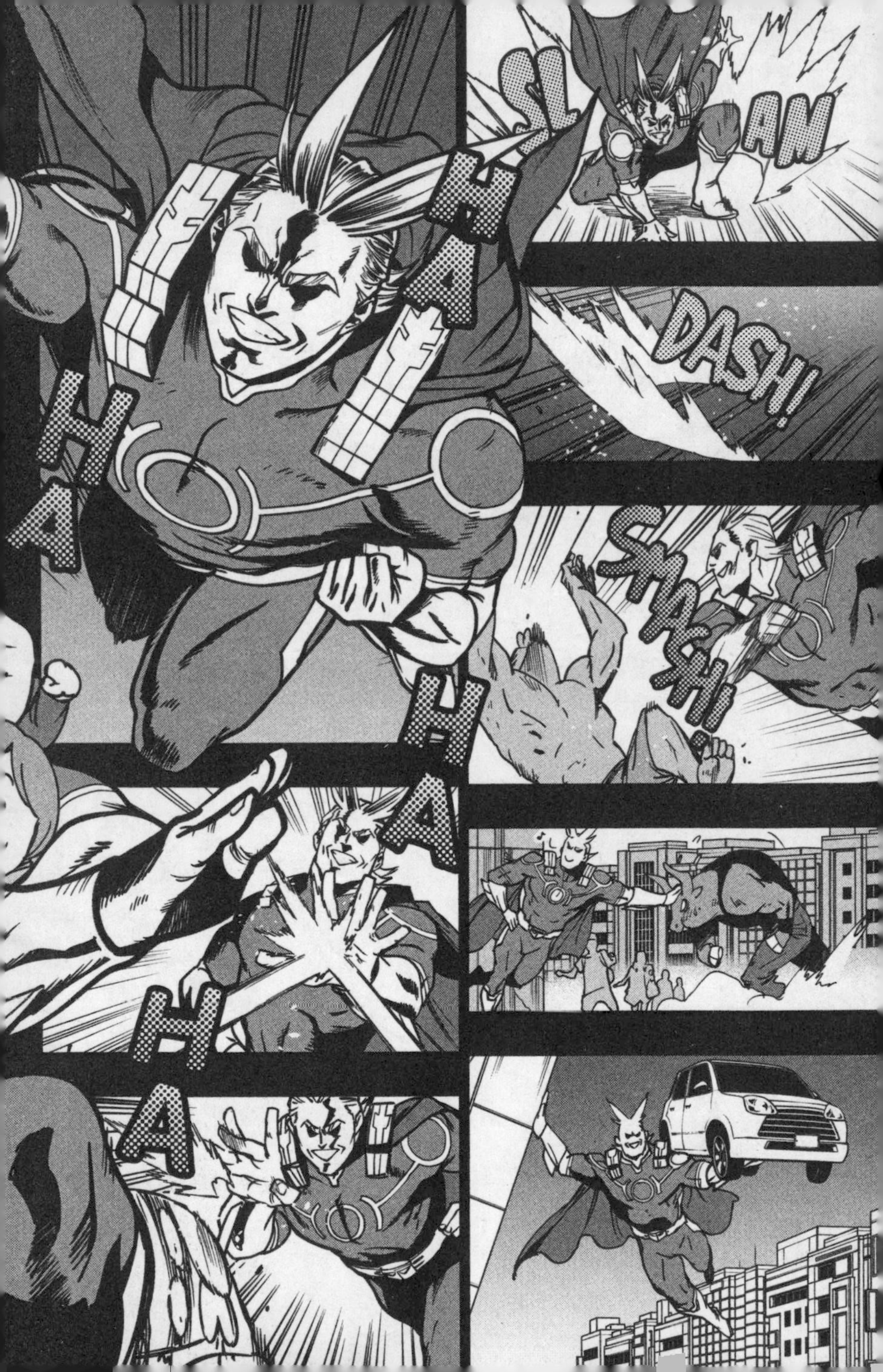
SLAM
DASH!
SMASH!
HAHAHAHA

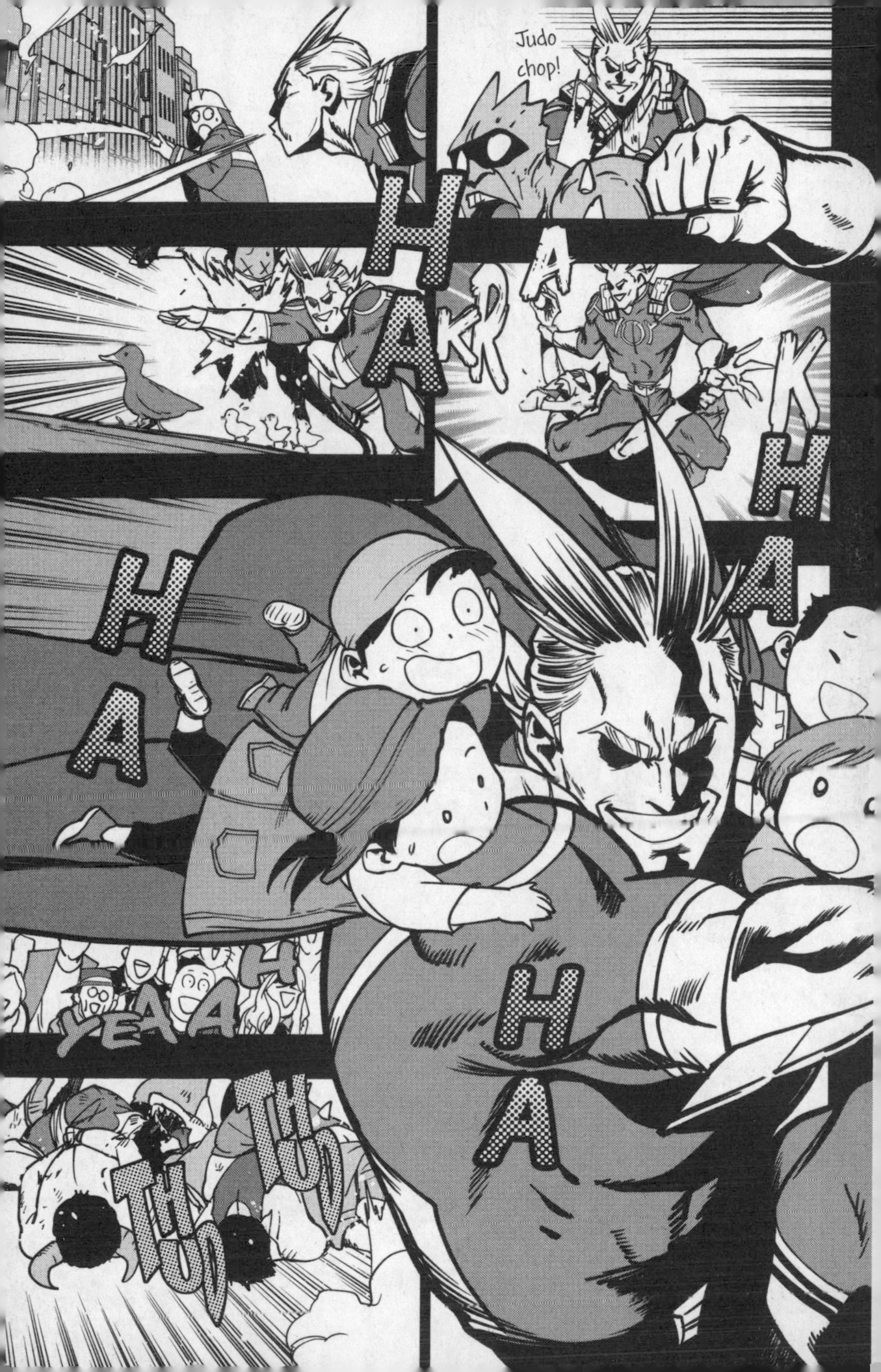
Judo chop!
HAHAHA
HAHAHA
YEAA
THUD
THUD

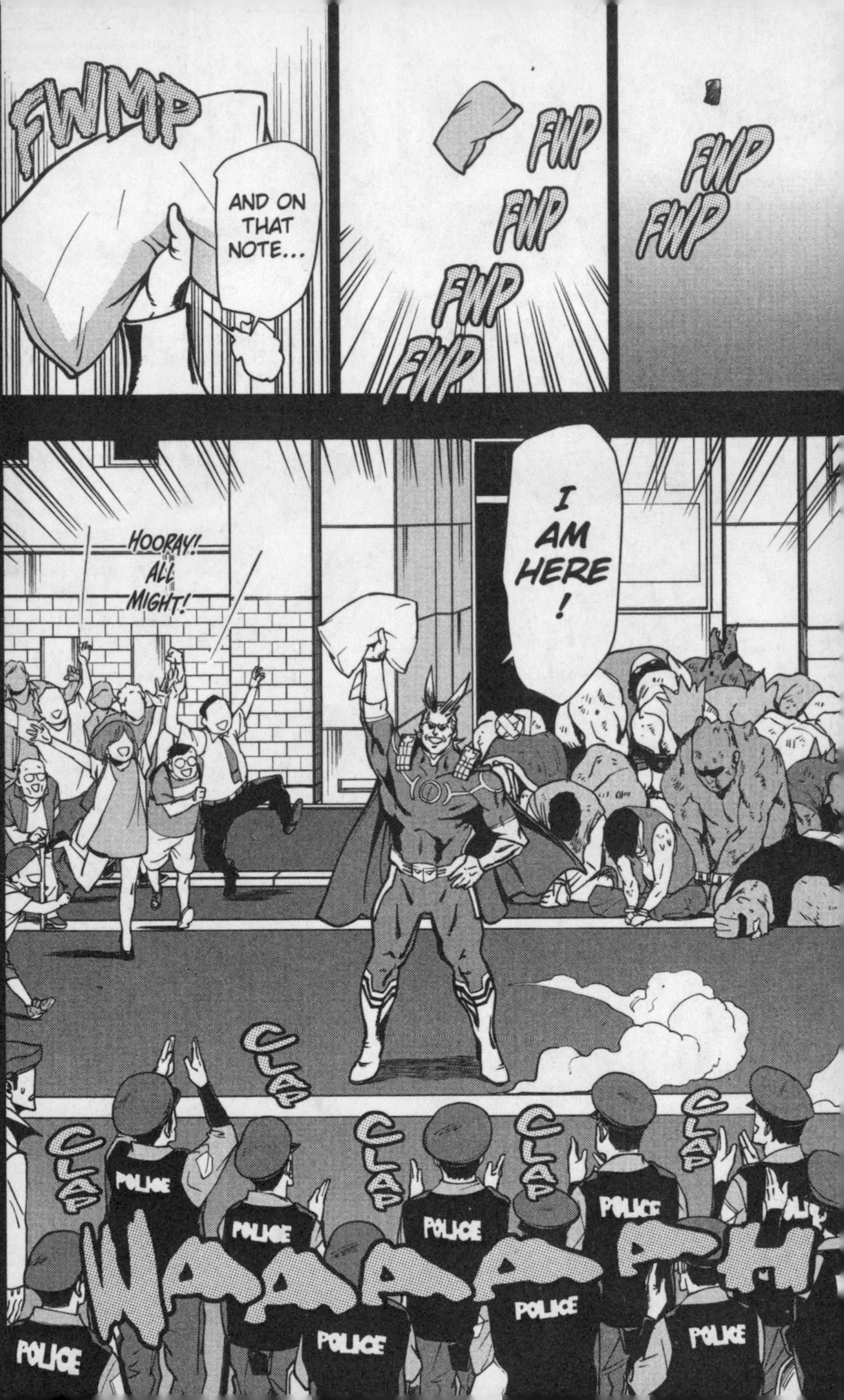
FWP
FWP
FWP
FWP
FWP
FWP
FWMP
AND ON THAT NOTE...
I AM HERE!
HOORAY! ALL MIGHT!
CLAP
CLAP
CLAP
CLAP
CLAP
POLICE

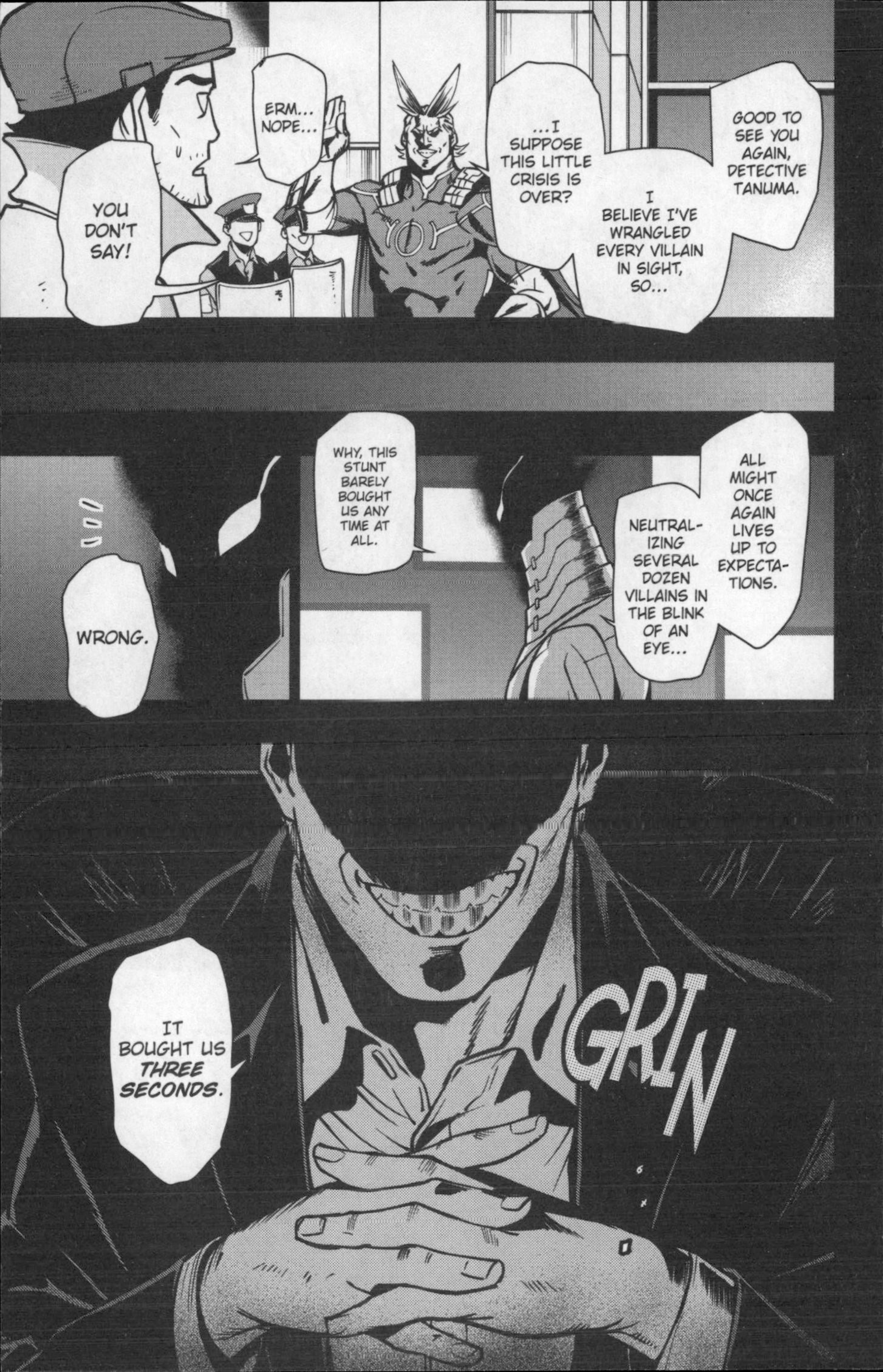
GOOD TO SEE YOU AGAIN, DETECTIVE TANUMA.
I BELIEVE I'VE WRANGLED EVERY VILLAIN IN SIGHT, SO...
...I SUPPOSE THIS LITTLE CRISIS IS OVER?
ERM... NOPE...
YOU DON'T SAY!
ALL MIGHT ONCE AGAIN LIVES UP TO EXPECTATIONS.
NEUTRALIZING SEVERAL DOZEN VILLAINS IN THE BLINK OF AN EYE...
WHY, THIS STUNT BARELY BOUGHT US ANY TIME AT ALL.
WRONG.
GRIN
IT BOUGHT US *THREE SECONDS*.

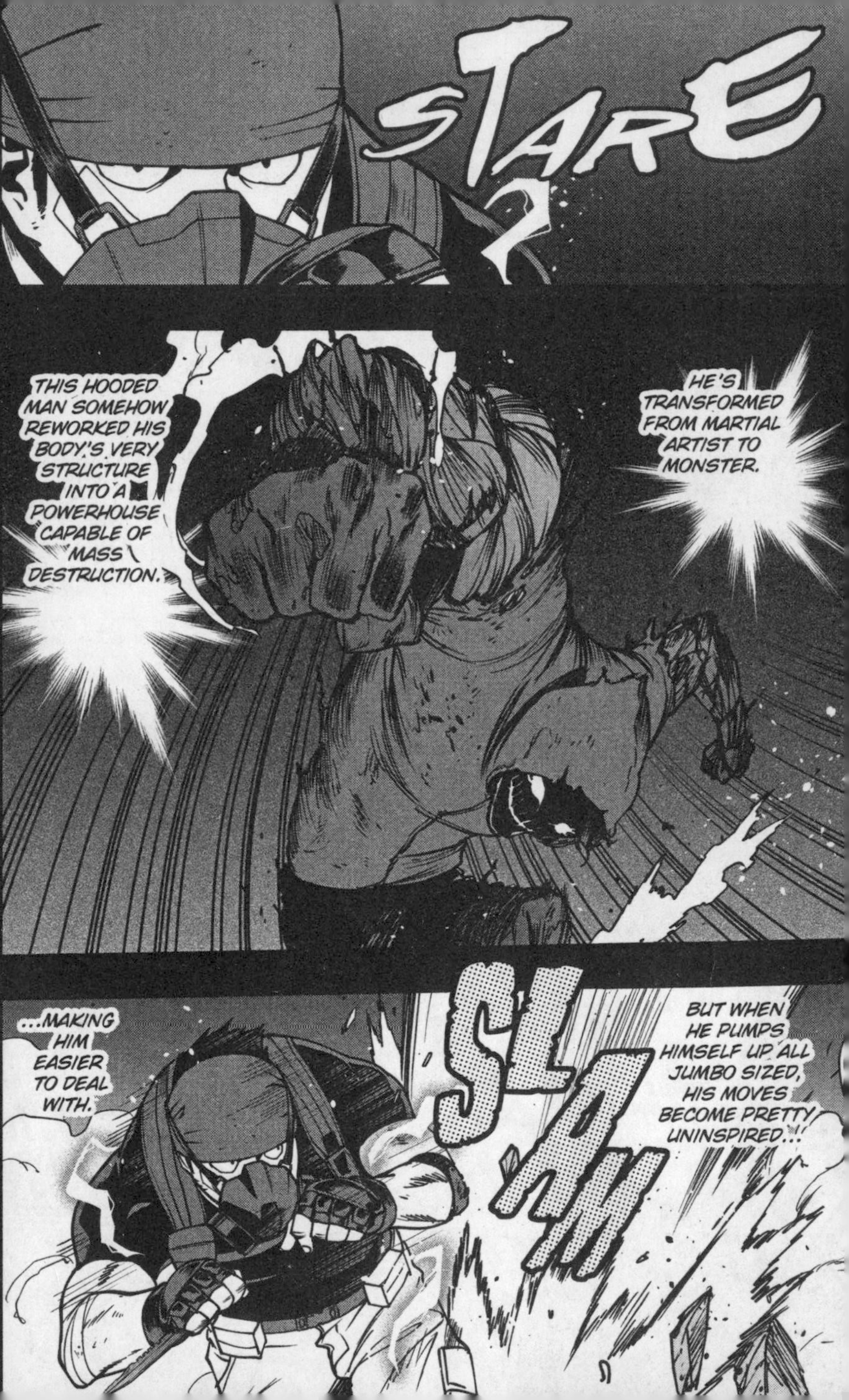
STARE
HE'S TRANSFORMED FROM MARTIAL ARTIST TO MONSTER.
THIS HOODED MAN SOMEHOW REWORKED HIS BODY'S VERY STRUCTURE INTO A POWERHOUSE CAPABLE OF MASS DESTRUCTION.
BUT WHEN HE PUMPS HIMSELF UP ALL JUMBO SIZED, HIS MOVES BECOME PRETTY UNINSPIRED...
SLAM
...MAKING HIM EASIER TO DEAL WITH.

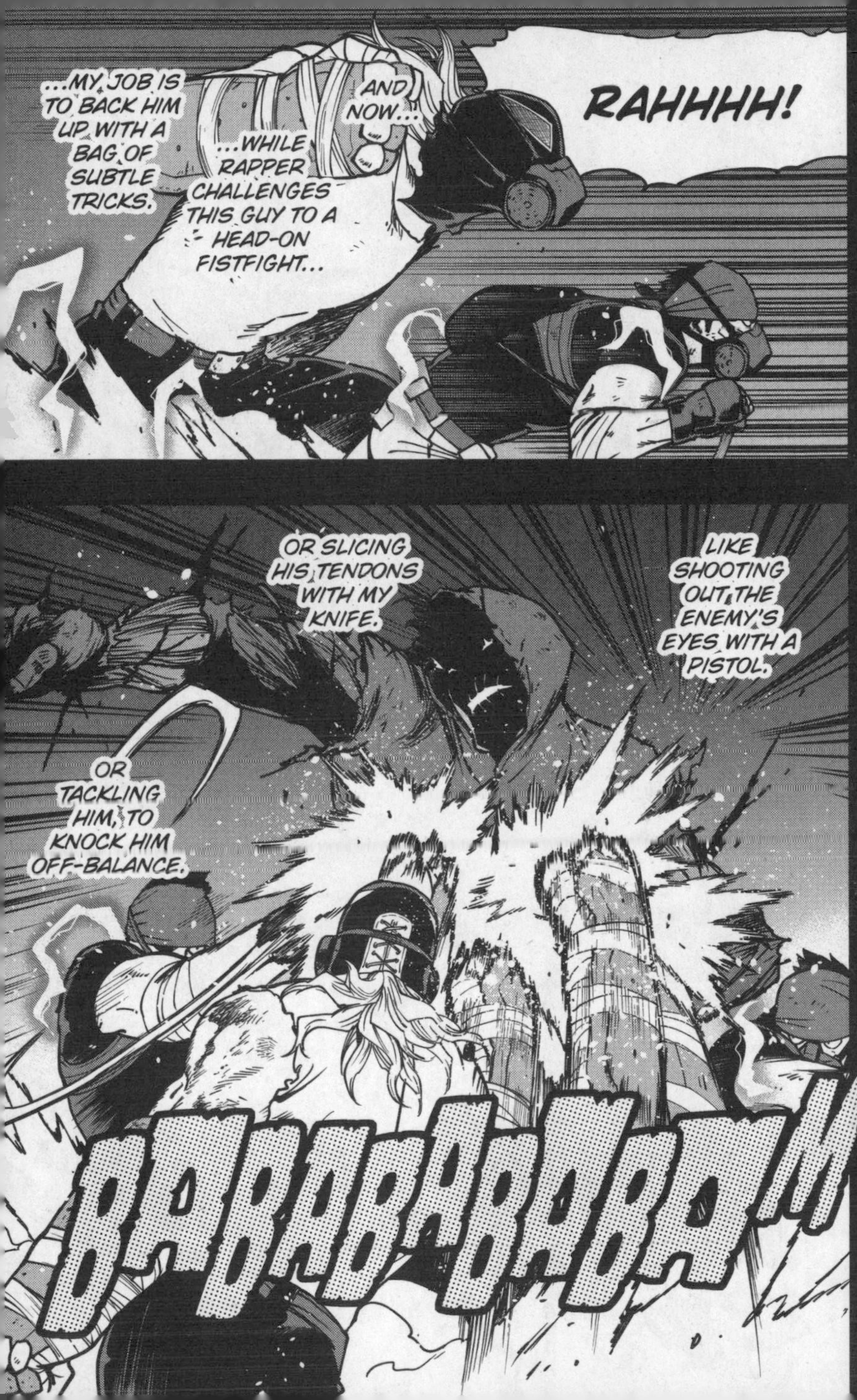
RAHHHH!
AND NOW...
...WHILE RAPPER CHALLENGES THIS GUY TO A HEAD-ON FISTFIGHT...
...MY JOB IS TO BACK HIM UP WITH A BAG OF SUBTLE TRICKS.
LIKE SHOOTING OUT THE ENEMY'S EYES WITH A PISTOL.
OR SLICING HIS TENDONS WITH MY KNIFE.
OR TACKLING HIM, TO KNOCK HIM OFF-BALANCE.
BABABABABOOM

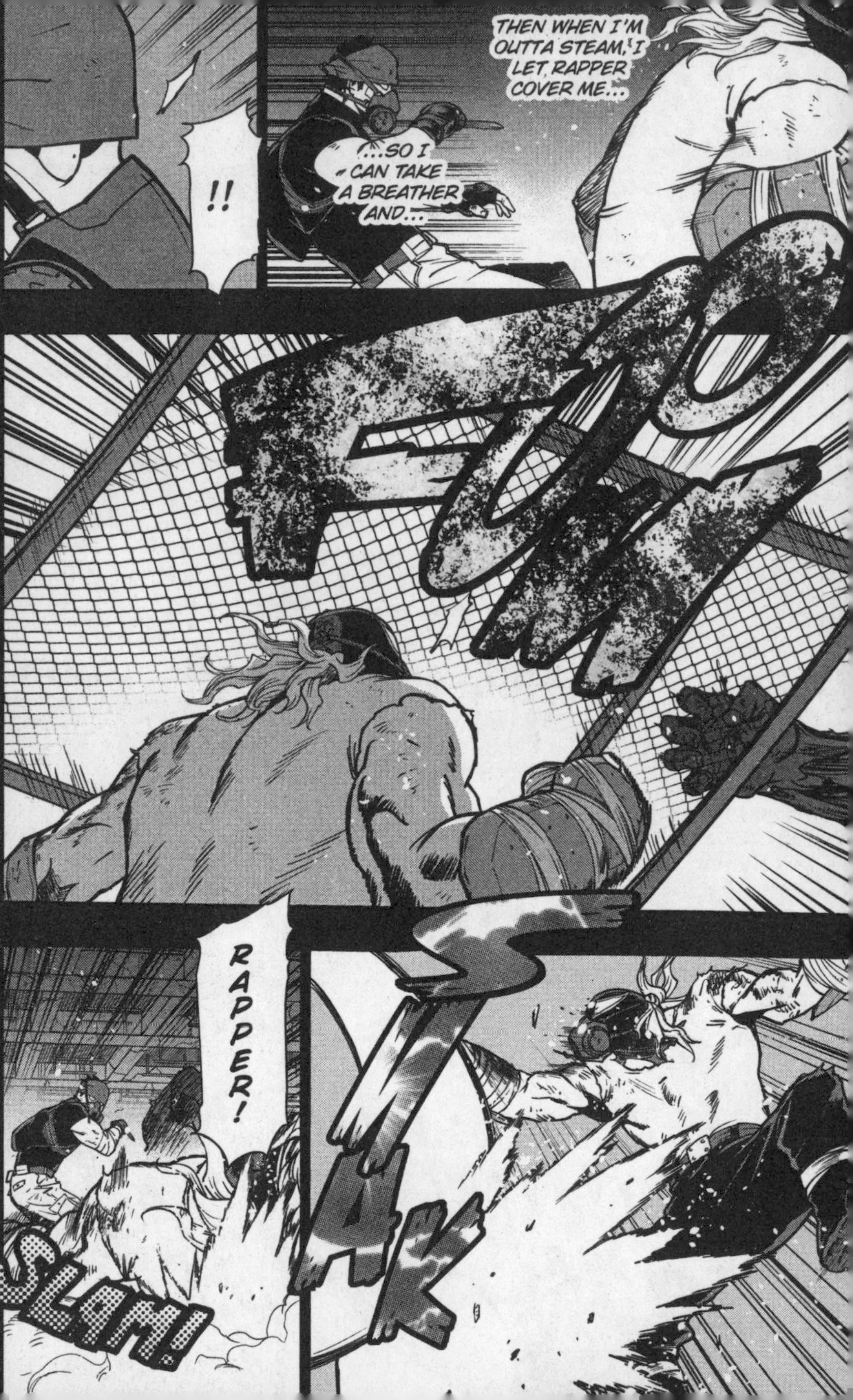
THEN WHEN I'M OUTTA STEAM, I LET RAPPER COVER ME...
...SO I CAN TAKE A BREATHER AND...
!!
RAPPER!
SLAM!

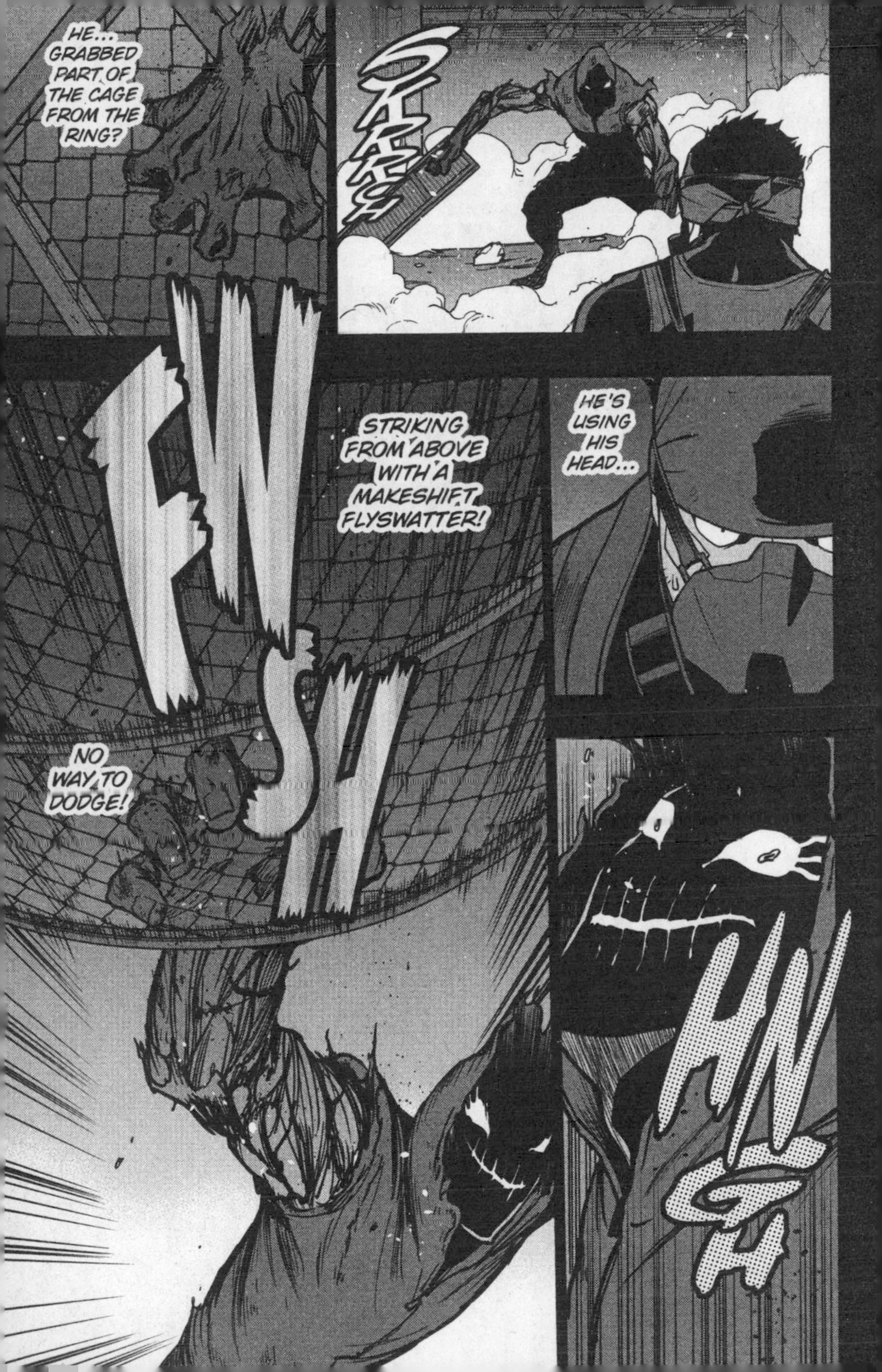
HE... GRABBED PART OF THE CAGE FROM THE RING?
HE'S USING HIS HEAD...
STRIKING FROM ABOVE WITH A MAKESHIFT FLYSWATTER!
FWSH
NO WAY TO DODGE!
HNGH

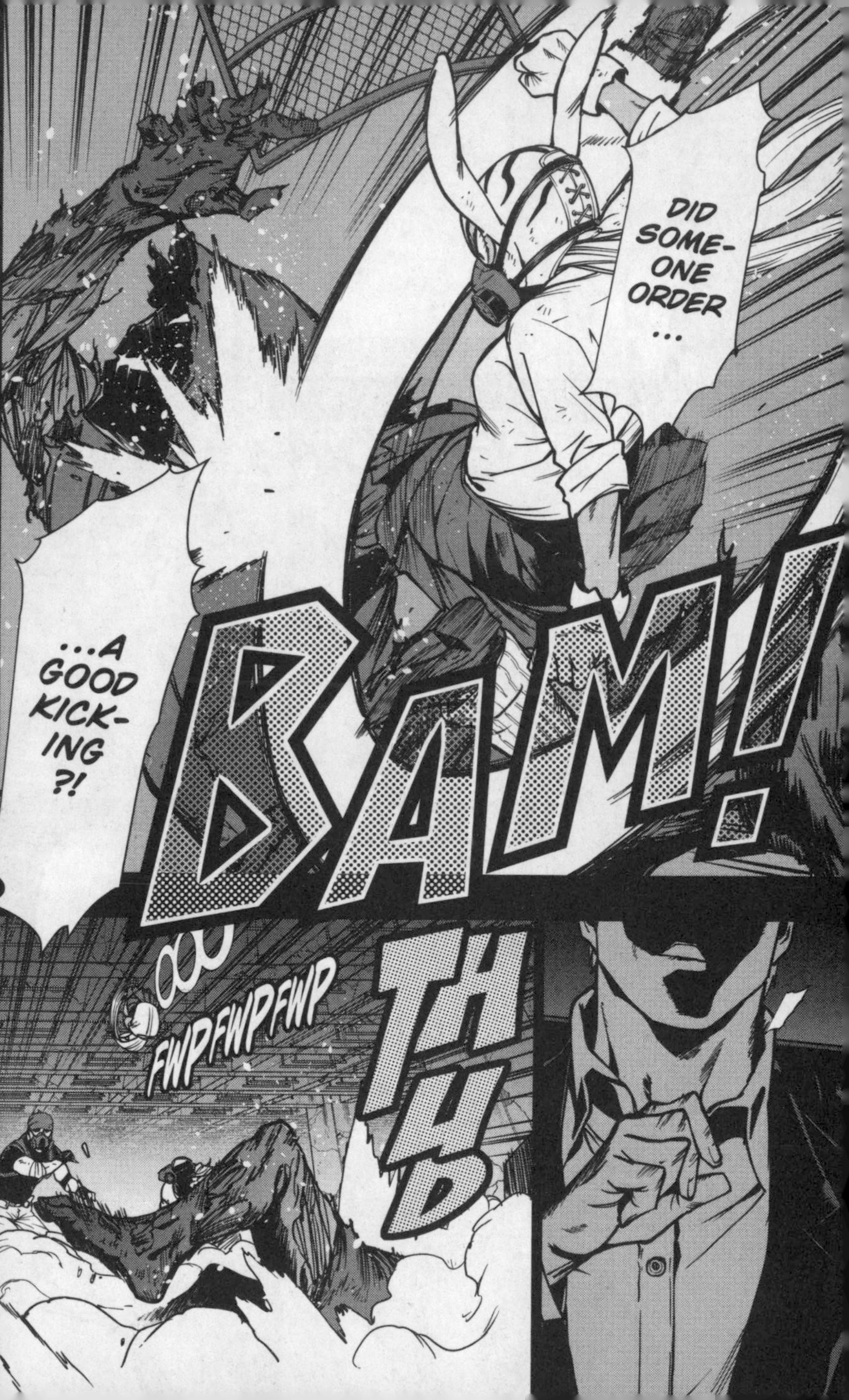

DID SOME-ONE ORDER ...
...A GOOD KICK-ING ?!
BAM!!
THUD
FWP FWP FWP

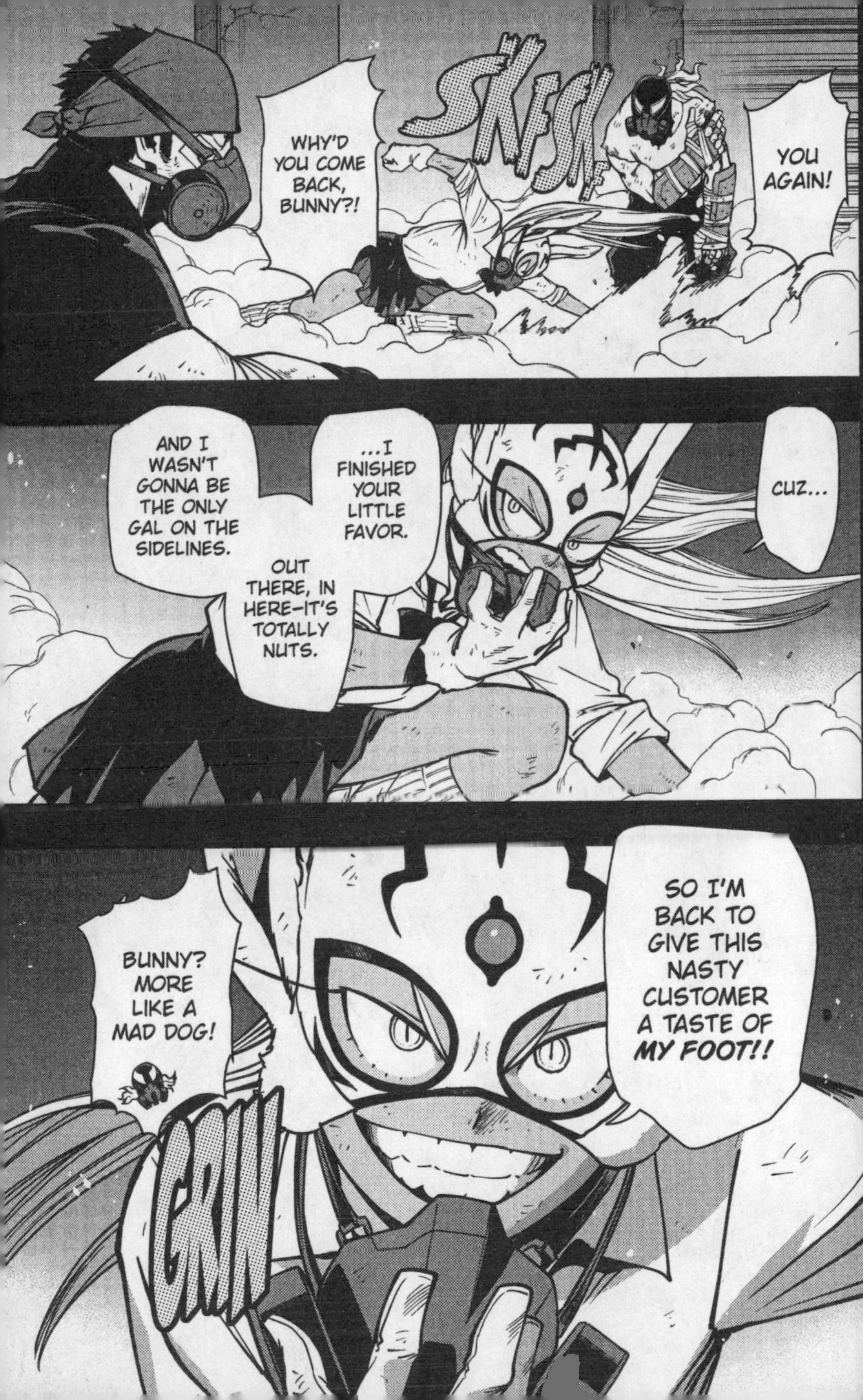
YOU AGAIN!
SKFSH
WHY'D YOU COME BACK, BUNNY?!
CUZ...
...I FINISHED YOUR LITTLE FAVOR.
OUT THERE, IN HERE–IT'S TOTALLY NUTS.
AND I WASN'T GONNA BE THE ONLY GAL ON THE SIDELINES.
SO I'M BACK TO GIVE THIS NASTY CUSTOMER A TASTE OF *MY FOOT!!*
GRIN
BUNNY? MORE LIKE A MAD DOG!

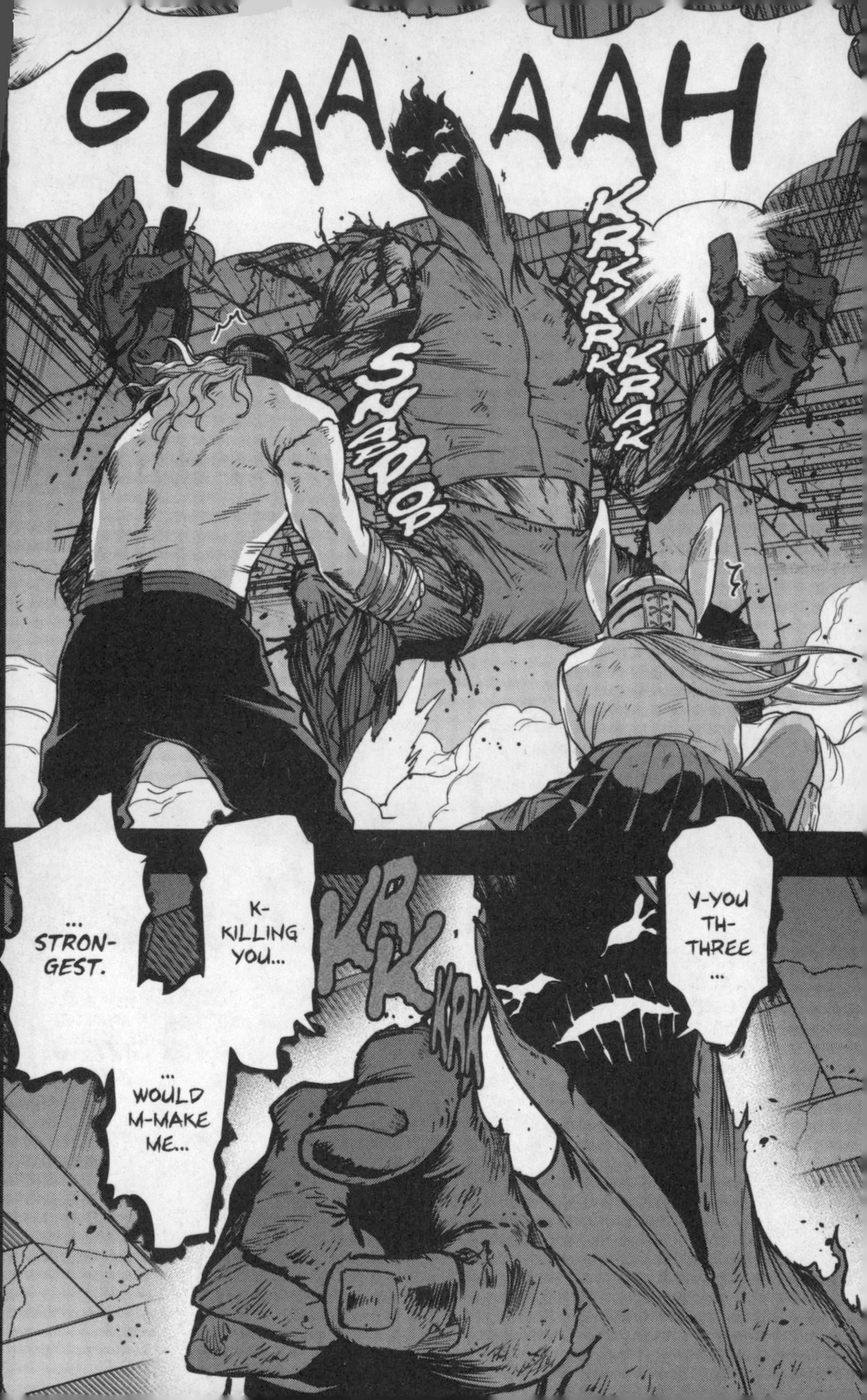
GRAAAAH
KRKKRKRK KRAK
SNAPPOP
Y-YOU TH-THREE ...
KRK
KRAK
K-KILLING YOU...
... WOULD M-MAKE ME...
... STRON-GEST.

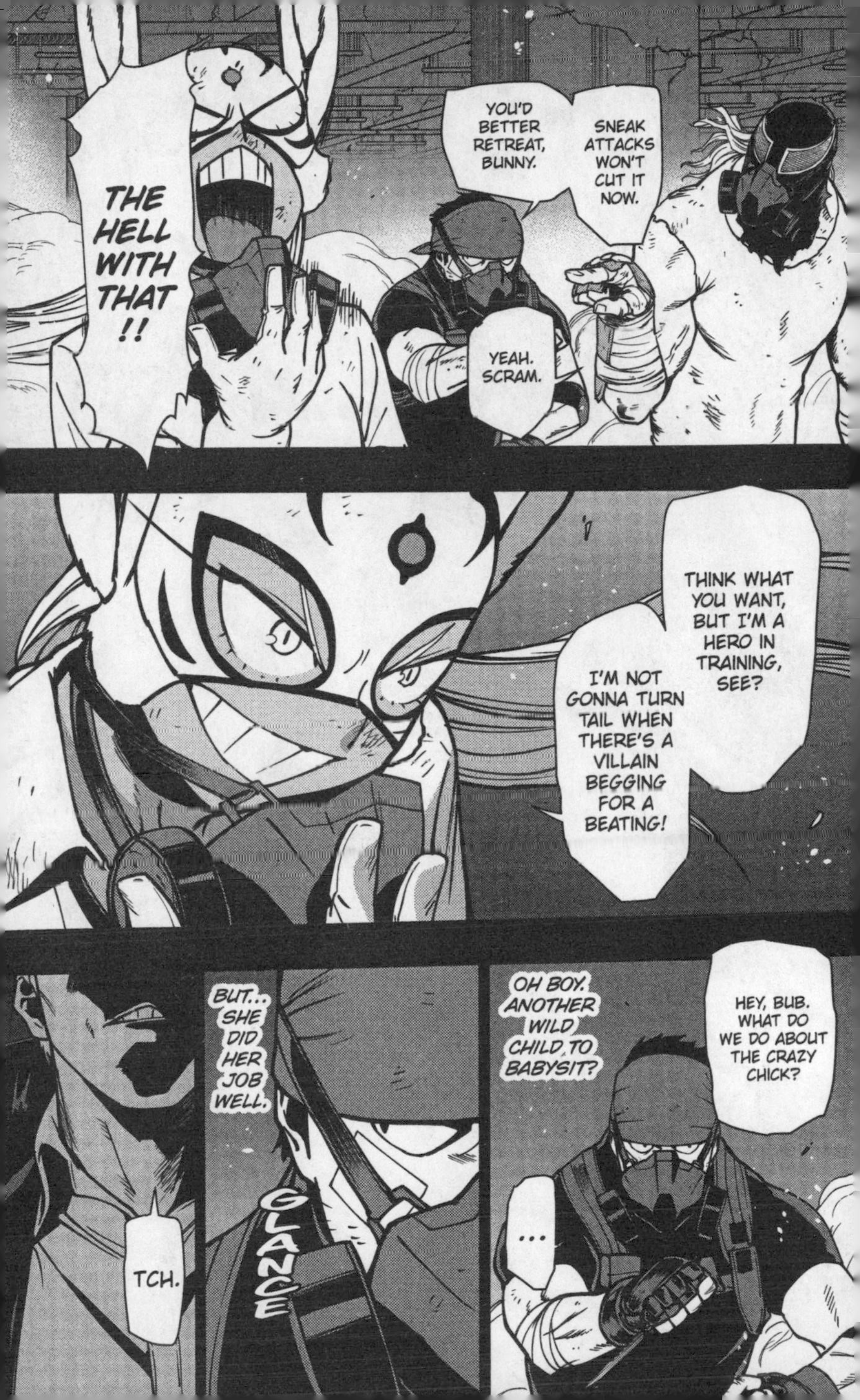
SNEAK ATTACKS WON'T CUT IT NOW.
YOU'D BETTER RETREAT, BUNNY.
YEAH. SCRAM.
THE HELL WITH THAT!!
THINK WHAT YOU WANT, BUT I'M A HERO IN TRAINING, SEE?
I'M NOT GONNA TURN TAIL WHEN THERE'S A VILLAIN BEGGING FOR A BEATING!
HEY, BUB. WHAT DO WE DO ABOUT THE CRAZY CHICK?
OH BOY. ANOTHER WILD CHILD TO BABYSIT?
...
BUT... SHE DID HER JOB WELL.
GLANCE
TCH.

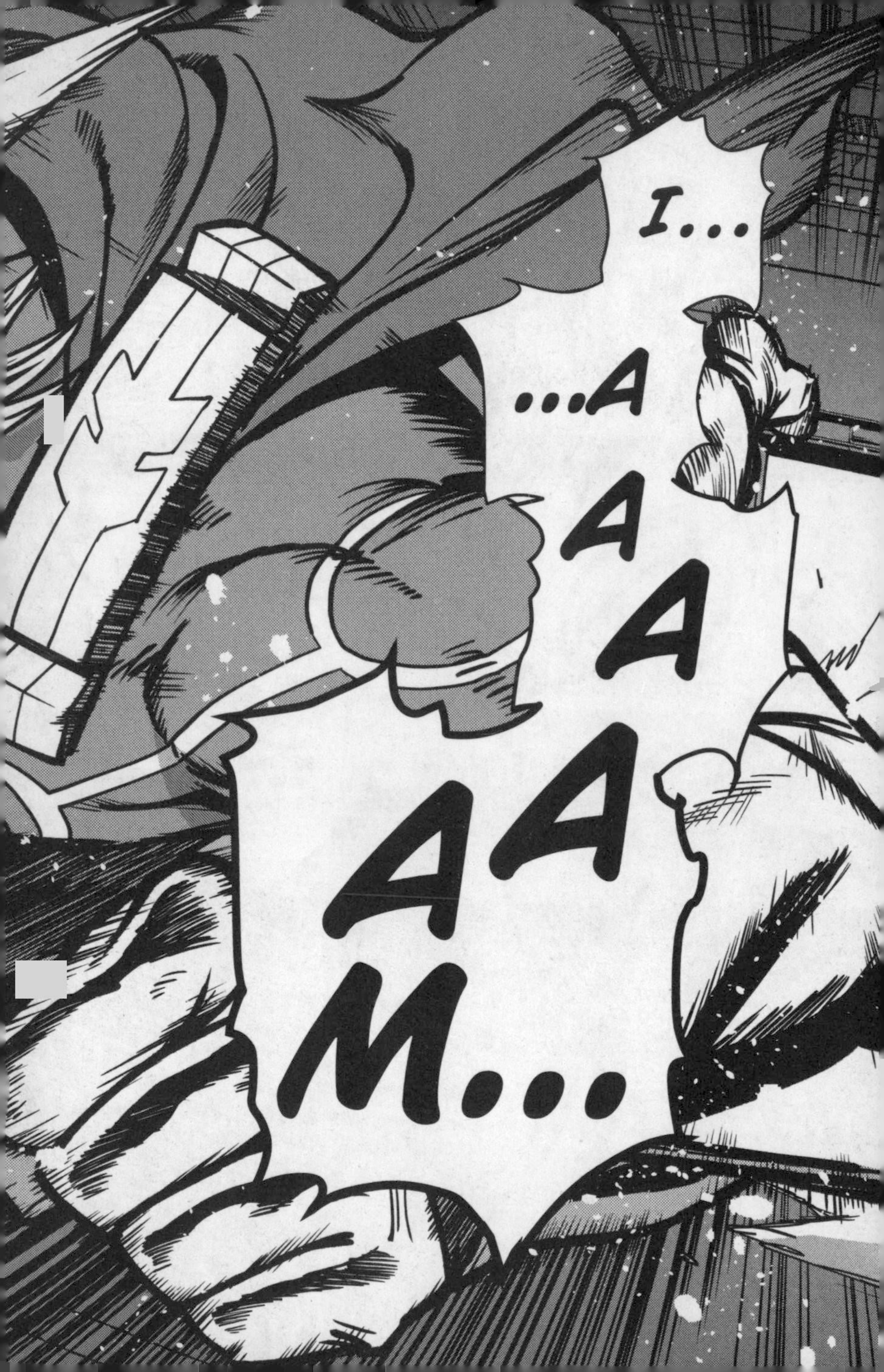
I...
...AAAAAAM...

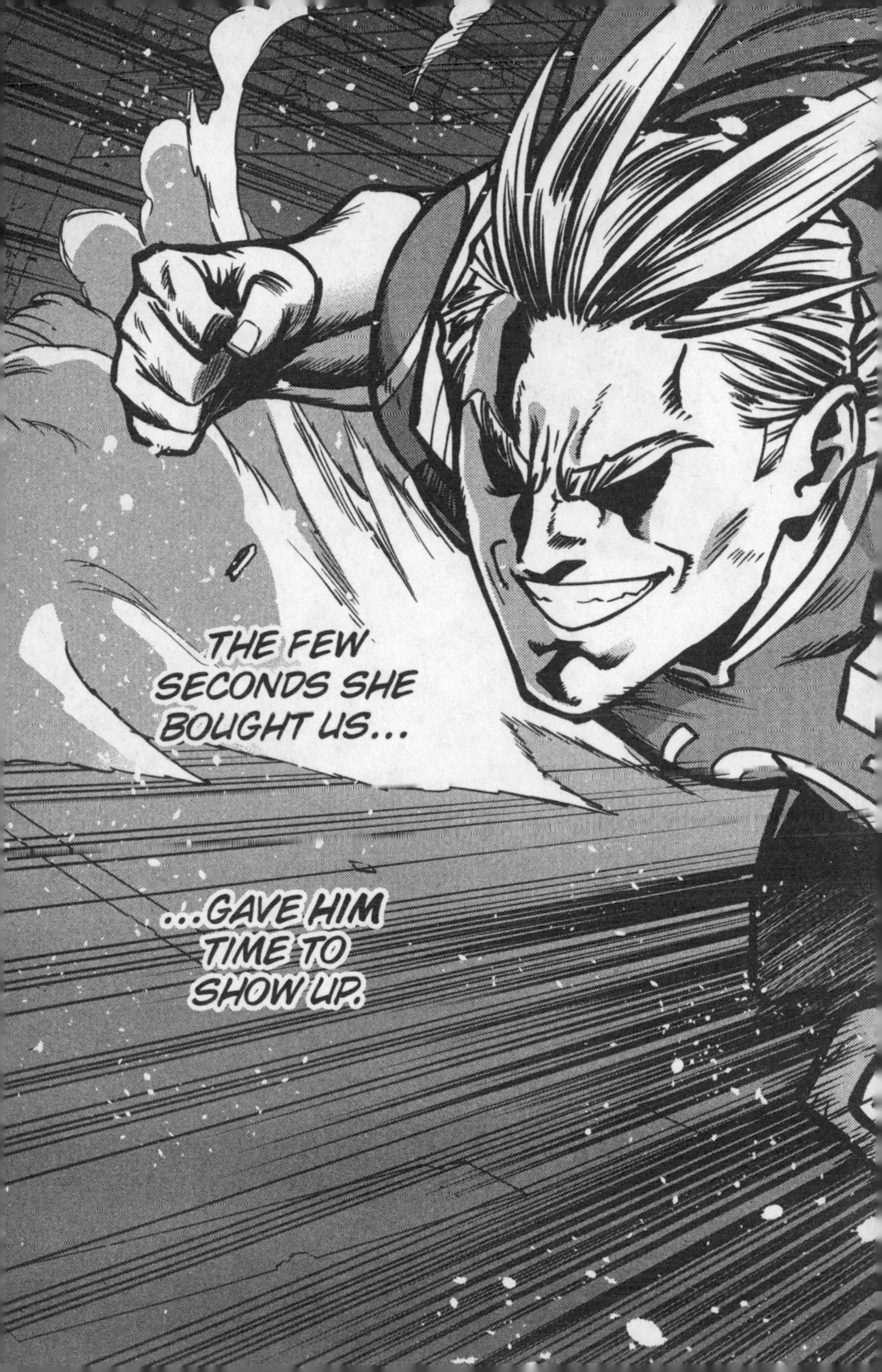
THE FEW SECONDS SHE BOUGHT US...
...GAVE HIM TIME TO SHOW UP.

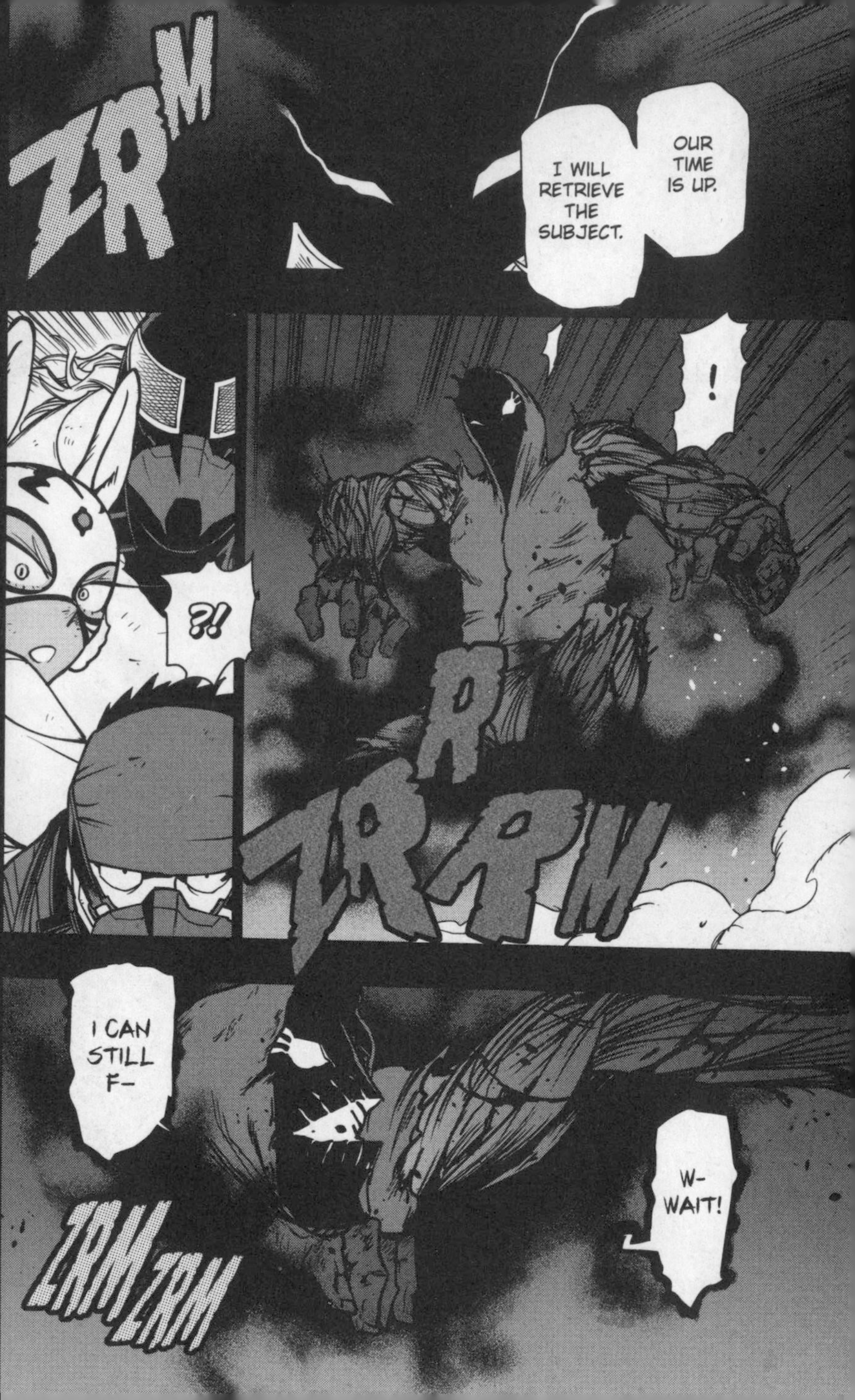
OUR TIME IS UP.
I WILL RETRIEVE THE SUBJECT.
ZRM
!
!
ZRRRM
?!
W- WAIT!
I CAN STILL F-
ZRM ZRM

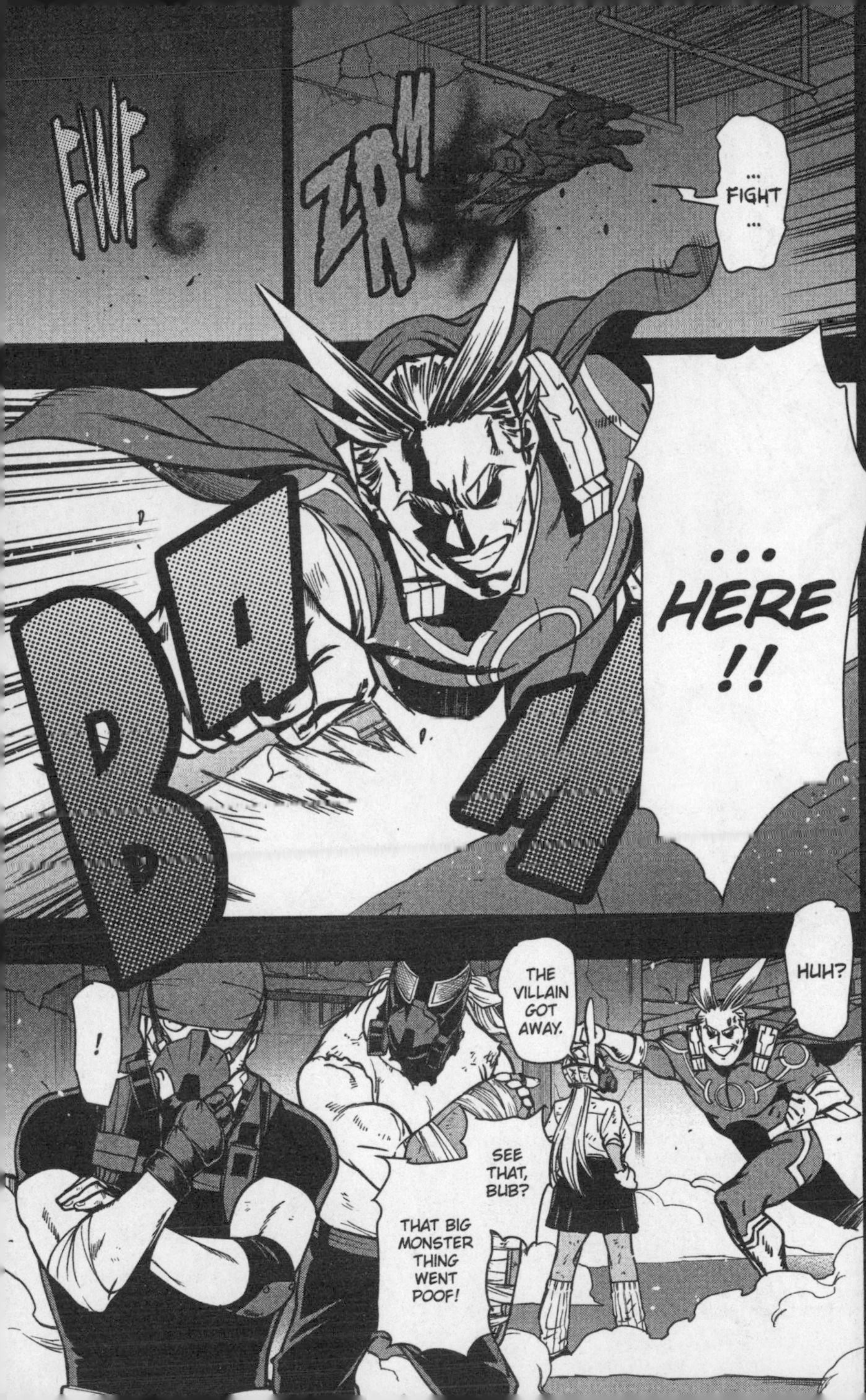

... FIGHT ...
ZRM
FWF
... HERE !!
BAM
HUH?
THE VILLAIN GOT AWAY.
!
SEE THAT, BUB?
THAT BIG MONSTER THING WENT POOF!

THE COLUMN

HOOD

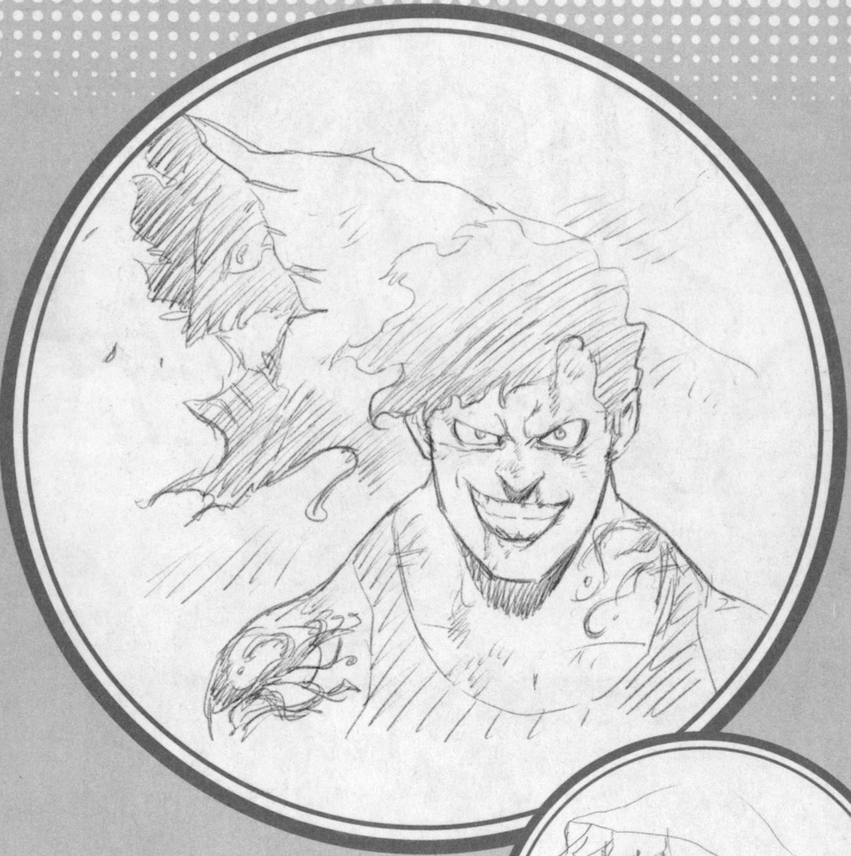

I was glad I decided to bring in the brawler who eventually becomes the Nomu called Hood and just have him wearing a sweatshirt with a hood. (LOL) But if that had been the extent of it, people might've been like, "Wait, who was that anyway?" so we needed to have him grow gigantic, as an extra hint.

—Furuhashi

Horikoshi Sensei went out of his way to provide us with concept art for a midway point of Hood's evolution, but the timing just didn't work out right on our end. Sorry!

—Betten

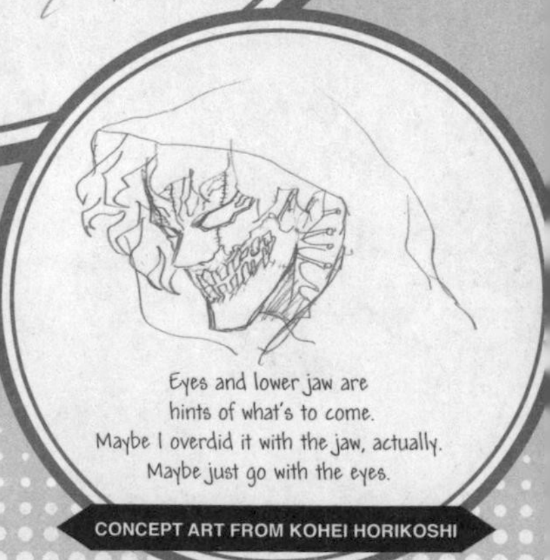
Eyes and lower jaw are
hints of what's to come.
Maybe I overdid it with the jaw, actually.
Maybe just go with the eyes.

CONCEPT ART FROM KOHEI HORIKOSHI

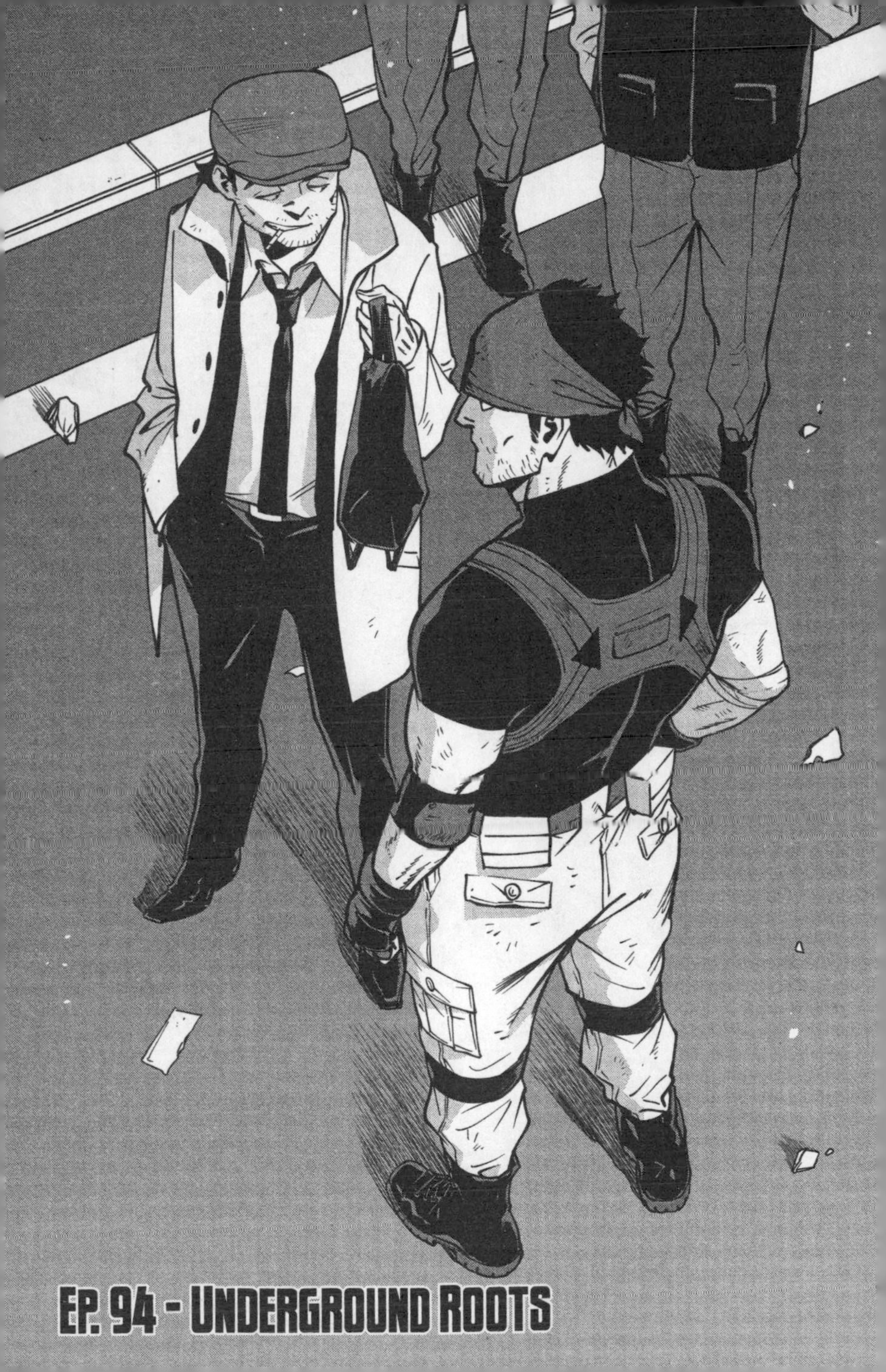

Ep. 94 - Underground Roots

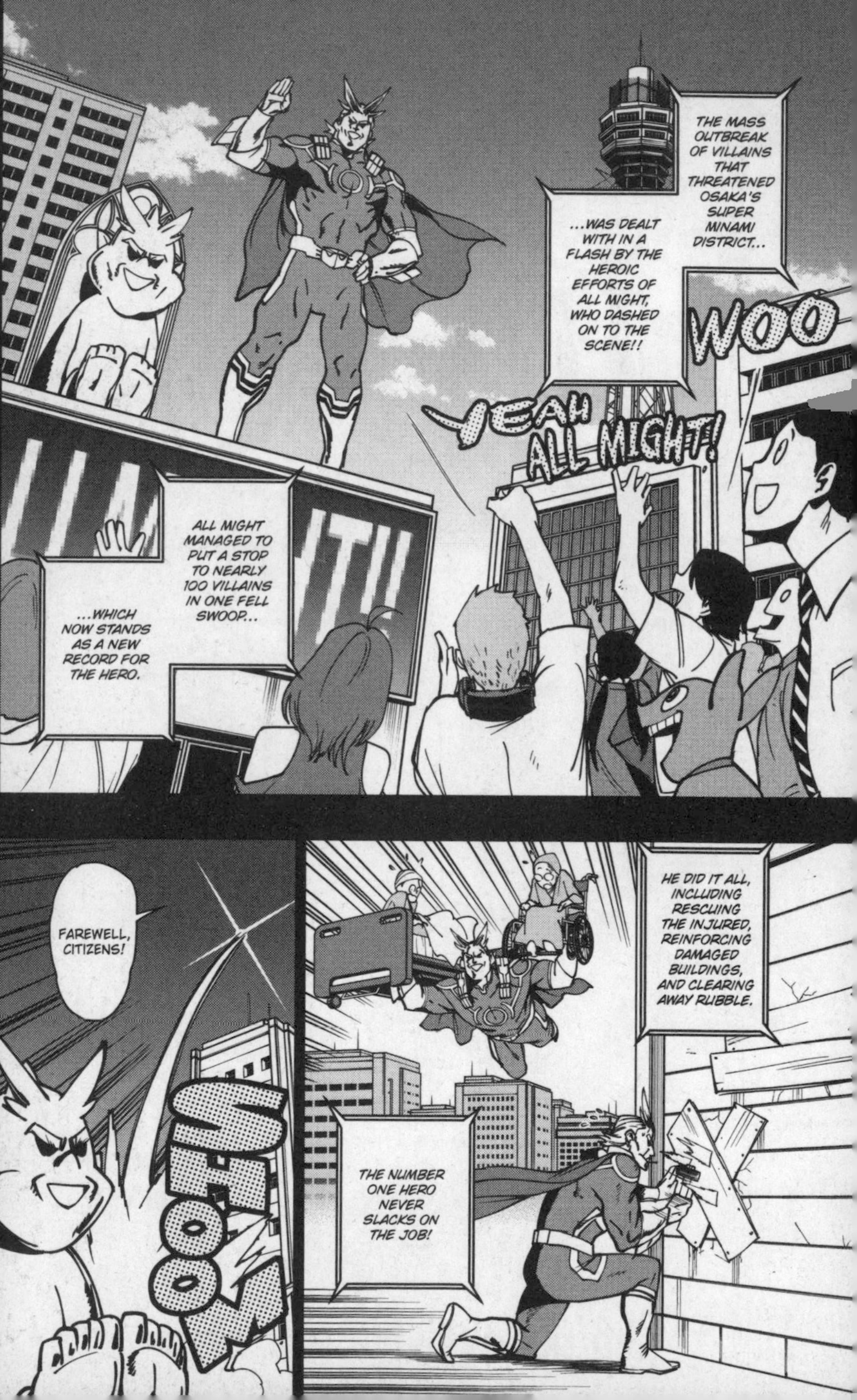
THE MASS OUTBREAK OF VILLAINS THAT THREATENED OSAKA'S SUPER MINAMI DISTRICT...
...WAS DEALT WITH IN A FLASH BY THE HEROIC EFFORTS OF ALL MIGHT, WHO DASHED ON TO THE SCENE!!
WOO
YEAH
ALL MIGHT!
ALL MIGHT MANAGED TO PUT A STOP TO NEARLY 100 VILLAINS IN ONE FELL SWOOP...
...WHICH NOW STANDS AS A NEW RECORD FOR THE HERO.
HE DID IT ALL, INCLUDING RESCUING THE INJURED, REINFORCING DAMAGED BUILDINGS, AND CLEARING AWAY RUBBLE.
THE NUMBER ONE HERO NEVER SLACKS ON THE JOB!
FAREWELL, CITIZENS!

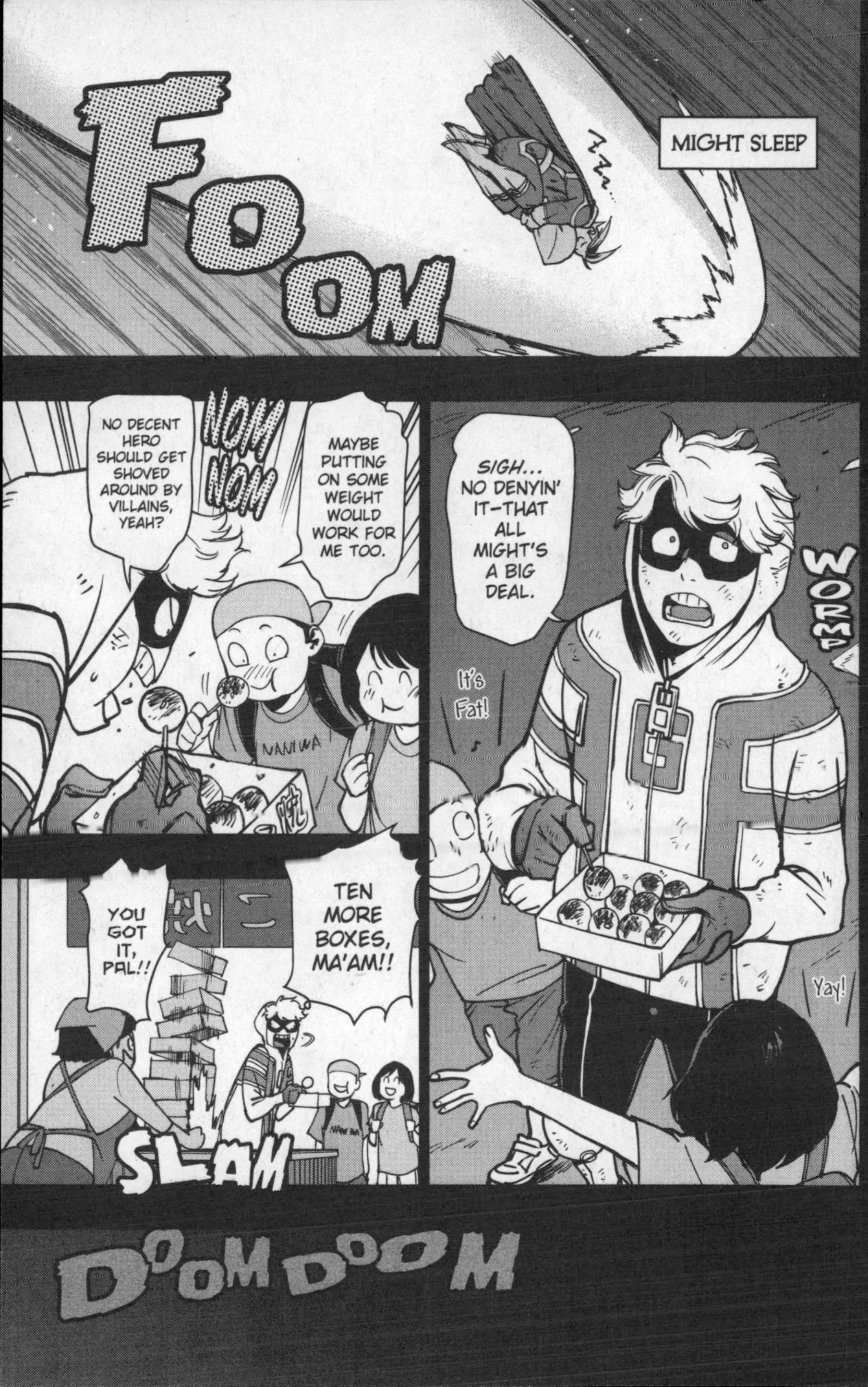
MIGHT SLEEP
ZZZ...
FOOM
SIGH... NO DENYIN' IT—THAT ALL MIGHT'S A BIG DEAL.
WORMP
It's Fat!
Yay!
MAYBE PUTTING ON SOME WEIGHT WOULD WORK FOR ME TOO.
NOM NOM
NO DECENT HERO SHOULD GET SHOVED AROUND BY VILLAINS, YEAH?
NANIWA
TEN MORE BOXES, MA'AM!!
YOU GOT IT, PAL!!
SLAM
DOOM DOOM

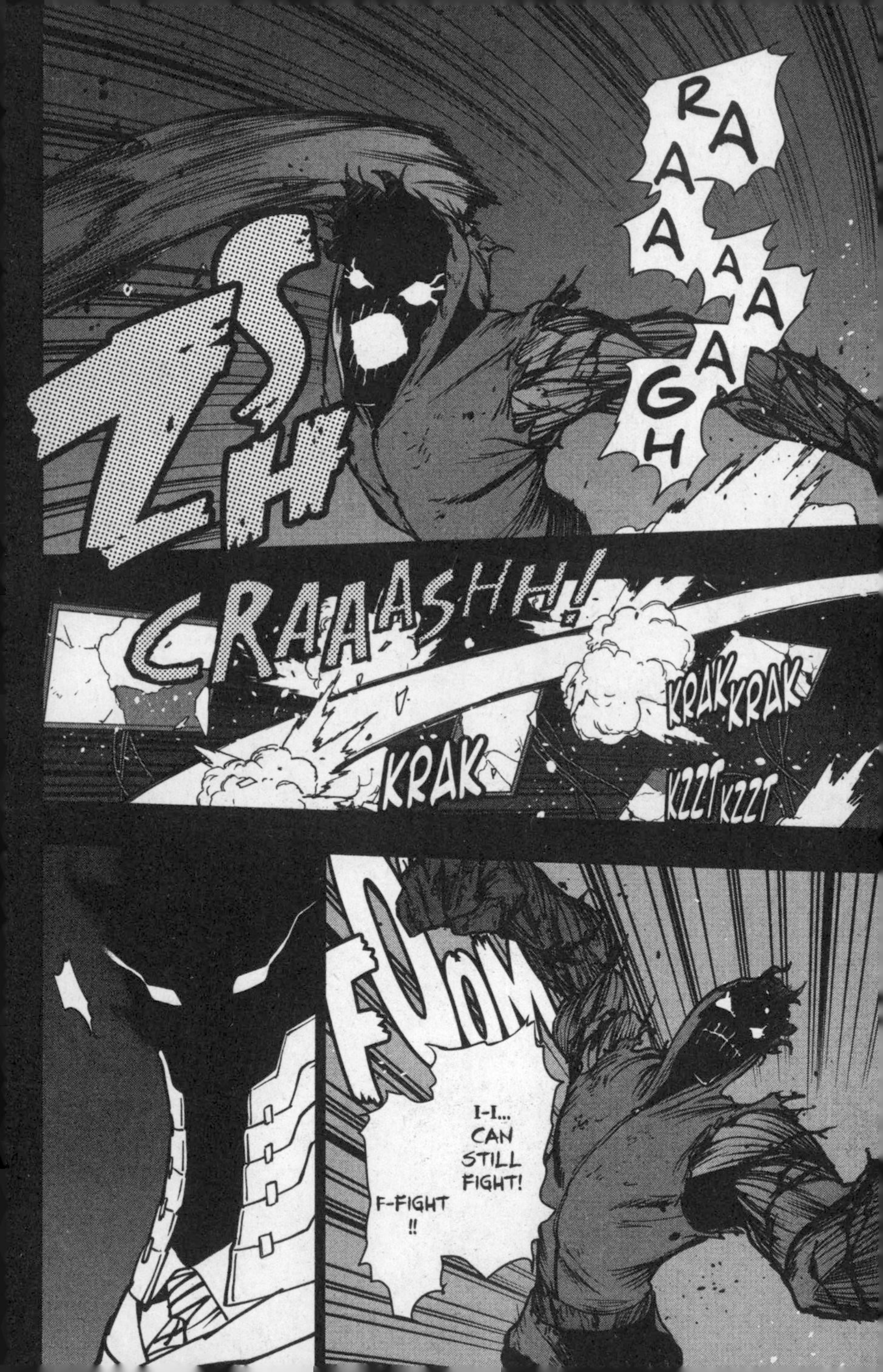
RAAAAAAAGH
ZSH
KRAKKRAK
KZZT KZZT
CRAAASHH!
KRAK
FOOM
I-I... CAN STILL FIGHT!
F-FIGHT !!

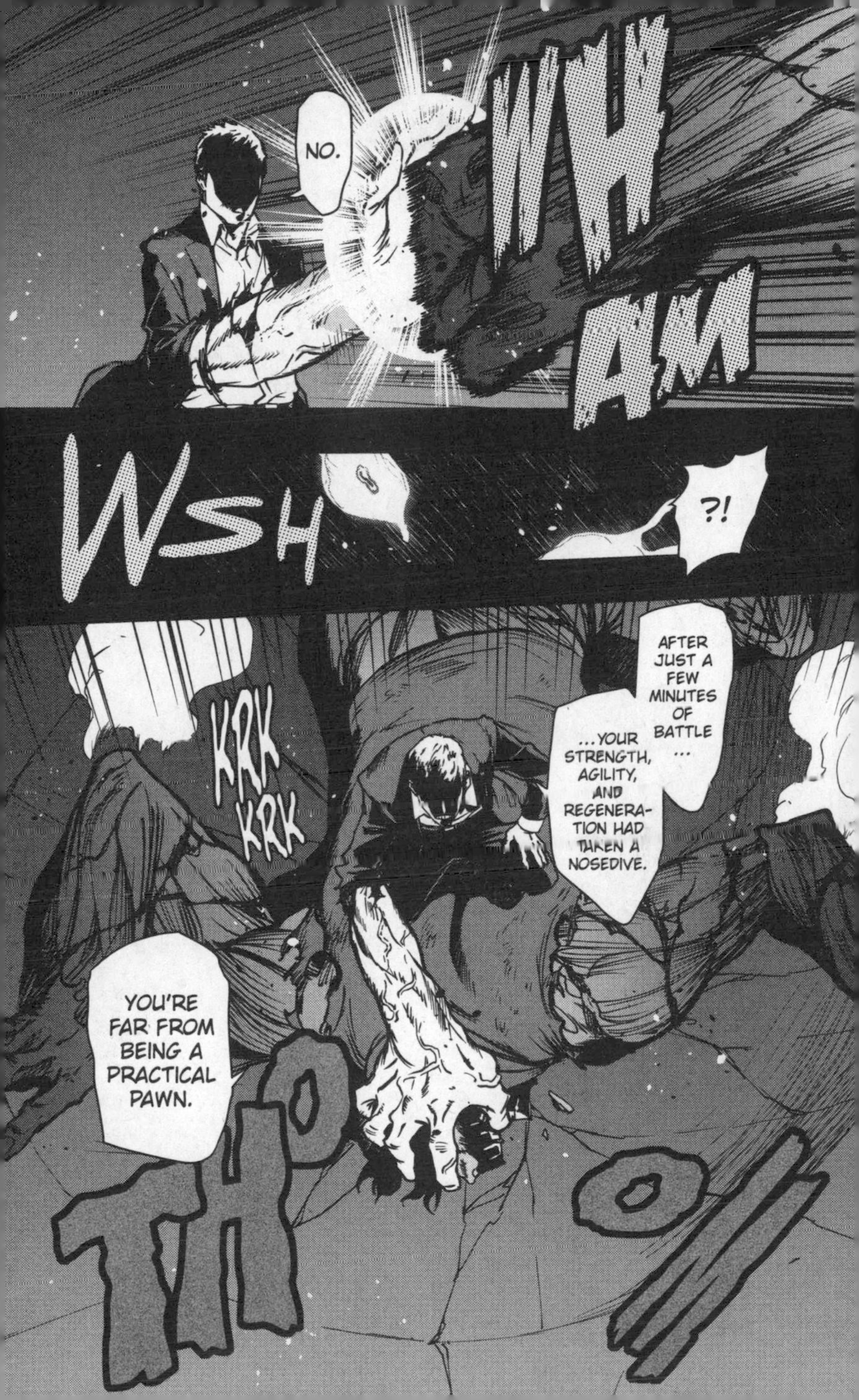
WHAM
NO.
?!
WSH
AFTER JUST A FEW MINUTES OF BATTLE...
...YOUR STRENGTH, AGILITY, AND REGENERATION HAD TAKEN A NOSEDIVE.
KRK KRK
YOU'RE FAR FROM BEING A PRACTICAL PAWN.
THO

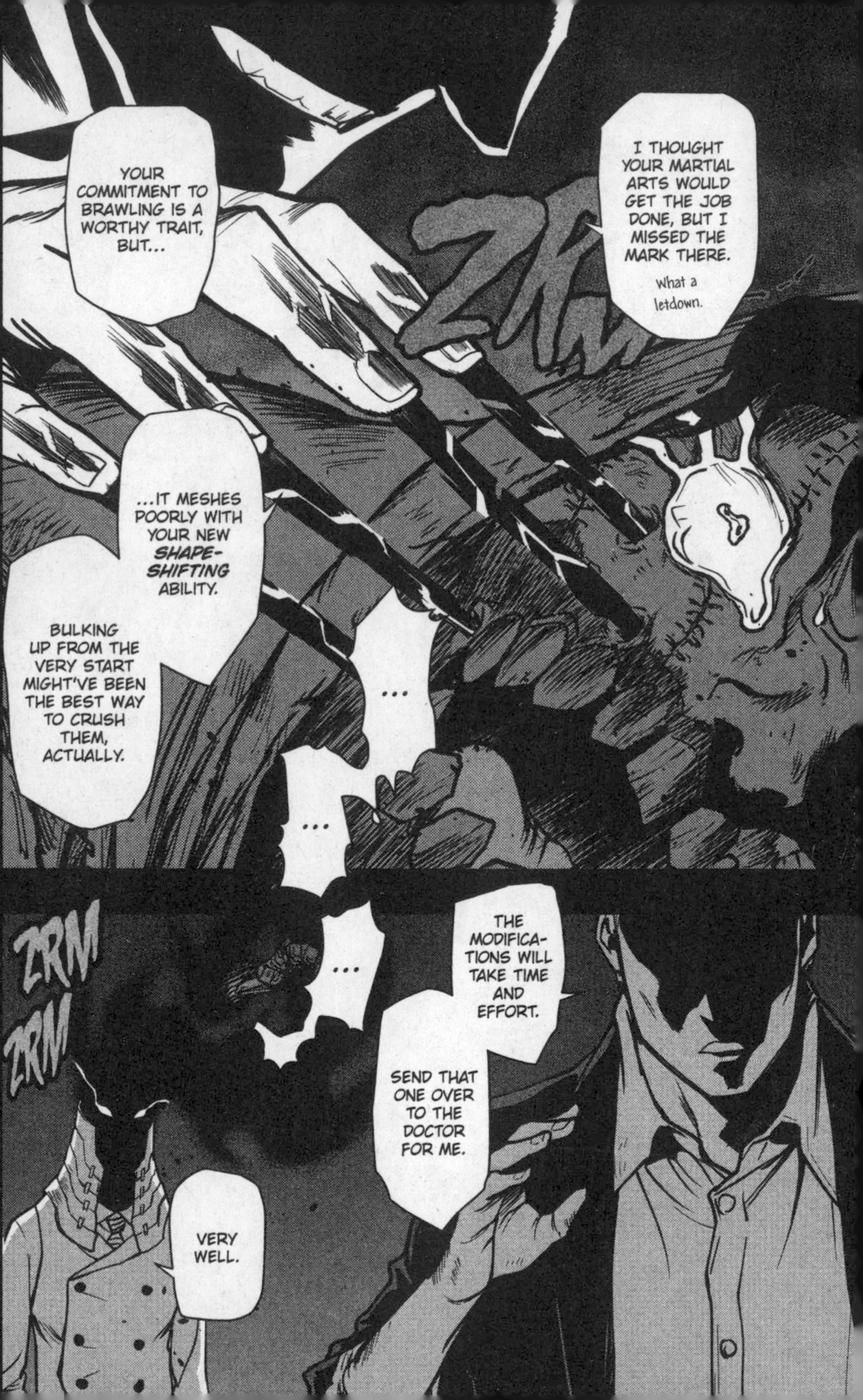
I THOUGHT YOUR MARTIAL ARTS WOULD GET THE JOB DONE, BUT I MISSED THE MARK THERE.
What a letdown.
YOUR COMMITMENT TO BRAWLING IS A WORTHY TRAIT, BUT...
...IT MESHES POORLY WITH YOUR NEW *SHAPE-SHIFTING* ABILITY.
BULKING UP FROM THE VERY START MIGHT'VE BEEN THE BEST WAY TO CRUSH THEM, ACTUALLY.
...
...
THE MODIFICATIONS WILL TAKE TIME AND EFFORT.
SEND THAT ONE OVER TO THE DOCTOR FOR ME.
...
ZRM ZRM
VERY WELL.

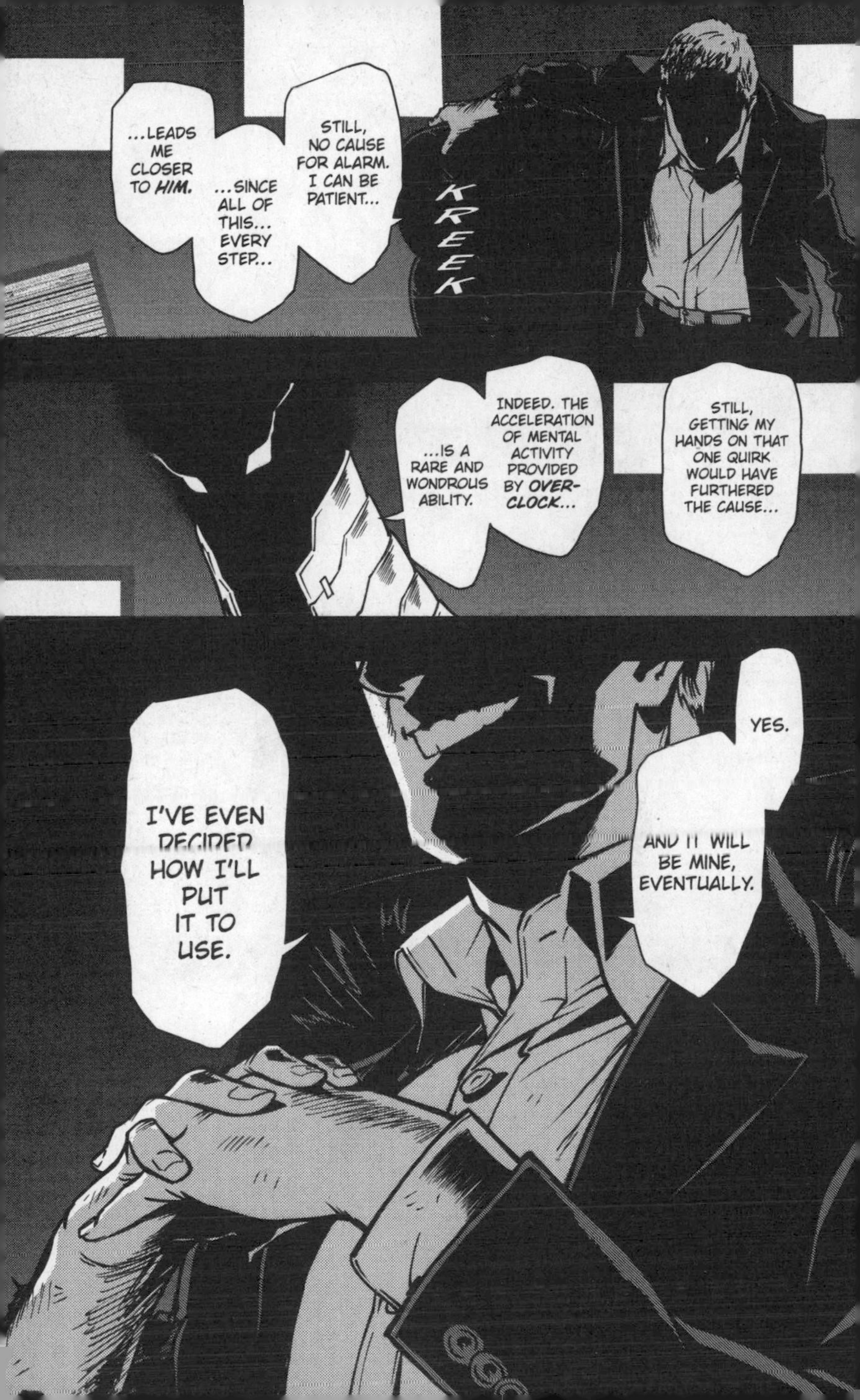
KREEK
STILL, NO CAUSE FOR ALARM. I CAN BE PATIENT...
...SINCE ALL OF THIS... EVERY STEP...
...LEADS ME CLOSER TO HIM.
STILL, GETTING MY HANDS ON THAT ONE QUIRK WOULD HAVE FURTHERED THE CAUSE...
INDEED. THE ACCELERATION OF MENTAL ACTIVITY PROVIDED BY OVER-CLOCK...
...IS A RARE AND WONDROUS ABILITY.
YES.
AND IT WILL BE MINE, EVENTUALLY.
I'VE EVEN DECIDED HOW I'LL PUT IT TO USE.

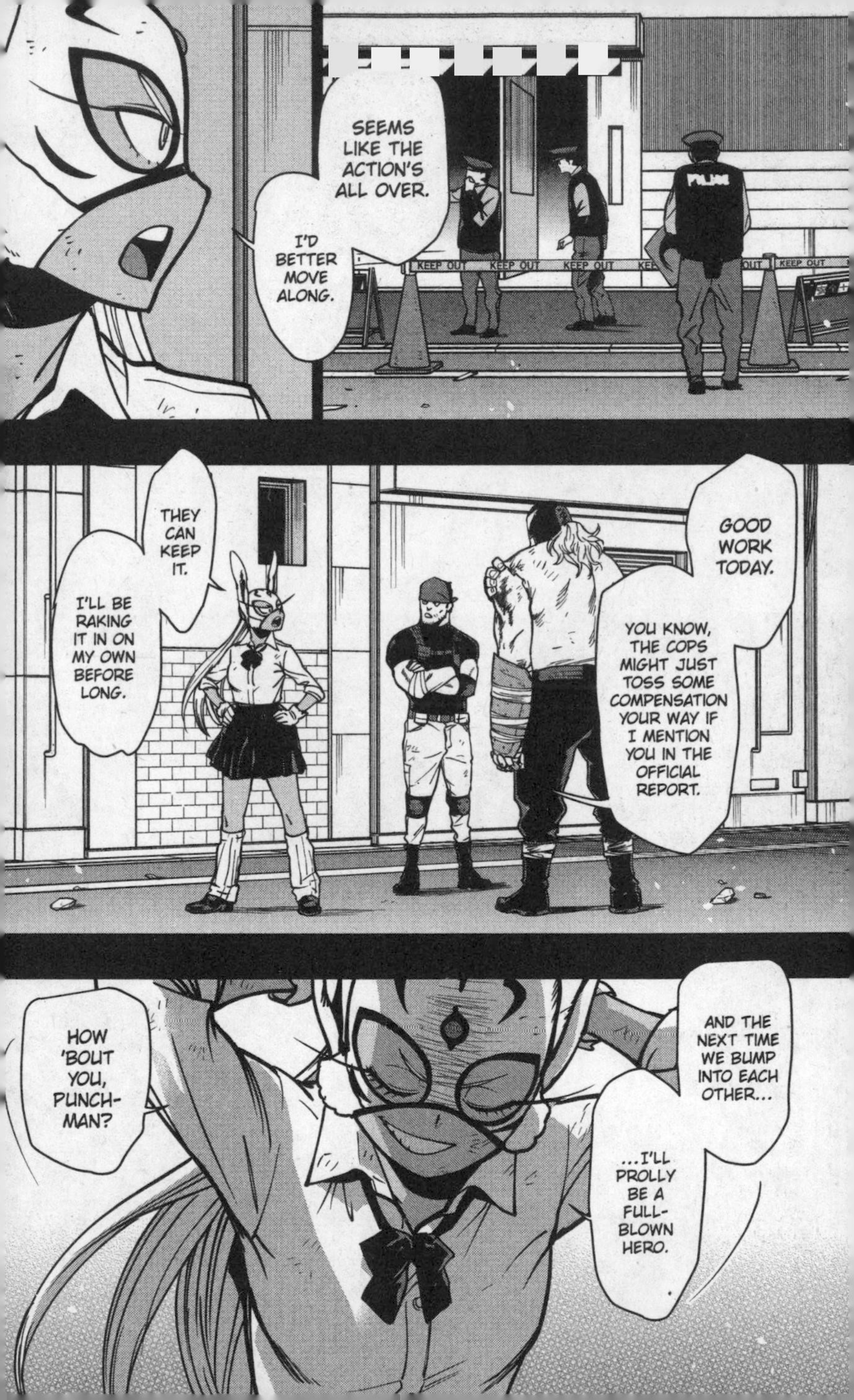
KEEP OUT
SEEMS LIKE THE ACTION'S ALL OVER.
I'D BETTER MOVE ALONG.
GOOD WORK TODAY.
YOU KNOW, THE COPS MIGHT JUST TOSS SOME COMPENSATION YOUR WAY IF I MENTION YOU IN THE OFFICIAL REPORT.
THEY CAN KEEP IT.
I'LL BE RAKING IT IN ON MY OWN BEFORE LONG.
AND THE NEXT TIME WE BUMP INTO EACH OTHER...
...I'LL PROLLY BE A FULL-BLOWN HERO.
HOW 'BOUT YOU, PUNCH-MAN?

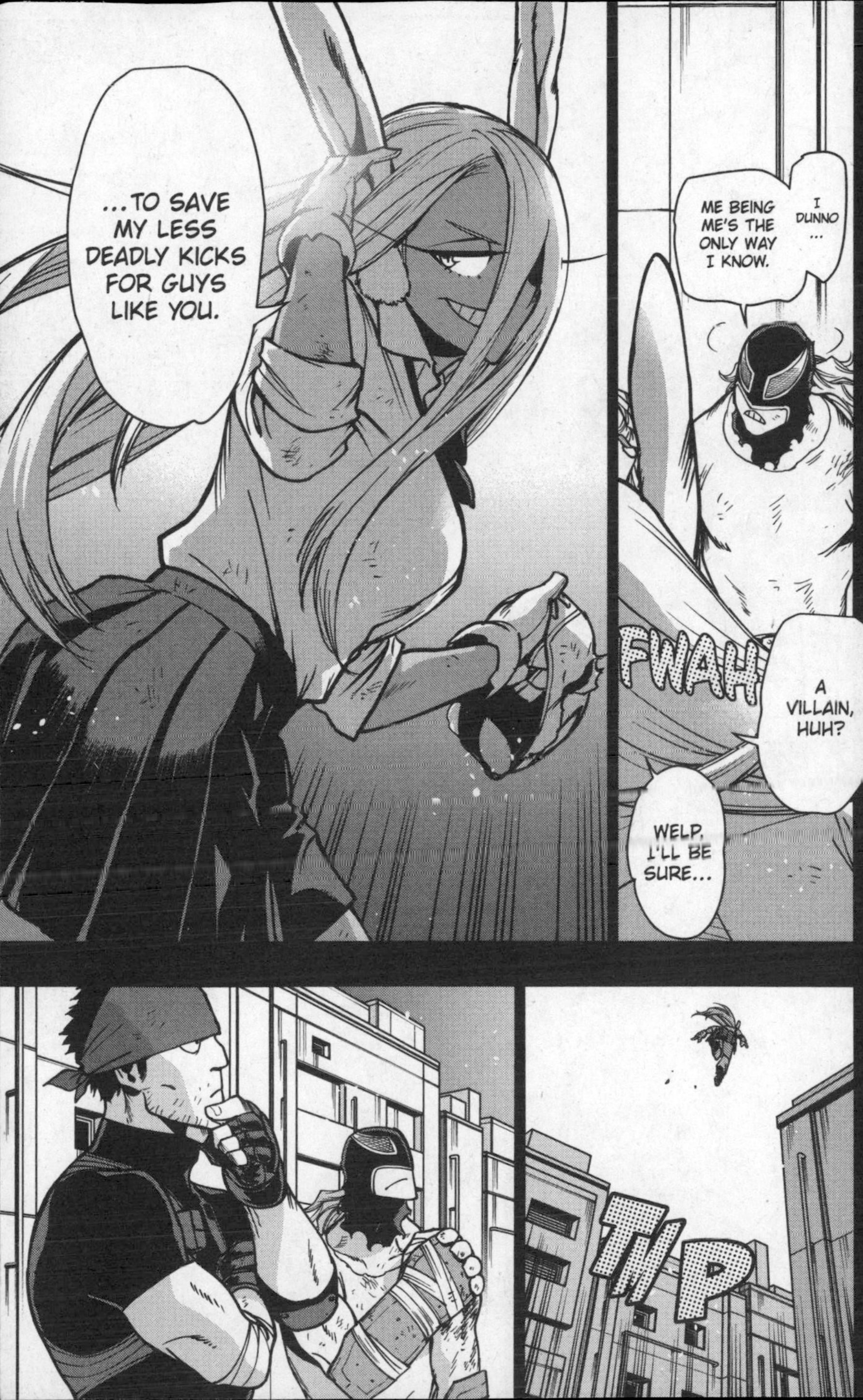
I DUNNO ...
ME BEING ME'S THE ONLY WAY I KNOW.
FWAH
A VILLAIN, HUH?
WELP, I'LL BE SURE...
...TO SAVE MY LESS DEADLY KICKS FOR GUYS LIKE YOU.
THP

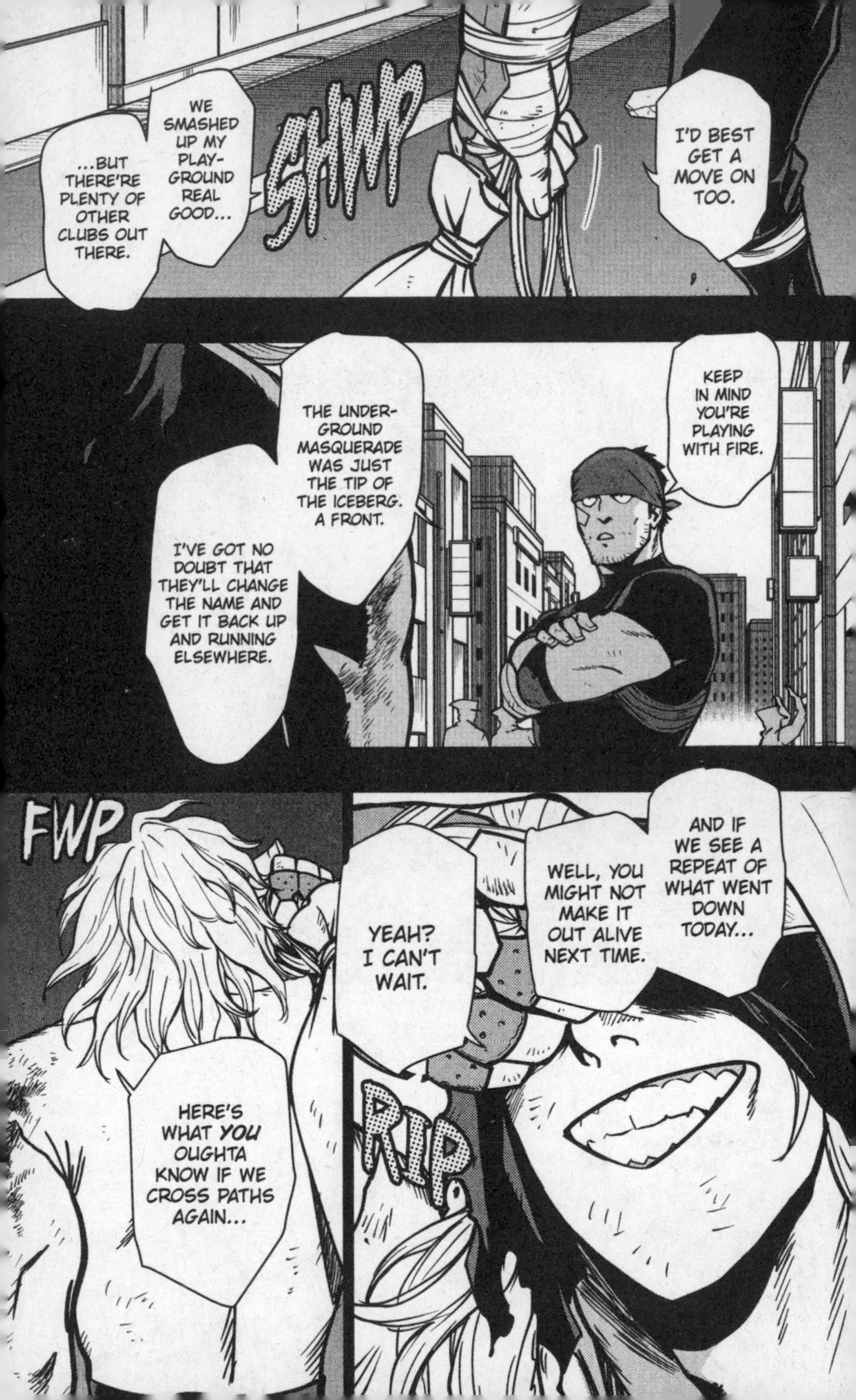
I'D BEST GET A MOVE ON TOO.
SHWP
WE SMASHED UP MY PLAY-GROUND REAL GOOD...
...BUT THERE'RE PLENTY OF OTHER CLUBS OUT THERE.
KEEP IN MIND YOU'RE PLAYING WITH FIRE.
THE UNDER-GROUND MASQUERADE WAS JUST THE TIP OF THE ICEBERG. A FRONT.
I'VE GOT NO DOUBT THAT THEY'LL CHANGE THE NAME AND GET IT BACK UP AND RUNNING ELSEWHERE.
AND IF WE SEE A REPEAT OF WHAT WENT DOWN TODAY...
WELL, YOU MIGHT NOT MAKE IT OUT ALIVE NEXT TIME.
YEAH? I CAN'T WAIT.
RIP
FWP
HERE'S WHAT *YOU* OUGHTA KNOW IF WE CROSS PATHS AGAIN...

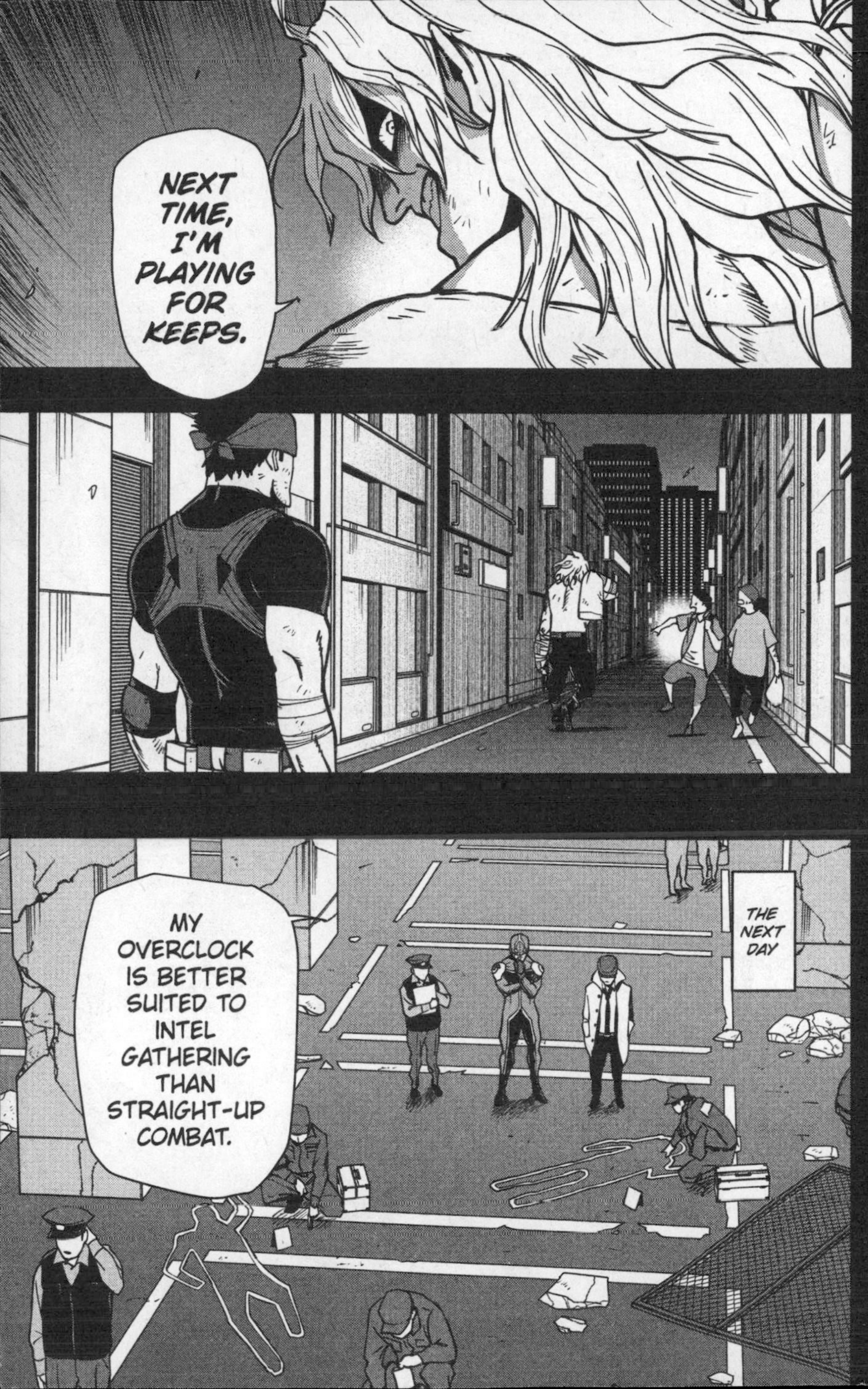
NEXT TIME, I'M PLAYING FOR KEEPS.
THE NEXT DAY
MY OVERCLOCK IS BETTER SUITED TO INTEL GATHERING THAN STRAIGHT-UP COMBAT.

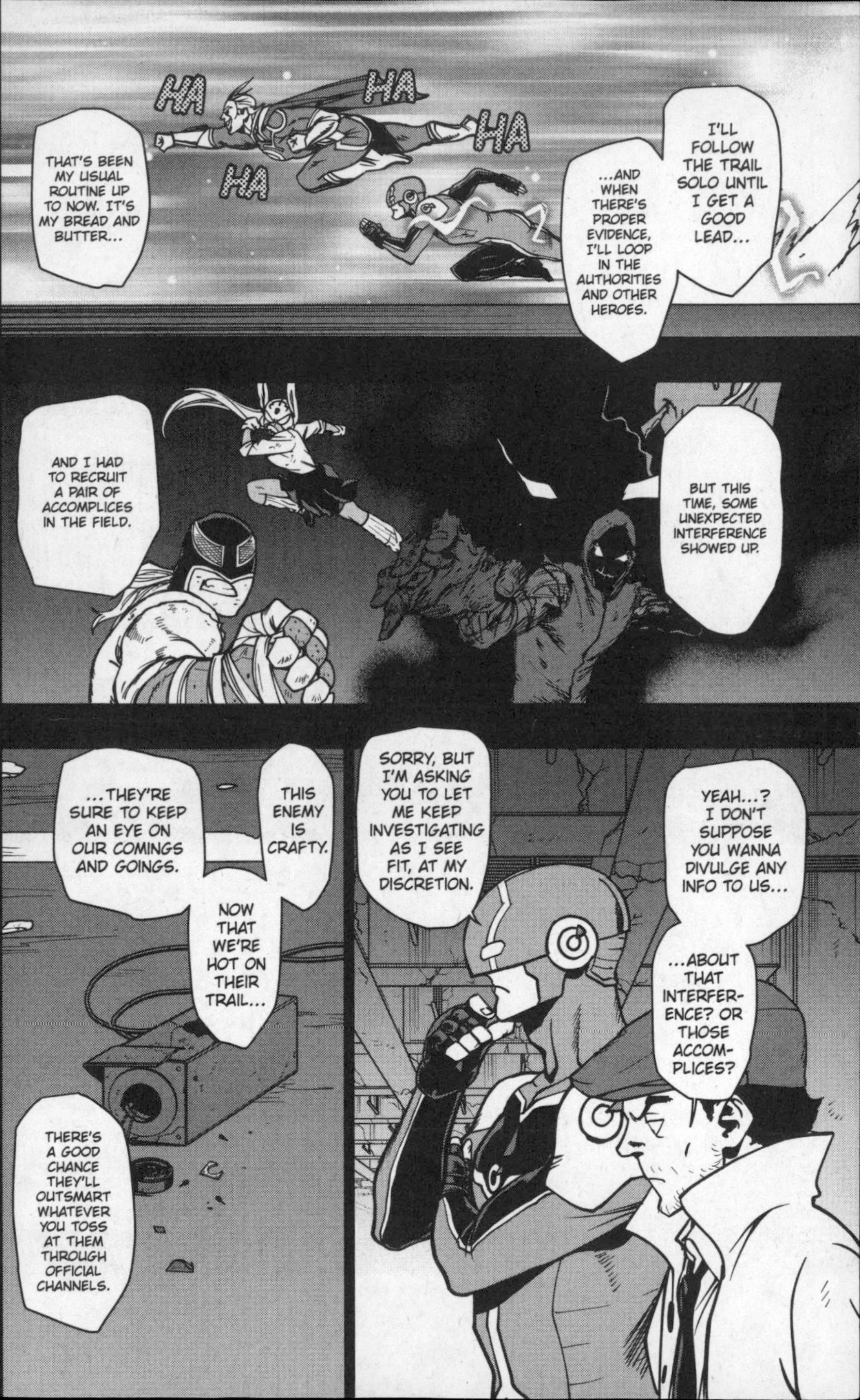
I'LL FOLLOW THE TRAIL SOLO UNTIL I GET A GOOD LEAD...
...AND WHEN THERE'S PROPER EVIDENCE, I'LL LOOP IN THE AUTHORITIES AND OTHER HEROES.
HA
HA
HA
HA
THAT'S BEEN MY USUAL ROUTINE UP TO NOW. IT'S MY BREAD AND BUTTER...
BUT THIS TIME, SOME UNEXPECTED INTERFERENCE SHOWED UP.
AND I HAD TO RECRUIT A PAIR OF ACCOMPLICES IN THE FIELD.
YEAH...? I DON'T SUPPOSE YOU WANNA DIVULGE ANY INFO TO US...
...ABOUT THAT INTERFER-ENCE? OR THOSE ACCOM-PLICES?
SORRY, BUT I'M ASKING YOU TO LET ME KEEP INVESTIGATING AS I SEE FIT, AT MY DISCRETION.
THIS ENEMY IS CRAFTY.
NOW THAT WE'RE HOT ON THEIR TRAIL...
...THEY'RE SURE TO KEEP AN EYE ON OUR COMINGS AND GOINGS.
THERE'S A GOOD CHANCE THEY'LL OUTSMART WHATEVER YOU TOSS AT THEM THROUGH OFFICIAL CHANNELS.

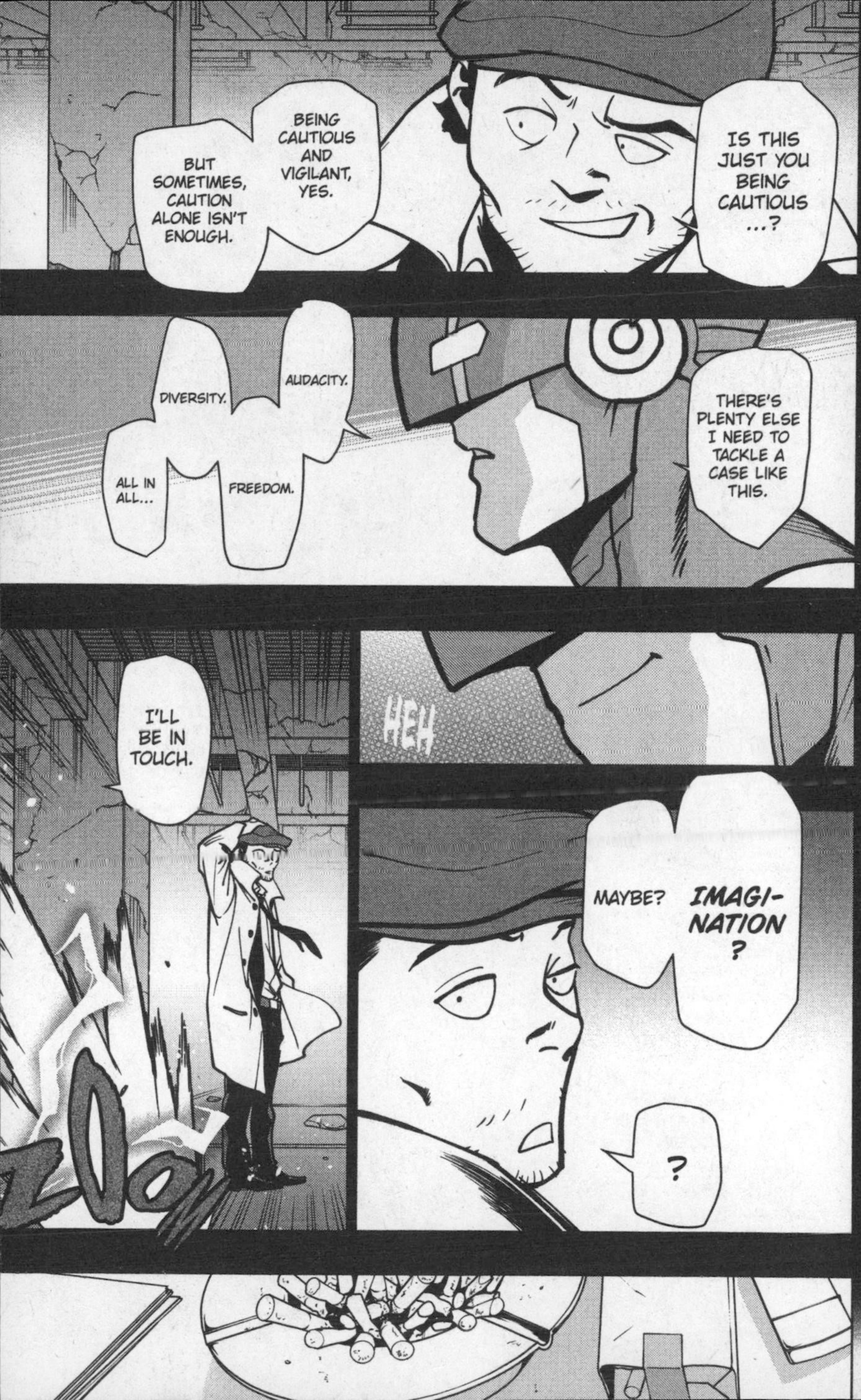
IS THIS JUST YOU BEING CAUTIOUS ...?
BEING CAUTIOUS AND VIGILANT, YES.
BUT SOMETIMES, CAUTION ALONE ISN'T ENOUGH.
THERE'S PLENTY ELSE I NEED TO TACKLE A CASE LIKE THIS.
AUDACITY.
DIVERSITY.
FREEDOM.
ALL IN ALL...
HEH
IMAGINATION ?
MAYBE?
?
I'LL BE IN TOUCH.

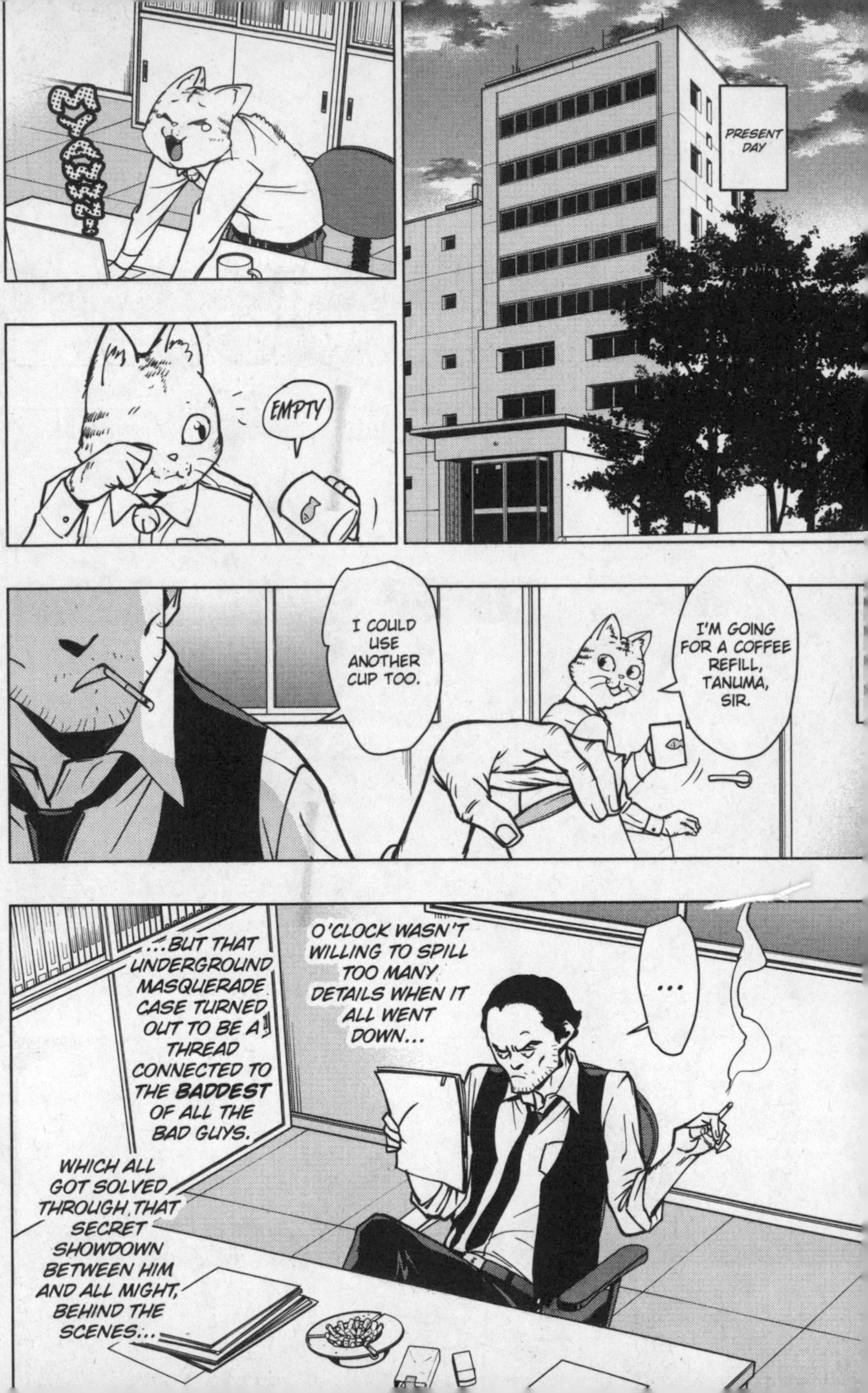
PRESENT DAY
EMPTY
I'M GOING FOR A COFFEE REFILL, TANUMA, SIR.
I COULD USE ANOTHER CUP TOO.
...
O'CLOCK WASN'T WILLING TO SPILL TOO MANY DETAILS WHEN IT ALL WENT DOWN...
...BUT THAT UNDERGROUND MASQUERADE CASE TURNED OUT TO BE A THREAD CONNECTED TO THE BADDEST OF ALL THE BAD GUYS.
WHICH ALL GOT SOLVED THROUGH THAT SECRET SHOWDOWN BETWEEN HIM AND ALL MIGHT, BEHIND THE SCENES...

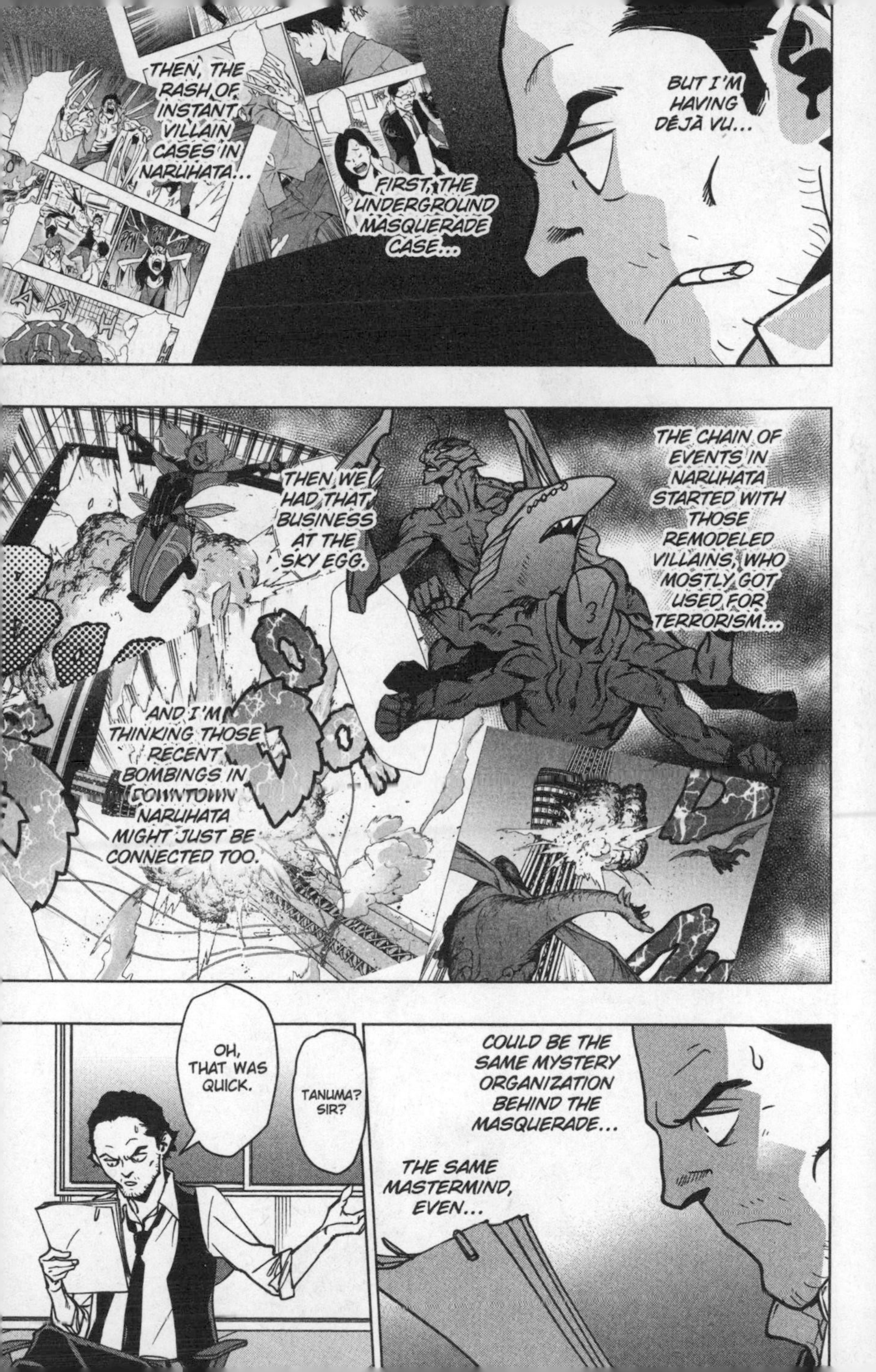
BUT I'M HAVING DÉJÀ VU...
FIRST, THE UNDERGROUND MASQUERADE CASE...
THEN, THE RASH OF INSTANT VILLAIN CASES IN NARUHATA...
THE CHAIN OF EVENTS IN NARUHATA STARTED WITH THOSE REMODELED VILLAINS, WHO MOSTLY GOT USED FOR TERRORISM...
THEN WE HAD THAT BUSINESS AT THE SKY EGG.
AND I'M THINKING THOSE RECENT BOMBINGS IN DOWNTOWN NARUHATA MIGHT JUST BE CONNECTED TOO.
COULD BE THE SAME MYSTERY ORGANIZATION BEHIND THE MASQUERADE...
THE SAME MASTERMIND, EVEN...
TANUMA? SIR?
OH, THAT WAS QUICK.

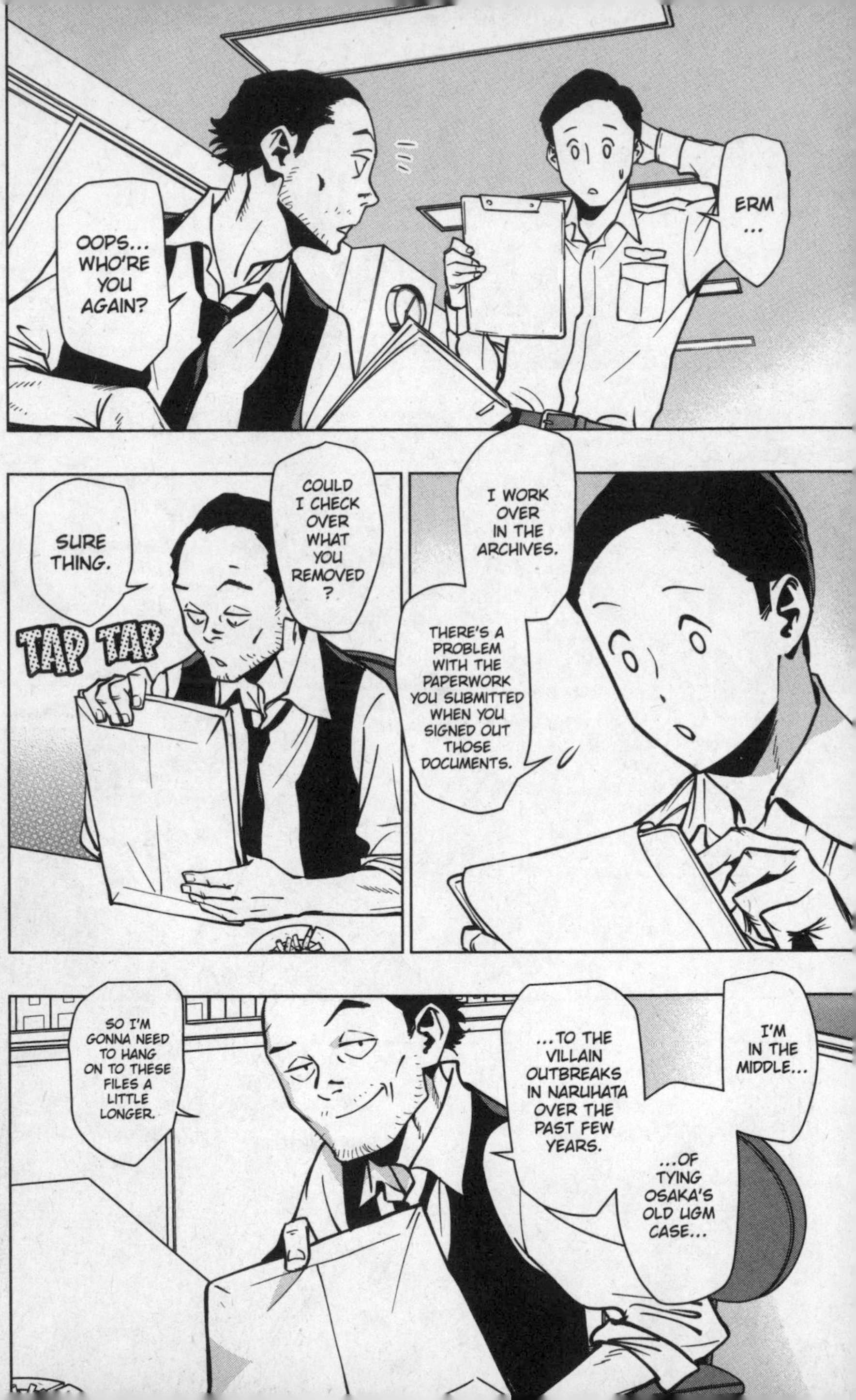
ERM ...
OOPS... WHO'RE YOU AGAIN?
I WORK OVER IN THE ARCHIVES.
THERE'S A PROBLEM WITH THE PAPERWORK YOU SUBMITTED WHEN YOU SIGNED OUT THOSE DOCUMENTS.
COULD I CHECK OVER WHAT YOU REMOVED ?
SURE THING.
TAP TAP
I'M IN THE MIDDLE...
...OF TYING OSAKA'S OLD UGM CASE...
...TO THE VILLAIN OUTBREAKS IN NARUHATA OVER THE PAST FEW YEARS.
SO I'M GONNA NEED TO HANG ON TO THESE FILES A LITTLE LONGER.

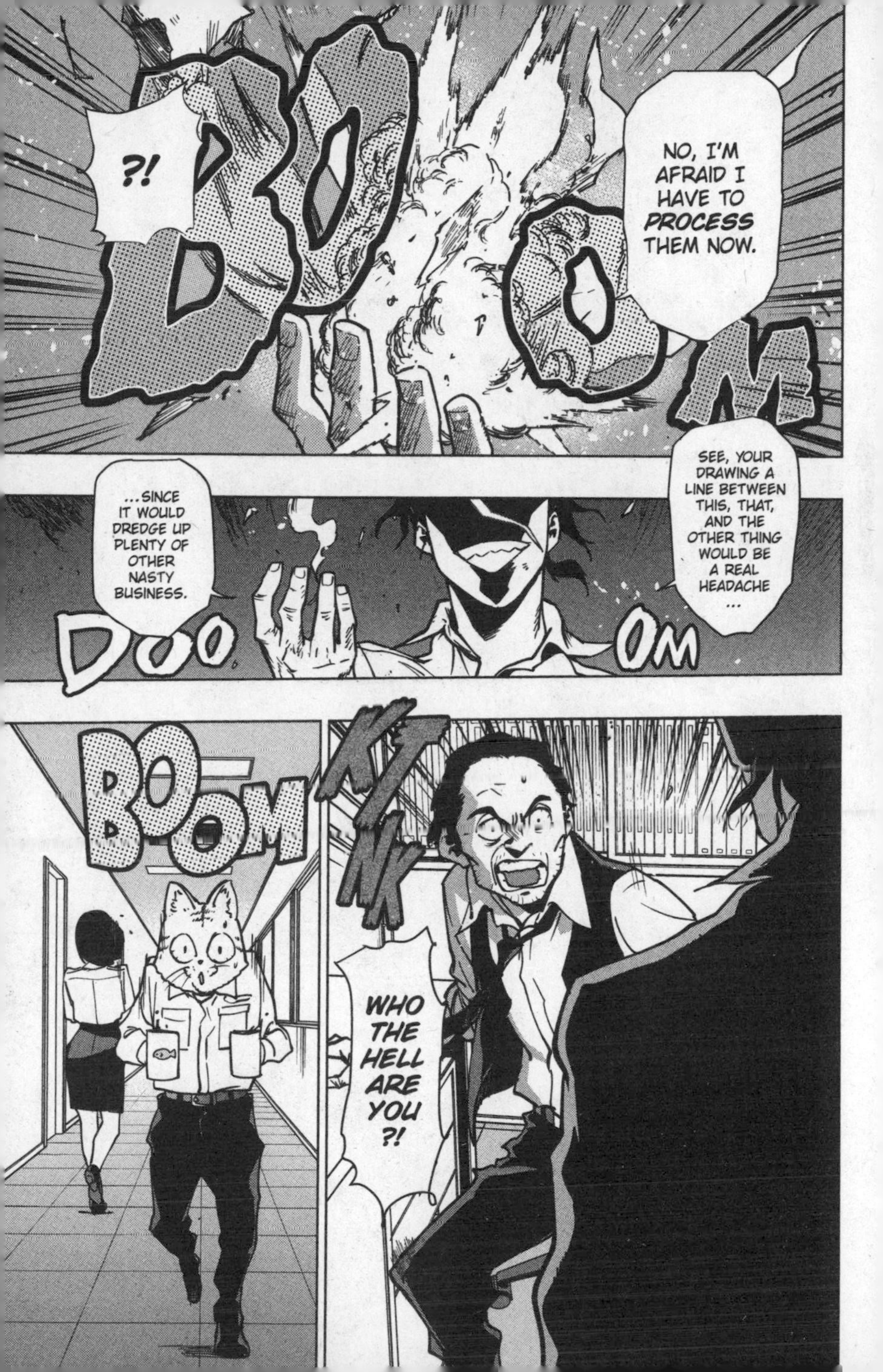
NO, I'M AFRAID I HAVE TO *PROCESS* THEM NOW.
?!
BOOM
SEE, YOUR DRAWING A LINE BETWEEN THIS, THAT, AND THE OTHER THING WOULD BE A REAL HEADACHE ...
...SINCE IT WOULD DREDGE UP PLENTY OF OTHER NASTY BUSINESS.
DOO OM
WHO THE HELL ARE YOU ?!
BOOM

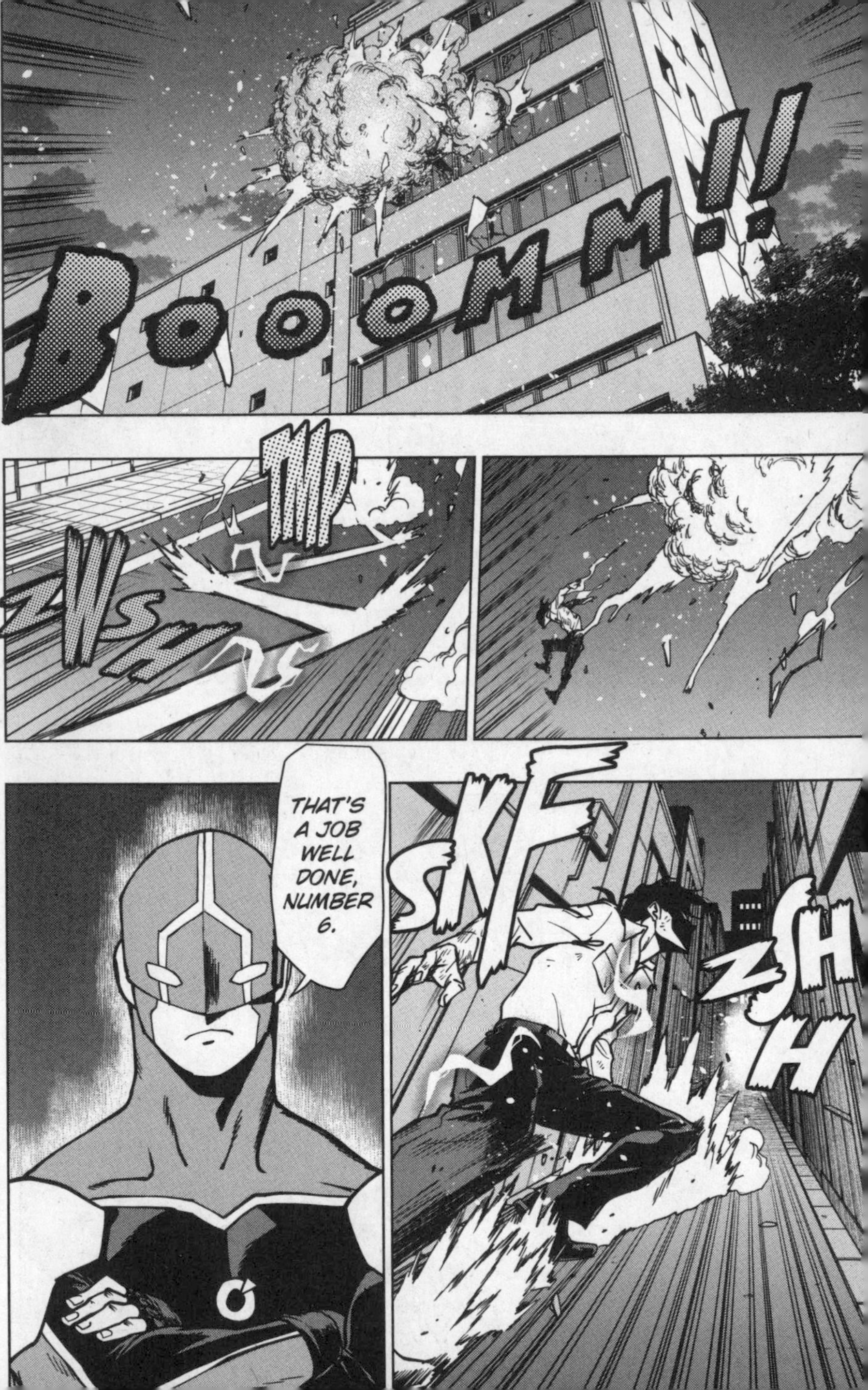
BOOOMM!!
TMP
ZWSSH
SKF
ZSHH
THAT'S A JOB WELL DONE, NUMBER 6.

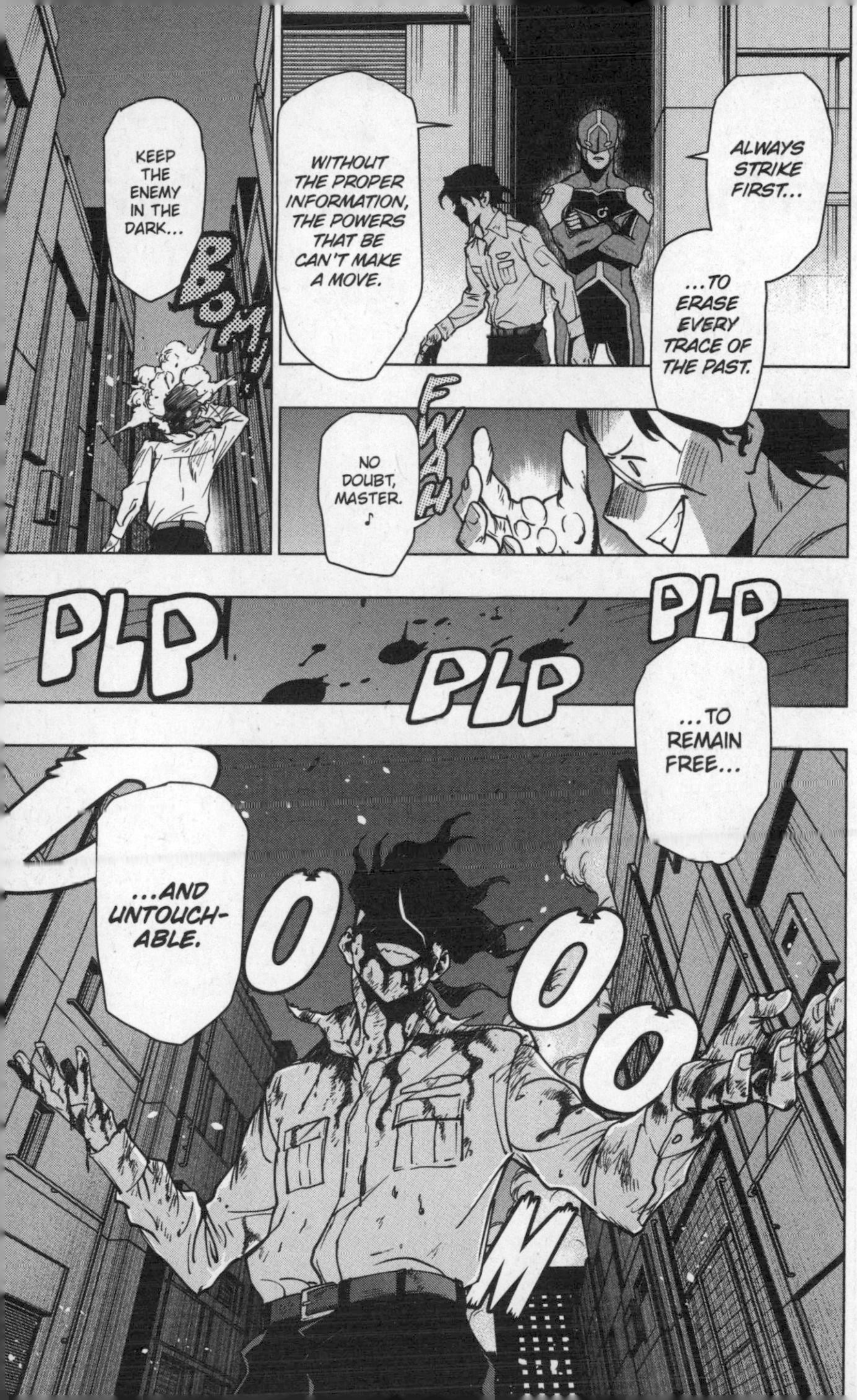

ALWAYS STRIKE FIRST...
...TO ERASE EVERY TRACE OF THE PAST.
WITHOUT THE PROPER INFORMATION, THE POWERS THAT BE CAN'T MAKE A MOVE.
FWAH
NO DOUBT, MASTER. ♪
KEEP THE ENEMY IN THE DARK...
BOOM
PLP
PLP
PLP
...TO REMAIN FREE...
...AND UNTOUCHABLE.
OOOM

KENDO RAPPA'S FACE REVEAL

The idea of the goofy masked man actually being kind of handsome was just too perfect. So when I heard that the anime offered a glimpse of his face (and he turned out to be good-looking), I thought, "Ooh, lucky us."

—Furuhashi

I went to check the video when I learned about Rappa's partial face reveal in the anime, but it's such a brief moment that I had to keep rewinding in my attempts to pause it perfectly. (LOL)

—Betten

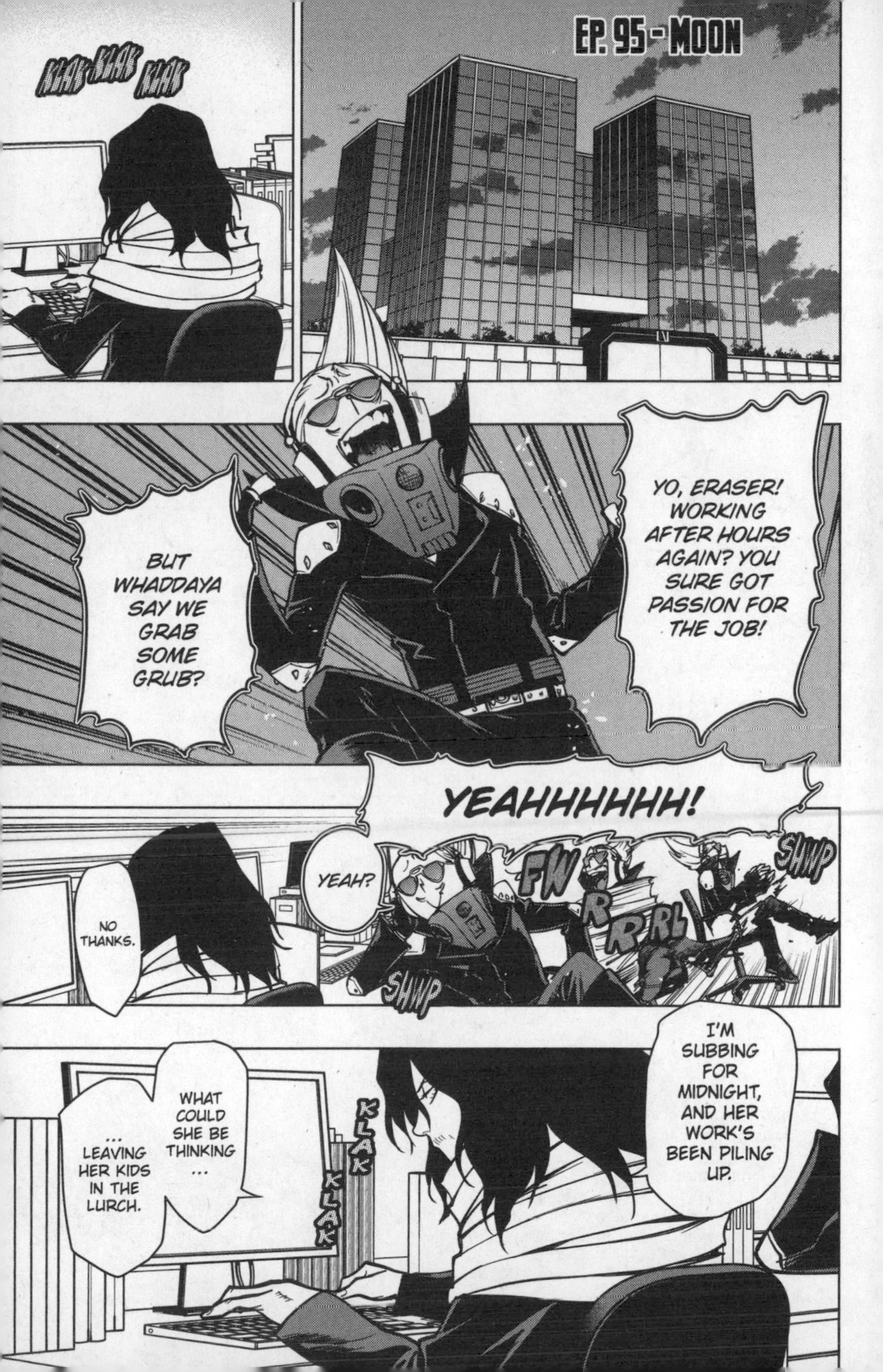
EP. 95 - MOON
KLAK KLAK KLAK
YO, ERASER! WORKING AFTER HOURS AGAIN? YOU SURE GOT PASSION FOR THE JOB!
BUT WHADDAYA SAY WE GRAB SOME GRUB?
YEAHHHHHHH!
SHWP
FWRRRRL
YEAH?
SHWP
NO THANKS.
I'M SUBBING FOR MIDNIGHT, AND HER WORK'S BEEN PILING UP.
KLAK
KLAK
WHAT COULD SHE BE THINKING...
...LEAVING HER KIDS IN THE LURCH.

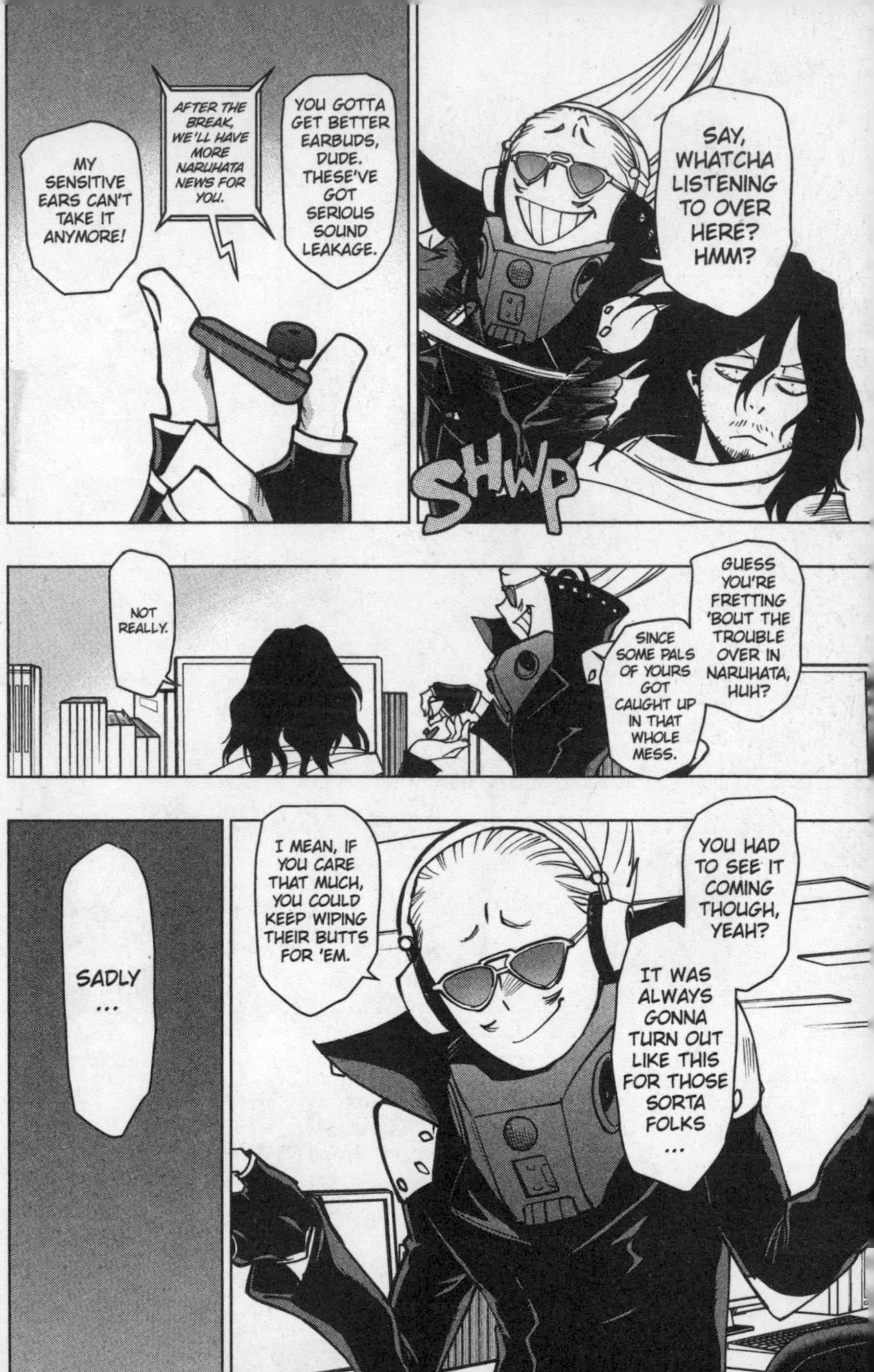
SAY, WHATCHA LISTENING TO OVER HERE? HMM?
SHWP
YOU GOTTA GET BETTER EARBUDS, DUDE. THESE'VE GOT SERIOUS SOUND LEAKAGE.
AFTER THE BREAK, WE'LL HAVE MORE NARUHATA NEWS FOR YOU.
MY SENSITIVE EARS CAN'T TAKE IT ANYMORE!
GUESS YOU'RE FRETTING 'BOUT THE TROUBLE OVER IN NARUHATA, HUH?
SINCE SOME PALS OF YOURS GOT CAUGHT UP IN THAT WHOLE MESS.
NOT REALLY.
YOU HAD TO SEE IT COMING THOUGH, YEAH?
IT WAS ALWAYS GONNA TURN OUT LIKE THIS FOR THOSE SORTA FOLKS ...
I MEAN, IF YOU CARE THAT MUCH, YOU COULD KEEP WIPING THEIR BUTTS FOR 'EM.
SADLY ...

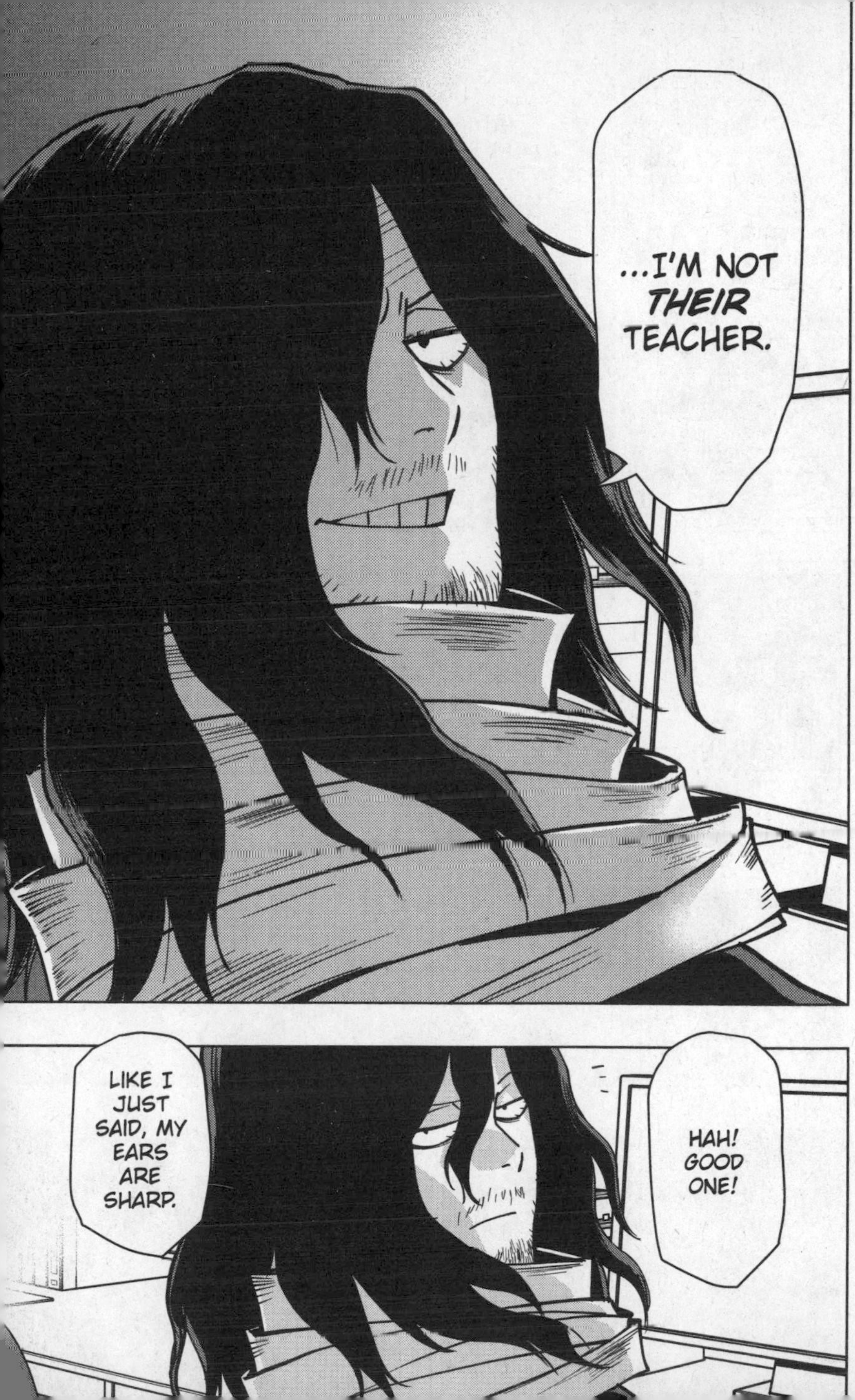
...I'M NOT *THEIR* TEACHER.
HAH! GOOD ONE!
LIKE I JUST SAID, MY EARS ARE SHARP.

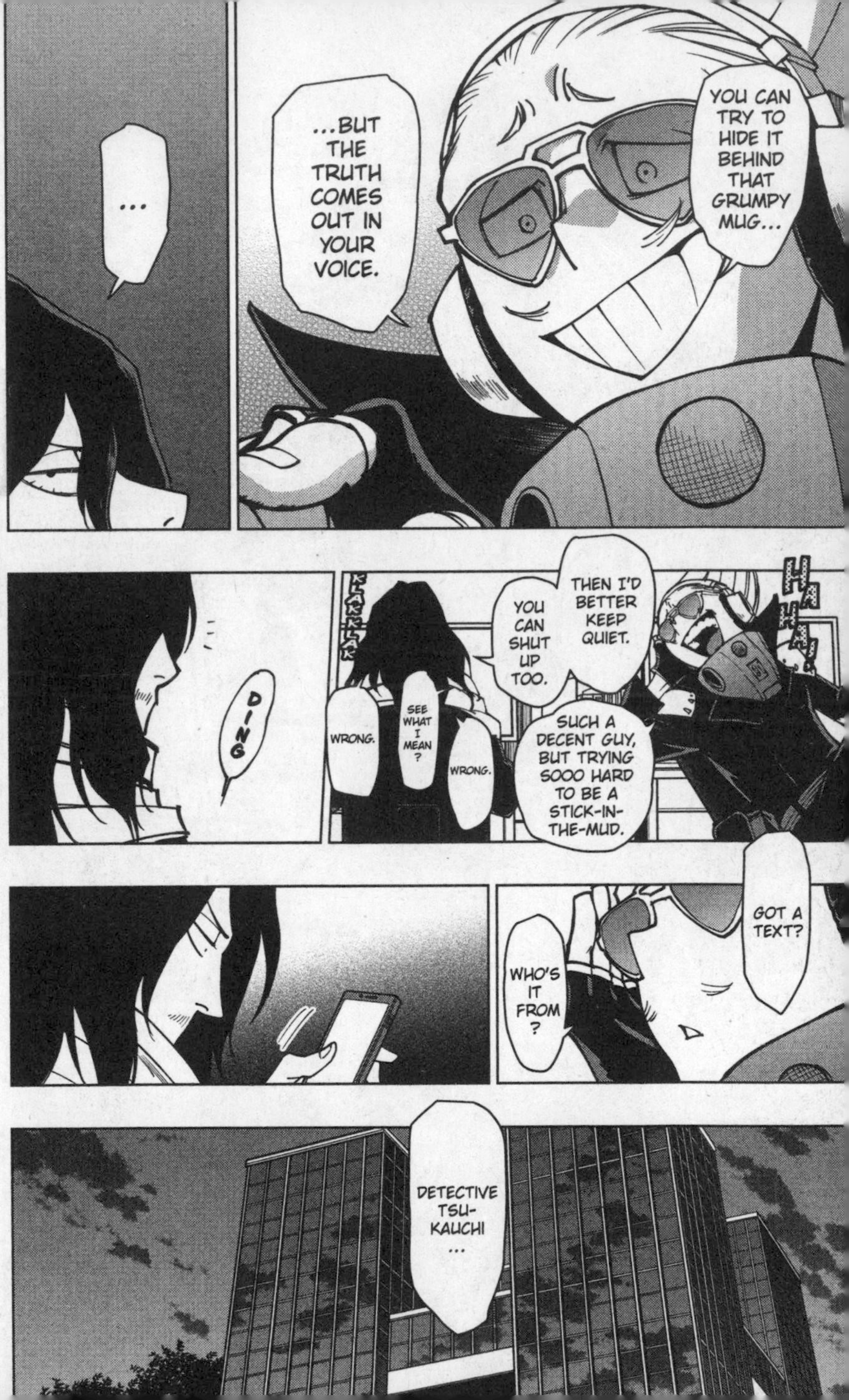
YOU CAN TRY TO HIDE IT BEHIND THAT GRUMPY MUG...
...BUT THE TRUTH COMES OUT IN YOUR VOICE.
...
HAHA!
THEN I'D BETTER KEEP QUIET.
YOU CAN SHUT UP TOO.
SUCH A DECENT GUY, BUT TRYING SOOO HARD TO BE A STICK-IN-THE-MUD.
WRONG.
SEE WHAT I MEAN?
WRONG.
KLAKKLAK
DING
GOT A TEXT?
WHO'S IT FROM?
DETECTIVE TSUKAUCHI...

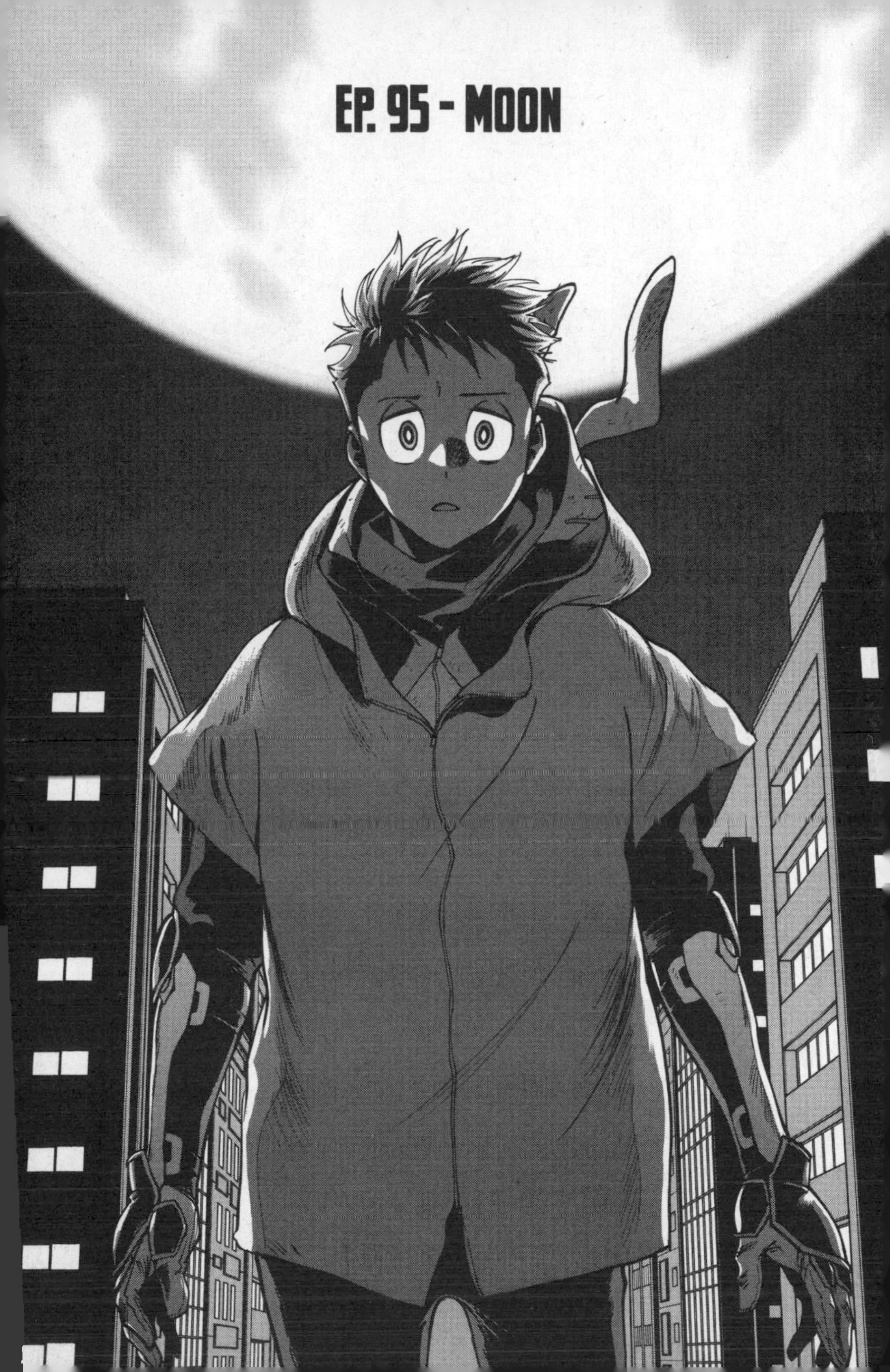
EP. 95 - MOON

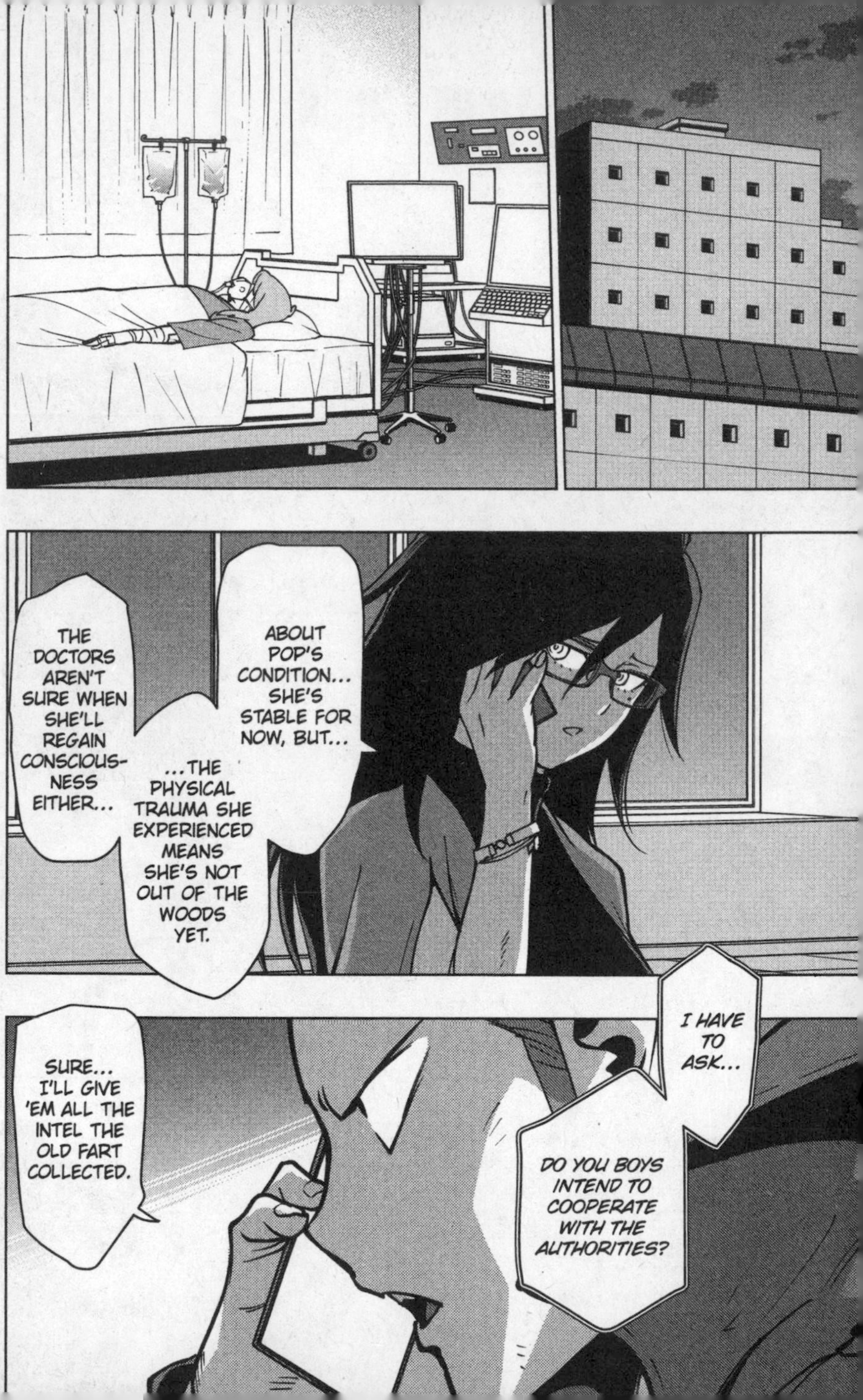
ABOUT POP'S CONDITION... SHE'S STABLE FOR NOW, BUT...
...THE PHYSICAL TRAUMA SHE EXPERIENCED MEANS SHE'S NOT OUT OF THE WOODS YET.
THE DOCTORS AREN'T SURE WHEN SHE'LL REGAIN CONSCIOUS-NESS EITHER...
I HAVE TO ASK...
DO YOU BOYS INTEND TO COOPERATE WITH THE AUTHORITIES?
SURE... I'LL GIVE 'EM ALL THE INTEL THE OLD FART COLLECTED.

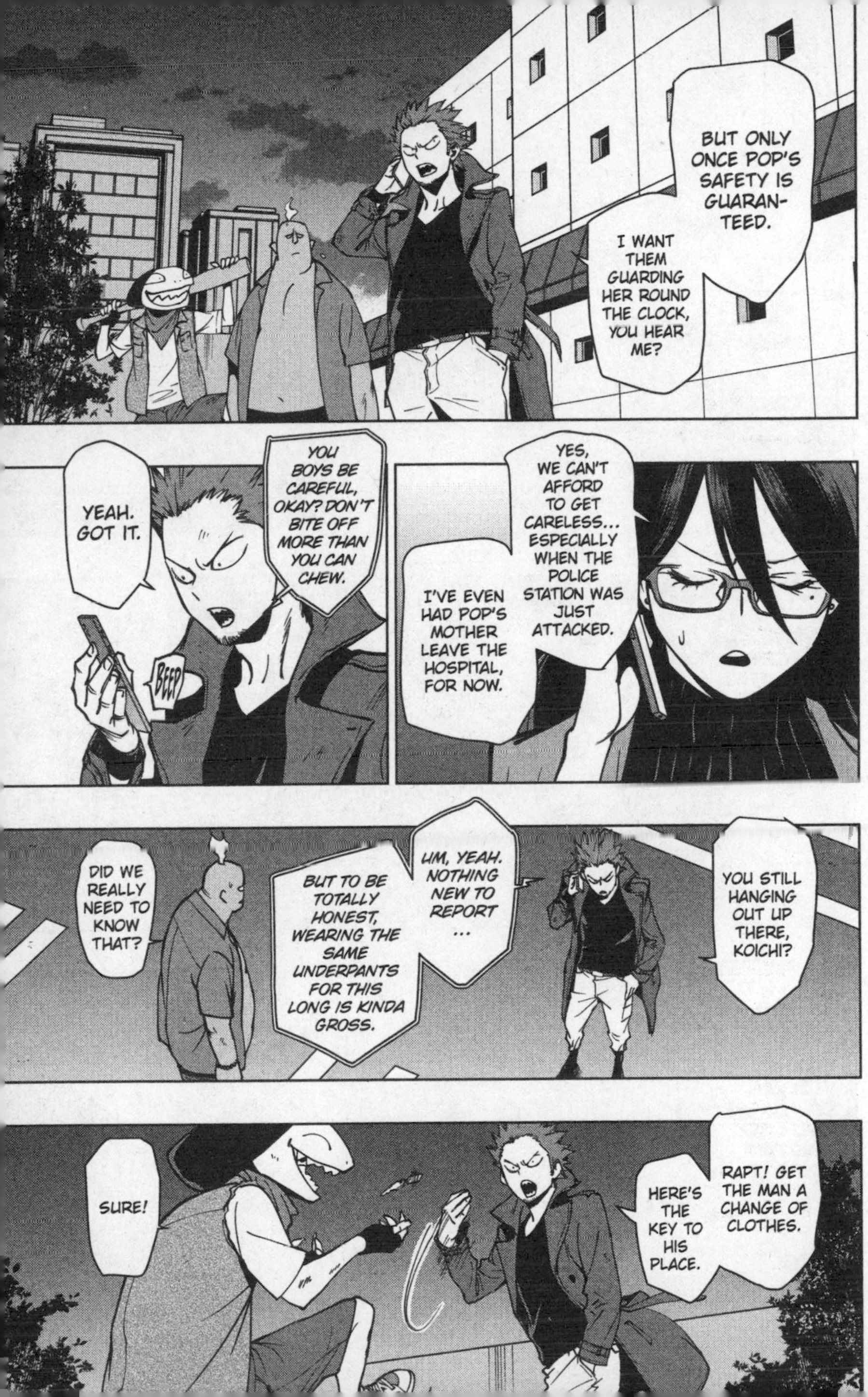
BUT ONLY ONCE POP'S SAFETY IS GUARAN-TEED.
I WANT THEM GUARDING HER ROUND THE CLOCK, YOU HEAR ME?
YES, WE CAN'T AFFORD TO GET CARELESS... ESPECIALLY WHEN THE POLICE STATION WAS JUST ATTACKED.
I'VE EVEN HAD POP'S MOTHER LEAVE THE HOSPITAL, FOR NOW.
YOU BOYS BE CAREFUL, OKAY? DON'T BITE OFF MORE THAN YOU CAN CHEW.
YEAH. GOT IT.
BEEP
YOU STILL HANGING OUT UP THERE, KOICHI?
UM, YEAH. NOTHING NEW TO REPORT ...
BUT TO BE TOTALLY HONEST, WEARING THE SAME UNDERPANTS FOR THIS LONG IS KINDA GROSS.
DID WE REALLY NEED TO KNOW THAT?
RAPT! GET THE MAN A CHANGE OF CLOTHES.
HERE'S THE KEY TO HIS PLACE.
SURE!

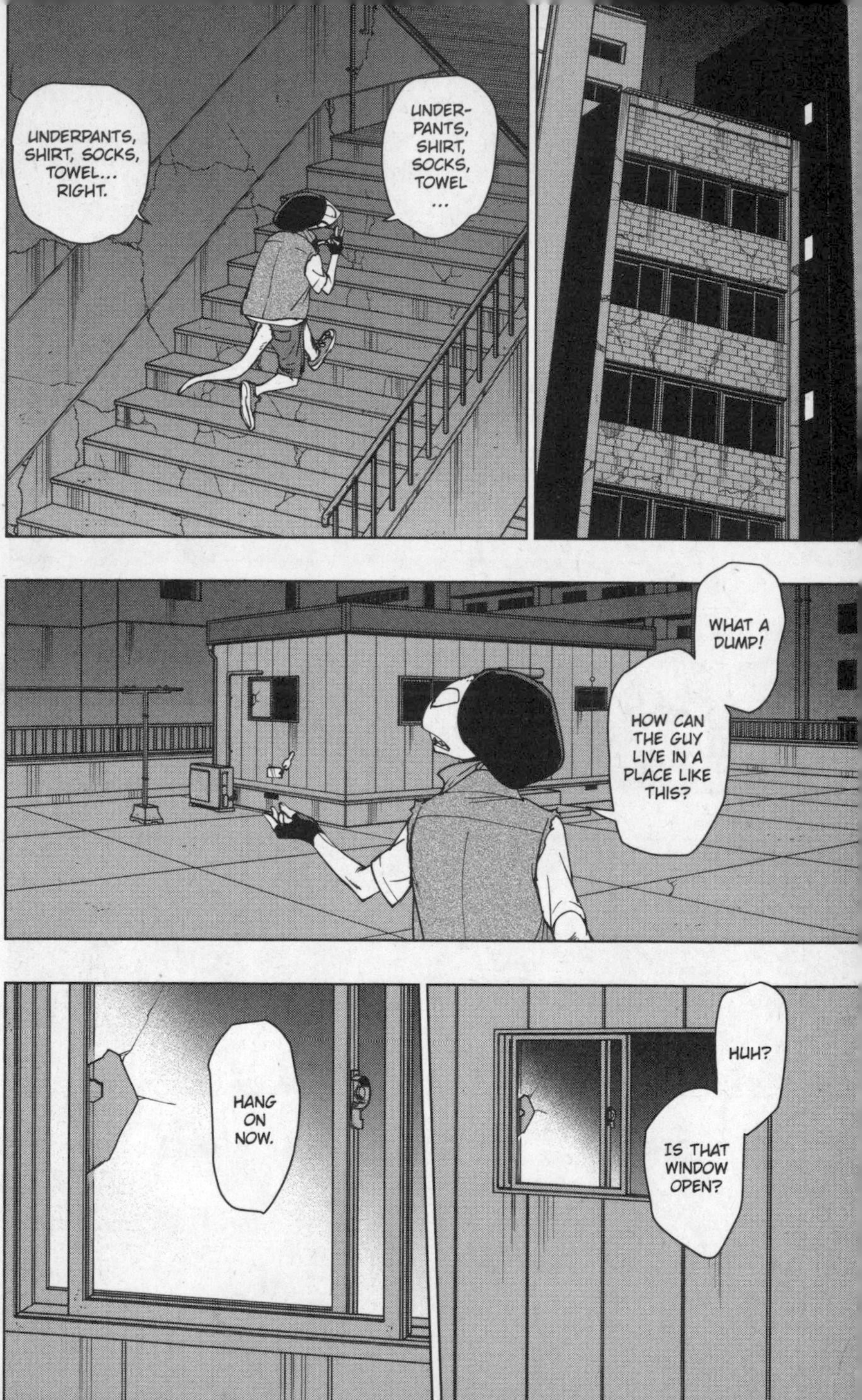
UNDER-PANTS, SHIRT, SOCKS, TOWEL ...
UNDERPANTS, SHIRT, SOCKS, TOWEL... RIGHT.
WHAT A DUMP!
HOW CAN THE GUY LIVE IN A PLACE LIKE THIS?
HUH?
IS THAT WINDOW OPEN?
HANG ON NOW.

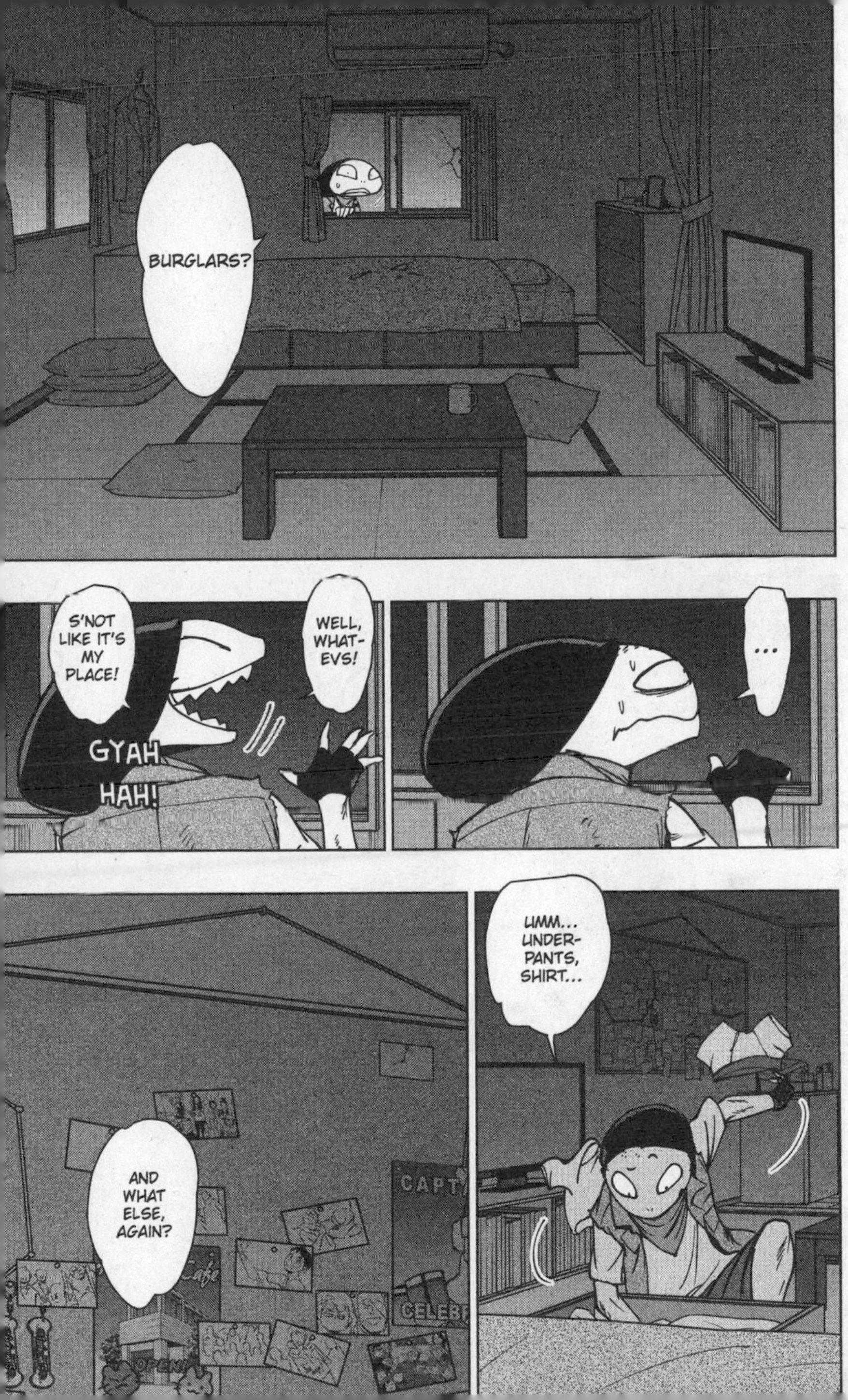
BURGLARS?
...
WELL, WHAT-EVS!
S'NOT LIKE IT'S MY PLACE!
GYAH HAH!
UMM... UNDER-PANTS, SHIRT...
AND WHAT ELSE, AGAIN?

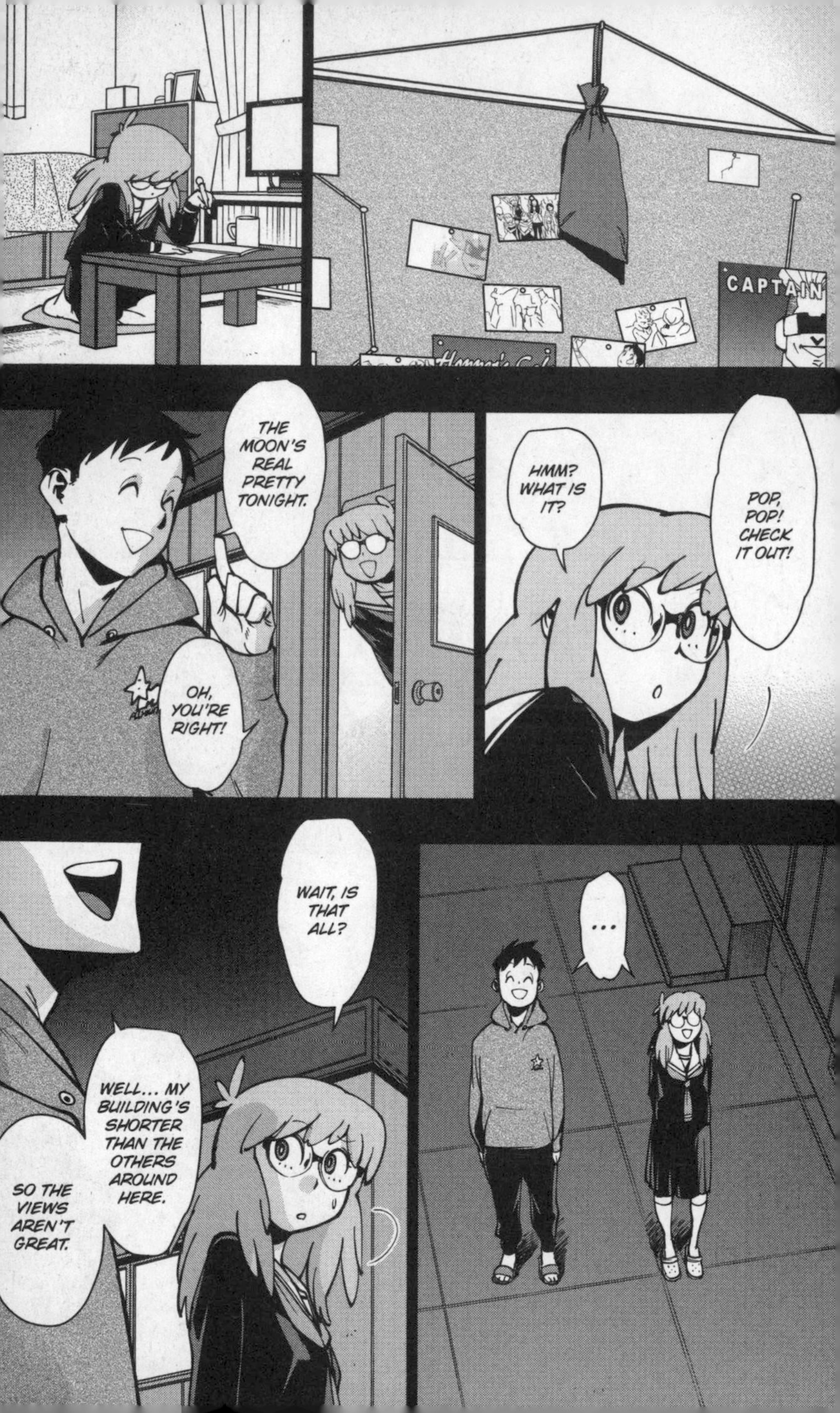
CAPTAIN
POP, POP! CHECK IT OUT!
HMM? WHAT IS IT?
THE MOON'S REAL PRETTY TONIGHT.
OH, YOU'RE RIGHT!
...
WAIT, IS THAT ALL?
WELL... MY BUILDING'S SHORTER THAN THE OTHERS AROUND HERE.
SO THE VIEWS AREN'T GREAT.

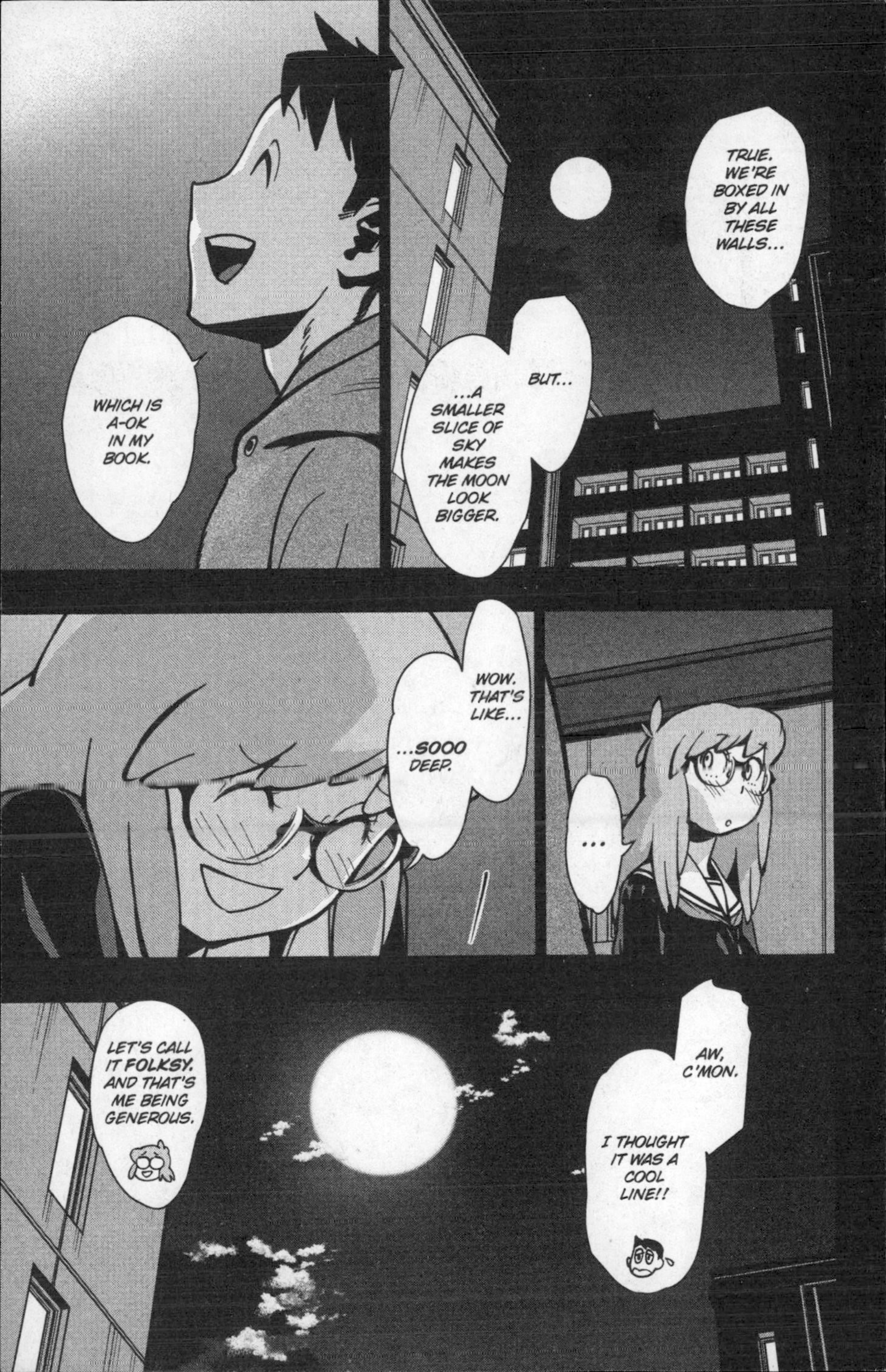
TRUE. WE'RE BOXED IN BY ALL THESE WALLS...
BUT...
...A SMALLER SLICE OF SKY MAKES THE MOON LOOK BIGGER.
WHICH IS A-OK IN MY BOOK.
...
WOW. THAT'S LIKE...
...SOOO DEEP.
LET'S CALL IT FOLKSY. AND THAT'S ME BEING GENEROUS.
AW, C'MON.
I THOUGHT IT WAS A COOL LINE!!

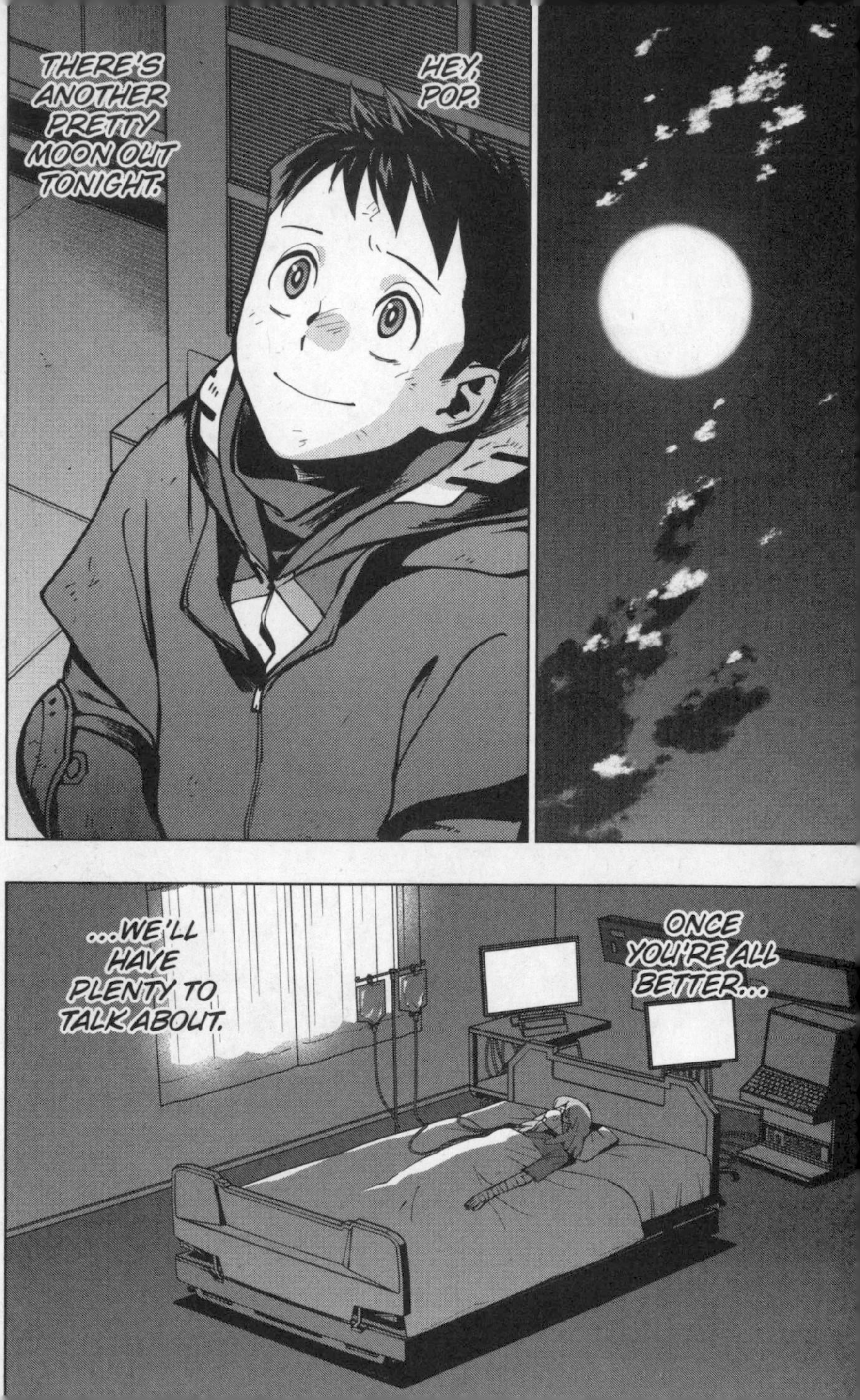
HEY, POP.
THERE'S ANOTHER PRETTY MOON OUT TONIGHT.
ONCE YOU'RE ALL BETTER...
...WE'LL HAVE PLENTY TO TALK ABOUT.

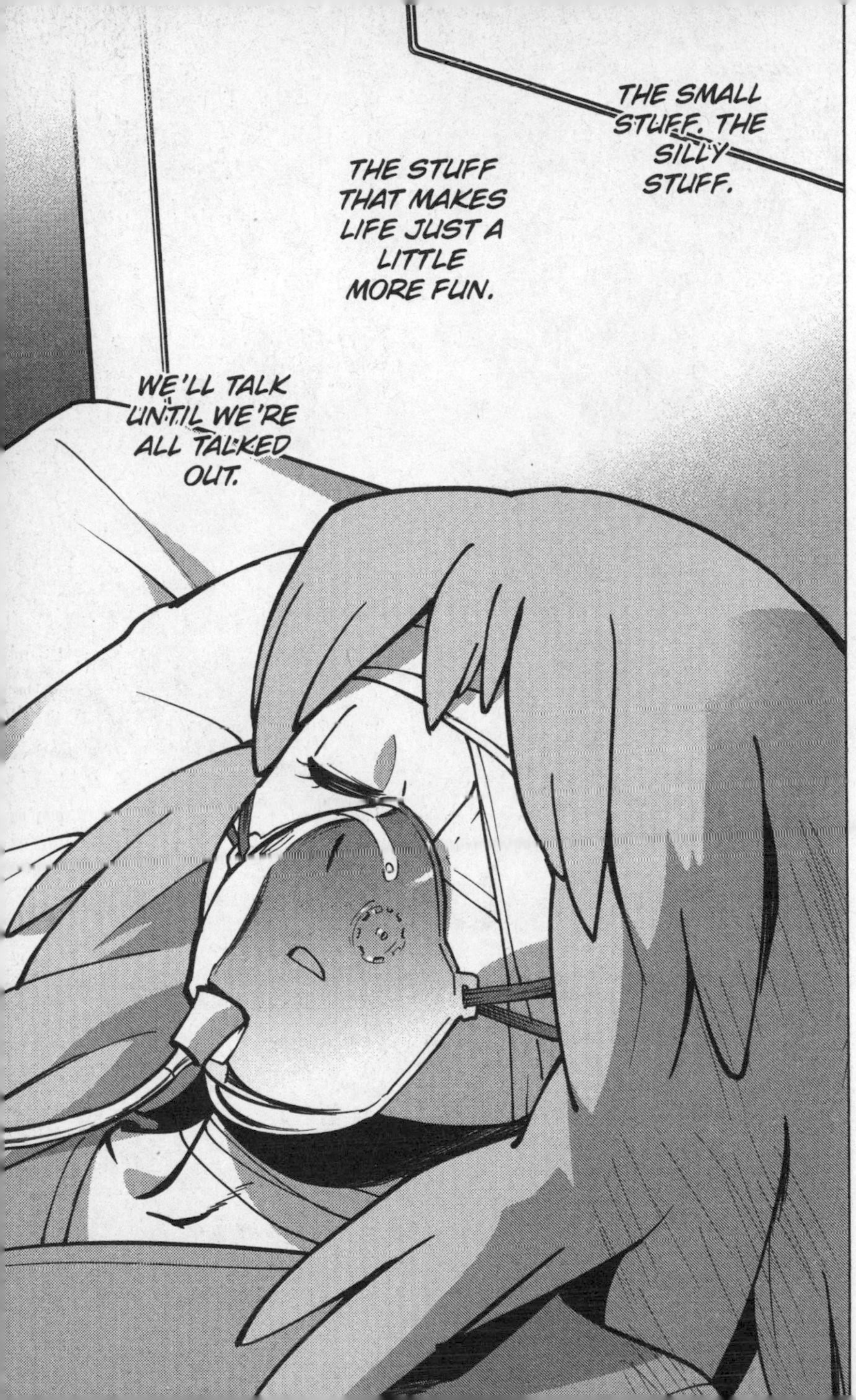
THE SMALL STUFF. THE SILLY STUFF.
THE STUFF THAT MAKES LIFE JUST A LITTLE MORE FUN.
WE'LL TALK UNTIL WE'RE ALL TALKED OUT.

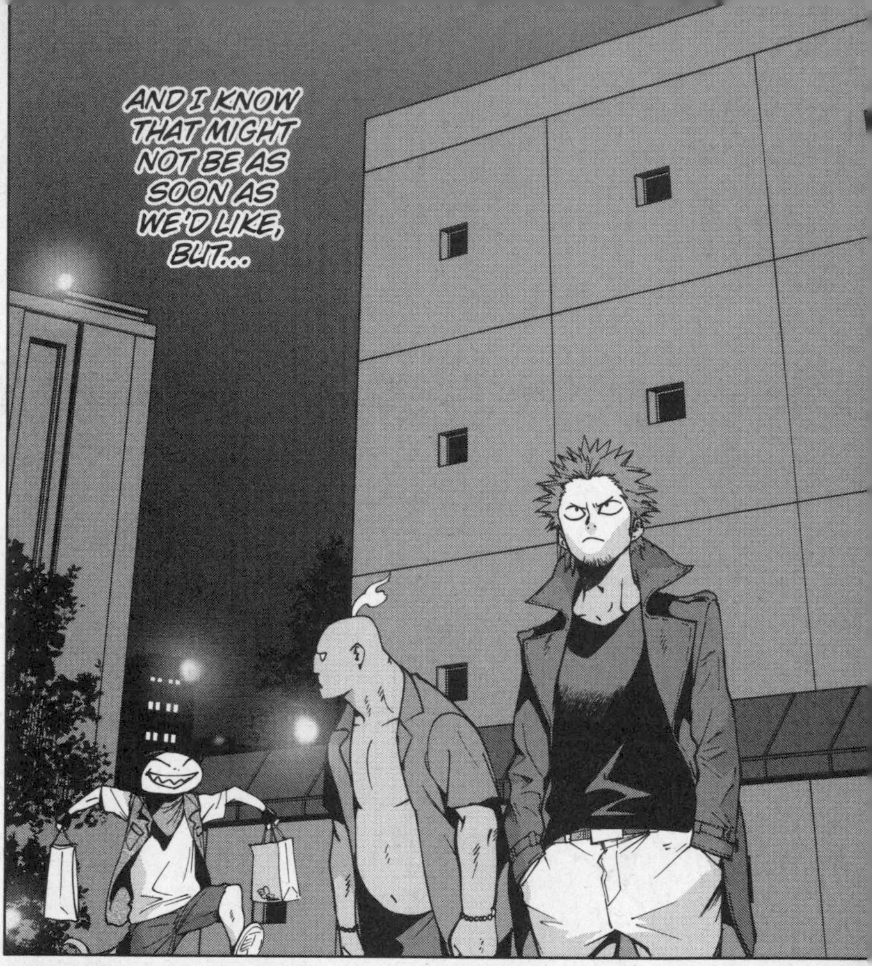
AND I KNOW THAT MIGHT NOT BE AS SOON AS WE'D LIKE, BUT...

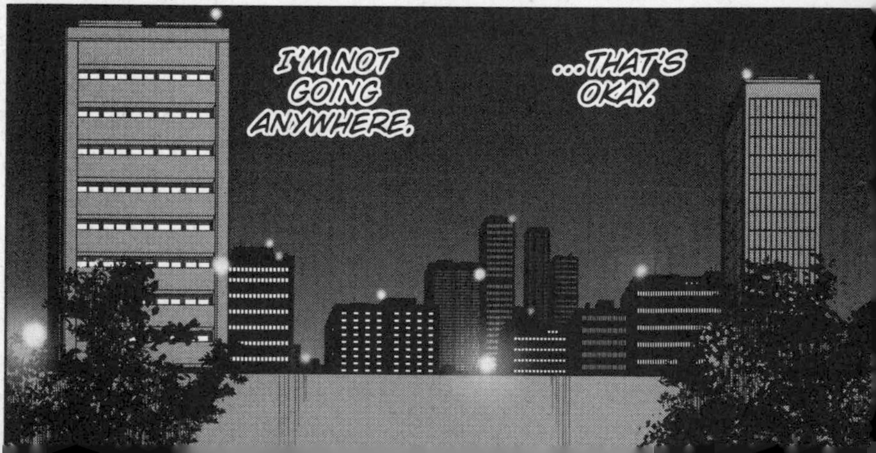
...THAT'S OKAY.
I'M NOT GOING ANYWHERE.

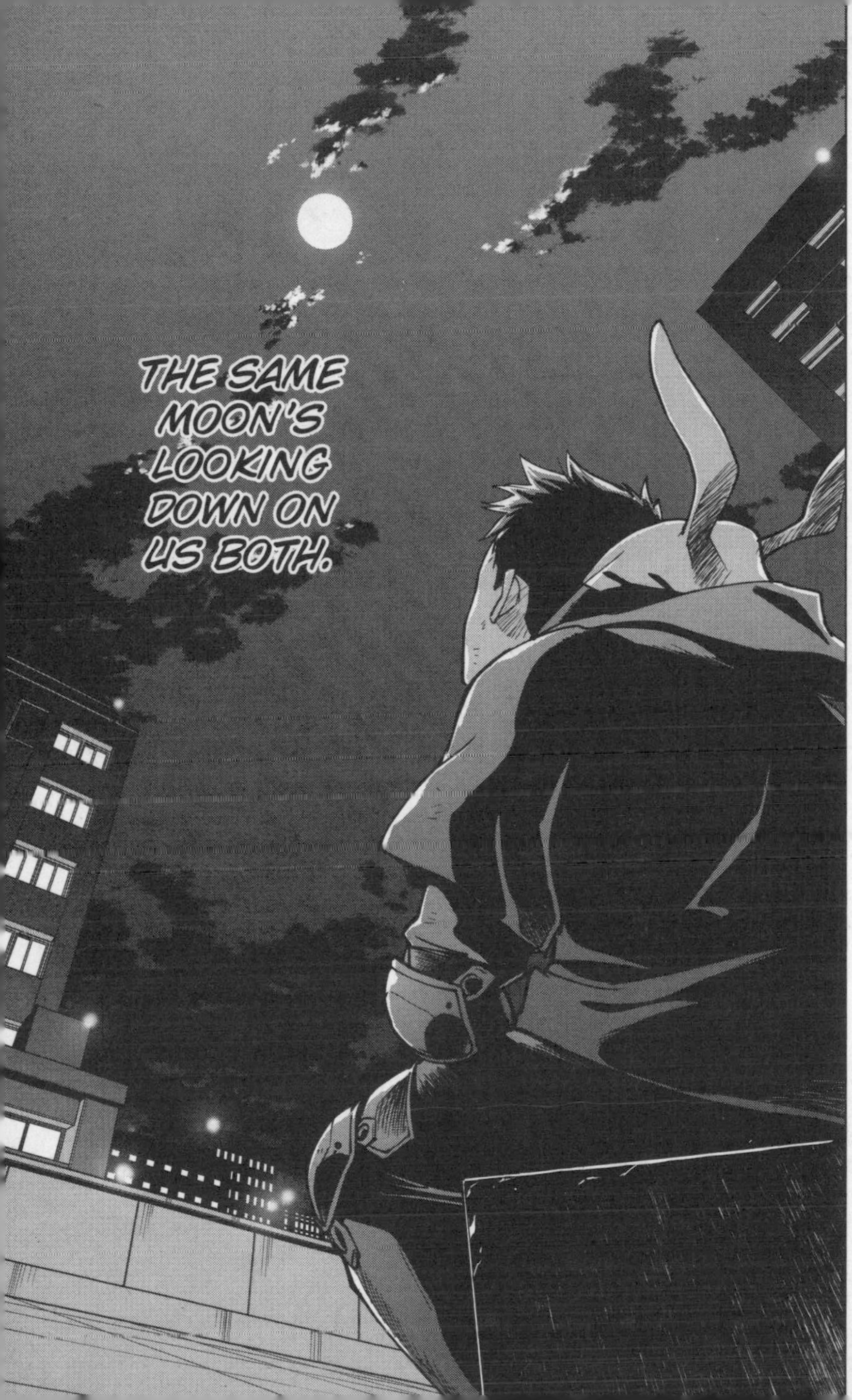
THE SAME MOON'S LOOKING DOWN ON US BOTH.

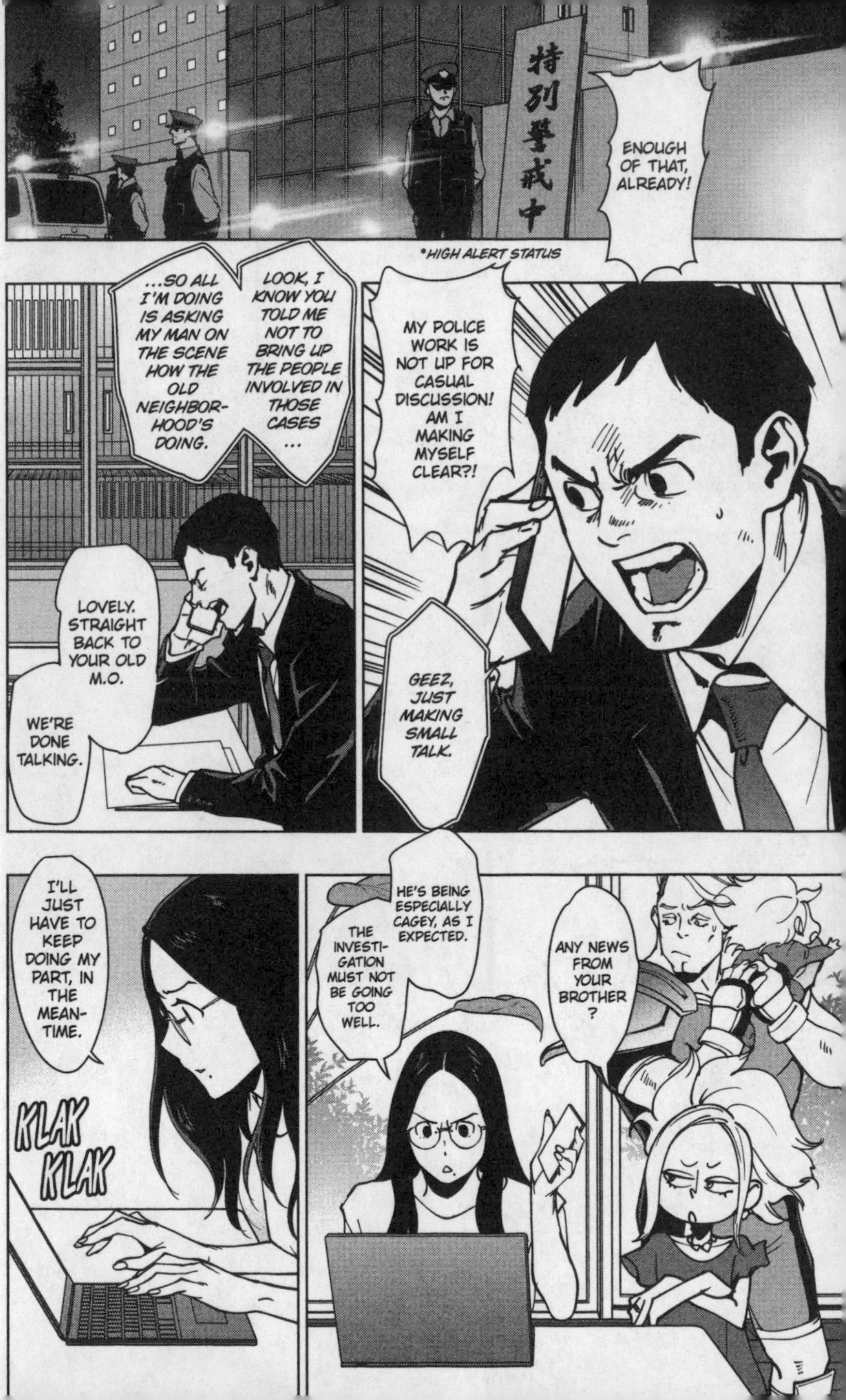
特別警戒中
*HIGH ALERT STATUS
ENOUGH OF THAT, ALREADY!
MY POLICE WORK IS NOT UP FOR CASUAL DISCUSSION! AM I MAKING MYSELF CLEAR?!
GEEZ, JUST MAKING SMALL TALK.
LOOK, I KNOW YOU TOLD ME NOT TO BRING UP THE PEOPLE INVOLVED IN THOSE CASES ...
...SO ALL I'M DOING IS ASKING MY MAN ON THE SCENE HOW THE OLD NEIGHBOR-HOOD'S DOING.
LOVELY. STRAIGHT BACK TO YOUR OLD M.O.
WE'RE DONE TALKING.
ANY NEWS FROM YOUR BROTHER?
HE'S BEING ESPECIALLY CAGEY, AS I EXPECTED.
THE INVESTI-GATION MUST NOT BE GOING TOO WELL.
I'LL JUST HAVE TO KEEP DOING MY PART, IN THE MEAN-TIME.
KLAK KLAK

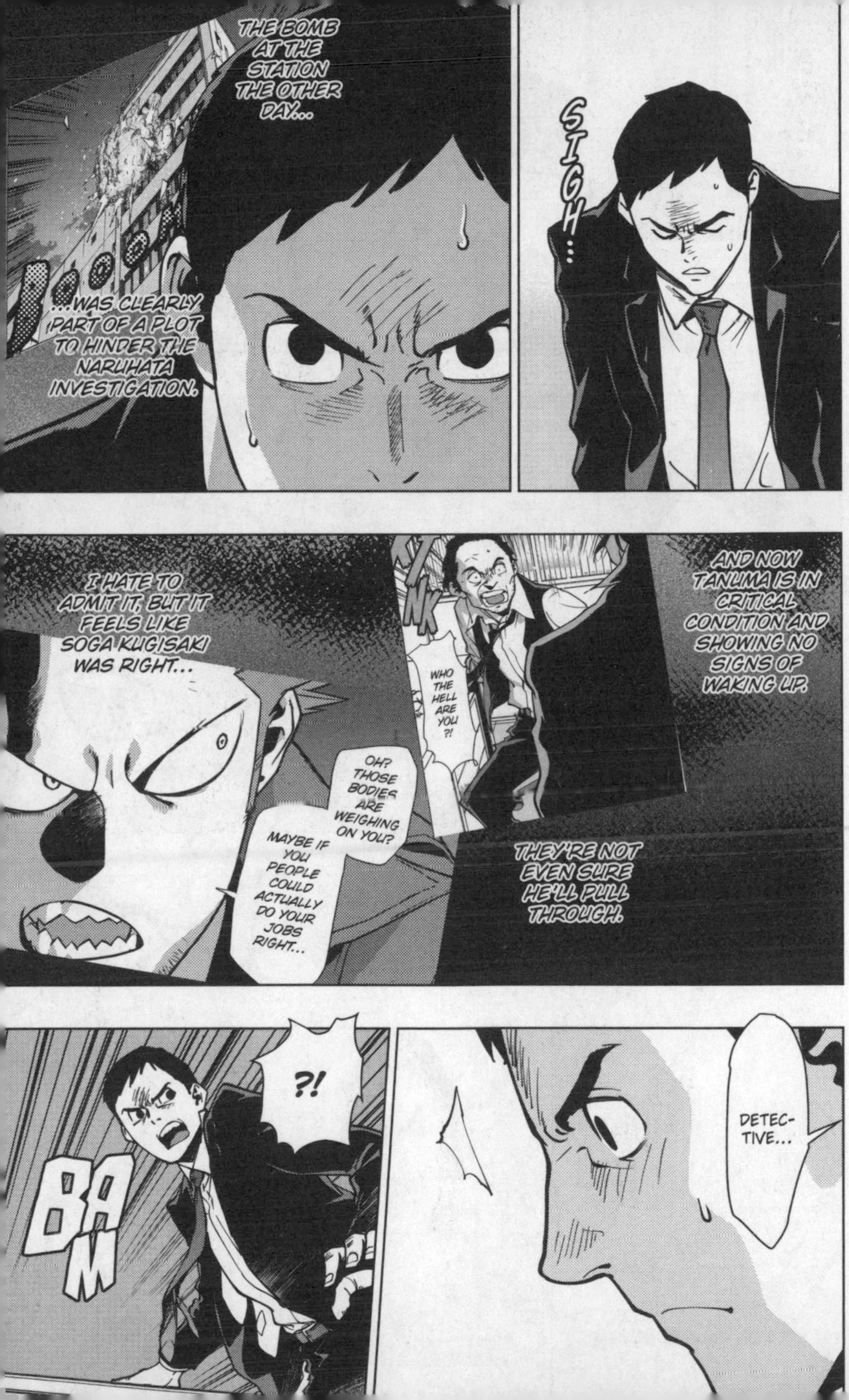
SIGH...
THE BOMB AT THE STATION THE OTHER DAY...
...WAS CLEARLY PART OF A PLOT TO HINDER THE NARUHATA INVESTIGATION.
AND NOW TANUMA IS IN CRITICAL CONDITION AND SHOWING NO SIGNS OF WAKING UP.
THEY'RE NOT EVEN SURE HE'LL PULL THROUGH.
WHO THE HELL ARE YOU ?!
I HATE TO ADMIT IT, BUT IT FEELS LIKE SOGA KUGISAKI WAS RIGHT...
OH? THOSE BODIES ARE WEIGHING ON YOU?
MAYBE IF YOU PEOPLE COULD ACTUALLY DO YOUR JOBS RIGHT...
DETEC-TIVE...
?!
BAM

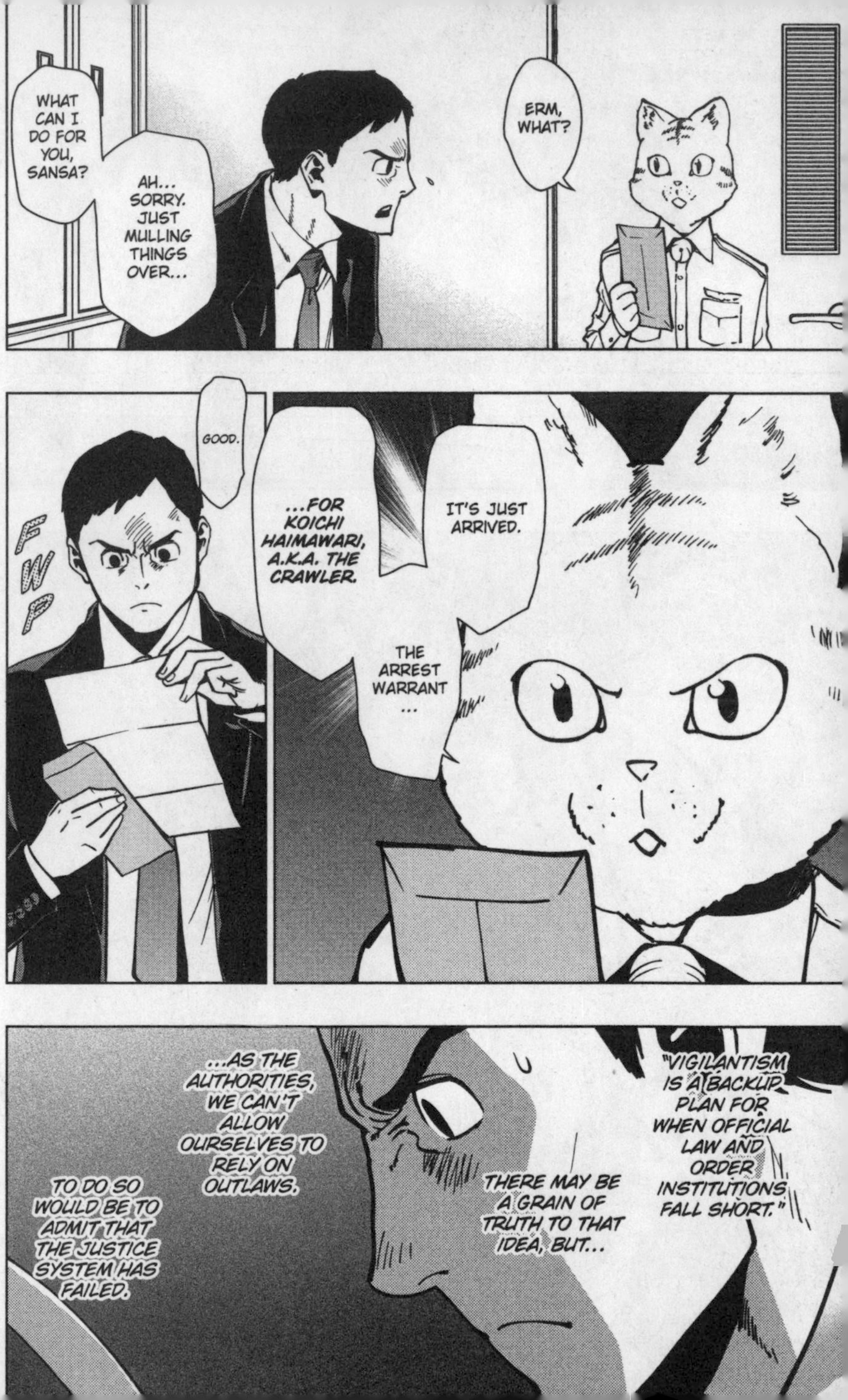
ERM, WHAT?
AH... SORRY. JUST MULLING THINGS OVER...
WHAT CAN I DO FOR YOU, SANSA?
IT'S JUST ARRIVED.
THE ARREST WARRANT...
...FOR KOICHI HAIMAWARI, A.K.A. THE CRAWLER.
GOOD.
FWP
"VIGILANTISM IS A BACKUP PLAN FOR WHEN OFFICIAL LAW AND ORDER INSTITUTIONS FALL SHORT."
THERE MAY BE A GRAIN OF TRUTH TO THAT IDEA, BUT...
...AS THE AUTHORITIES, WE CAN'T ALLOW OURSELVES TO RELY ON OUTLAWS.
TO DO SO WOULD BE TO ADMIT THAT THE JUSTICE SYSTEM HAS FAILED.

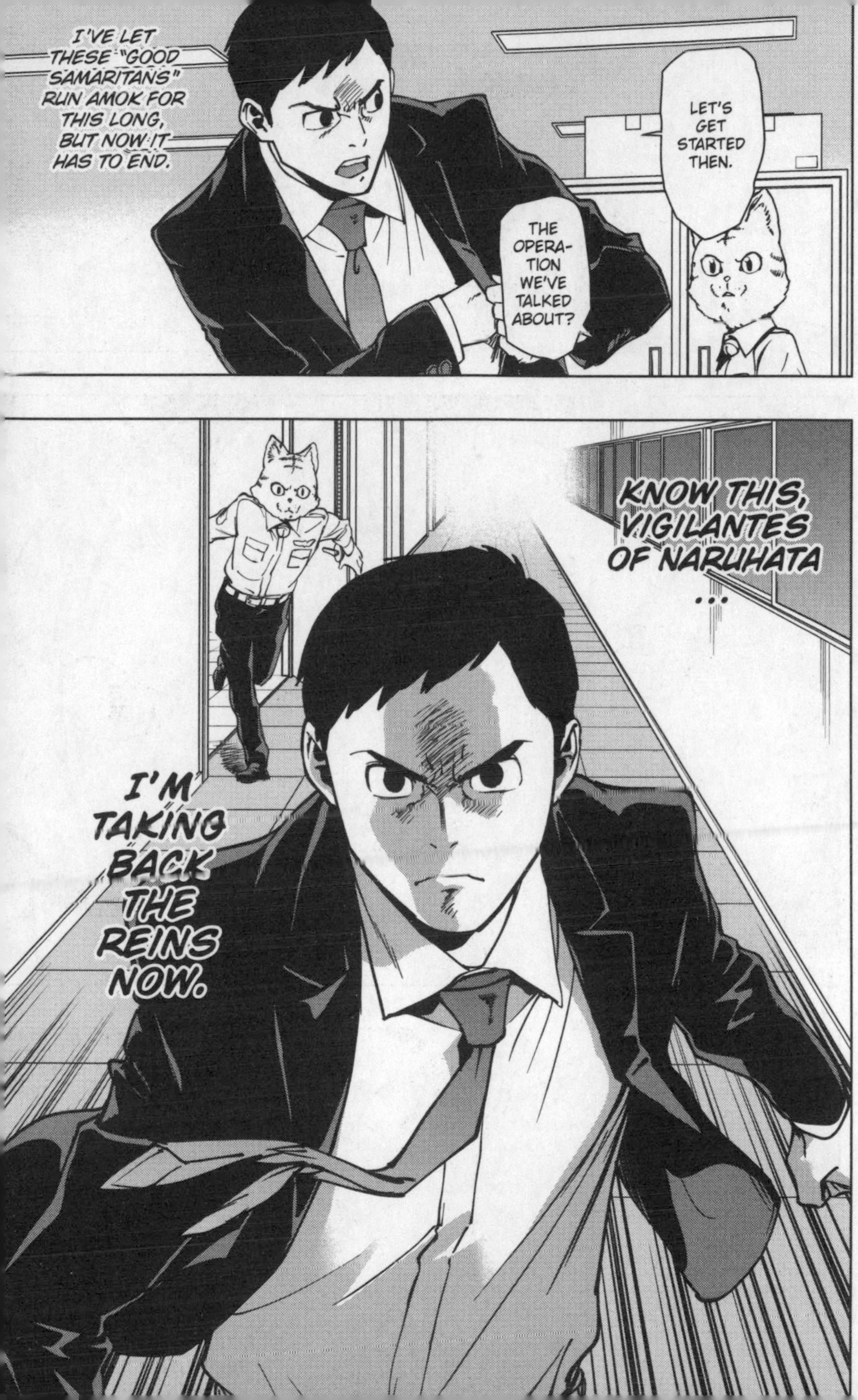
LET'S GET STARTED THEN.
THE OPERATION WE'VE TALKED ABOUT?
I'VE LET THESE "GOOD SAMARITANS" RUN AMOK FOR THIS LONG, BUT NOW IT HAS TO END.
KNOW THIS, VIGILANTES OF NARUHATA...
I'M TAKING BACK THE REINS NOW.

THE COLUMN

THE COPS

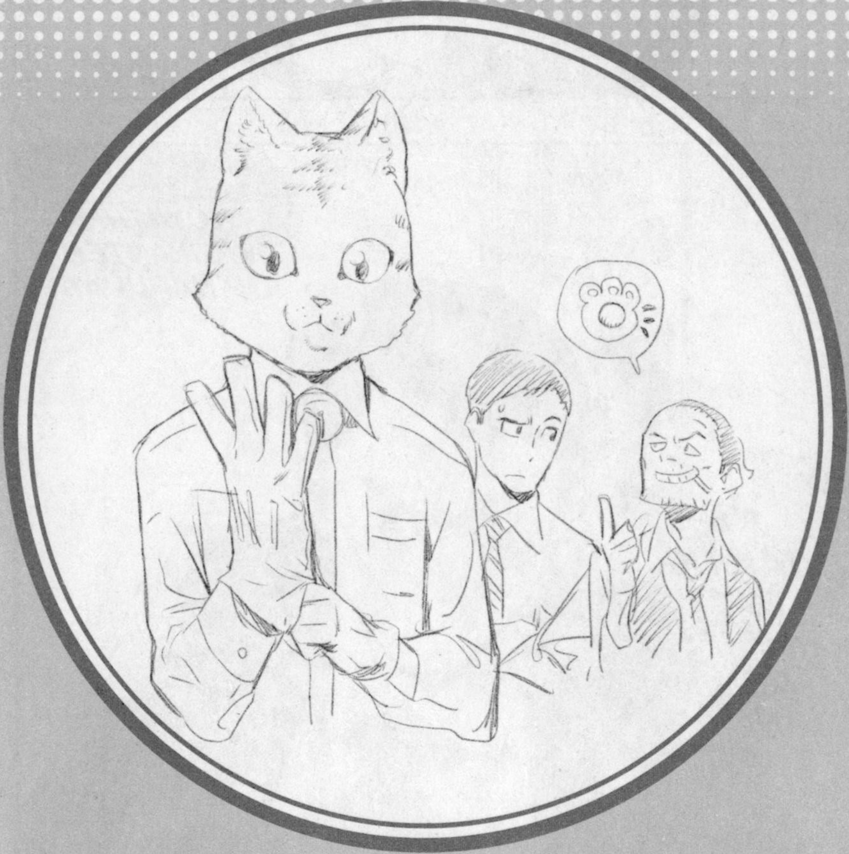

I've gotten lots of feedback about Sansa along the lines of "cute kitty cat ♪" but he's no spring chicken, actually. He's a full-grown adult. Tsukauchi is also in his thirties.

And Tanuma is genuinely deserving of being called "old dude."

—Furuhashi

Sansa is visually striking, but we have basically no other info about him. Which led to lots of moments while drawing where I was like, "Eh, this is probably fine, I guess?"

—Betten

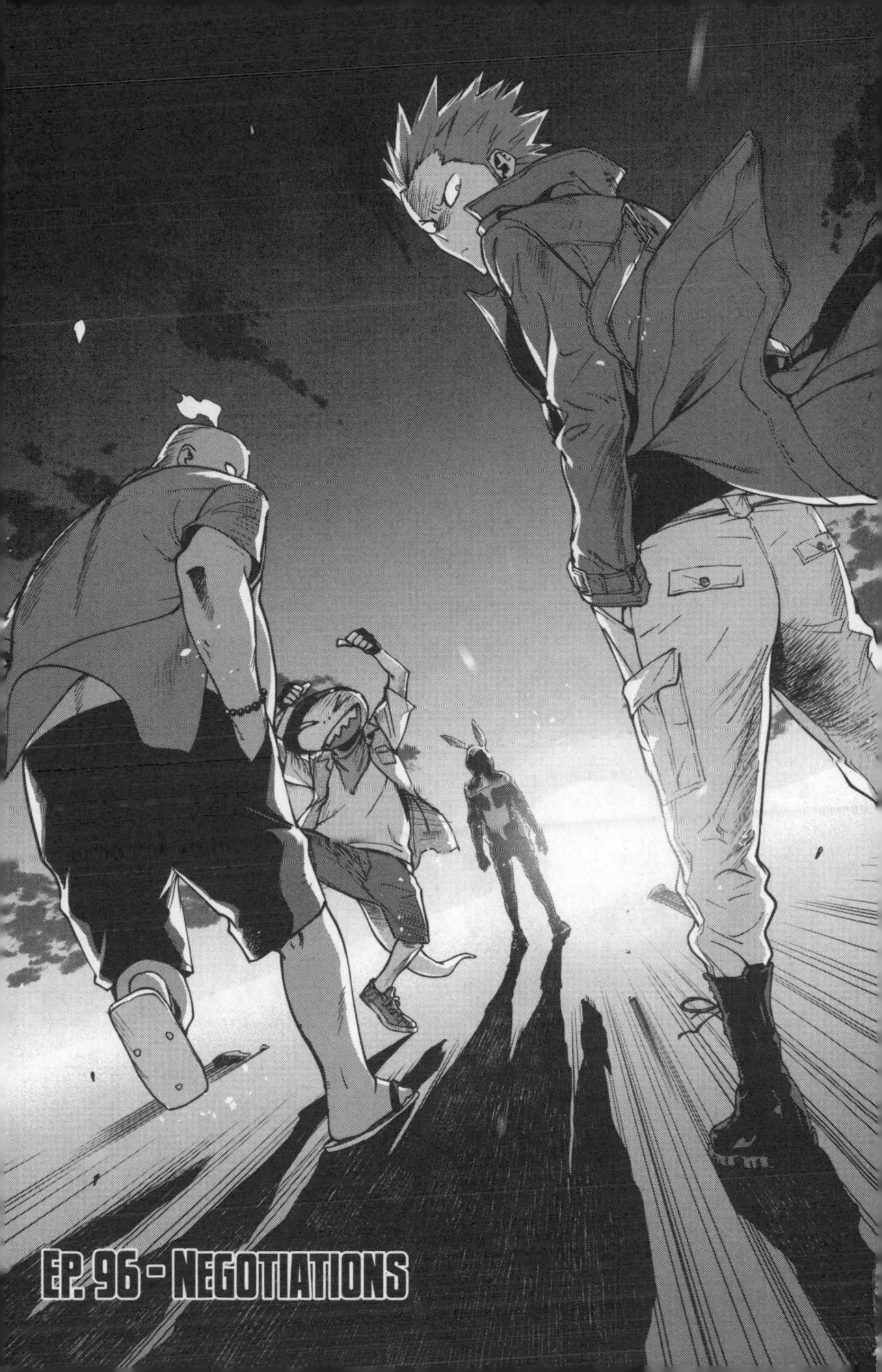
EP. 96 - NEGOTIATIONS

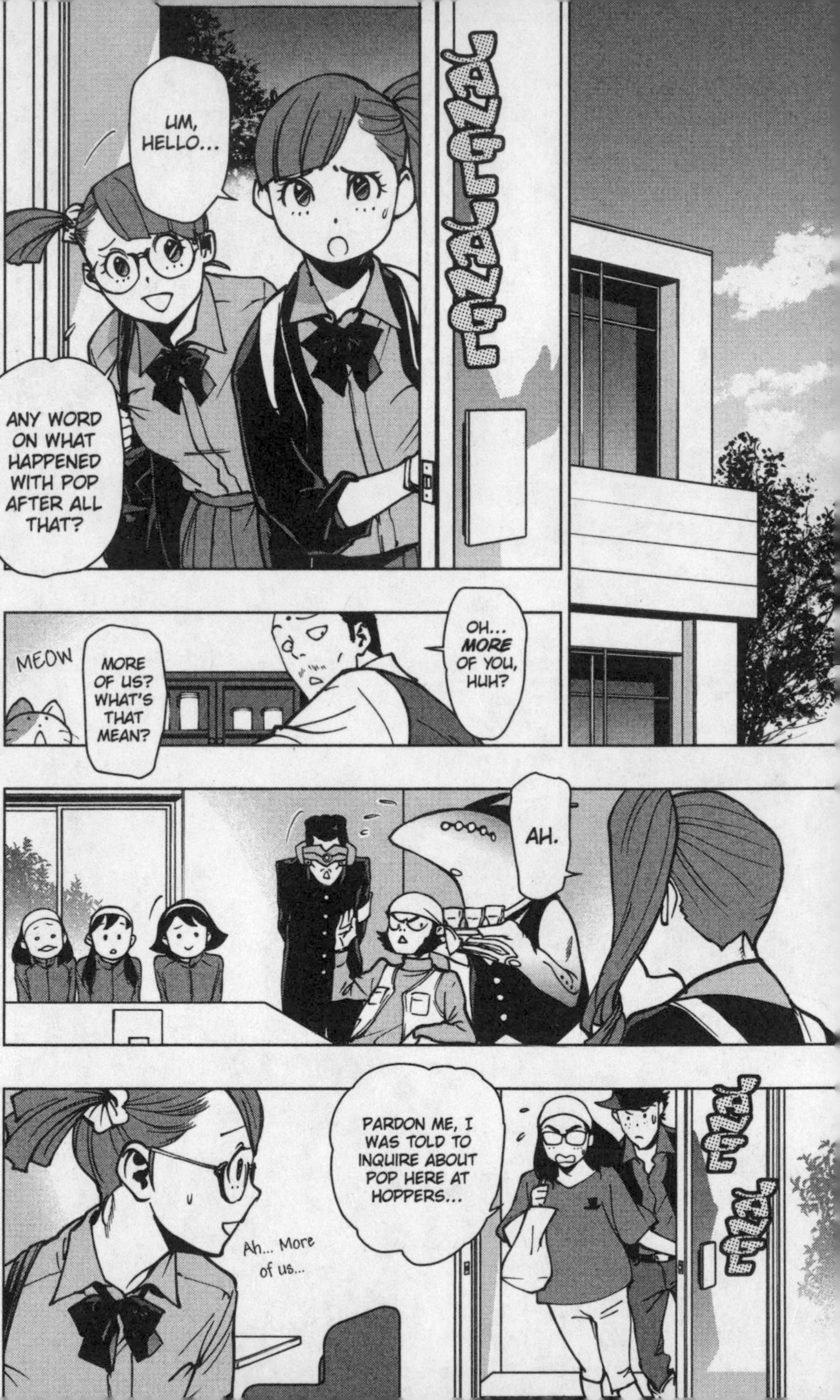
UM, HELLO...
ANY WORD ON WHAT HAPPENED WITH POP AFTER ALL THAT?
OH... *MORE* OF YOU, HUH?
MEOW
MORE OF US? WHAT'S THAT MEAN?
AH.
PARDON ME, I WAS TOLD TO INQUIRE ABOUT POP HERE AT HOPPERS...
Ah... More of us...

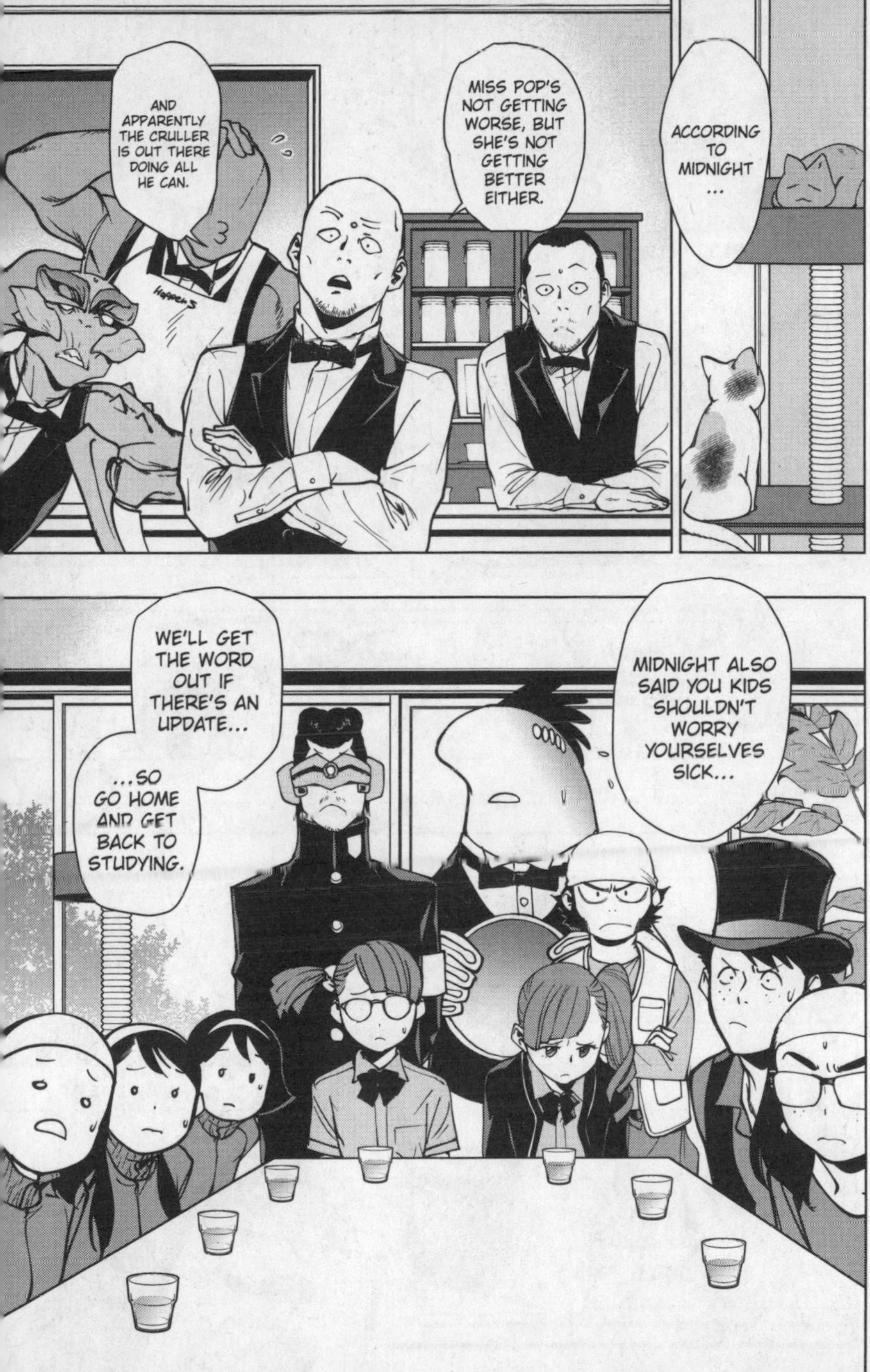
ACCORDING TO MIDNIGHT...
MISS POP'S NOT GETTING WORSE, BUT SHE'S NOT GETTING BETTER EITHER.
AND APPARENTLY THE CRULLER IS OUT THERE DOING ALL HE CAN.
MIDNIGHT ALSO SAID YOU KIDS SHOULDN'T WORRY YOURSELVES SICK...
WE'LL GET THE WORD OUT IF THERE'S AN UPDATE...
...SO GO HOME AND GET BACK TO STUDYING.

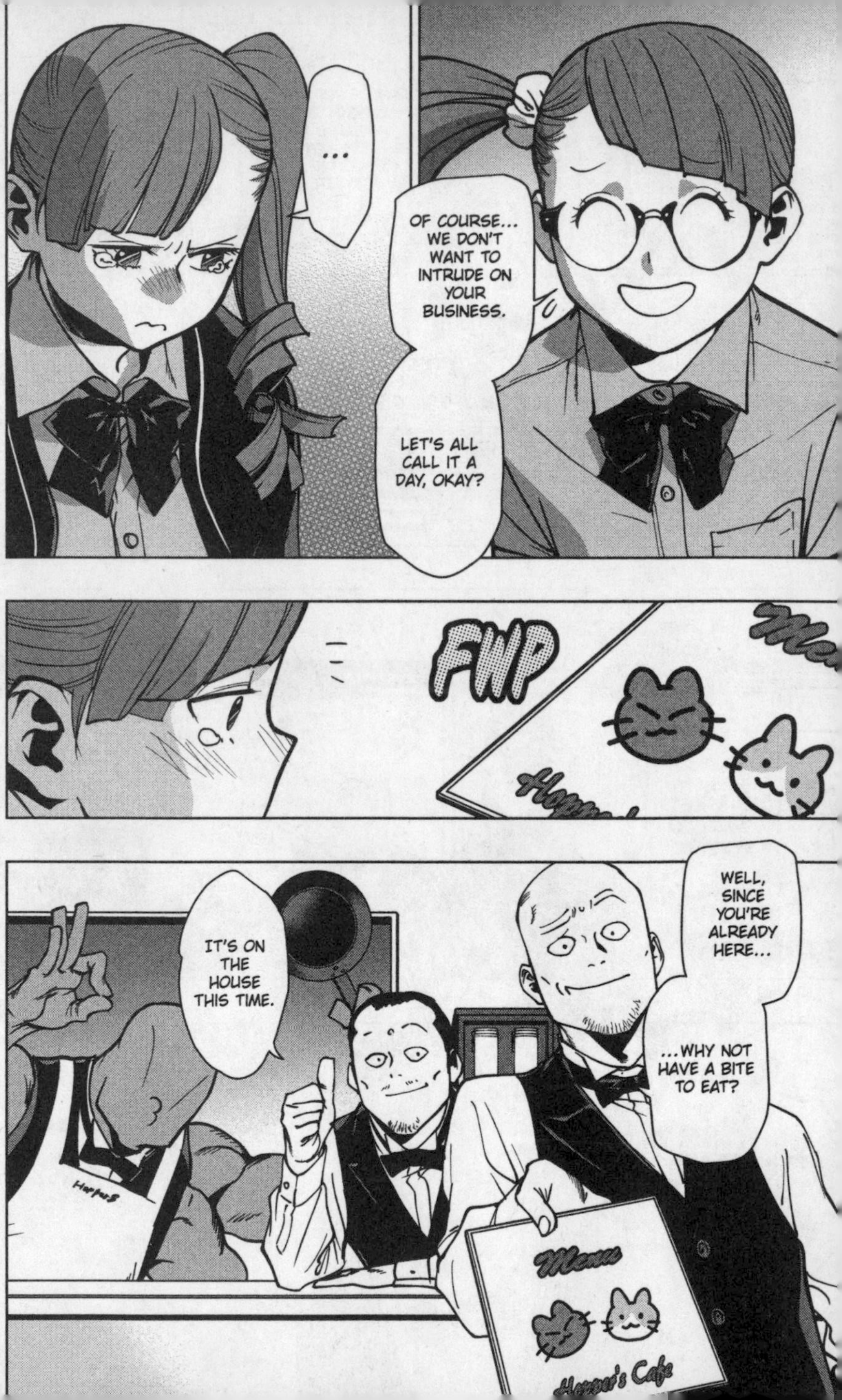
OF COURSE... WE DON'T WANT TO INTRUDE ON YOUR BUSINESS.
LET'S ALL CALL IT A DAY, OKAY?
...
FWP
WELL, SINCE YOU'RE ALREADY HERE...
...WHY NOT HAVE A BITE TO EAT?
IT'S ON THE HOUSE THIS TIME.
Menu
Hopper's Cafe

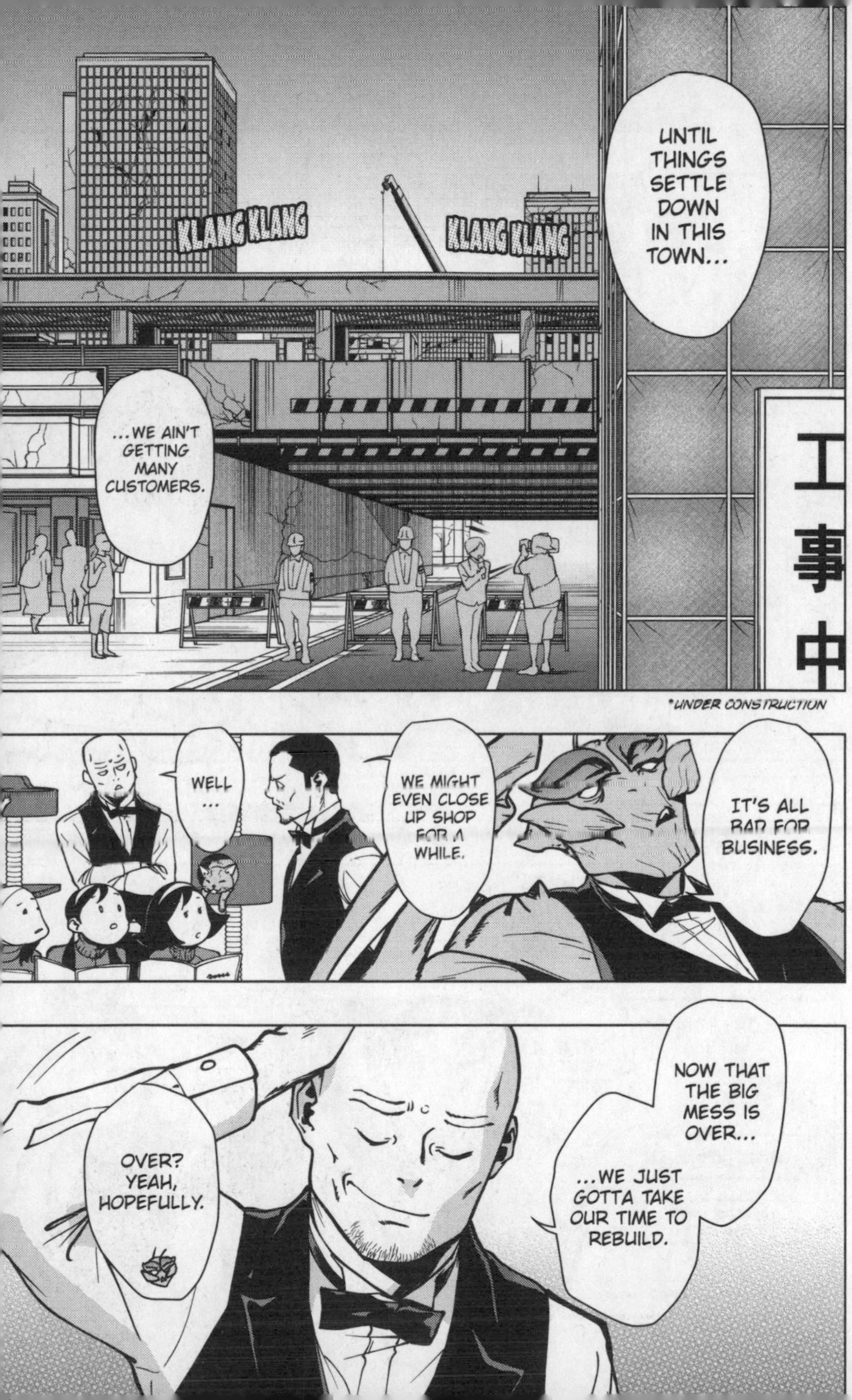
UNTIL THINGS SETTLE DOWN IN THIS TOWN...
工事中
KLANG KLANG
KLANG KLANG
...WE AIN'T GETTING MANY CUSTOMERS.
*UNDER CONSTRUCTION
IT'S ALL BAD FOR BUSINESS.
WE MIGHT EVEN CLOSE UP SHOP FOR A WHILE.
WELL...
NOW THAT THE BIG MESS IS OVER...
...WE JUST GOTTA TAKE OUR TIME TO REBUILD.
OVER? YEAH, HOPEFULLY.

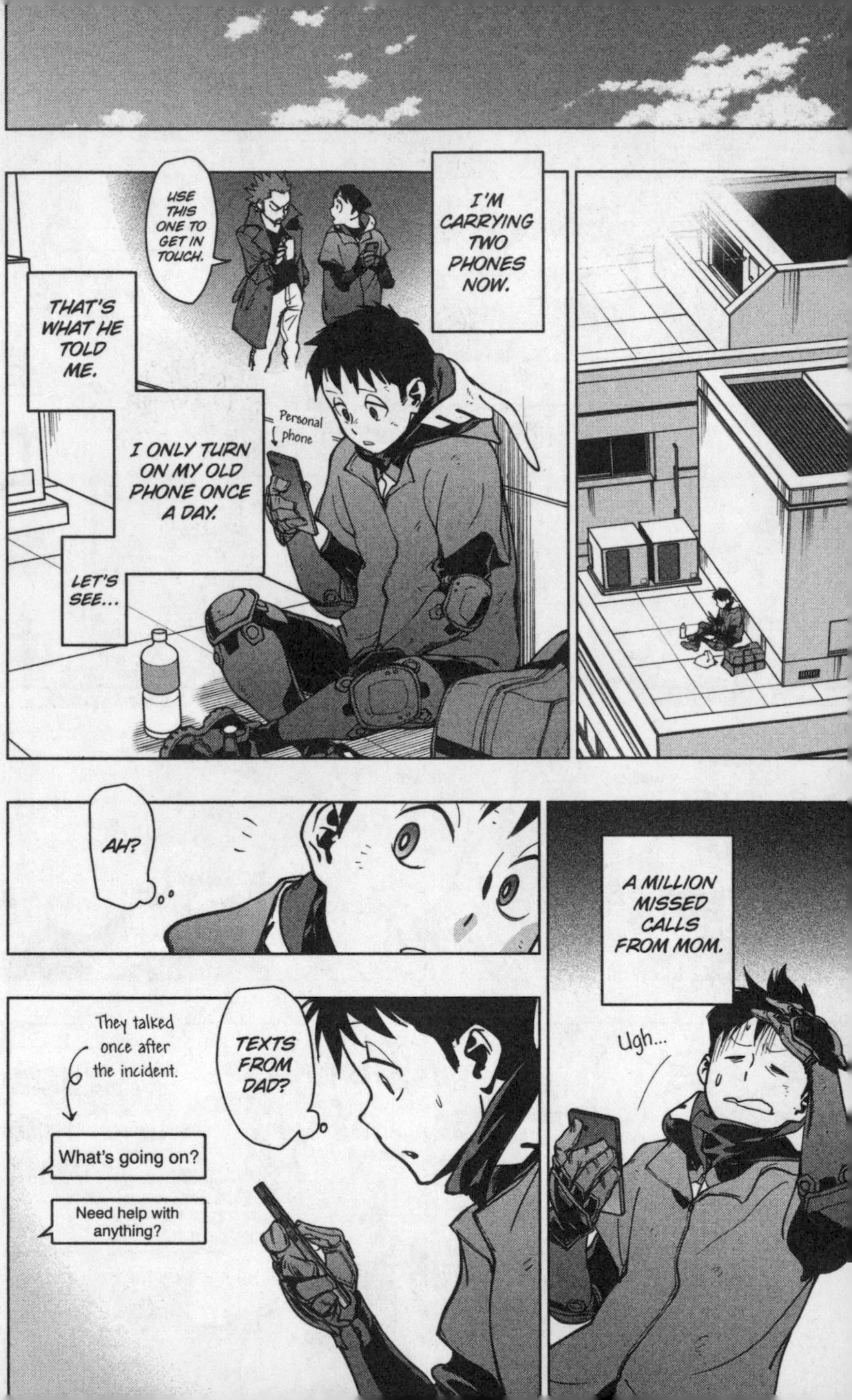
I'M CARRYING TWO PHONES NOW.
USE THIS ONE TO GET IN TOUCH.
THAT'S WHAT HE TOLD ME.
Personal phone
I ONLY TURN ON MY OLD PHONE ONCE A DAY.
LET'S SEE...
A MILLION MISSED CALLS FROM MOM.
Ugh...
AH?
TEXTS FROM DAD?
They talked once after the incident.
What's going on?
Need help with anything?

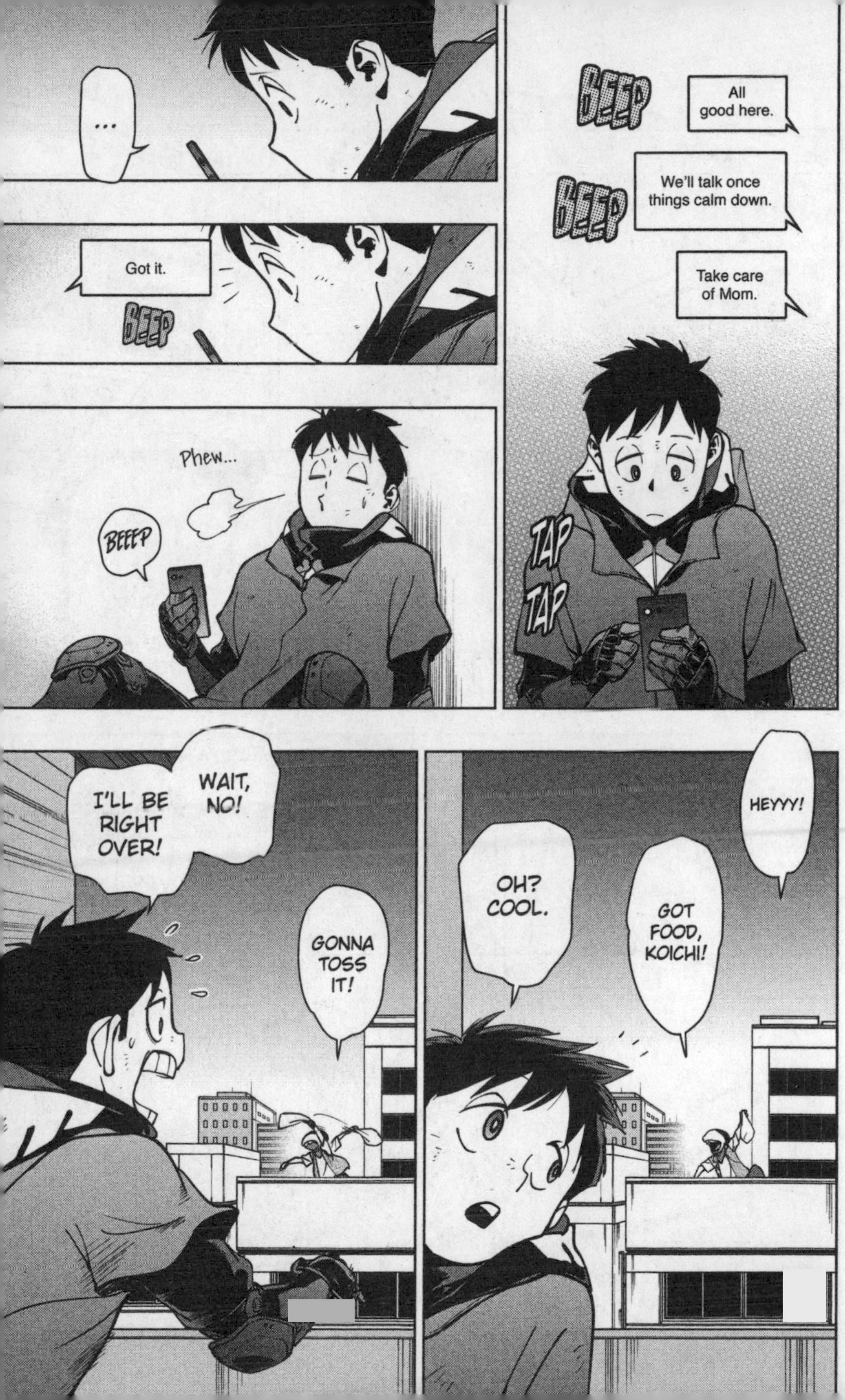
BEEP
All good here.
BEEP
We'll talk once things calm down.
Take care of Mom.
TAP
TAP
...
Got it.
BEEP
Phew...
BEEEP
HEYYY!
GOT FOOD, KOICHI!
OH? COOL.
GONNA TOSS IT!
WAIT, NO!
I'LL BE RIGHT OVER!

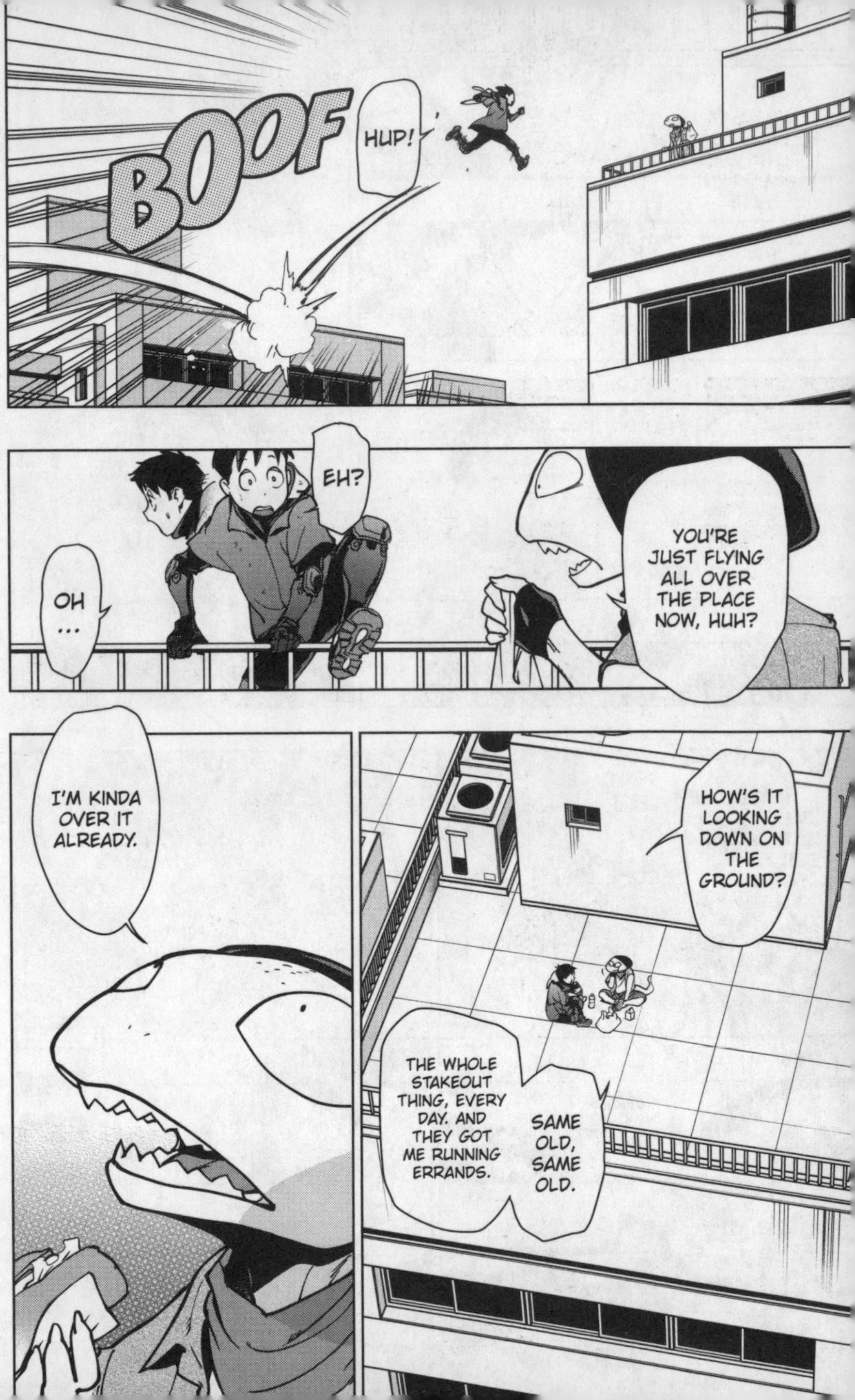
HUP!
BOOF
YOU'RE JUST FLYING ALL OVER THE PLACE NOW, HUH?
EH?
OH ...
HOW'S IT LOOKING DOWN ON THE GROUND?
SAME OLD, SAME OLD.
THE WHOLE STAKEOUT THING, EVERY DAY. AND THEY GOT ME RUNNING ERRANDS.
I'M KINDA OVER IT ALREADY.

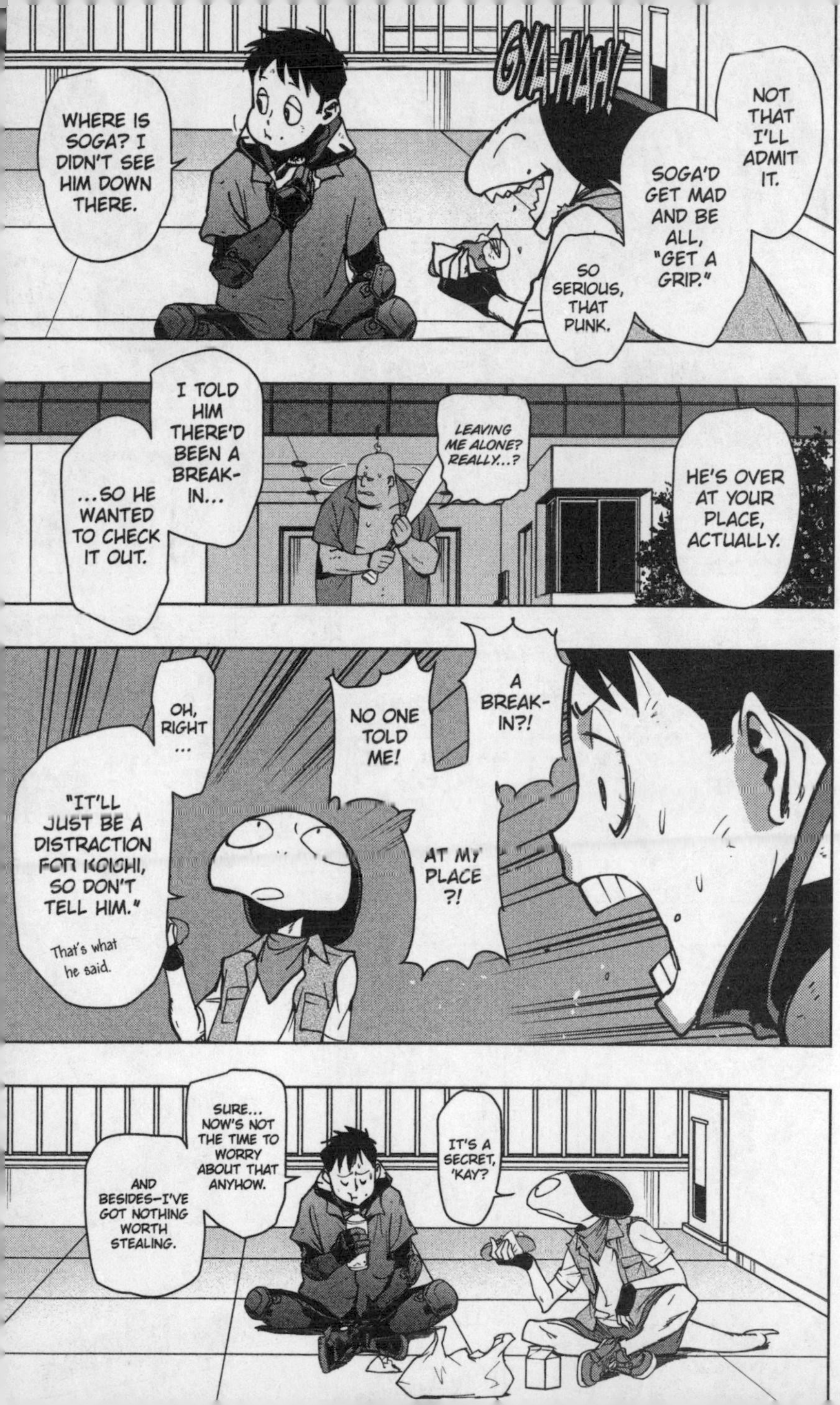
GYA HAH!
NOT THAT I'LL ADMIT IT.
SOGA'D GET MAD AND BE ALL, "GET A GRIP."
SO SERIOUS, THAT PUNK.
WHERE IS SOGA? I DIDN'T SEE HIM DOWN THERE.
HE'S OVER AT YOUR PLACE, ACTUALLY.
LEAVING ME ALONE? REALLY...?
I TOLD HIM THERE'D BEEN A BREAK-IN...
...SO HE WANTED TO CHECK IT OUT.
A BREAK-IN?!
NO ONE TOLD ME!
AT MY PLACE?!
OH, RIGHT...
"IT'LL JUST BE A DISTRACTION FOR KOICHI, SO DON'T TELL HIM."
That's what he said.
IT'S A SECRET, 'KAY?
SURE... NOW'S NOT THE TIME TO WORRY ABOUT THAT ANYHOW.
AND BESIDES—I'VE GOT NOTHING WORTH STEALING.

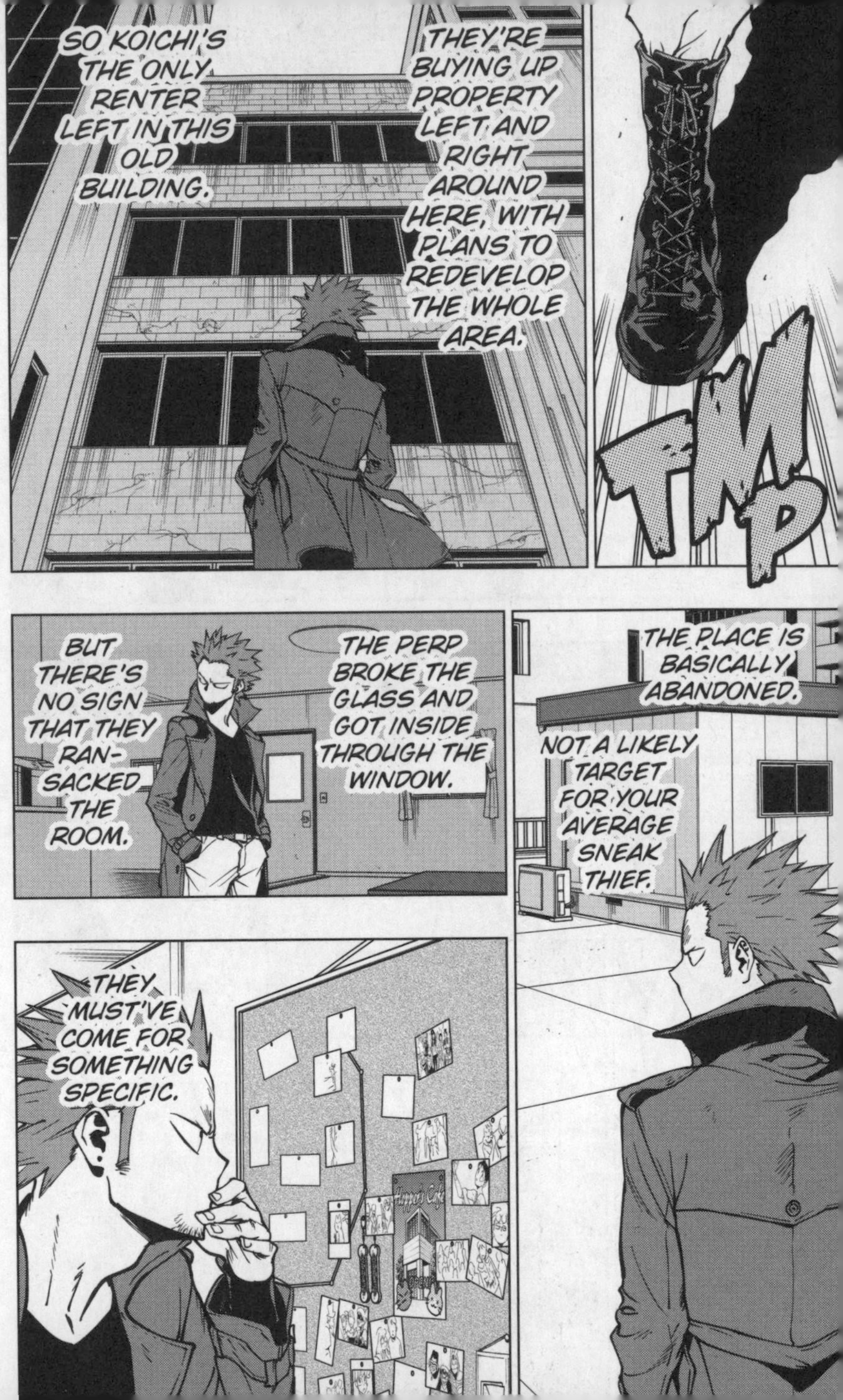
TMP
THEY'RE BUYING UP PROPERTY LEFT AND RIGHT AROUND HERE, WITH PLANS TO REDEVELOP THE WHOLE AREA.
SO KOICHI'S THE ONLY RENTER LEFT IN THIS OLD BUILDING.
THE PLACE IS BASICALLY ABANDONED.
NOT A LIKELY TARGET FOR YOUR AVERAGE SNEAK THIEF.
THE PERP BROKE THE GLASS AND GOT INSIDE THROUGH THE WINDOW.
BUT THERE'S NO SIGN THAT THEY RAN-SACKED THE ROOM.
THEY MUST'VE COME FOR SOMETHING SPECIFIC.

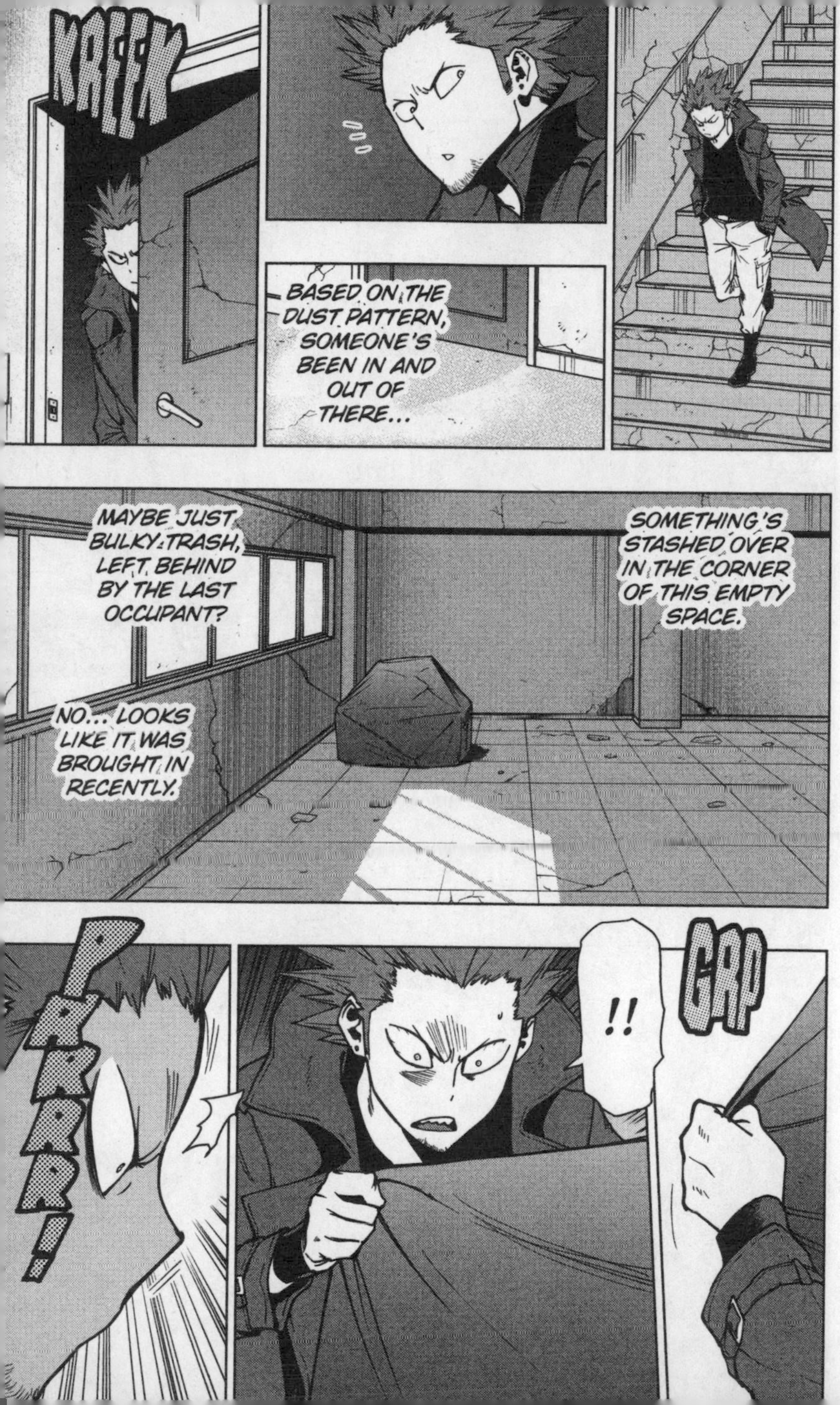
BASED ON THE DUST PATTERN, SOMEONE'S BEEN IN AND OUT OF THERE...
KREEK
SOMETHING'S STASHED OVER IN THE CORNER OF THIS EMPTY SPACE.
MAYBE JUST BULKY TRASH, LEFT BEHIND BY THE LAST OCCUPANT?
NO... LOOKS LIKE IT WAS BROUGHT IN RECENTLY.
GRP
!!

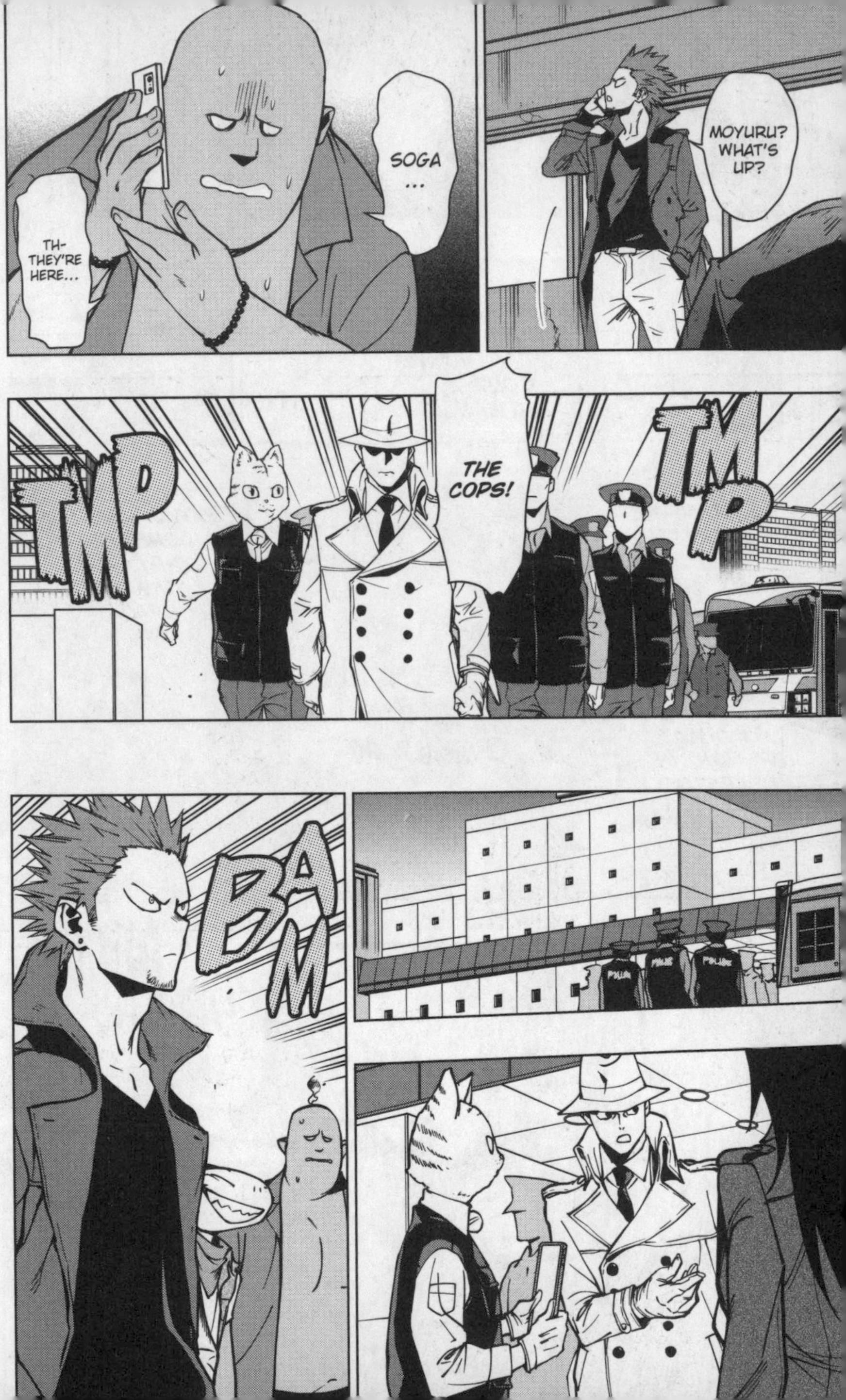
MOYURU? WHAT'S UP?
SOGA ...
TH- THEY'RE HERE...
TMP
THE COPS!
TMP
BAM

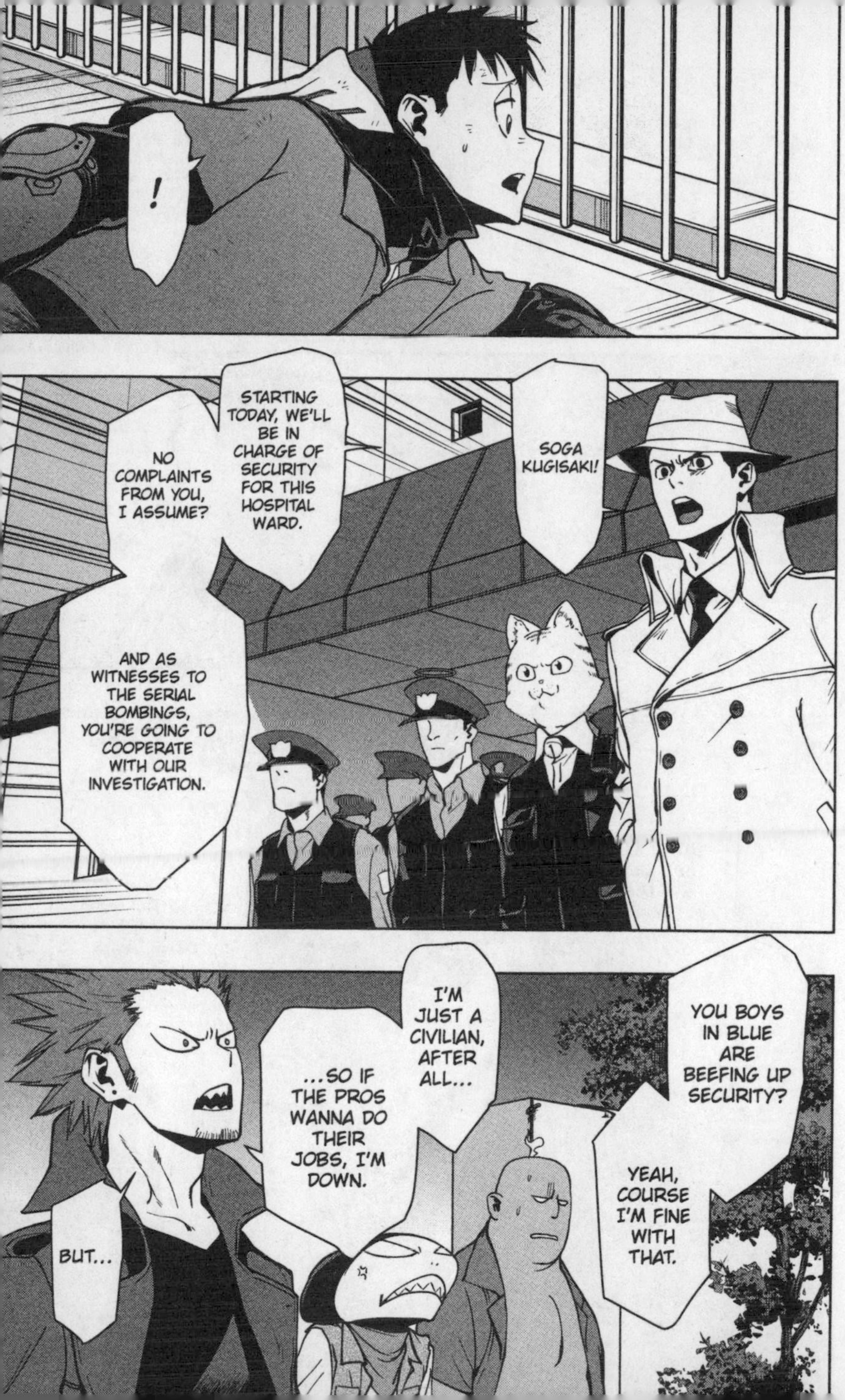
!
SOGA KUGISAKI!
STARTING TODAY, WE'LL BE IN CHARGE OF SECURITY FOR THIS HOSPITAL WARD.
NO COMPLAINTS FROM YOU, I ASSUME?
AND AS WITNESSES TO THE SERIAL BOMBINGS, YOU'RE GOING TO COOPERATE WITH OUR INVESTIGATION.
YOU BOYS IN BLUE ARE BEEFING UP SECURITY?
YEAH, COURSE I'M FINE WITH THAT.
I'M JUST A CIVILIAN, AFTER ALL...
...SO IF THE PROS WANNA DO THEIR JOBS, I'M DOWN.
BUT...

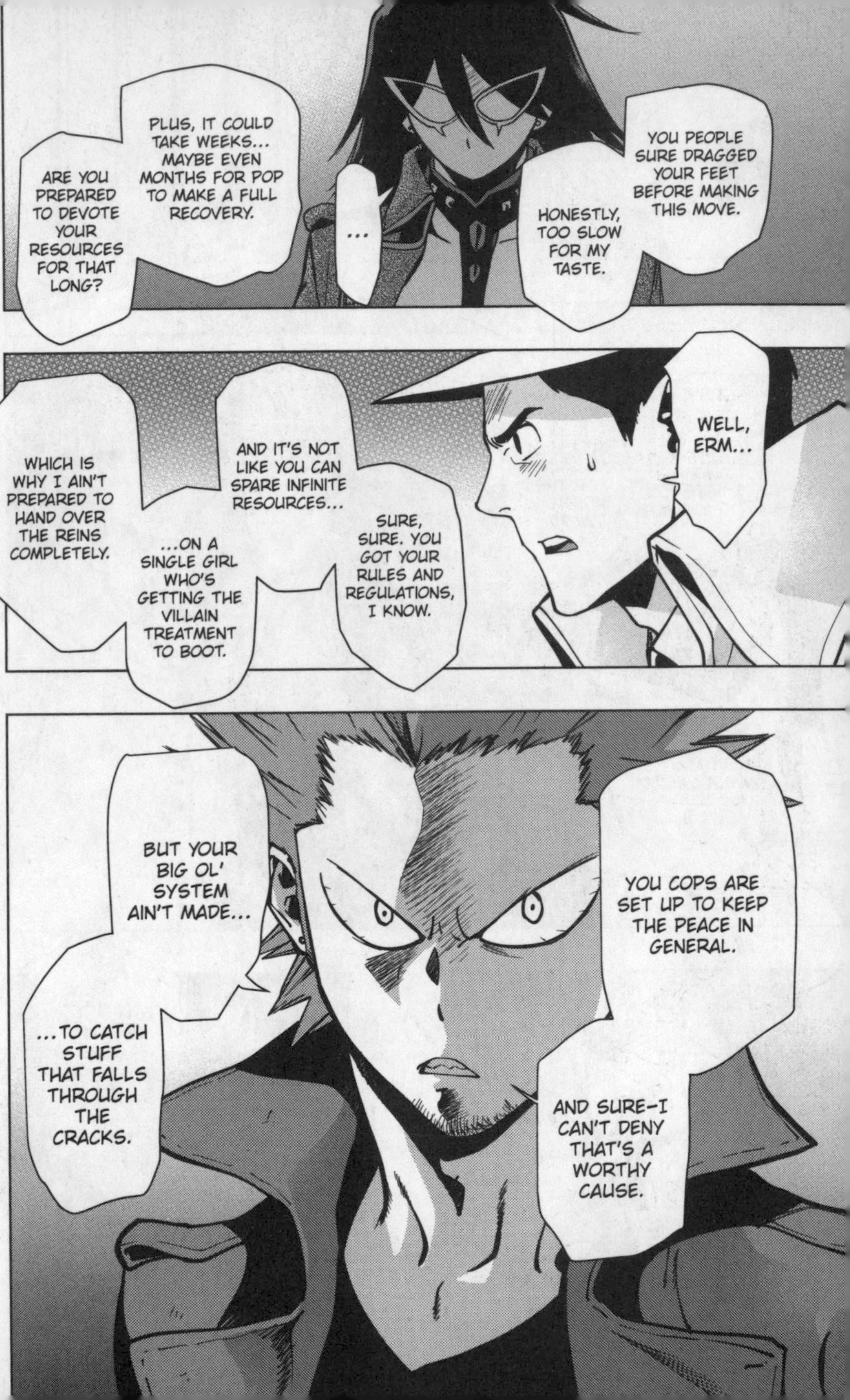
YOU PEOPLE SURE DRAGGED YOUR FEET BEFORE MAKING THIS MOVE.
HONESTLY, TOO SLOW FOR MY TASTE.
...
PLUS, IT COULD TAKE WEEKS... MAYBE EVEN MONTHS FOR POP TO MAKE A FULL RECOVERY.
ARE YOU PREPARED TO DEVOTE YOUR RESOURCES FOR THAT LONG?
WELL, ERM...
SURE, SURE. YOU GOT YOUR RULES AND REGULATIONS, I KNOW.
AND IT'S NOT LIKE YOU CAN SPARE INFINITE RESOURCES...
...ON A SINGLE GIRL WHO'S GETTING THE VILLAIN TREATMENT TO BOOT.
WHICH IS WHY I AIN'T PREPARED TO HAND OVER THE REINS COMPLETELY.
YOU COPS ARE SET UP TO KEEP THE PEACE IN GENERAL.
AND SURE—I CAN'T DENY THAT'S A WORTHY CAUSE.
BUT YOUR BIG OL' SYSTEM AIN'T MADE...
...TO CATCH STUFF THAT FALLS THROUGH THE CRACKS.

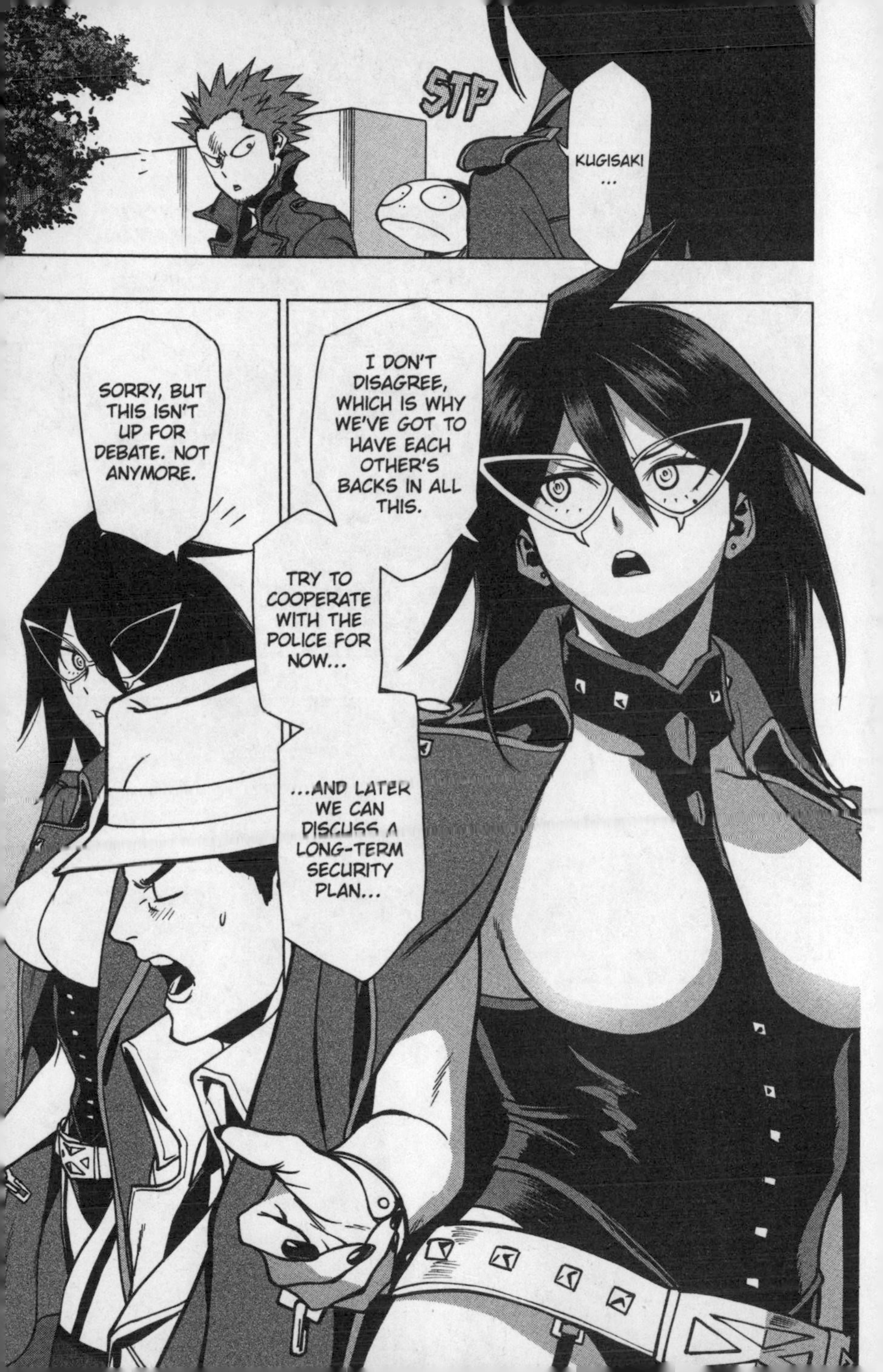
STP
KUGISAKI ...
I DON'T DISAGREE, WHICH IS WHY WE'VE GOT TO HAVE EACH OTHER'S BACKS IN ALL THIS.
TRY TO COOPERATE WITH THE POLICE FOR NOW...
...AND LATER WE CAN DISCUSS A LONG-TERM SECURITY PLAN...
SORRY, BUT THIS ISN'T UP FOR DEBATE. NOT ANYMORE.

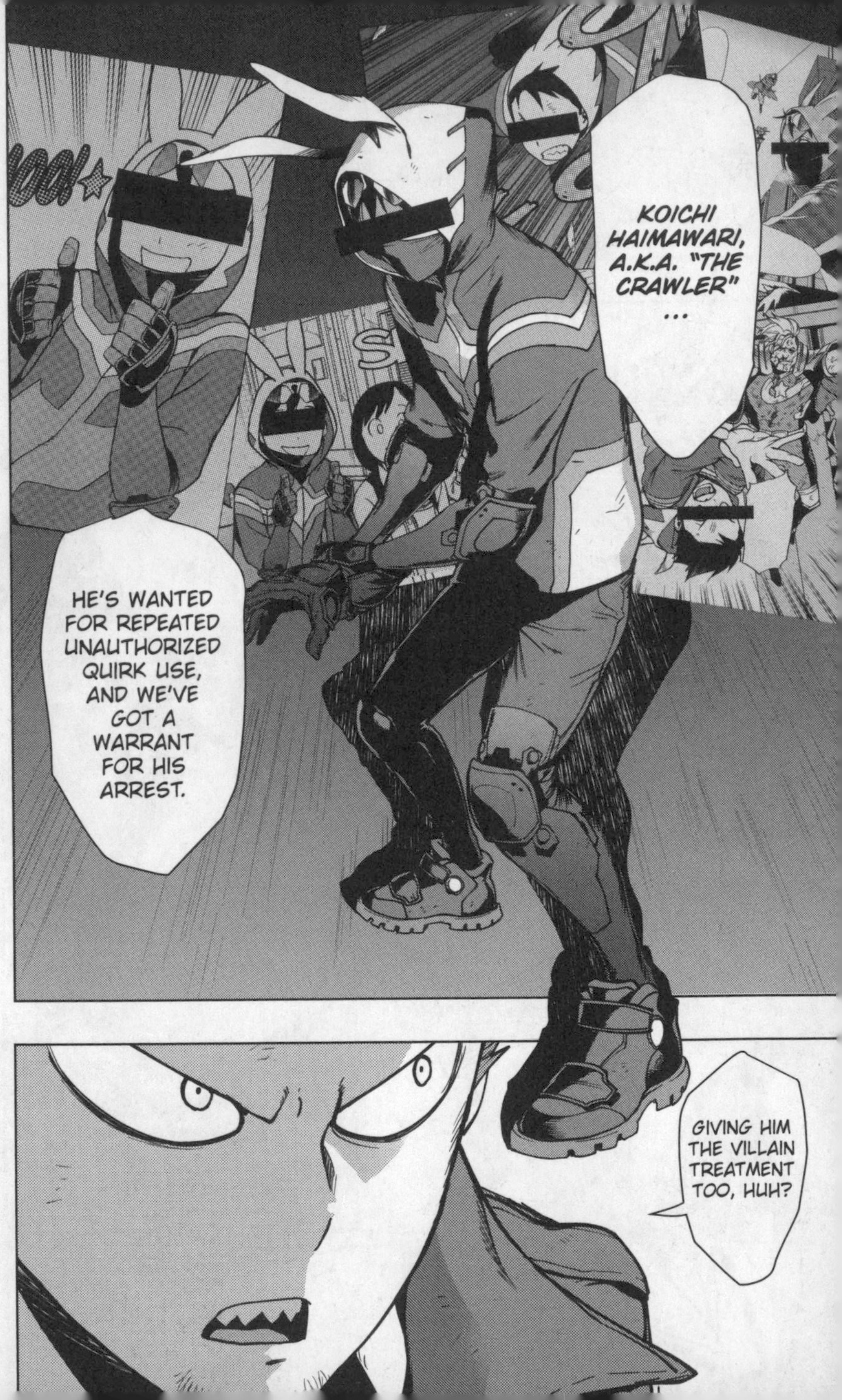
KOICHI HAIMAWARI, A.K.A. "THE CRAWLER" ...
HE'S WANTED FOR REPEATED UNAUTHORIZED QUIRK USE, AND WE'VE GOT A WARRANT FOR HIS ARREST.
GIVING HIM THE VILLAIN TREATMENT TOO, HUH?

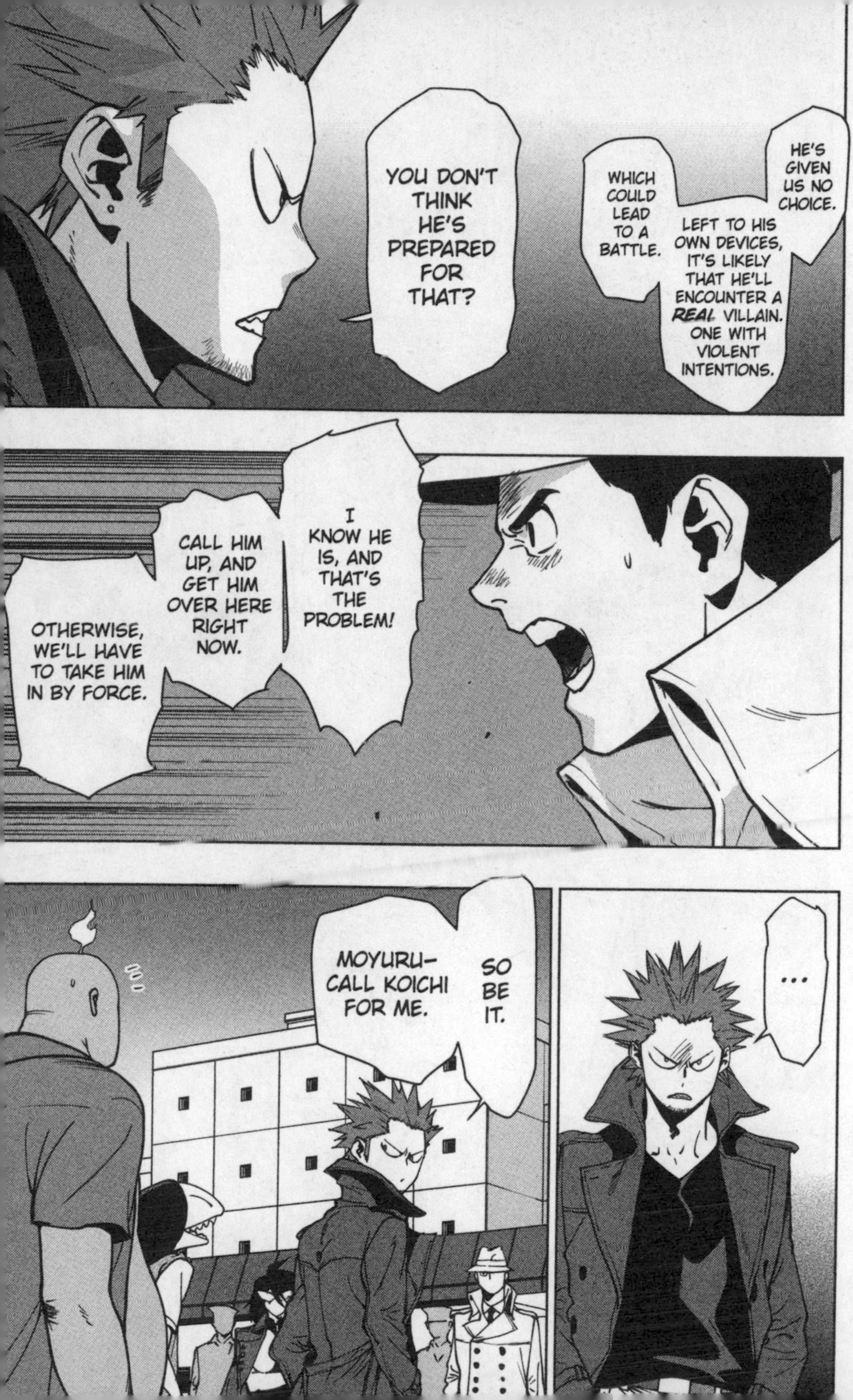

HE'S GIVEN US NO CHOICE.
LEFT TO HIS OWN DEVICES, IT'S LIKELY THAT HE'LL ENCOUNTER A *REAL* VILLAIN. ONE WITH VIOLENT INTENTIONS.
WHICH COULD LEAD TO A BATTLE.
YOU DON'T THINK HE'S PREPARED FOR THAT?
I KNOW HE IS, AND THAT'S THE PROBLEM!
CALL HIM UP, AND GET HIM OVER HERE RIGHT NOW.
OTHERWISE, WE'LL HAVE TO TAKE HIM IN BY FORCE.
...
SO BE IT.
MOYURU-CALL KOICHI FOR ME.

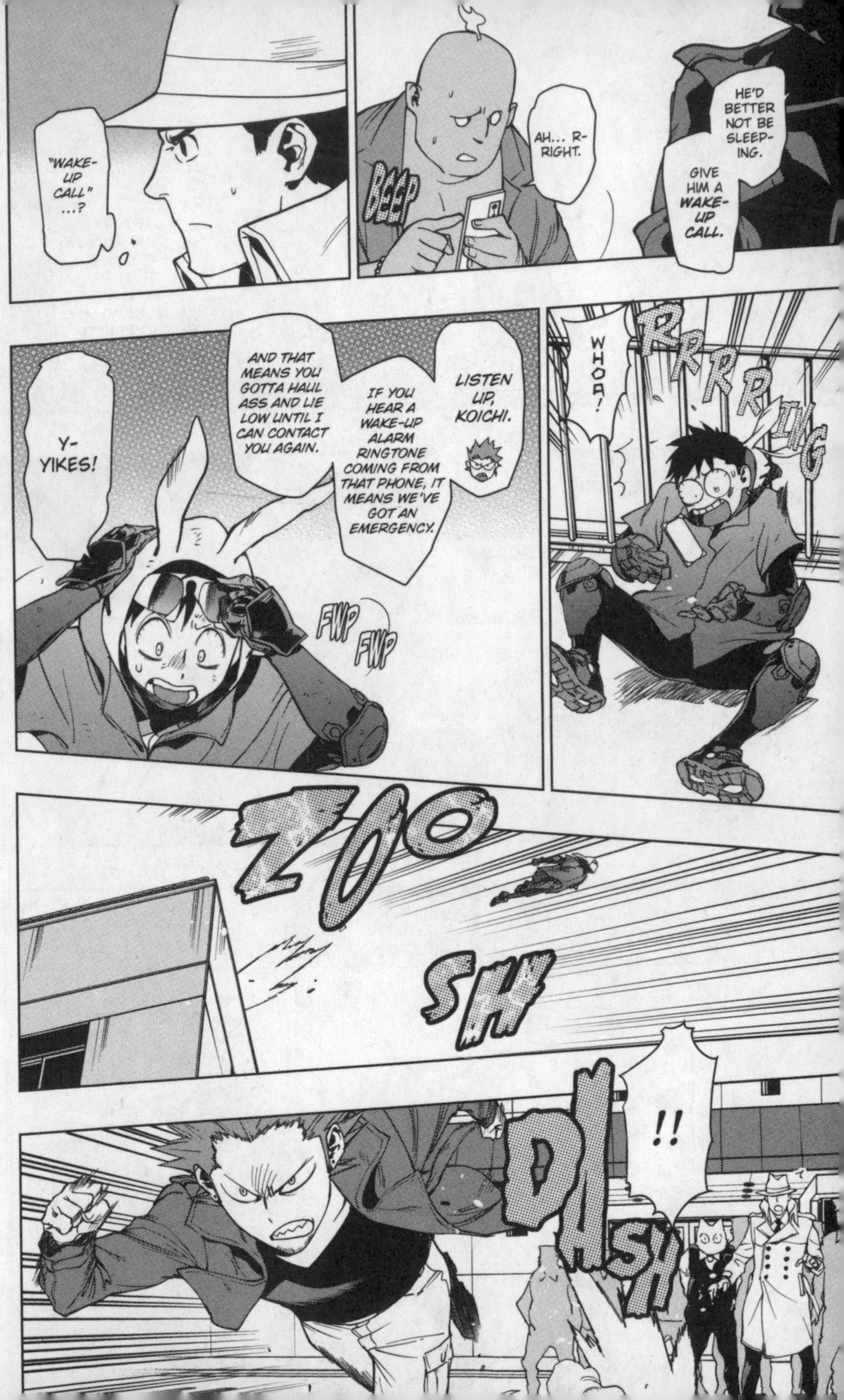
HE'D BETTER NOT BE SLEEPING.
GIVE HIM A WAKE-UP CALL.
BEEP
AH... R-RIGHT.
"WAKE-UP CALL"...?
RRRRRING
WHOA!
LISTEN UP, KOICHI.
IF YOU HEAR A WAKE-UP ALARM RINGTONE COMING FROM THAT PHONE, IT MEANS WE'VE GOT AN EMERGENCY.
AND THAT MEANS YOU GOTTA HAUL ASS AND LIE LOW UNTIL I CAN CONTACT YOU AGAIN.
FWP FWP
Y-YIKES!
ZOOSH
!!
DASH

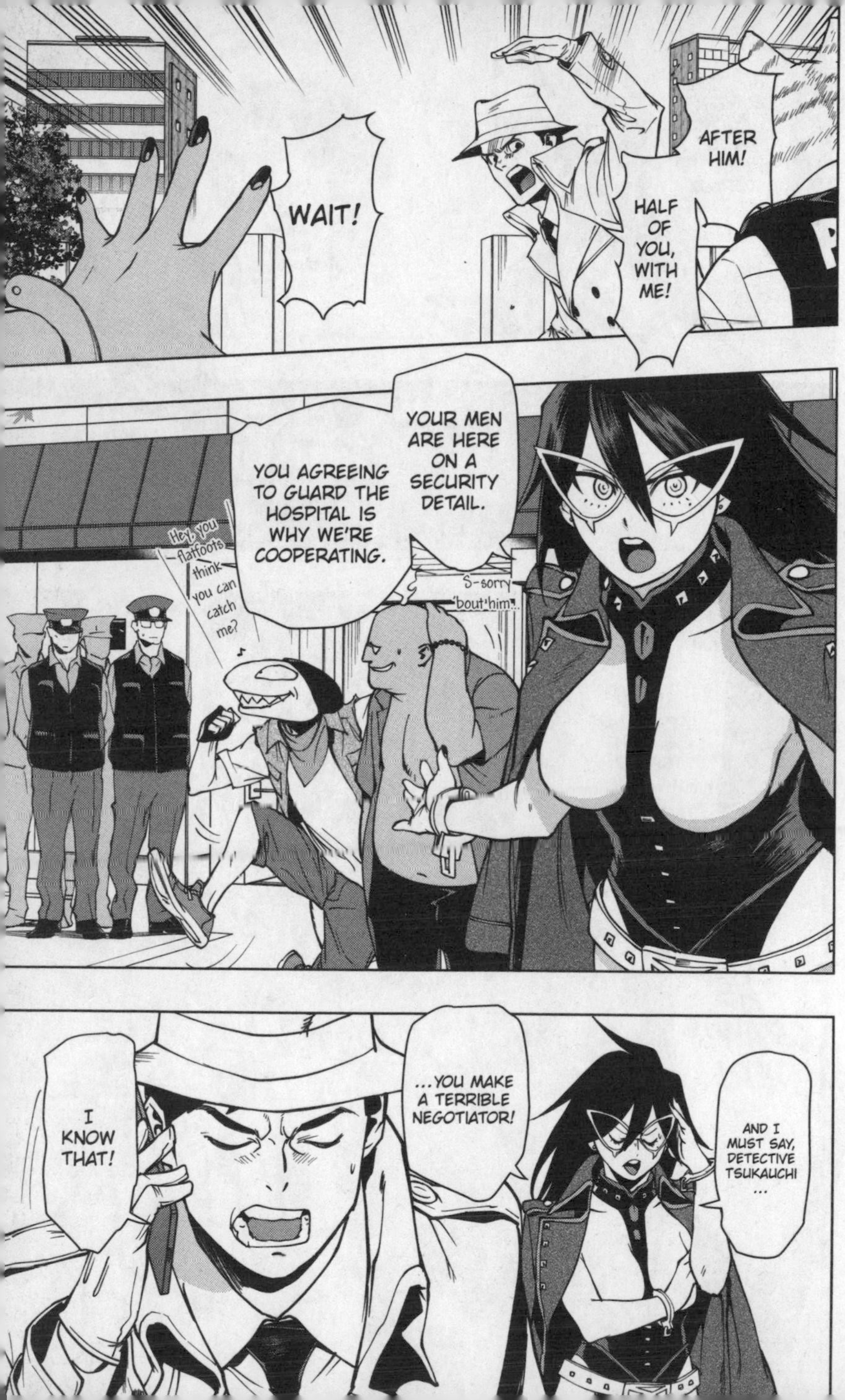
AFTER HIM!
HALF OF YOU, WITH ME!
WAIT!
YOUR MEN ARE HERE ON A SECURITY DETAIL.
YOU AGREEING TO GUARD THE HOSPITAL IS WHY WE'RE COOPERATING.
S-sorry 'bout him...
Hey, you flatfoots think you can catch me?
AND I MUST SAY, DETECTIVE TSUKAUCHI ...
...YOU MAKE A TERRIBLE NEGOTIATOR!
I KNOW THAT!

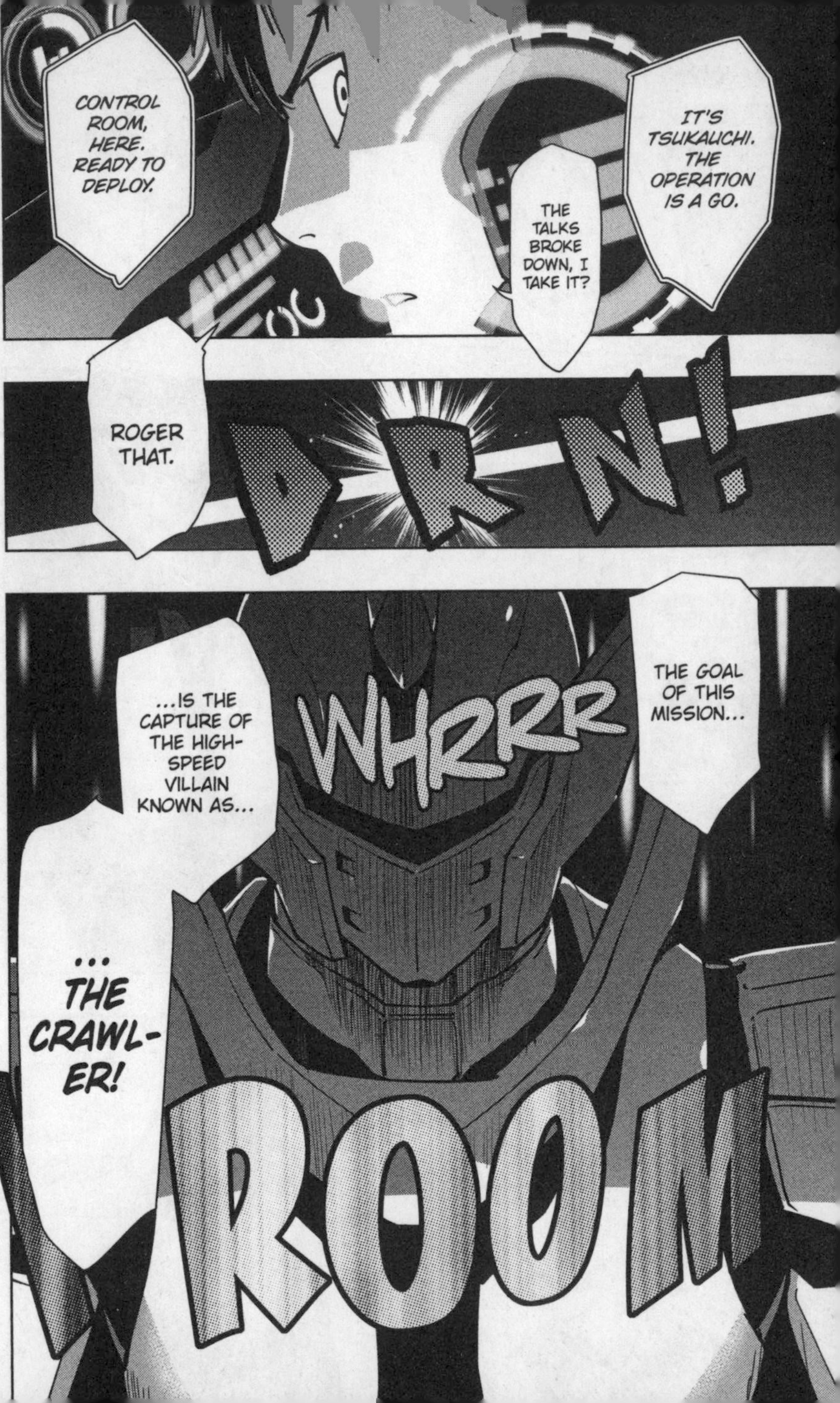
IT'S TSUKAUCHI. THE OPERATION IS A GO.
THE TALKS BROKE DOWN, I TAKE IT?
CONTROL ROOM, HERE. READY TO DEPLOY.
DRRN!
ROGER THAT.
THE GOAL OF THIS MISSION...
WHRRR
...IS THE CAPTURE OF THE HIGH-SPEED VILLAIN KNOWN AS...
...THE CRAWL-ER!
ROOM

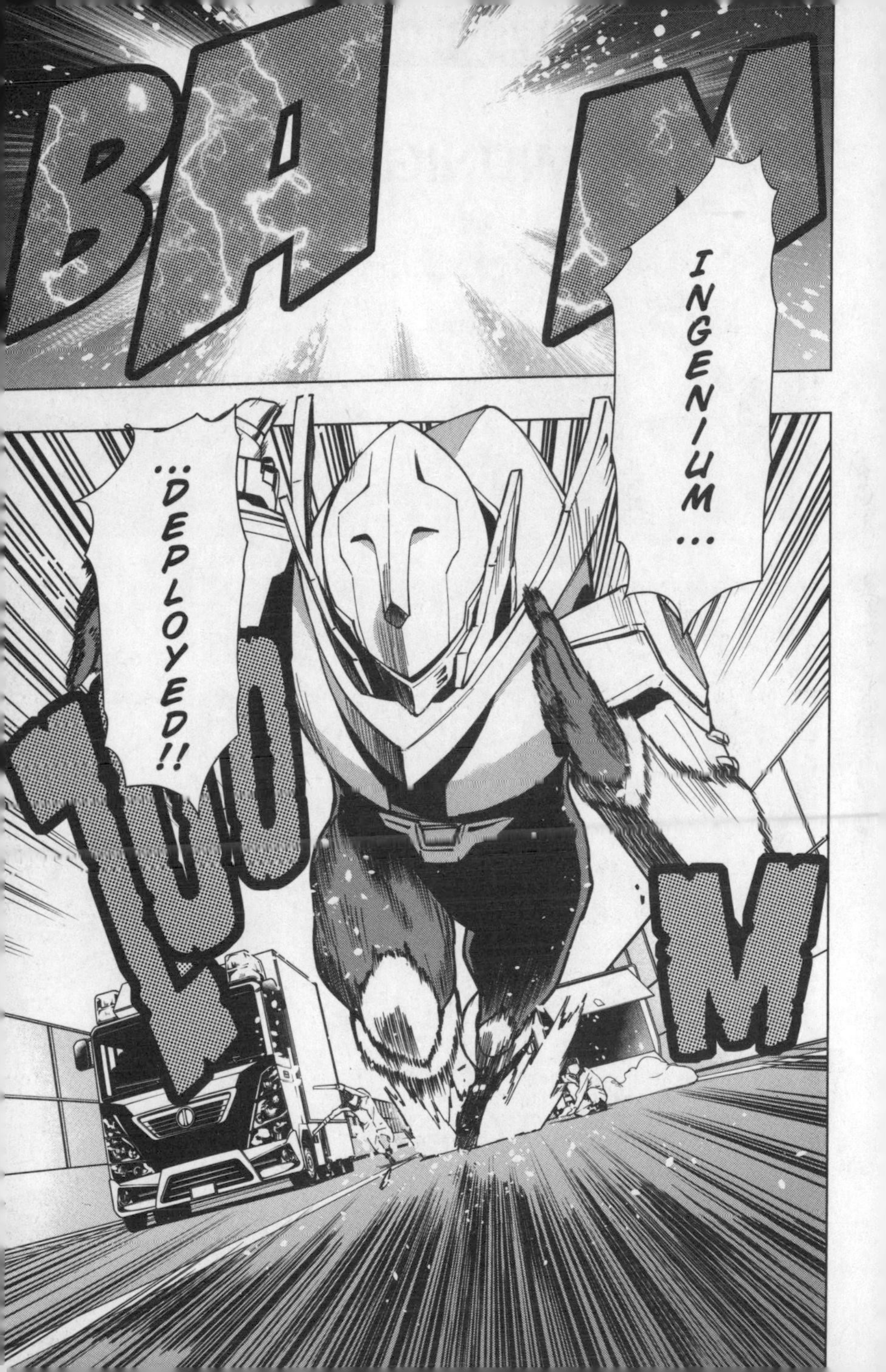
BAM
INGENIUM...
...DEPLOYED!!

MIDNIGHT

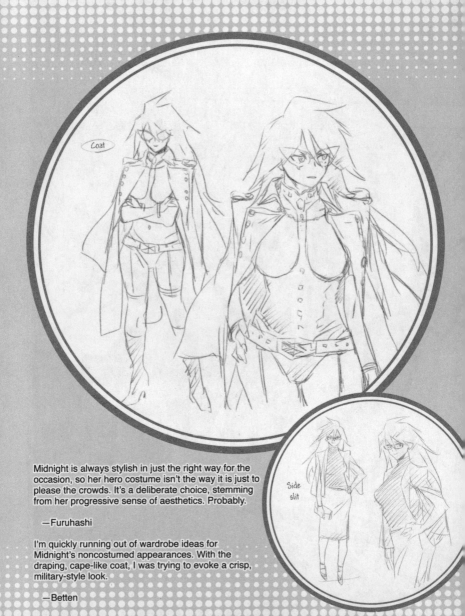

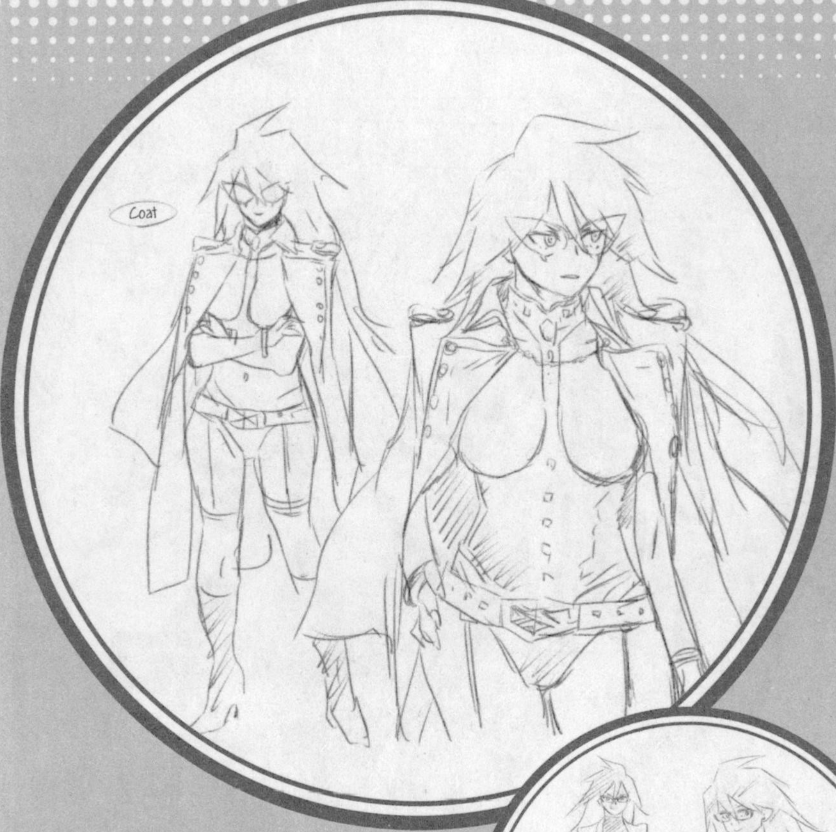
Coat

Midnight is always stylish in just the right way for the occasion, so her hero costume isn't the way it is just to please the crowds. It's a deliberate choice, stemming from her progressive sense of aesthetics. Probably.

—Furuhashi

I'm quickly running out of wardrobe ideas for Midnight's noncostumed appearances. With the draping, cape-like coat, I was trying to evoke a crisp, military-style look.

—Betten

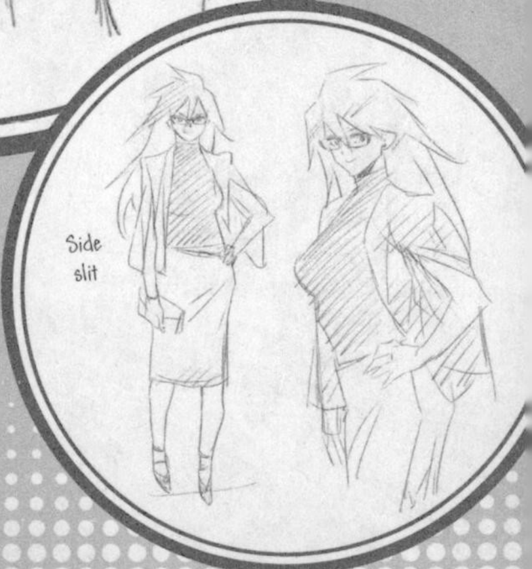
Side
slit

EP. 97 - PURSUERS

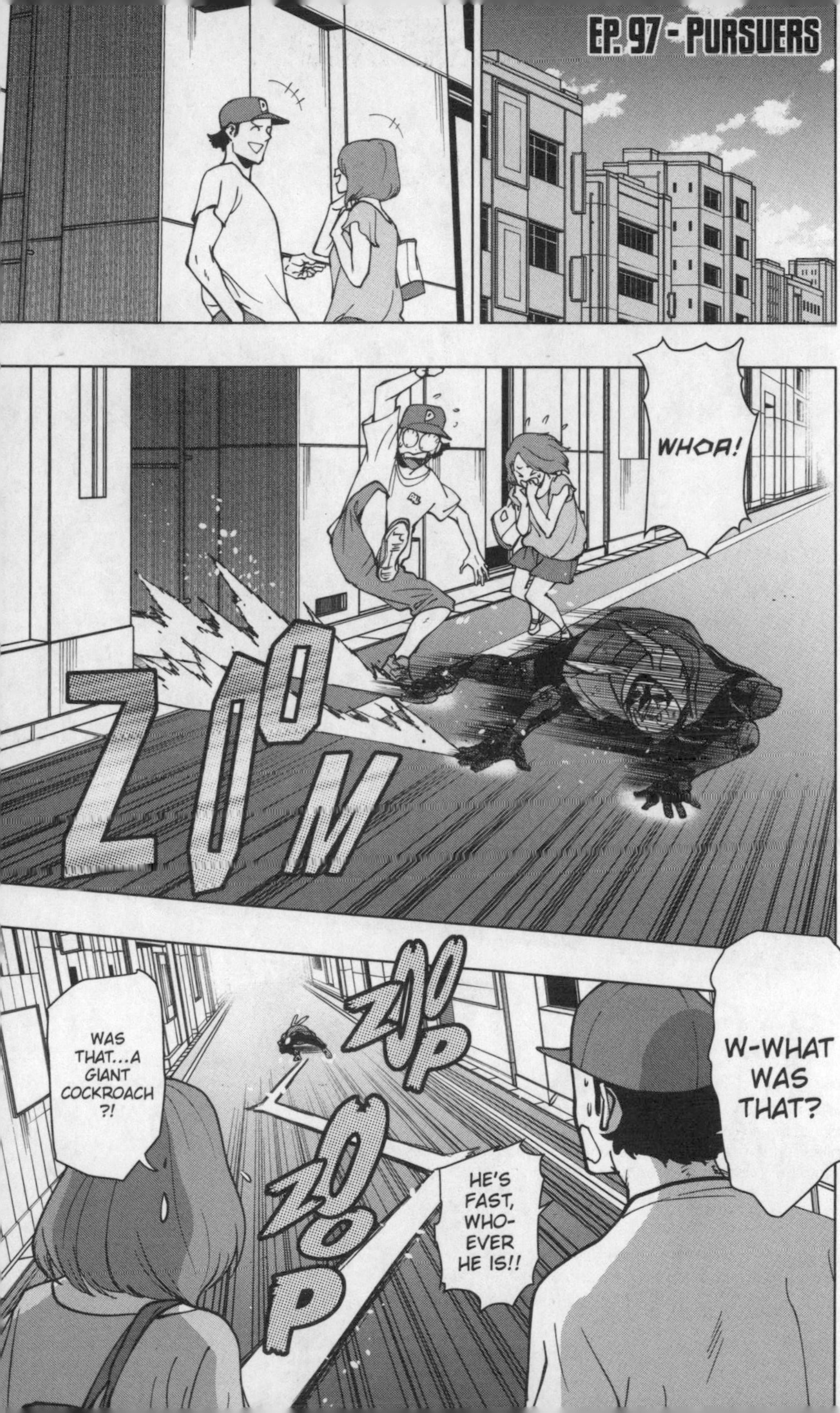
WHOA!
ZOOM
W-WHAT WAS THAT?
ZOOP
HE'S FAST, WHO-EVER HE IS!!
ZOOP
WAS THAT...A GIANT COCKROACH?!

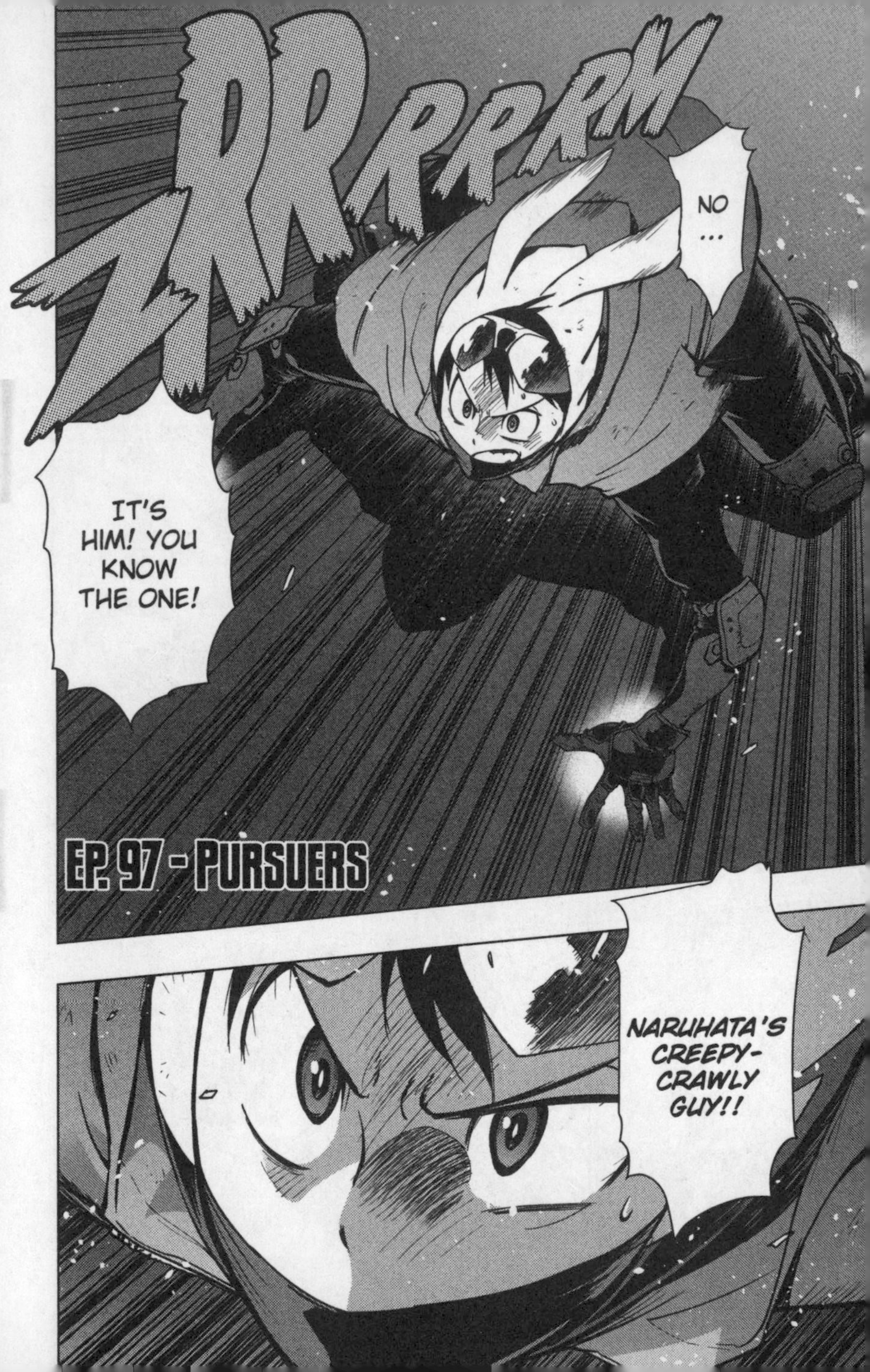
ZRRRRRM
NO ...
IT'S HIM! YOU KNOW THE ONE!
EP. 97 - PURSUERS
NARUHATA'S CREEPY-CRAWLY GUY!!

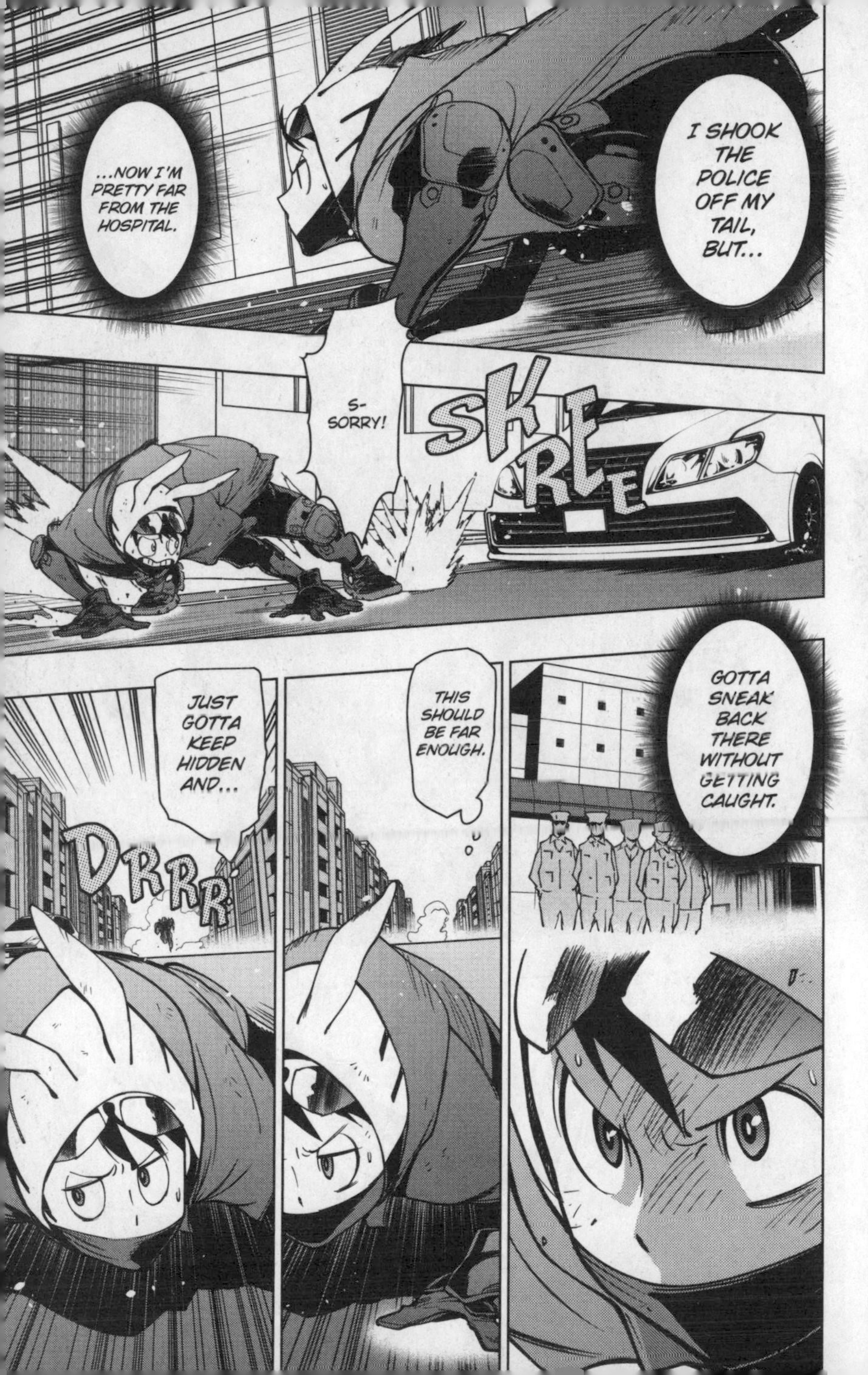
I SHOOK THE POLICE OFF MY TAIL, BUT...
...NOW I'M PRETTY FAR FROM THE HOSPITAL.
SKREE
S-SORRY!
GOTTA SNEAK BACK THERE WITHOUT GETTING CAUGHT.
THIS SHOULD BE FAR ENOUGH.
JUST GOTTA KEEP HIDDEN AND...
DRRRR

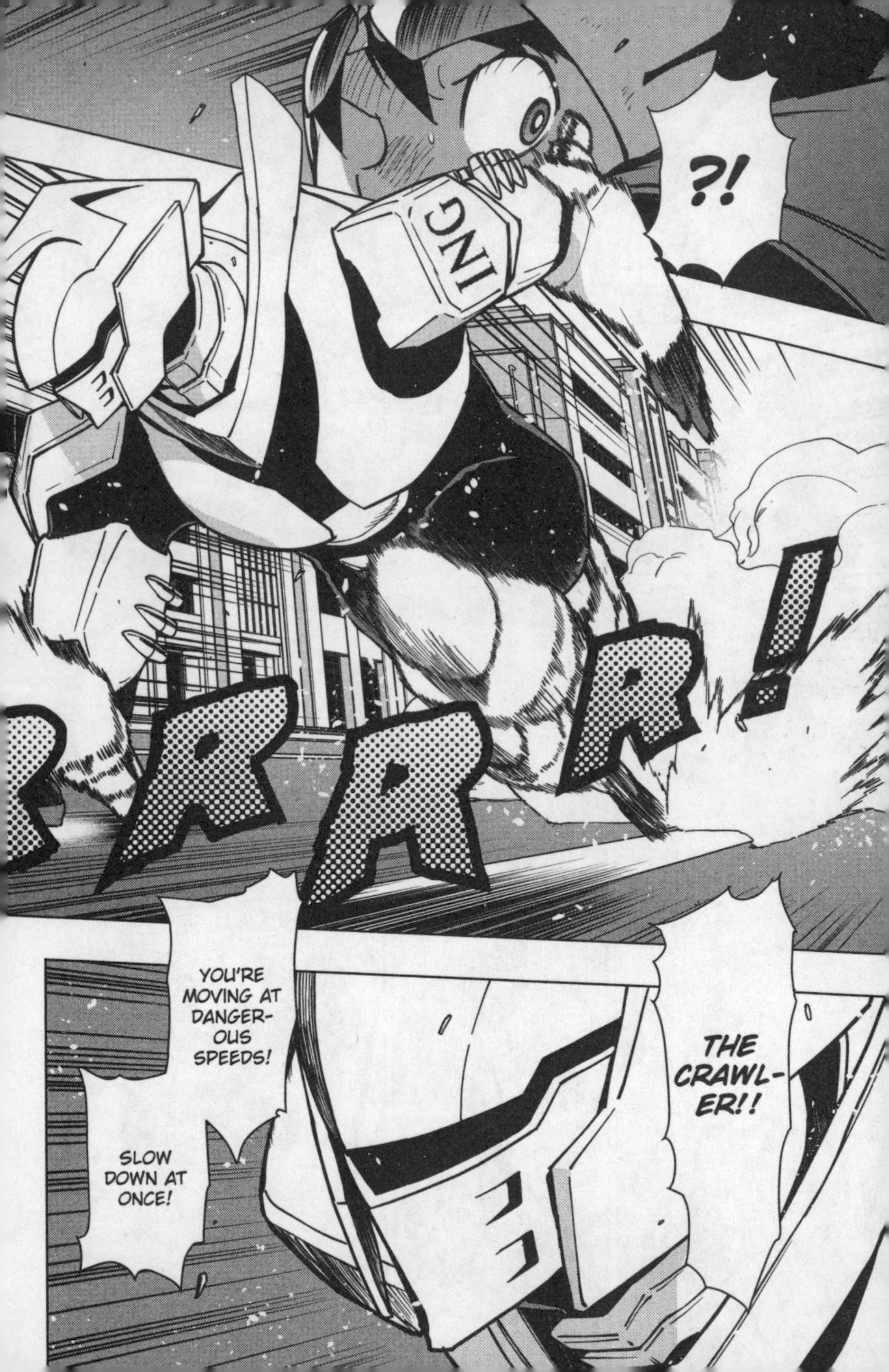
?!
ING
RRR!
THE CRAWL-ER!!
YOU'RE MOVING AT DANGER-OUS SPEEDS!
SLOW DOWN AT ONCE!

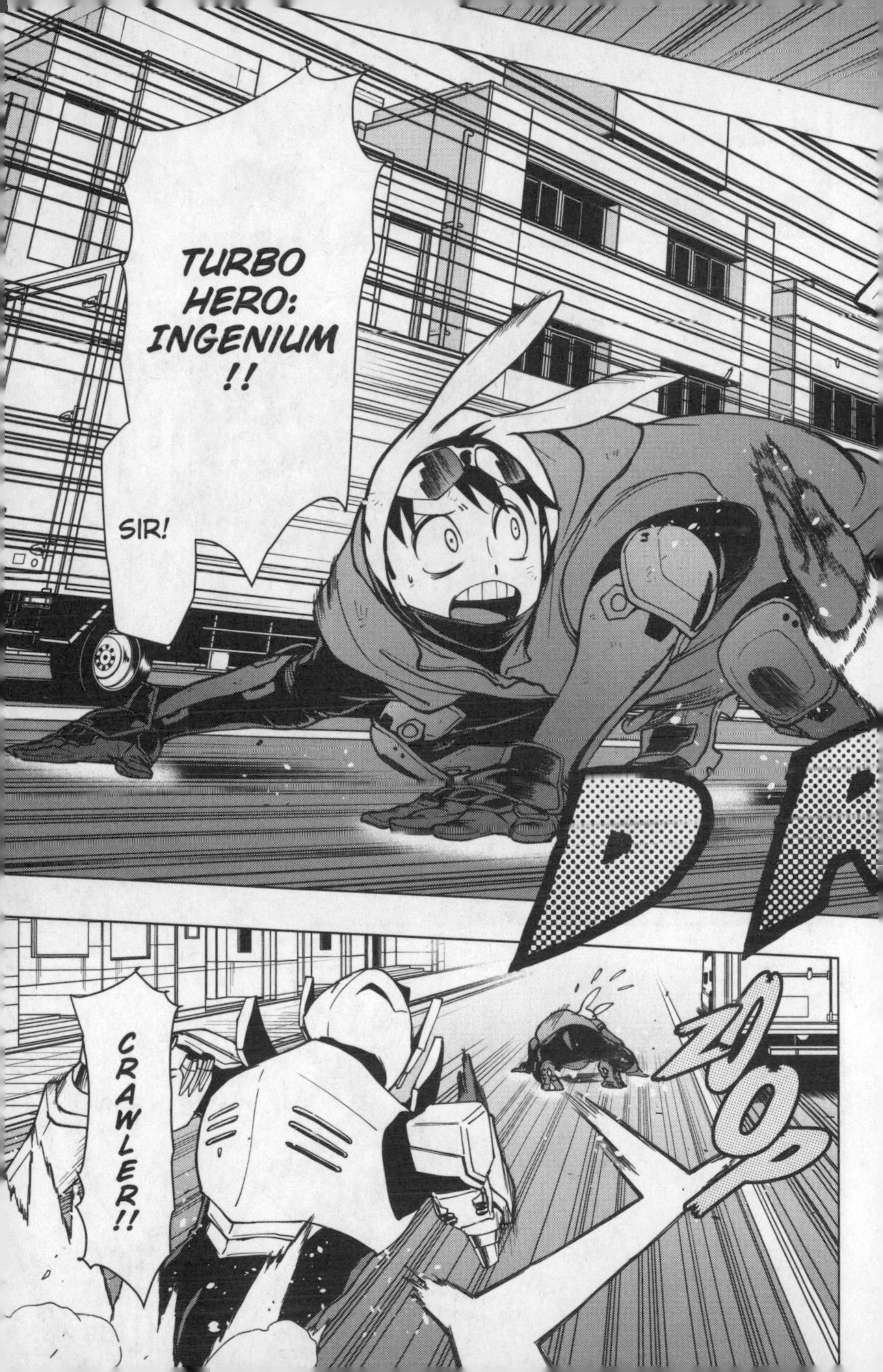
TURBO HERO: INGENIUM!!
SIR!
DR
ZOOP
CRAWLER!!

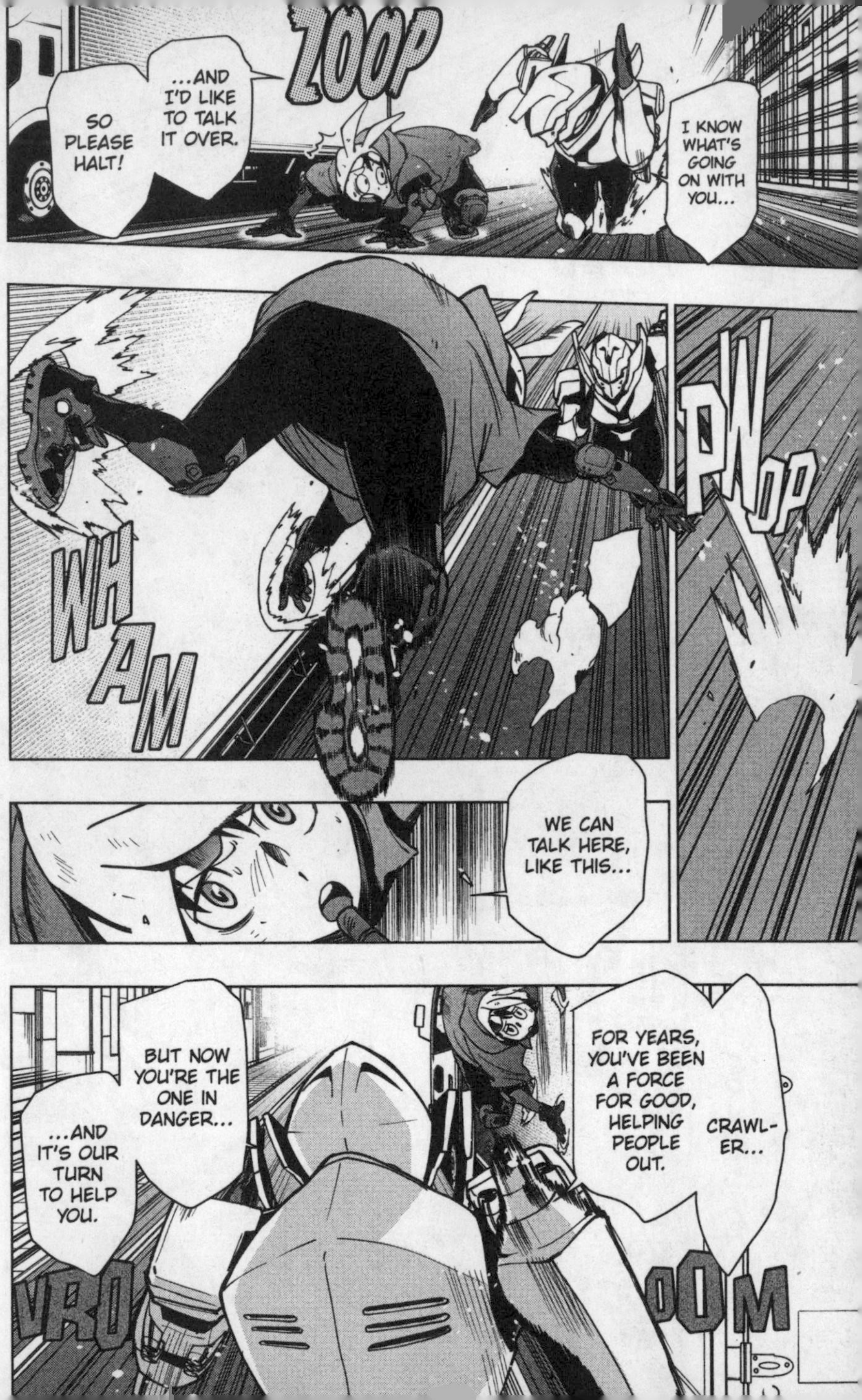
I KNOW WHAT'S GOING ON WITH YOU...
ZOOP
...AND I'D LIKE TO TALK IT OVER.
SO PLEASE HALT!
PWOP
WHAM
WE CAN TALK HERE, LIKE THIS...
CRAWL-ER...
FOR YEARS, YOU'VE BEEN A FORCE FOR GOOD, HELPING PEOPLE OUT.
BUT NOW YOU'RE THE ONE IN DANGER...
...AND IT'S OUR TURN TO HELP YOU.
VROOOM

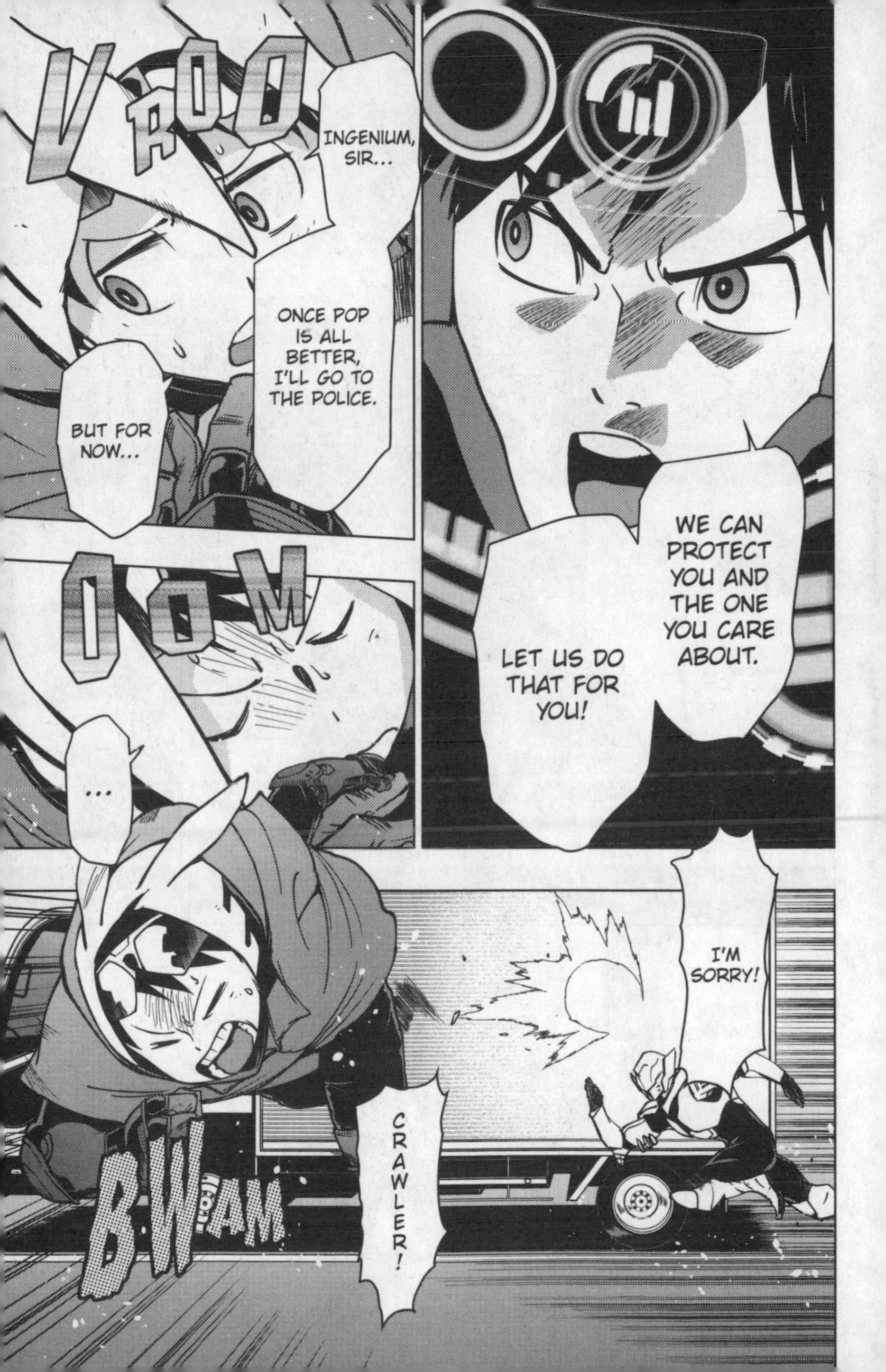
WE CAN PROTECT YOU AND THE ONE YOU CARE ABOUT.
LET US DO THAT FOR YOU!
VROO
INGENIUM, SIR...
ONCE POP IS ALL BETTER, I'LL GO TO THE POLICE.
BUT FOR NOW...
OOM
...
I'M SORRY!
CRAWLER!
BWAM

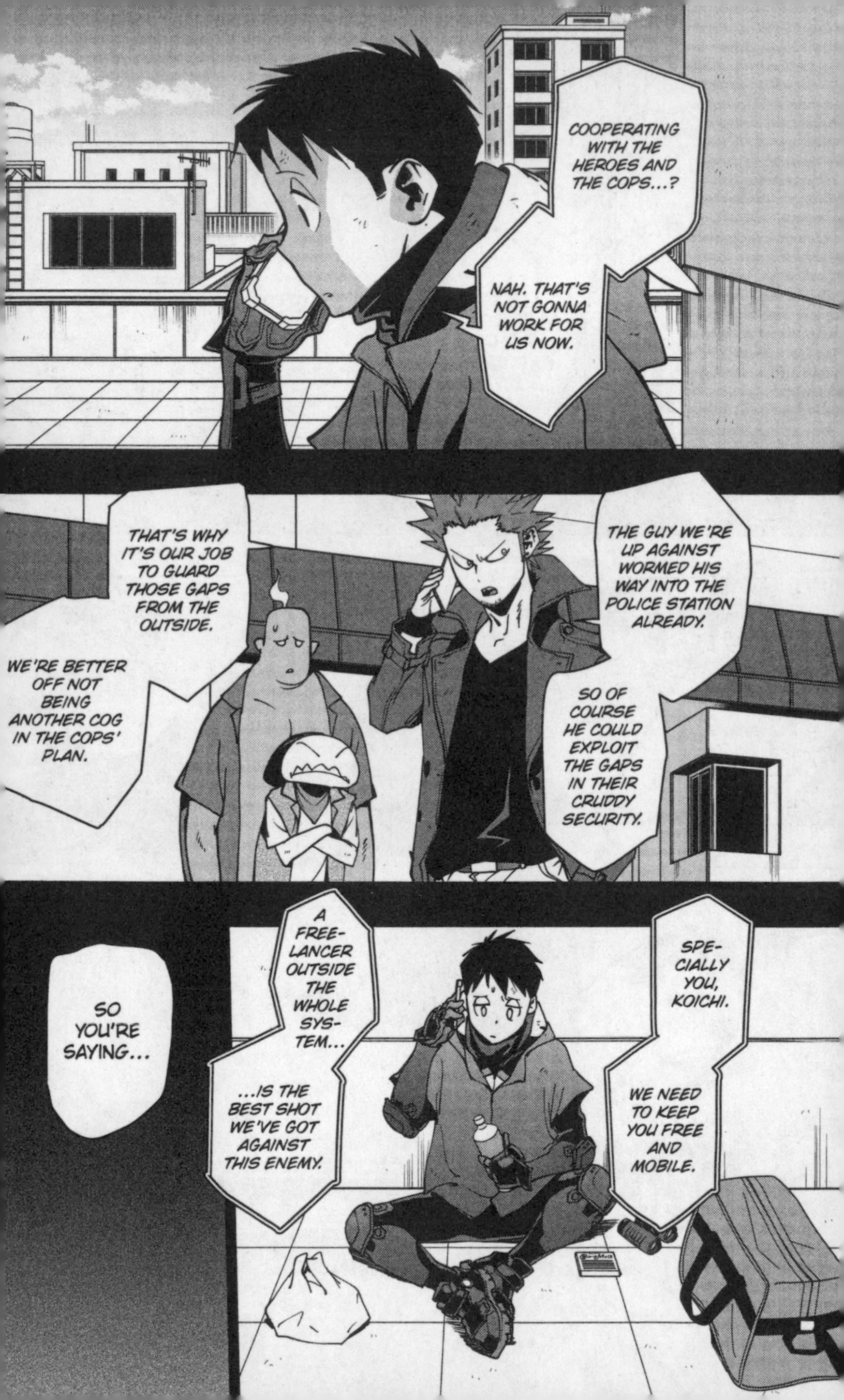
COOPERATING WITH THE HEROES AND THE COPS...?
NAH. THAT'S NOT GONNA WORK FOR US NOW.
THE GUY WE'RE UP AGAINST WORMED HIS WAY INTO THE POLICE STATION ALREADY.
SO OF COURSE HE COULD EXPLOIT THE GAPS IN THEIR CRUDDY SECURITY.
THAT'S WHY IT'S OUR JOB TO GUARD THOSE GAPS FROM THE OUTSIDE.
WE'RE BETTER OFF NOT BEING ANOTHER COG IN THE COPS' PLAN.
SPECIALLY YOU, KOICHI.
WE NEED TO KEEP YOU FREE AND MOBILE.
A FREELANCER OUTSIDE THE WHOLE SYSTEM...
...IS THE BEST SHOT WE'VE GOT AGAINST THIS ENEMY.
SO YOU'RE SAYING...

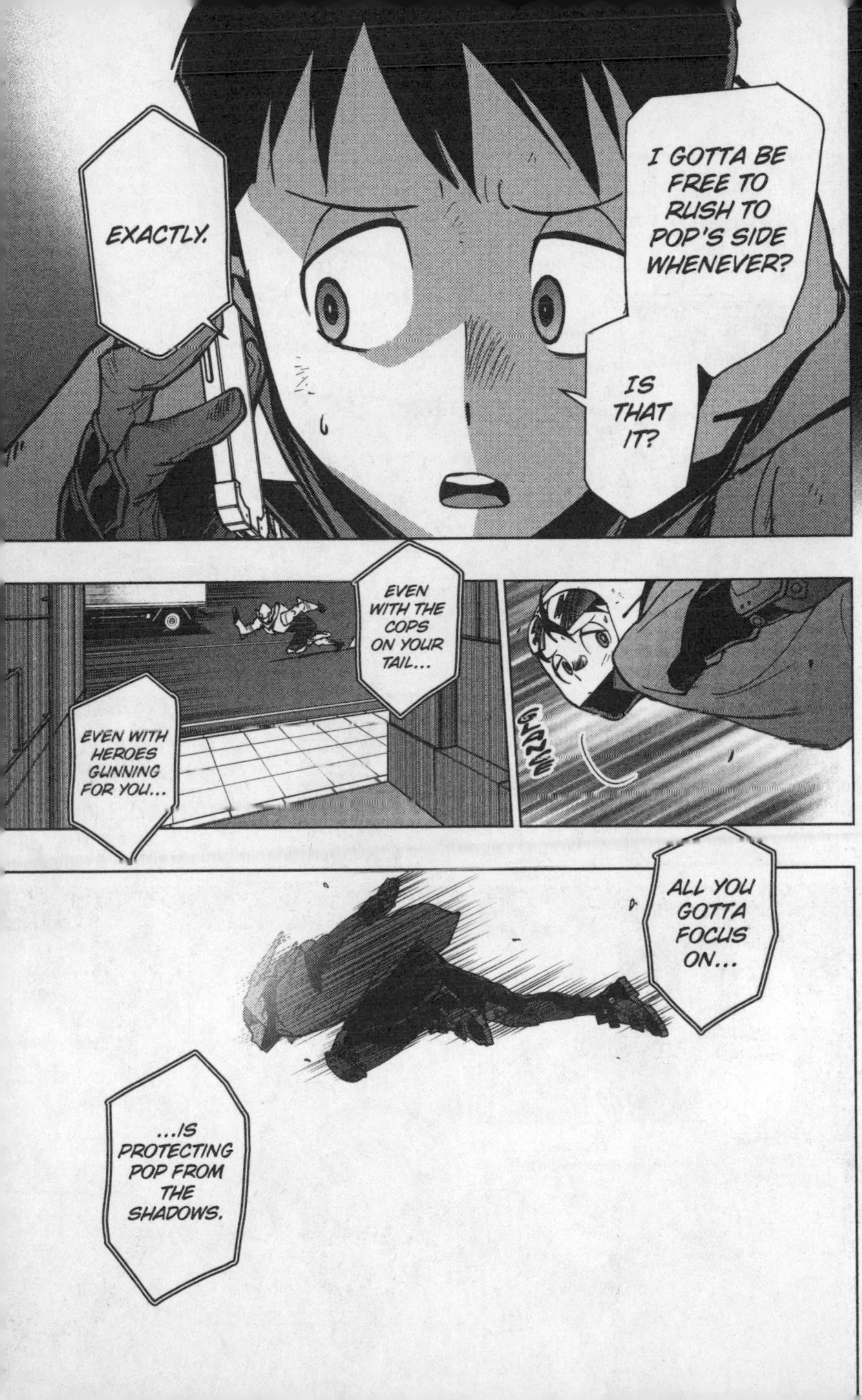
I GOTTA BE FREE TO RUSH TO POP'S SIDE WHENEVER?
IS THAT IT?
EXACTLY.
EVEN WITH THE COPS ON YOUR TAIL...
EVEN WITH HEROES GUNNING FOR YOU...
ALL YOU GOTTA FOCUS ON...
...IS PROTECTING POP FROM THE SHADOWS.

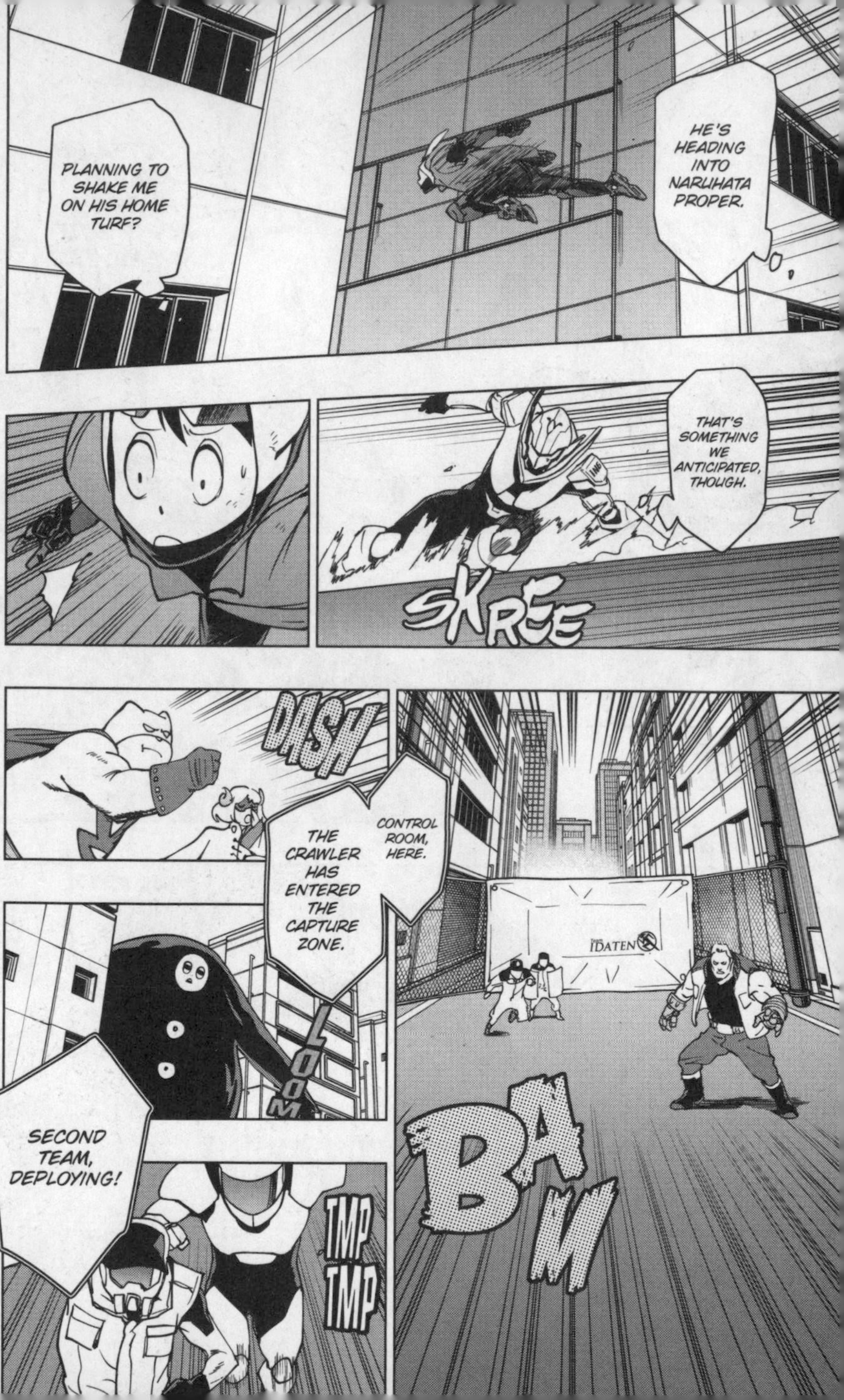
HE'S HEADING INTO NARUHATA PROPER.
PLANNING TO SHAKE ME ON HIS HOME TURF?
THAT'S SOMETHING WE ANTICIPATED, THOUGH.
SKREE
CONTROL ROOM, HERE.
THE CRAWLER HAS ENTERED THE CAPTURE ZONE.
BAM
IDATEN
DASH
LOOOM
SECOND TEAM, DEPLOYING!
TMP TMP

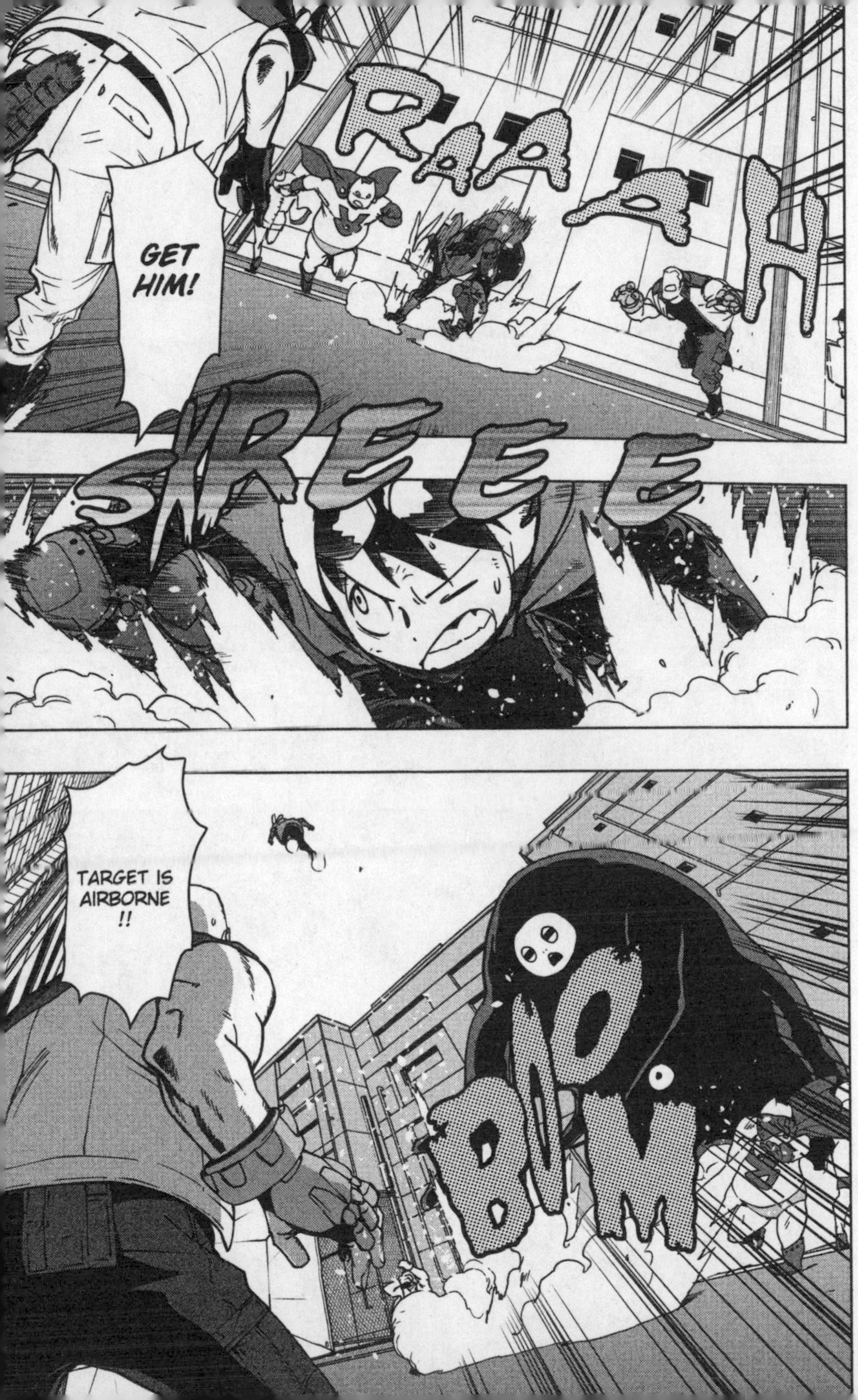
RAAAH
GET HIM!
SREEE
TARGET IS AIRBORNE !!
BOOM

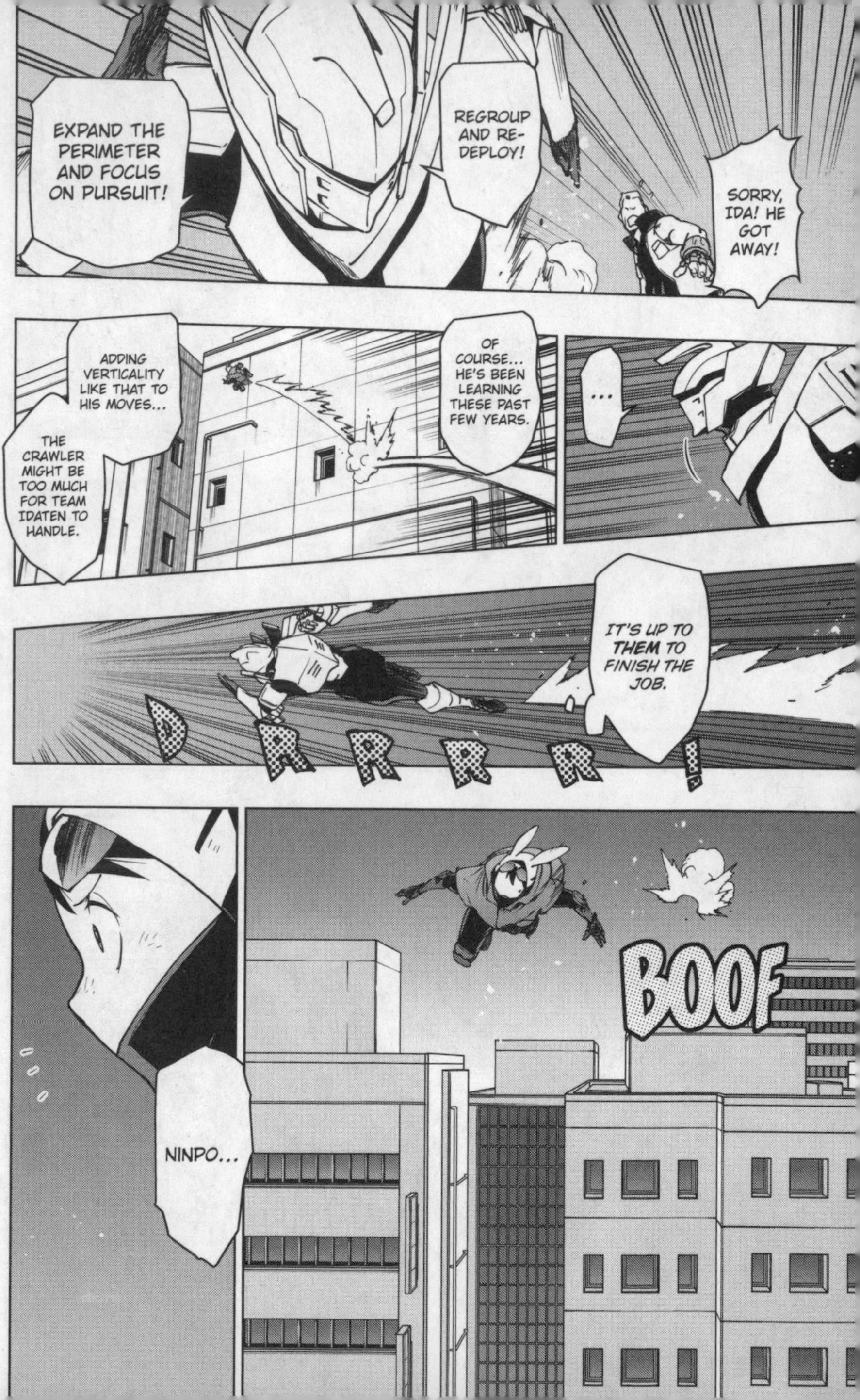
SORRY, IDA! HE GOT AWAY!
REGROUP AND RE-DEPLOY!
EXPAND THE PERIMETER AND FOCUS ON PURSUIT!
...
OF COURSE... HE'S BEEN LEARNING THESE PAST FEW YEARS.
ADDING VERTICALITY LIKE THAT TO HIS MOVES...
THE CRAWLER MIGHT BE TOO MUCH FOR TEAM IDATEN TO HANDLE.
IT'S UP TO **THEM** TO FINISH THE JOB.
DRRRRR!
BOOF
NINPO...

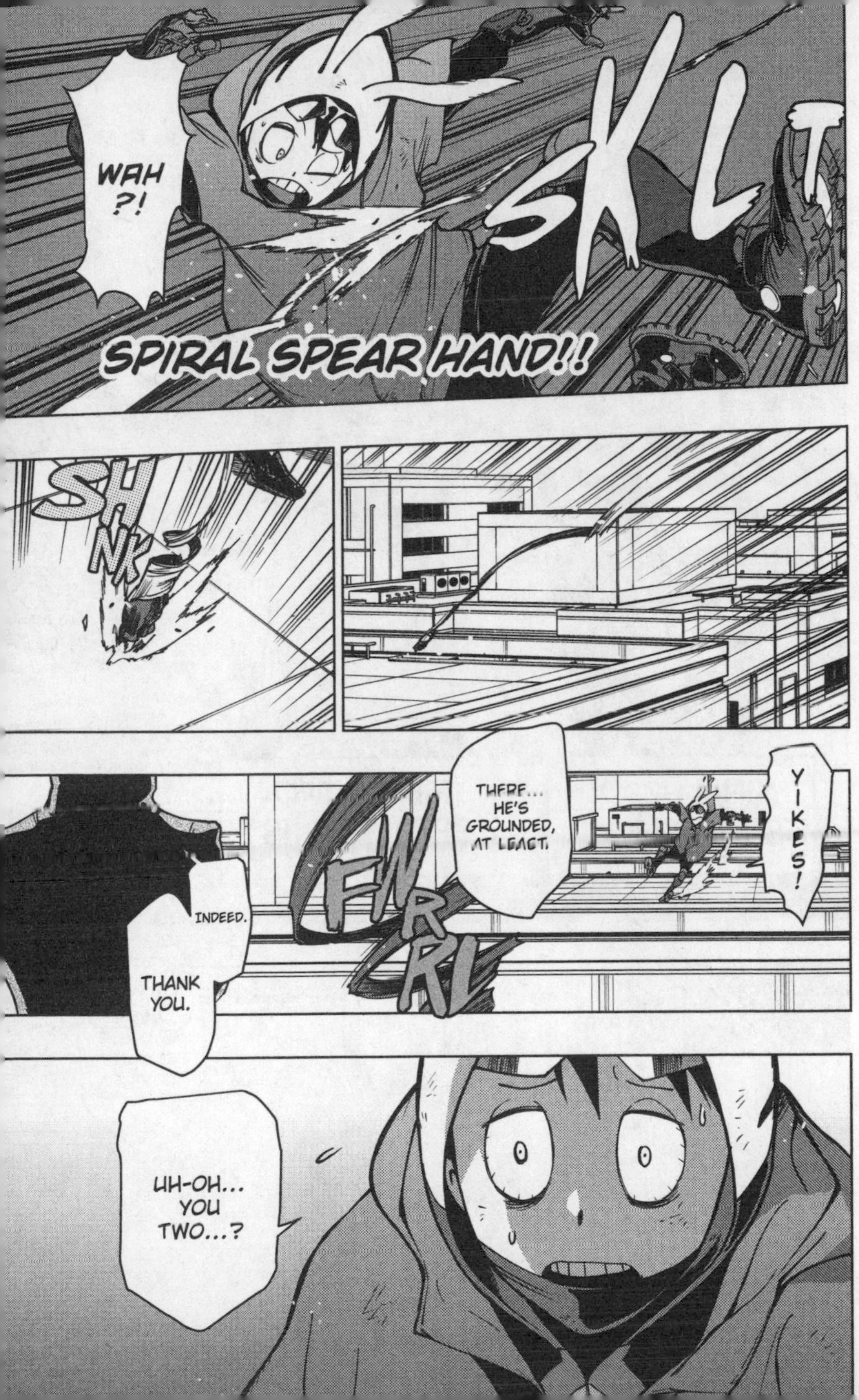
SKLT
WAH ?!
SPIRAL SPEAR HAND!!
SHNK
YIKES!
THERE... HE'S GROUNDED, AT LEAST.
FWRRL
INDEED.
THANK YOU.
UH-OH... YOU TWO...?

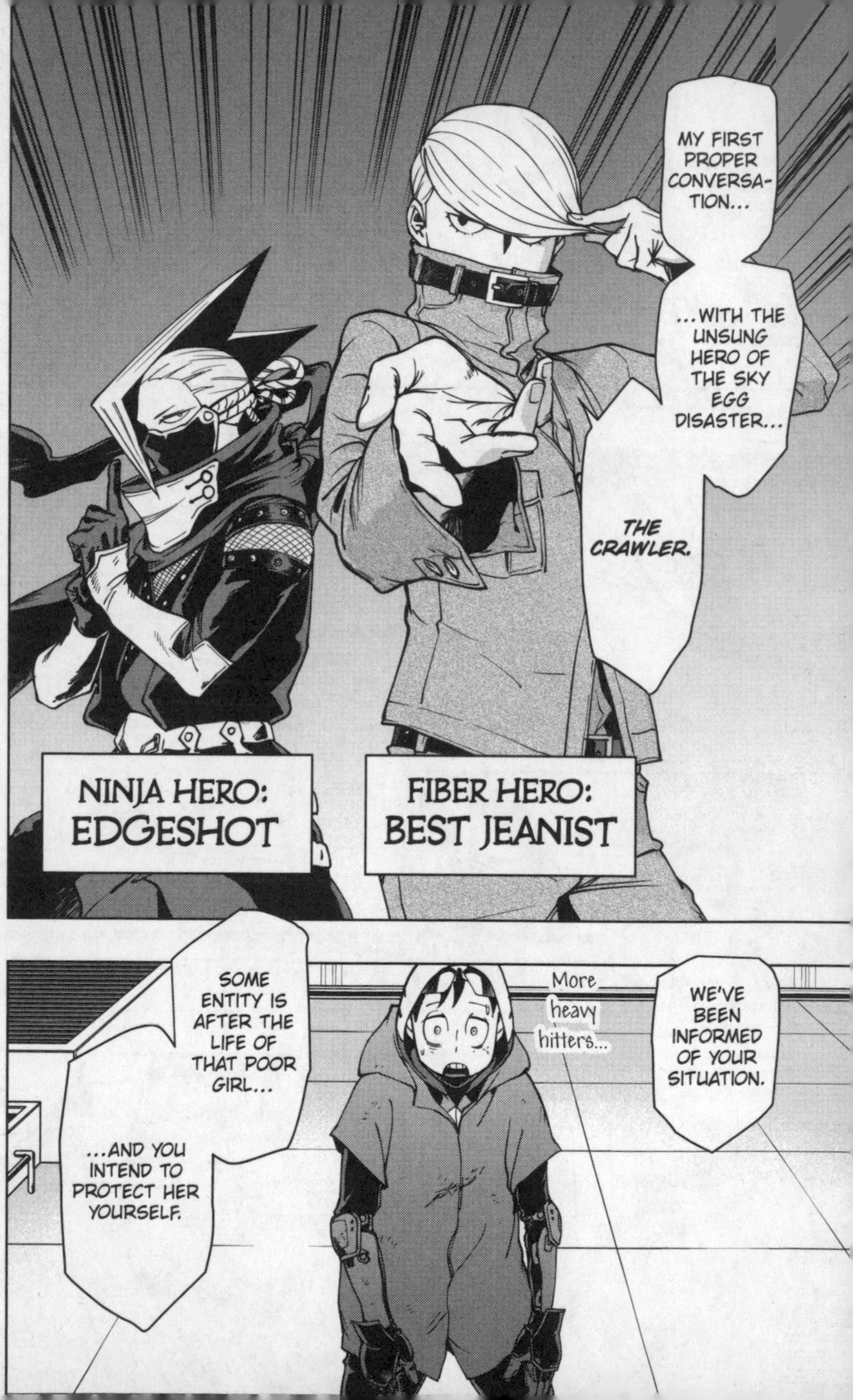
MY FIRST PROPER CONVERSATION...
...WITH THE UNSUNG HERO OF THE SKY EGG DISASTER...
THE CRAWLER.
FIBER HERO: BEST JEANIST
NINJA HERO: EDGESHOT
WE'VE BEEN INFORMED OF YOUR SITUATION.
More heavy hitters...
SOME ENTITY IS AFTER THE LIFE OF THAT POOR GIRL...
...AND YOU INTEND TO PROTECT HER YOURSELF.

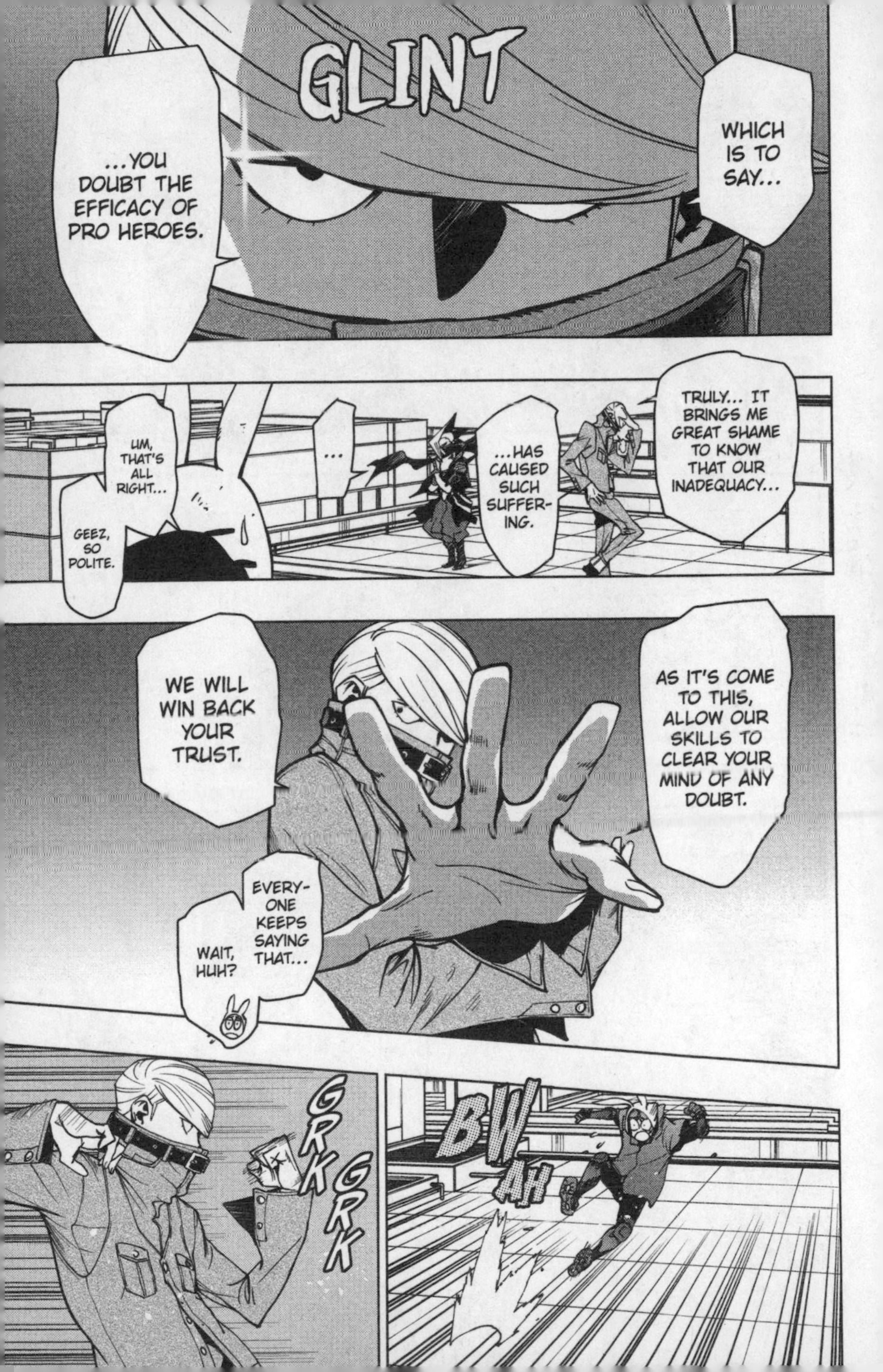
WHICH IS TO SAY...
GLINT
...YOU DOUBT THE EFFICACY OF PRO HEROES.
TRULY... IT BRINGS ME GREAT SHAME TO KNOW THAT OUR INADEQUACY...
...HAS CAUSED SUCH SUFFER-ING.
...
UM, THAT'S ALL RIGHT...
GEEZ, SO POLITE.
AS IT'S COME TO THIS, ALLOW OUR SKILLS TO CLEAR YOUR MIND OF ANY DOUBT.
WE WILL WIN BACK YOUR TRUST.
EVERY-ONE KEEPS SAYING THAT...
WAIT, HUH?
BWAH
GRK GRK

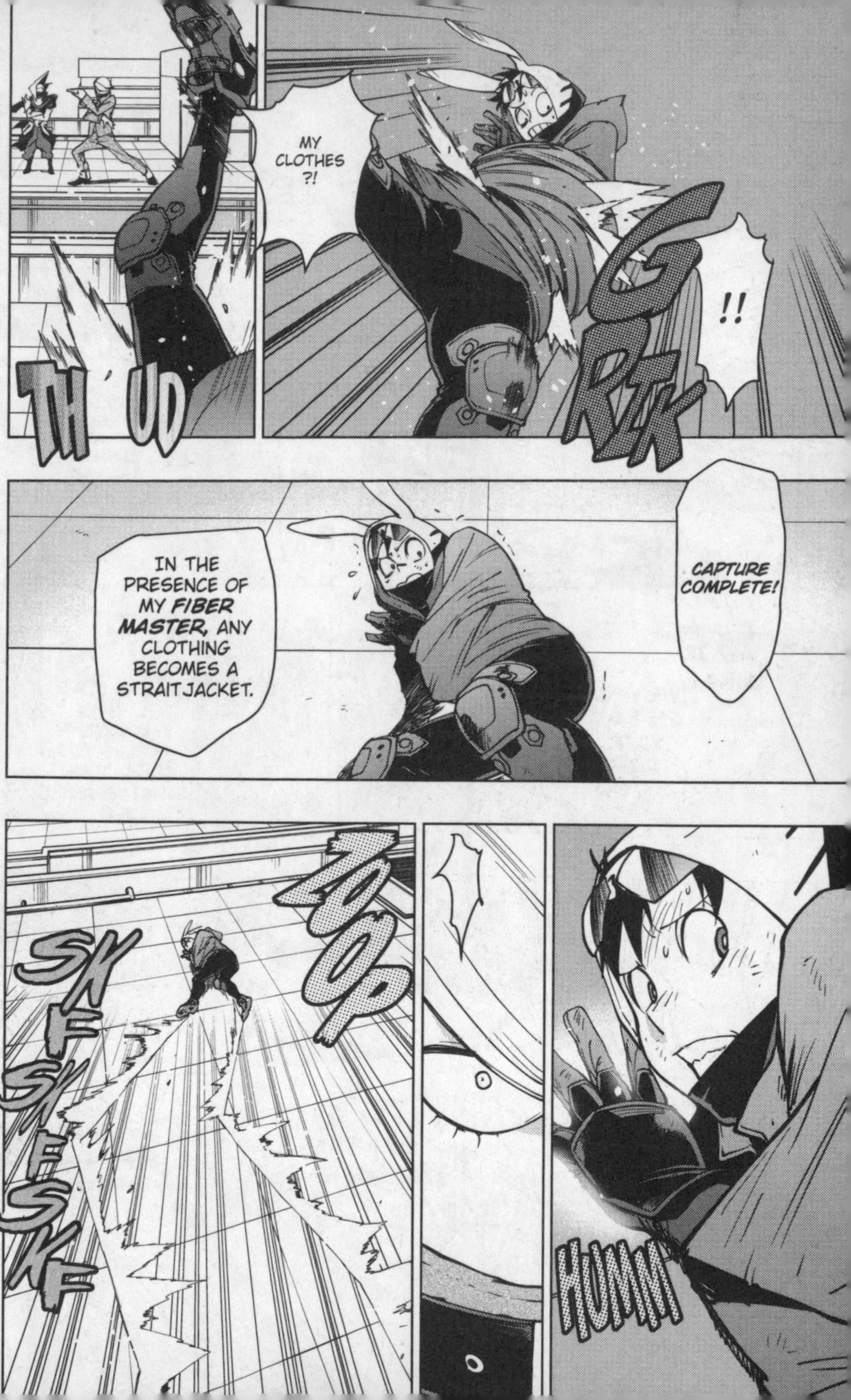
MY CLOTHES ?!
GRIK
!!
THUD
CAPTURE COMPLETE!
IN THE PRESENCE OF MY *FIBER MASTER,* ANY CLOTHING BECOMES A STRAITJACKET.
HUMM
ZOOP
SKF SKF SKF

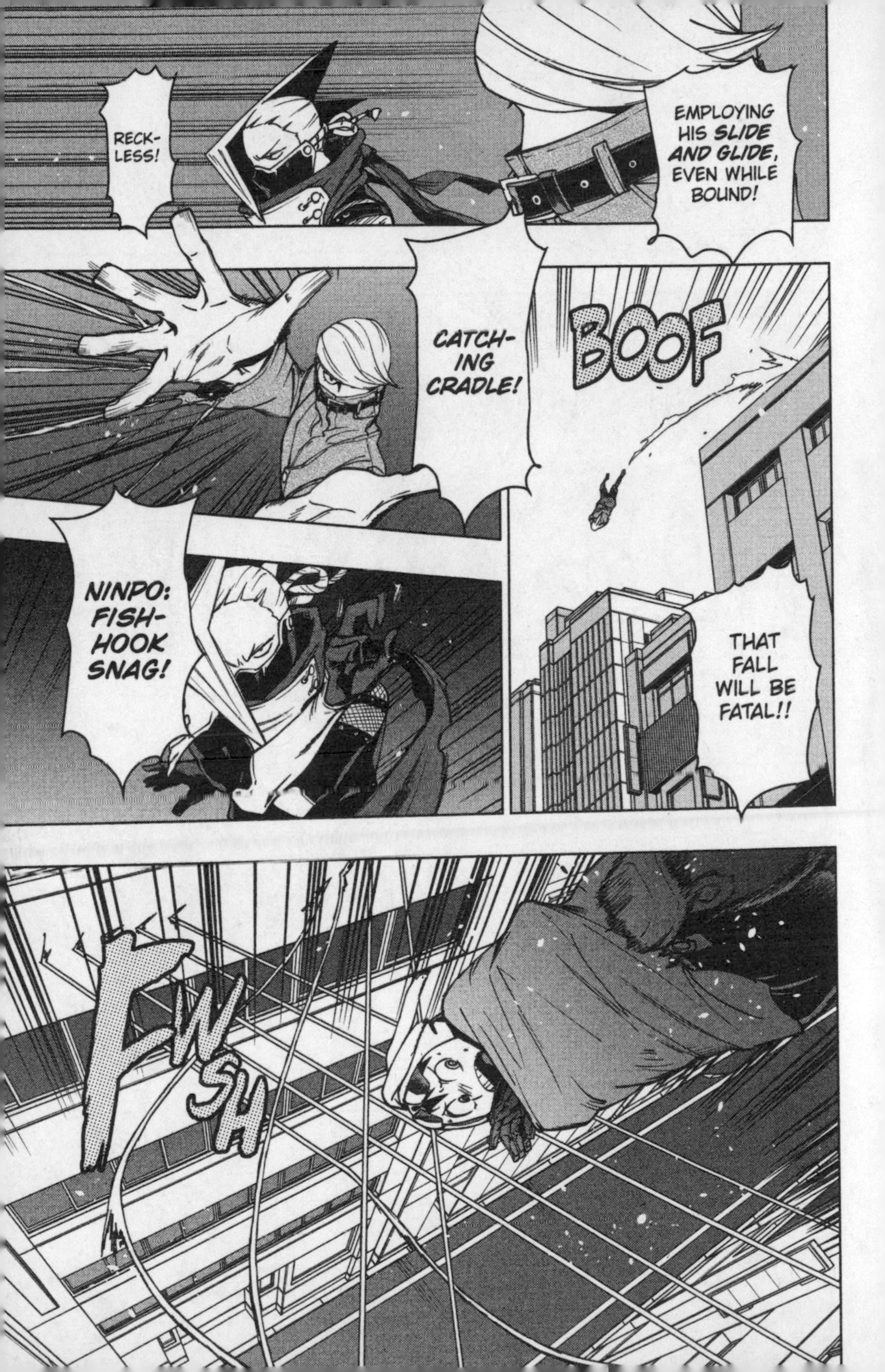
EMPLOYING HIS SLIDE AND GLIDE, EVEN WHILE BOUND!
RECK-LESS!
BOOF
THAT FALL WILL BE FATAL!!
CATCH-ING CRADLE!
NINPO: FISH-HOOK SNAG!
FWSH

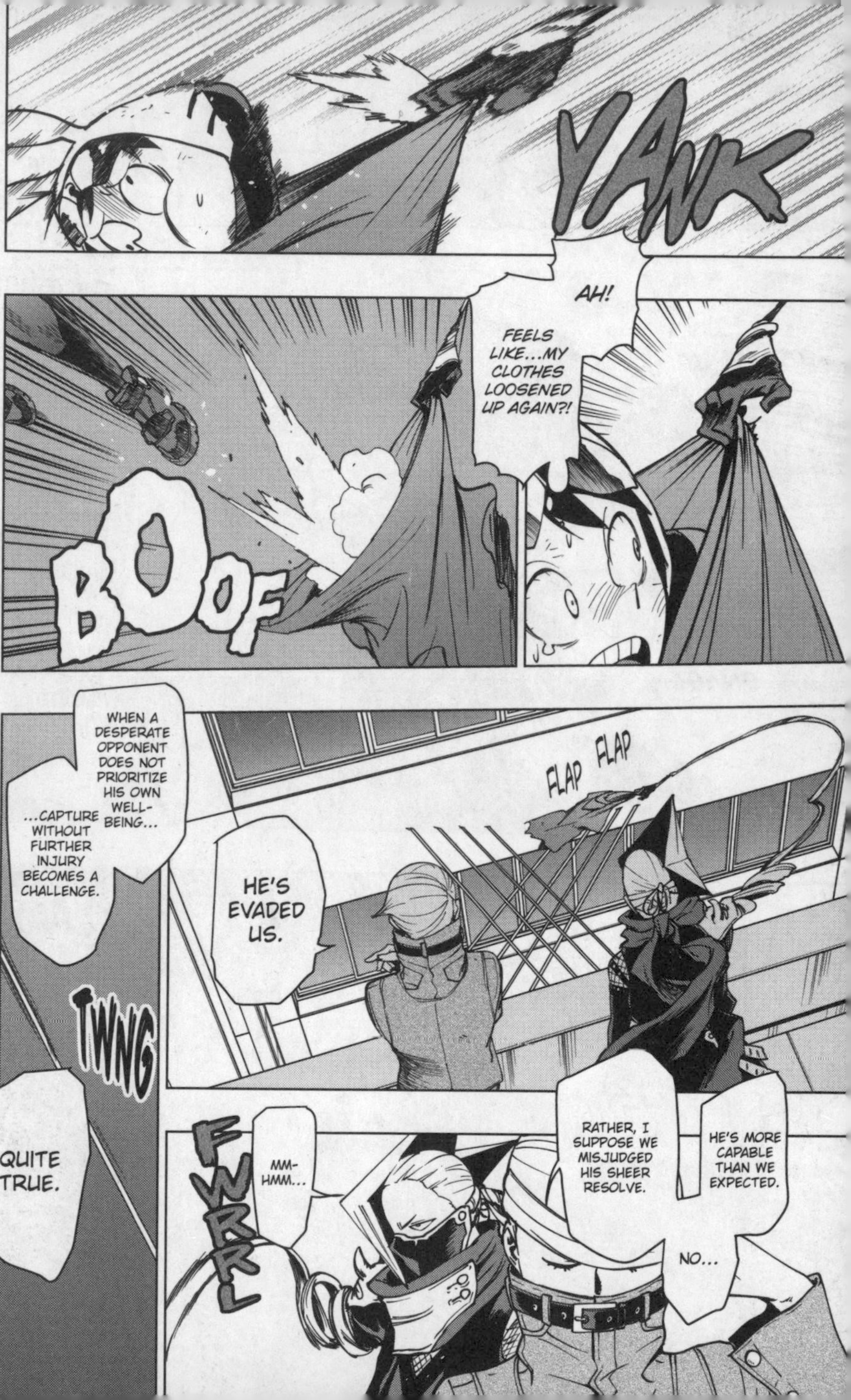

YANK
AH!
FEELS LIKE...MY CLOTHES LOOSENED UP AGAIN?!
BOOF
FLAP FLAP
HE'S EVADED US.
WHEN A DESPERATE OPPONENT DOES NOT PRIORITIZE HIS OWN WELL-BEING...
...CAPTURE WITHOUT FURTHER INJURY BECOMES A CHALLENGE.
TWNG
HE'S MORE CAPABLE THAN WE EXPECTED.
NO...
RATHER, I SUPPOSE WE MISJUDGED HIS SHEER RESOLVE.
MM-HMM...
FWRRL
QUITE TRUE.

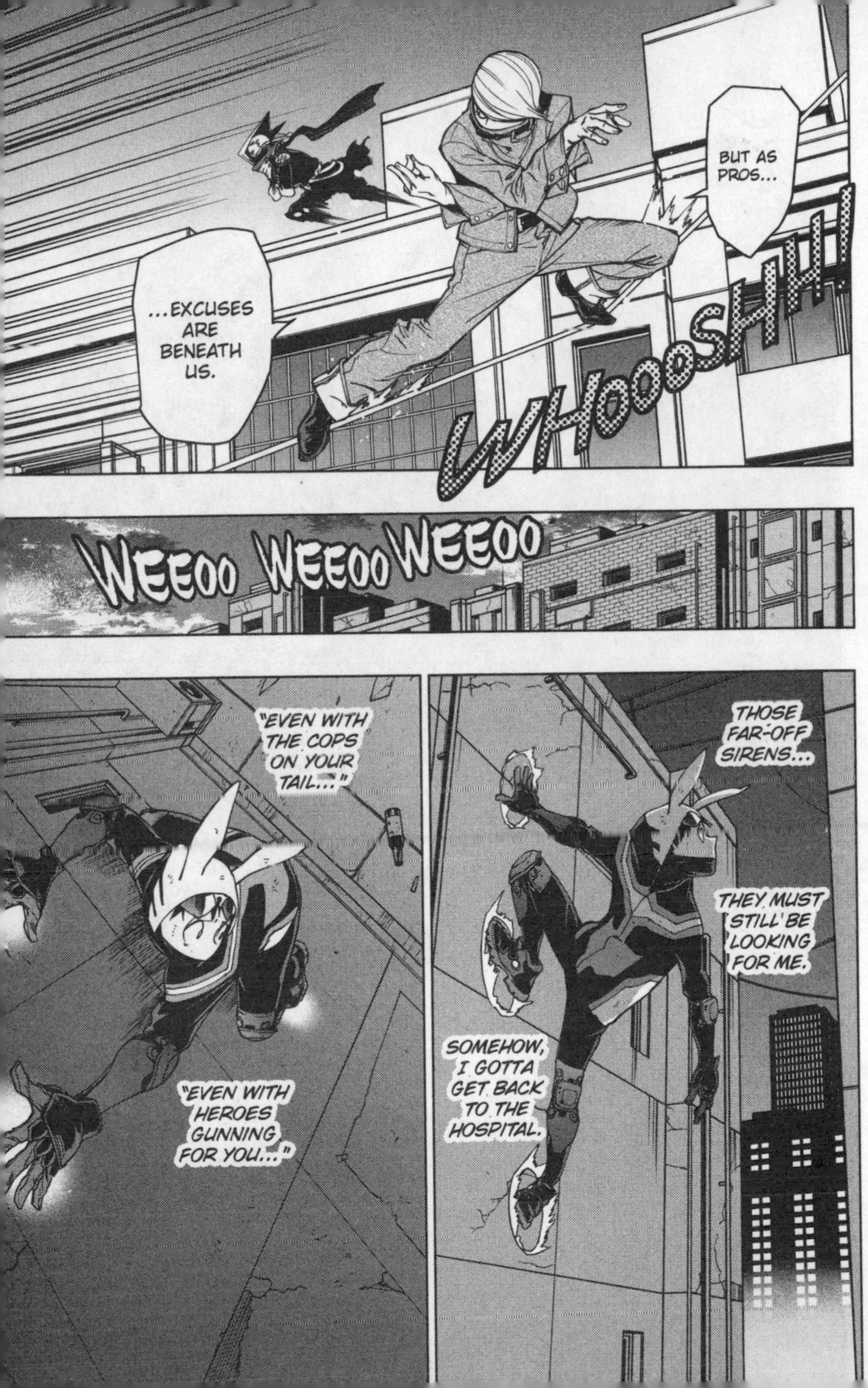
BUT AS PROS...
...EXCUSES ARE BENEATH US.
WHOOOSHH!!
WEEOO WEEOO WEEOO
THOSE FAR-OFF SIRENS...
THEY MUST STILL BE LOOKING FOR ME.
SOMEHOW, I GOTTA GET BACK TO THE HOSPITAL.
"EVEN WITH THE COPS ON YOUR TAIL..."
"EVEN WITH HEROES GUNNING FOR YOU..."

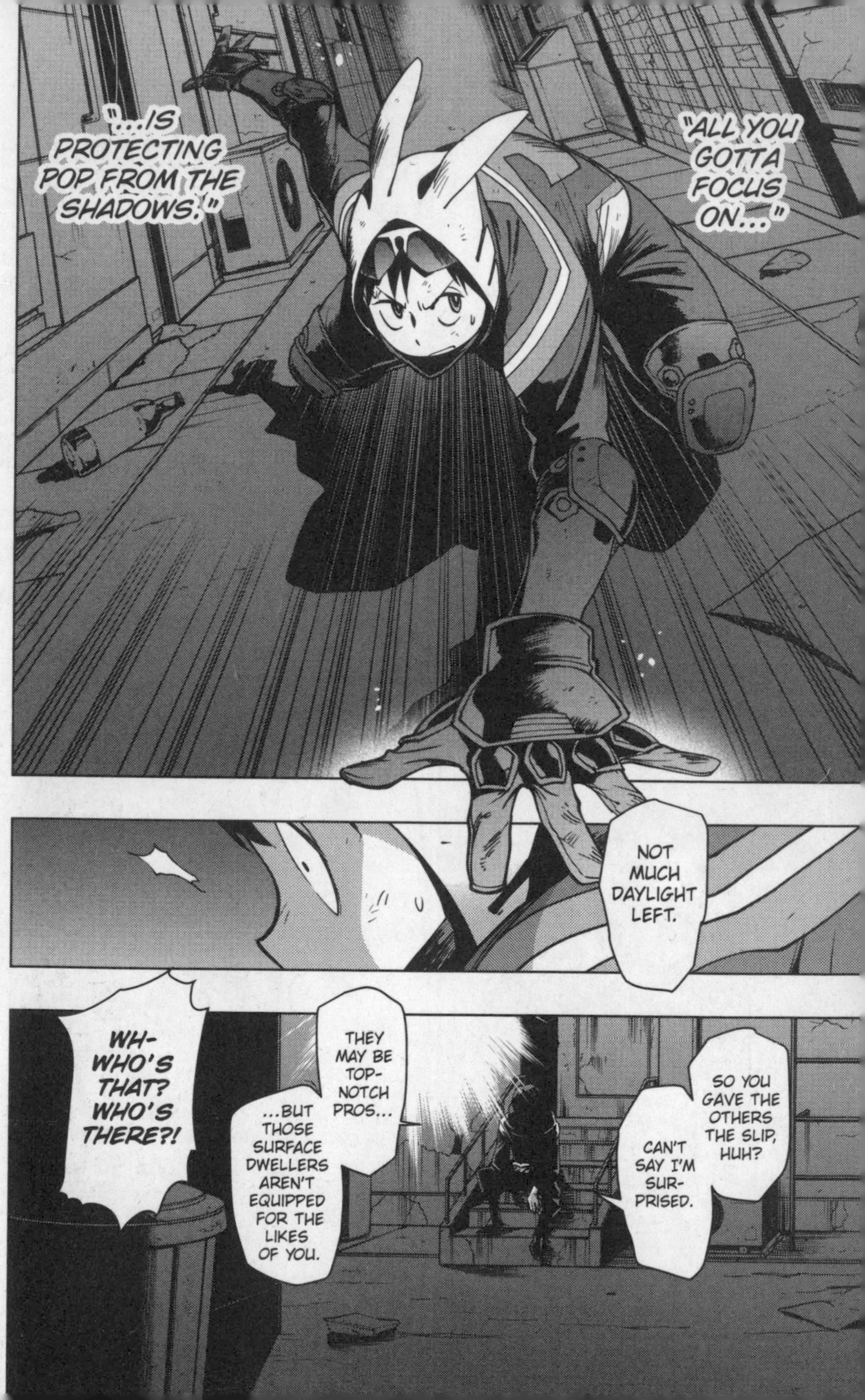
"ALL YOU GOTTA FOCUS ON..."
"...IS PROTECTING POP FROM THE SHADOWS."
NOT MUCH DAYLIGHT LEFT.
SO YOU GAVE THE OTHERS THE SLIP, HUH?
CAN'T SAY I'M SUR-PRISED.
THEY MAY BE TOP-NOTCH PROS...
...BUT THOSE SURFACE DWELLERS AREN'T EQUIPPED FOR THE LIKES OF YOU.
WH-WHO'S THAT? WHO'S THERE?!

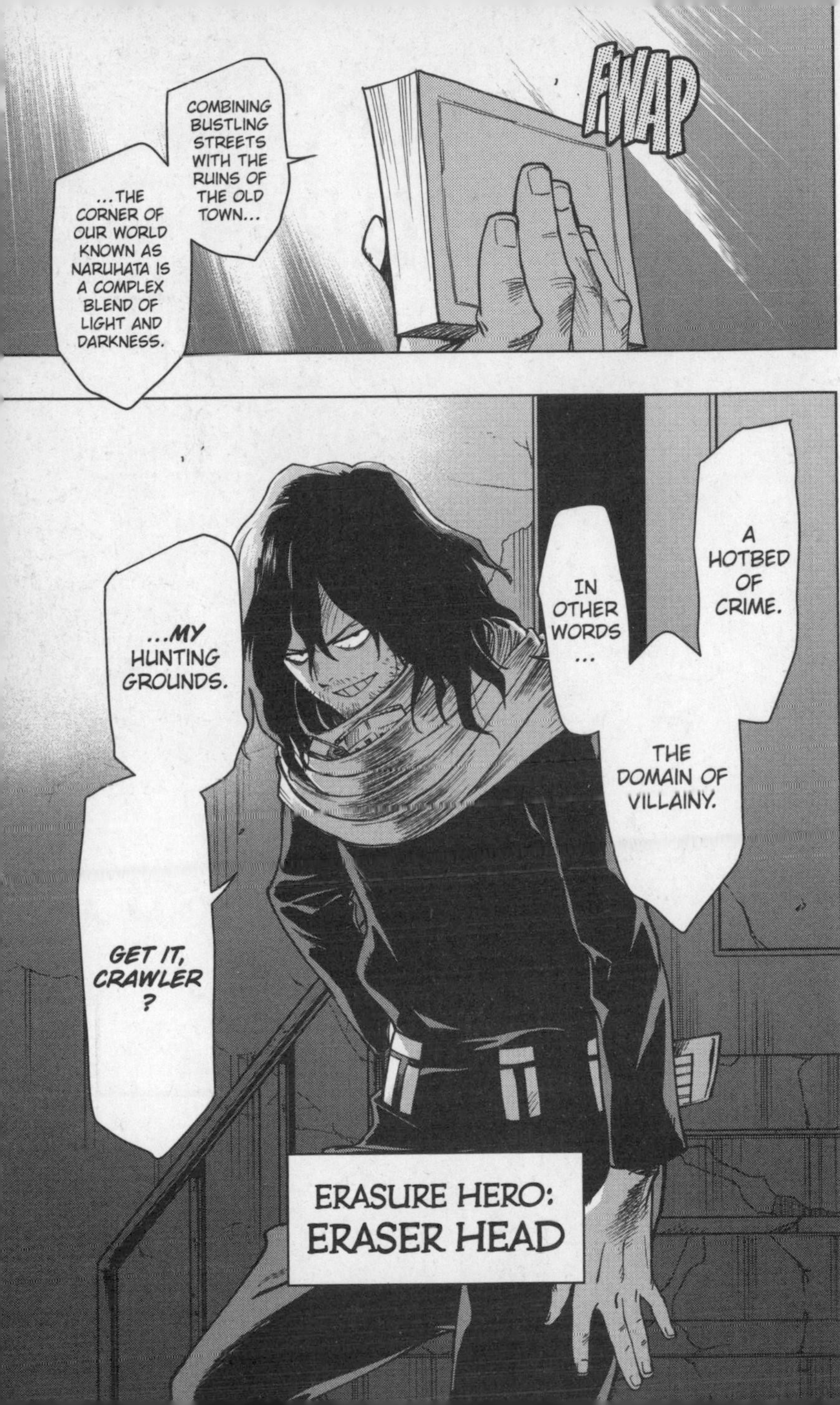
FWAP
COMBINING BUSTLING STREETS WITH THE RUINS OF THE OLD TOWN...
...THE CORNER OF OUR WORLD KNOWN AS NARUHATA IS A COMPLEX BLEND OF LIGHT AND DARKNESS.
A HOTBED OF CRIME.
IN OTHER WORDS...
THE DOMAIN OF VILLAINY.
...MY HUNTING GROUNDS.
GET IT, CRAWLER?
ERASURE HERO: ERASER HEAD

The BAD BOYS in "WHAT-IF" WORLD

THE RUFFIANS, AS SIDEKICKS.

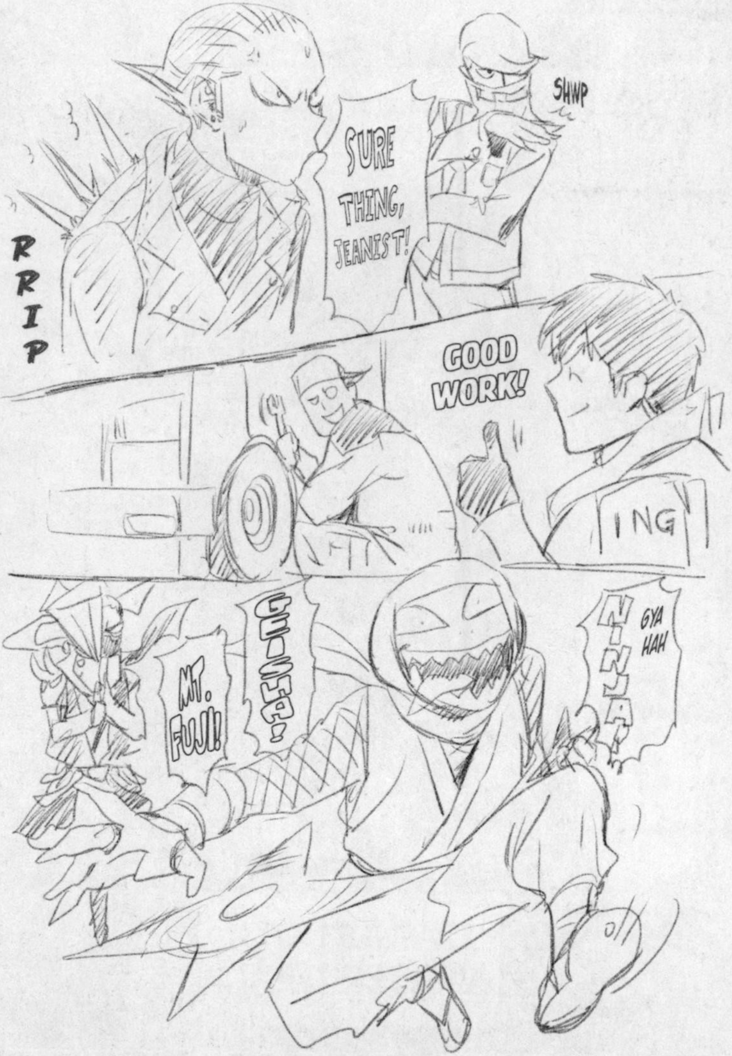
SHWP
SURE THING, JEANIST!
RRIP
GOOD WORK!
ING
NINJA!
GYA HAH
GEISHA!
MT. FUJI!

ILLUSTRATION: BETTEN COURT

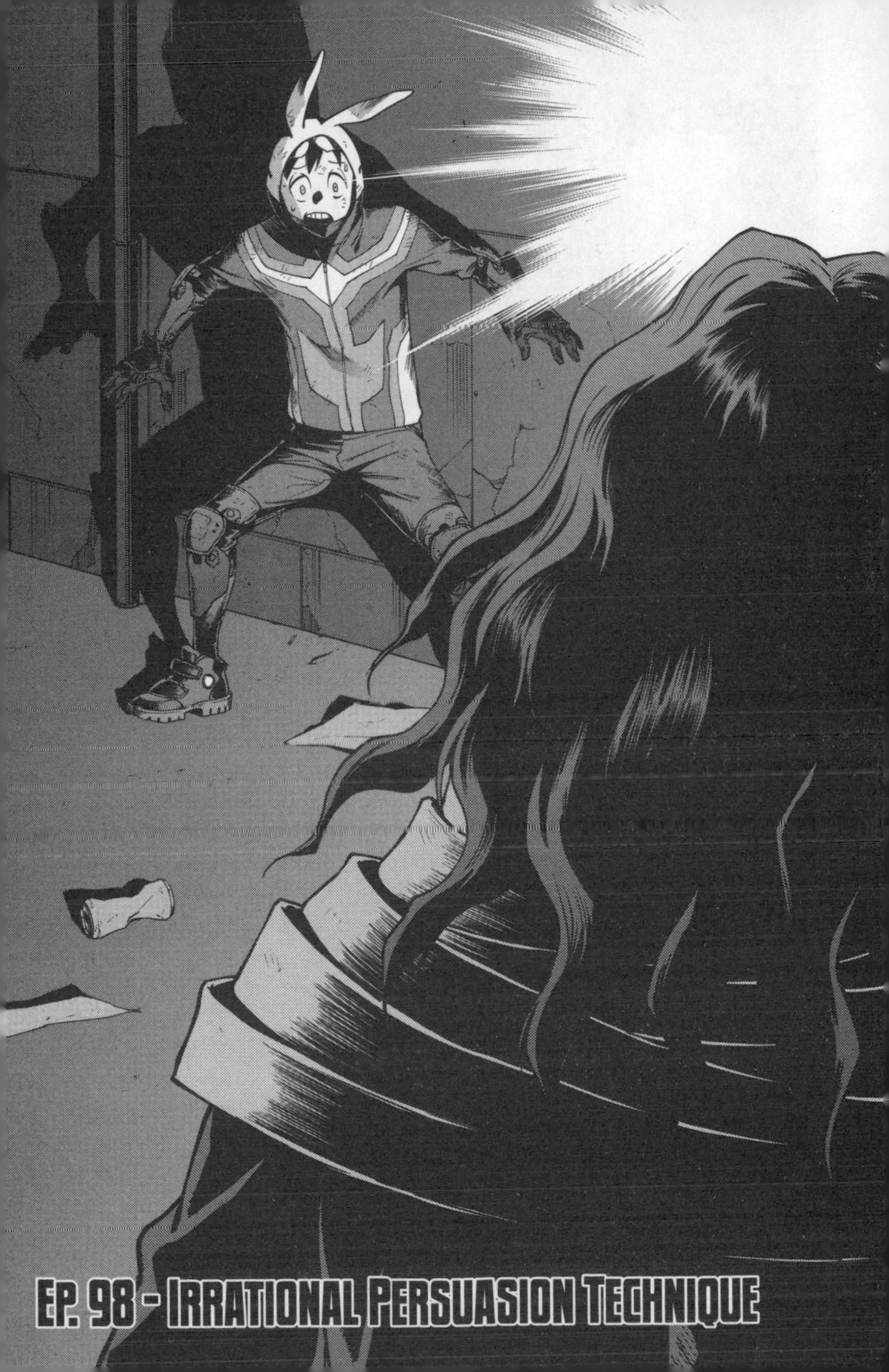

Ep. 98 - Irrational Persuasion Technique

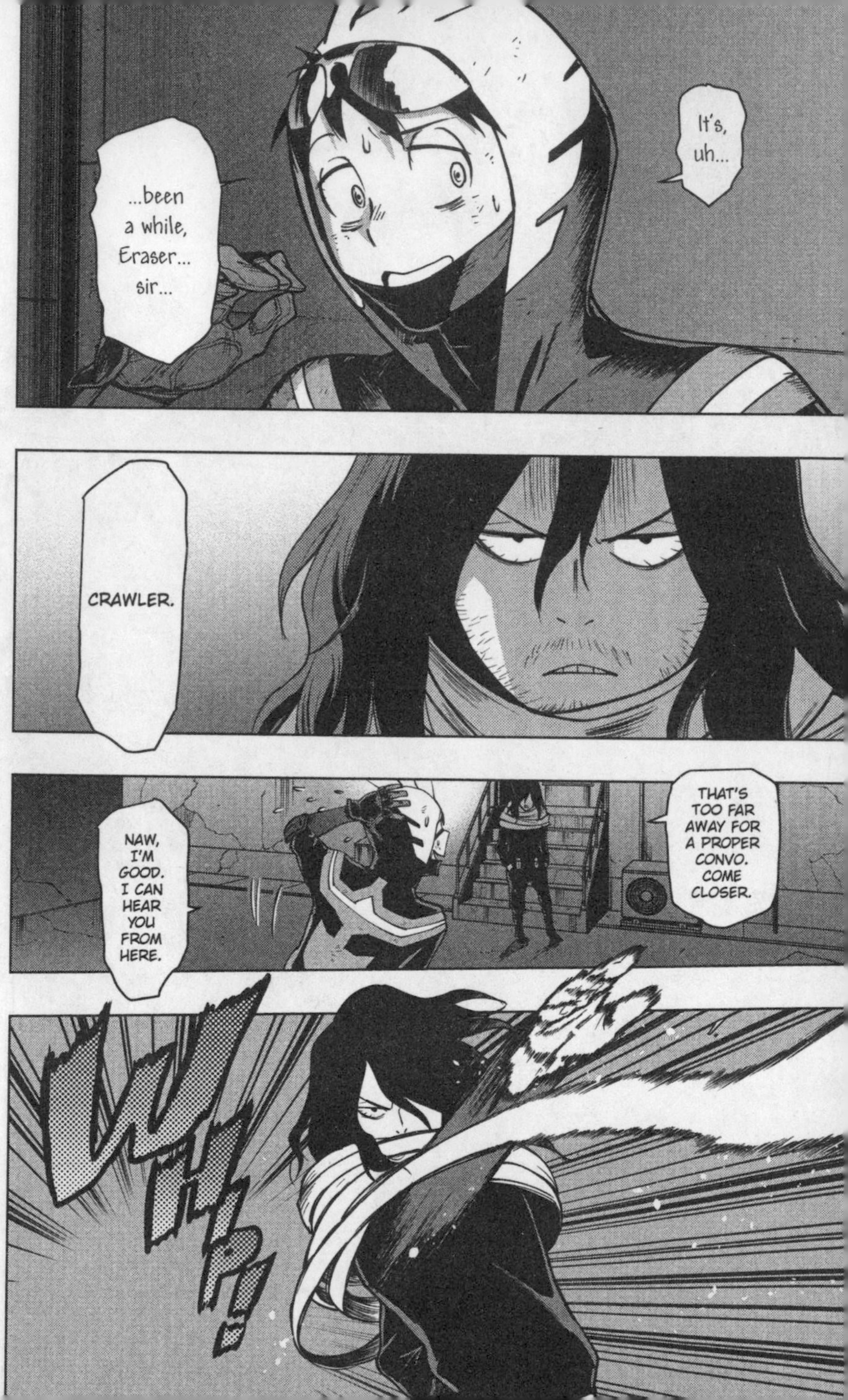
It's, uh...
...been a while, Eraser... sir...
CRAWLER.
THAT'S TOO FAR AWAY FOR A PROPER CONVO. COME CLOSER.
NAW, I'M GOOD. I CAN HEAR YOU FROM HERE.

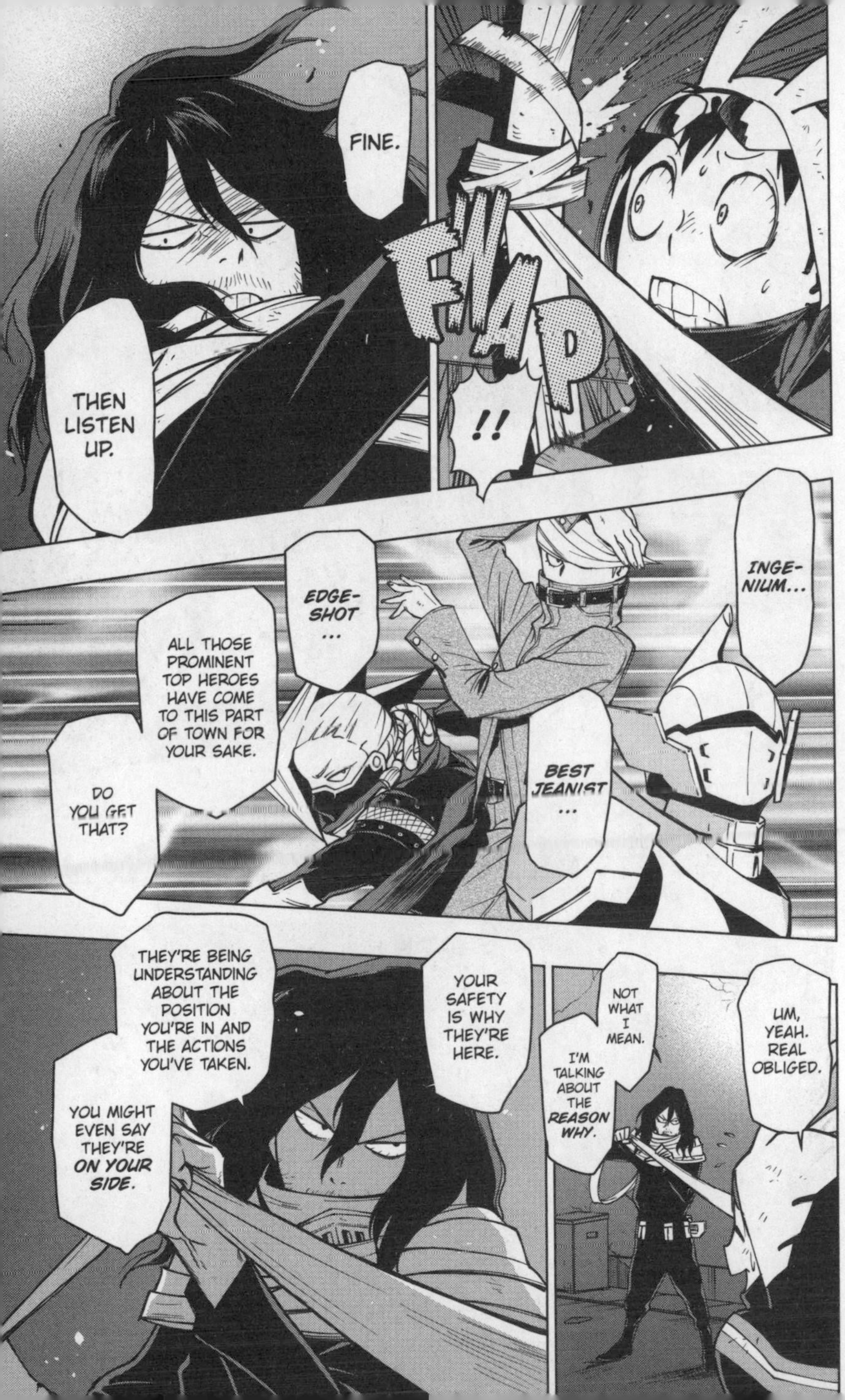
FWAP
!!
FINE.
THEN LISTEN UP.
INGE-NIUM...
BEST JEANIST ...
EDGE-SHOT ...
ALL THOSE PROMINENT TOP HEROES HAVE COME TO THIS PART OF TOWN FOR YOUR SAKE.
DO YOU GET THAT?
UM, YEAH. REAL OBLIGED.
NOT WHAT I MEAN.
I'M TALKING ABOUT THE *REASON WHY*.
YOUR SAFETY IS WHY THEY'RE HERE.
THEY'RE BEING UNDERSTANDING ABOUT THE POSITION YOU'RE IN AND THE ACTIONS YOU'VE TAKEN.
YOU MIGHT EVEN SAY THEY'RE *ON YOUR SIDE*.

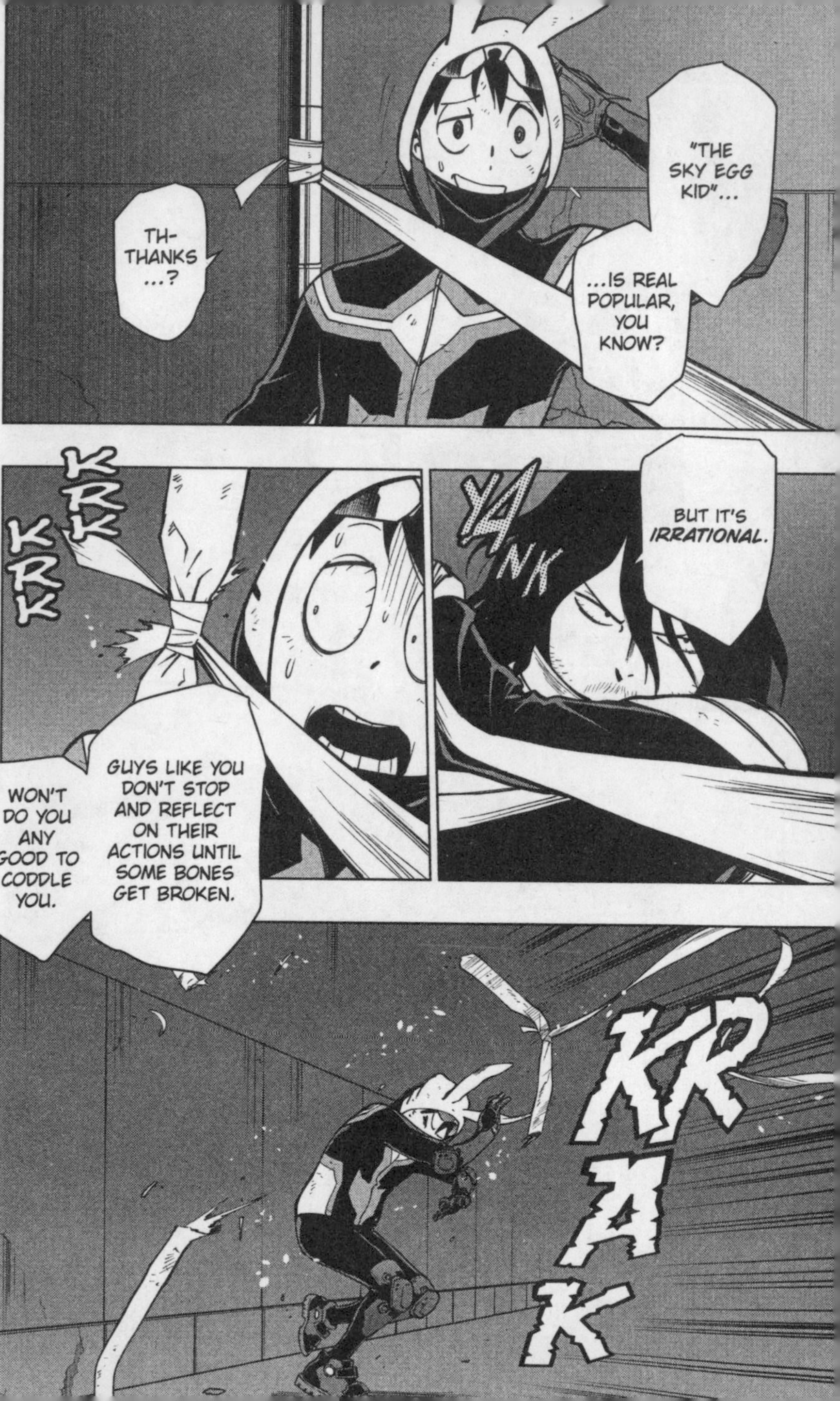
"THE SKY EGG KID"...
...IS REAL POPULAR, YOU KNOW?
TH-THANKS ...?
YANK
BUT IT'S *IRRATIONAL.*
KRK
KRK
GUYS LIKE YOU DON'T STOP AND REFLECT ON THEIR ACTIONS UNTIL SOME BONES GET BROKEN.
WON'T DO YOU ANY GOOD TO CODDLE YOU.
KRAK

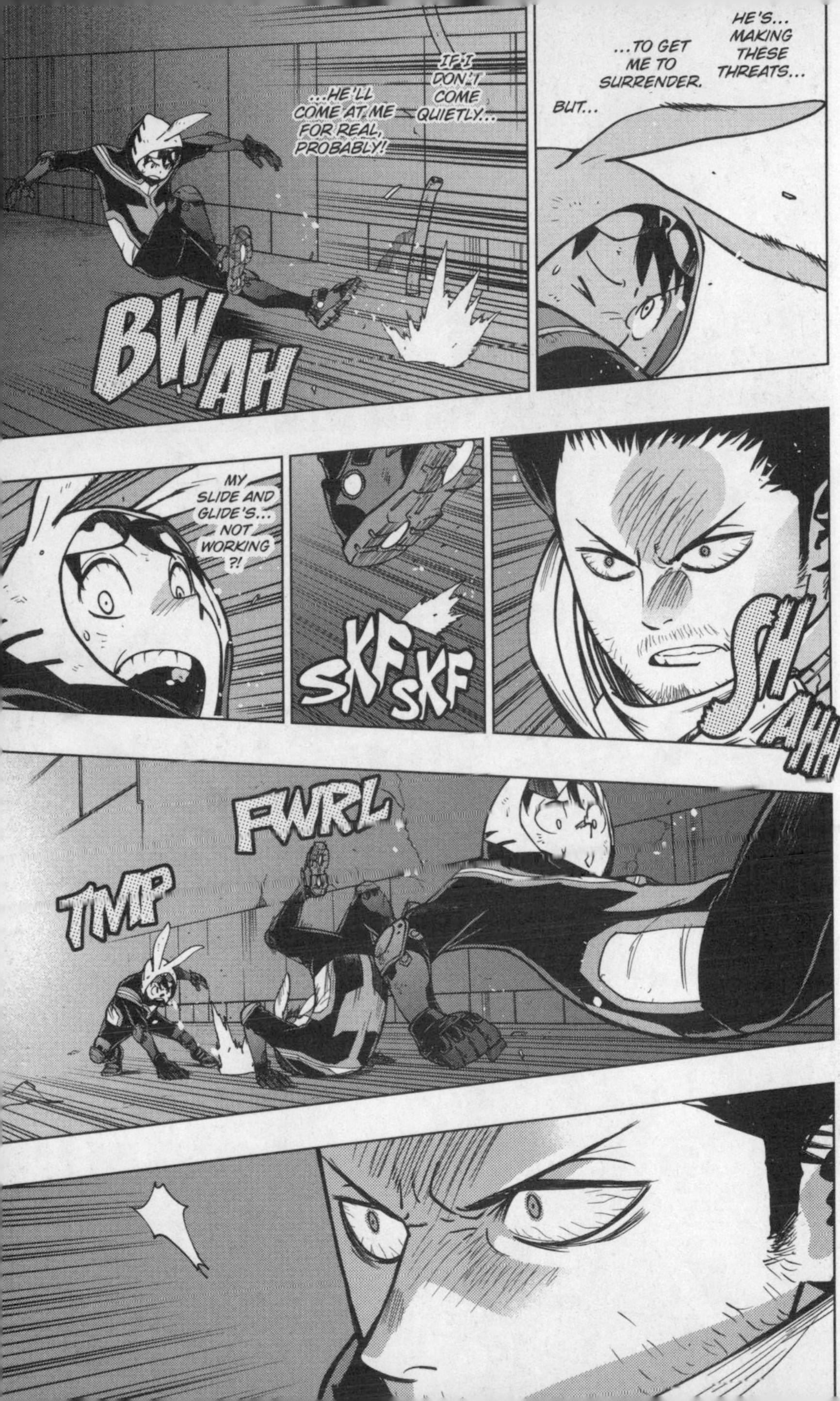
HE'S... MAKING THESE THREATS...
...TO GET ME TO SURRENDER.
BUT...
IF I DON'T COME QUIETLY...
...HE'LL COME AT ME FOR REAL, PROBABLY!
BWAH
SHAHH
SKF SKF
MY SLIDE AND GLIDE'S... NOT WORKING ?!
FWRL
TMP

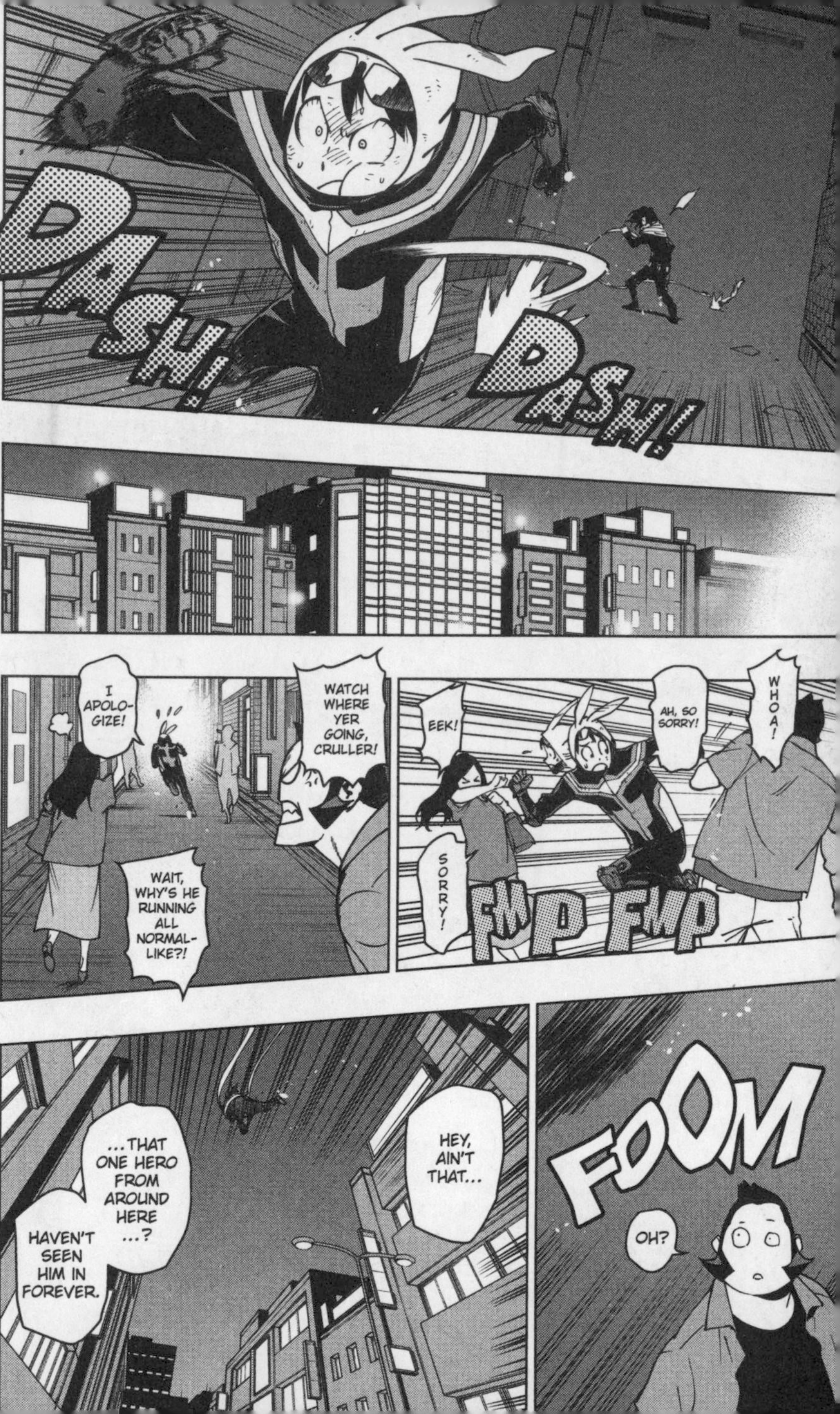
DASH!
DASH!
WHOA!
AH, SO SORRY!
EEK!
SORRY!
FMP FMP
WATCH WHERE YER GOING, CRULLER!
I APOLOGIZE!
WAIT, WHY'S HE RUNNING ALL NORMAL-LIKE?!
FOOM
OH?
HEY, AIN'T THAT...
...THAT ONE HERO FROM AROUND HERE ...?
HAVEN'T SEEN HIM IN FOREVER.

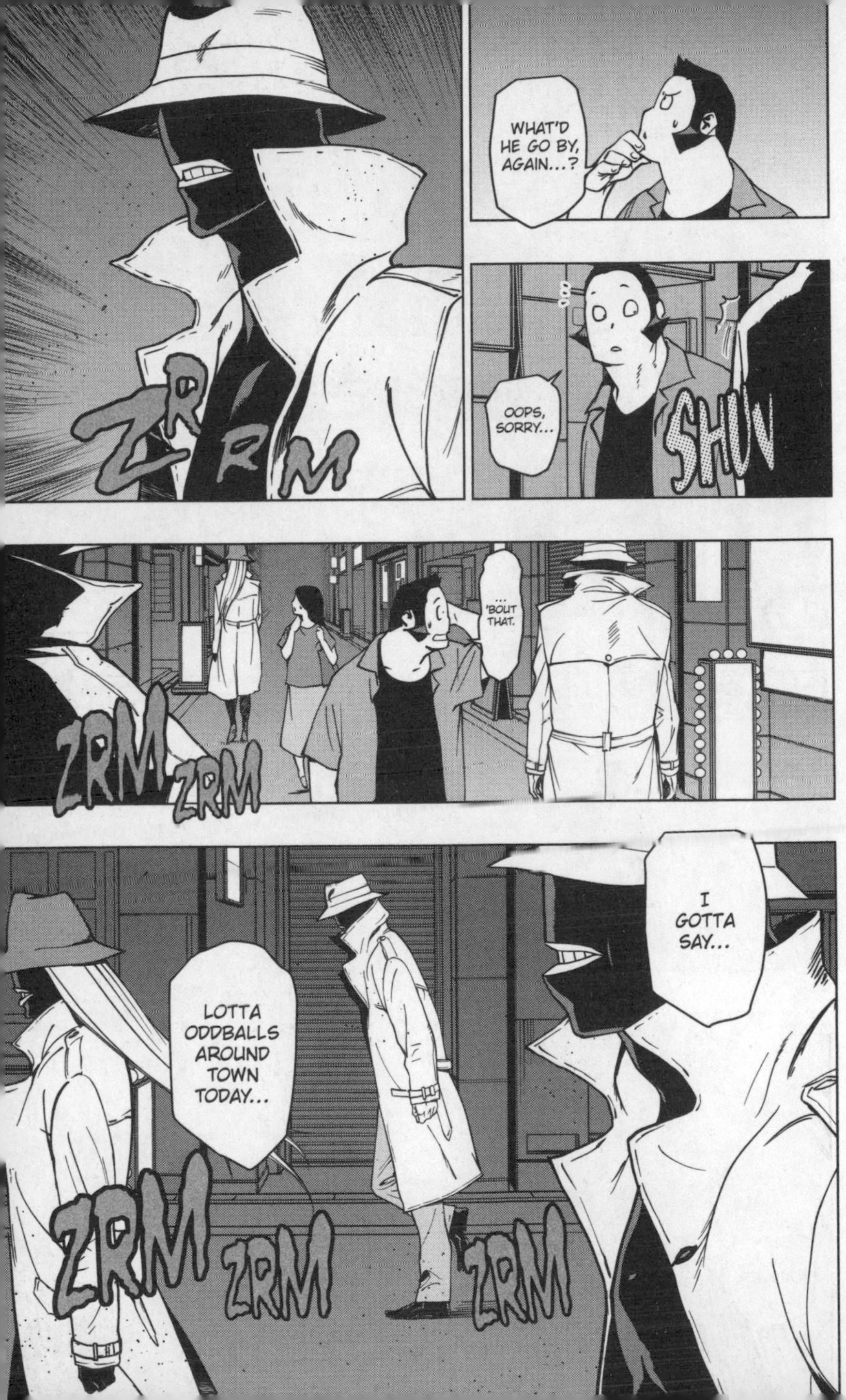
WHAT'D HE GO BY, AGAIN...?
OOPS, SORRY...
SHUV
ZRRM
...'BOUT THAT.
ZRM
ZRM
I GOTTA SAY...
LOTTA ODDBALLS AROUND TOWN TODAY...
ZRM
ZRM
ZRM

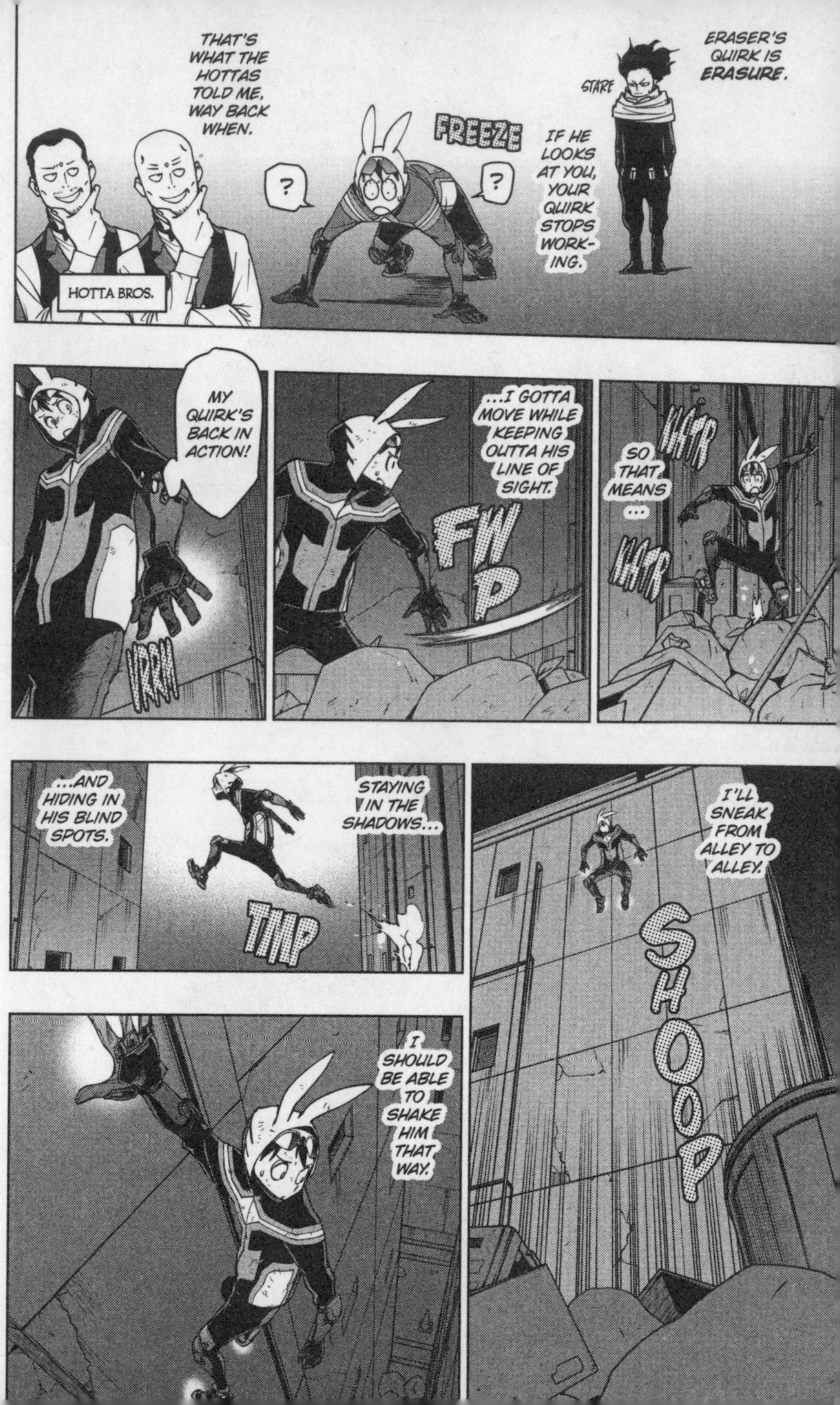
ERASER'S QUIRK IS ERASURE.
STARE
IF HE LOOKS AT YOU, YOUR QUIRK STOPS WORK-ING.
FREEZE
?
?
THAT'S WHAT THE HOTTAS TOLD ME, WAY BACK WHEN.
HOTTA BROS.
SO THAT MEANS...
WHR
WHR
...I GOTTA MOVE WHILE KEEPING OUTTA HIS LINE OF SIGHT.
FWIP
MY QUIRK'S BACK IN ACTION!
VRRM
I'LL SNEAK FROM ALLEY TO ALLEY.
SHOOP
STAYING IN THE SHADOWS...
...AND HIDING IN HIS BLIND SPOTS.
TMP
I SHOULD BE ABLE TO SHAKE HIM THAT WAY.

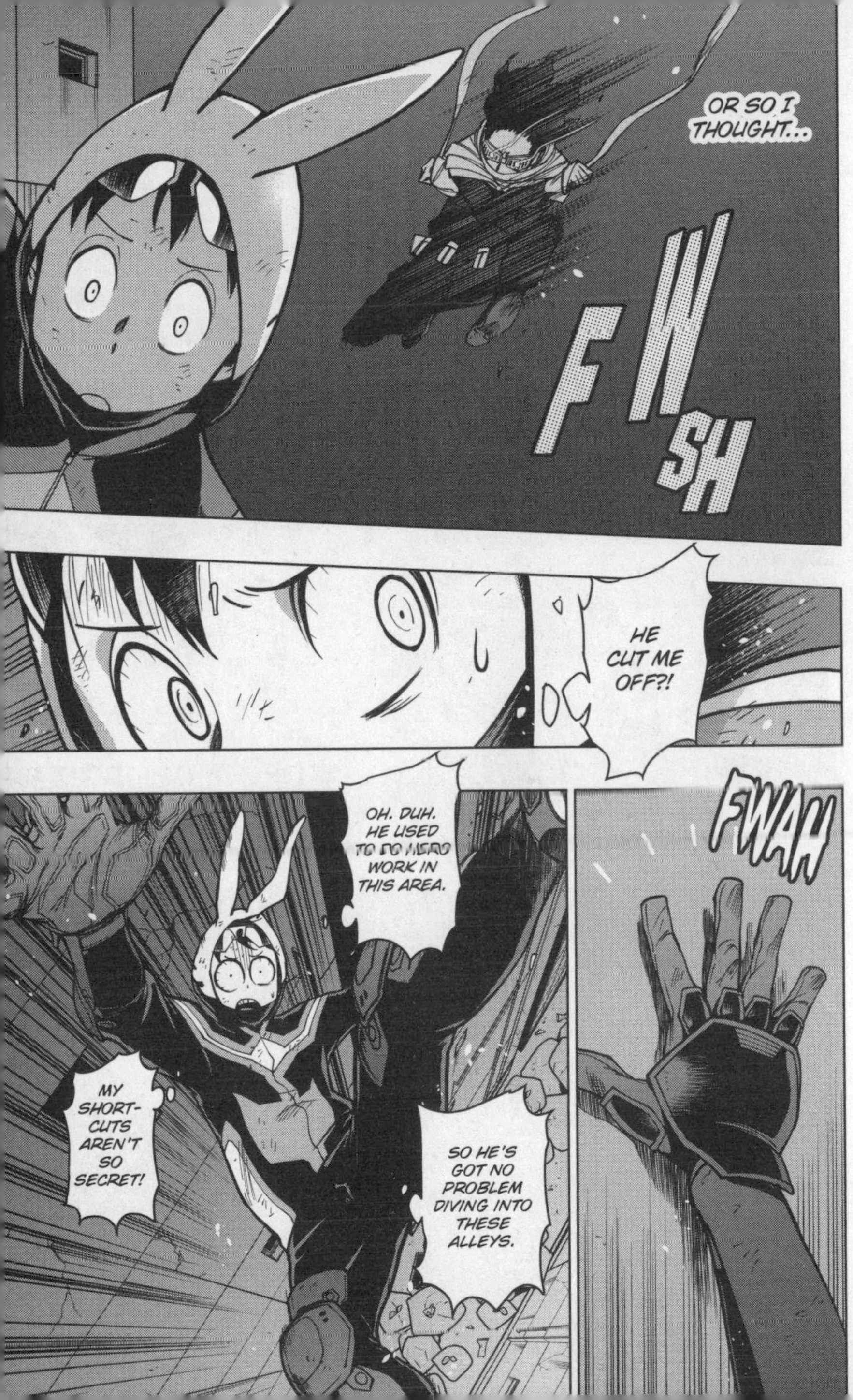
OR SO I THOUGHT...
FWSH
HE CUT ME OFF?!
FWAH
OH. DUH. HE USED TO DO HERO WORK IN THIS AREA.
SO HE'S GOT NO PROBLEM DIVING INTO THESE ALLEYS.
MY SHORT-CUTS AREN'T SO SECRET!

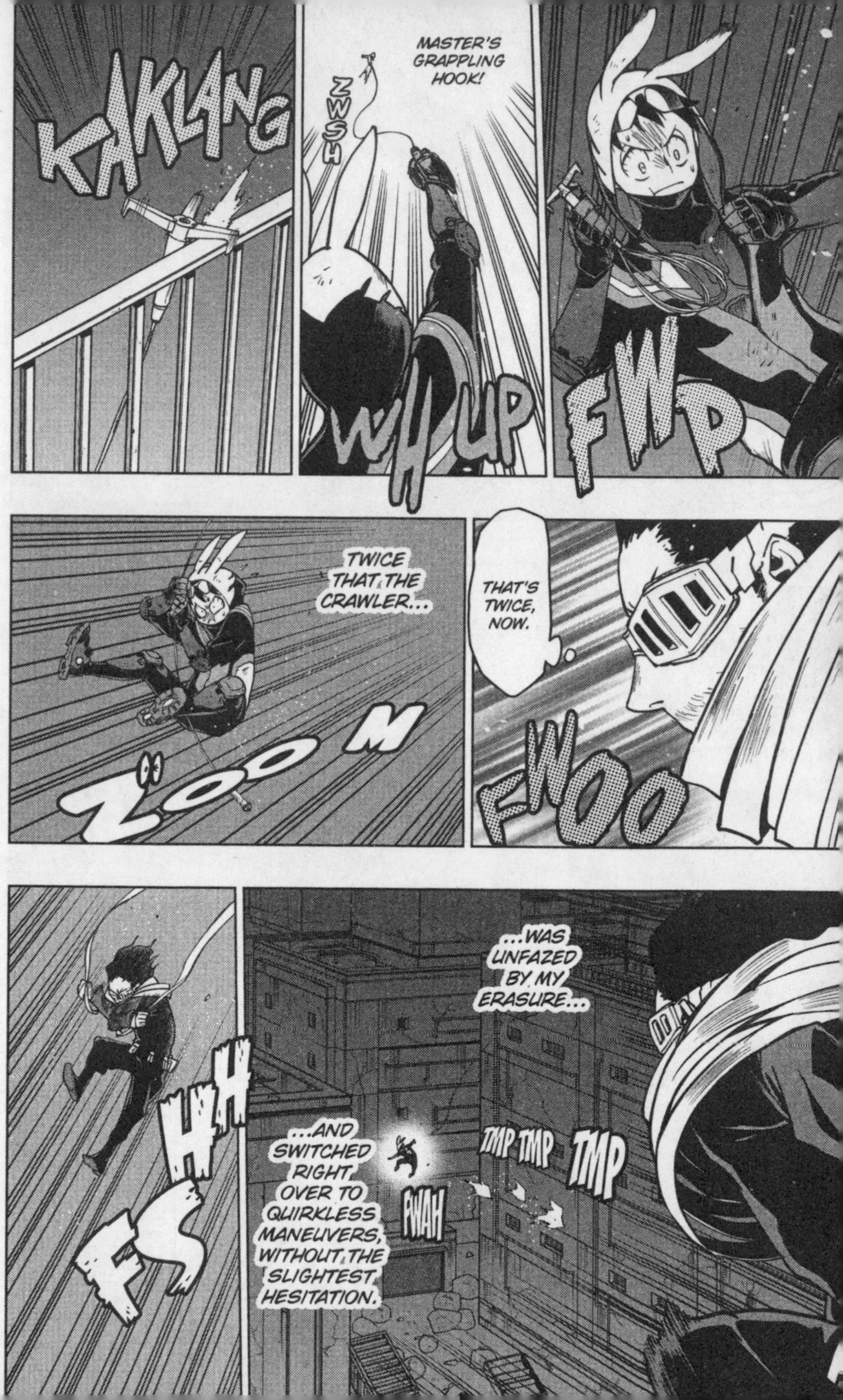
FWP
MASTER'S GRAPPLING HOOK!
ZWSH
WHUP
KAKLANG
THAT'S TWICE, NOW.
FWOO
TWICE THAT THE CRAWLER...
ZOOM
...WAS UNFAZED BY MY ERASURE...
...AND SWITCHED RIGHT OVER TO QUIRKLESS MANEUVERS, WITHOUT THE SLIGHTEST HESITATION.
TMP TMP TMP
PWAH
FSHH

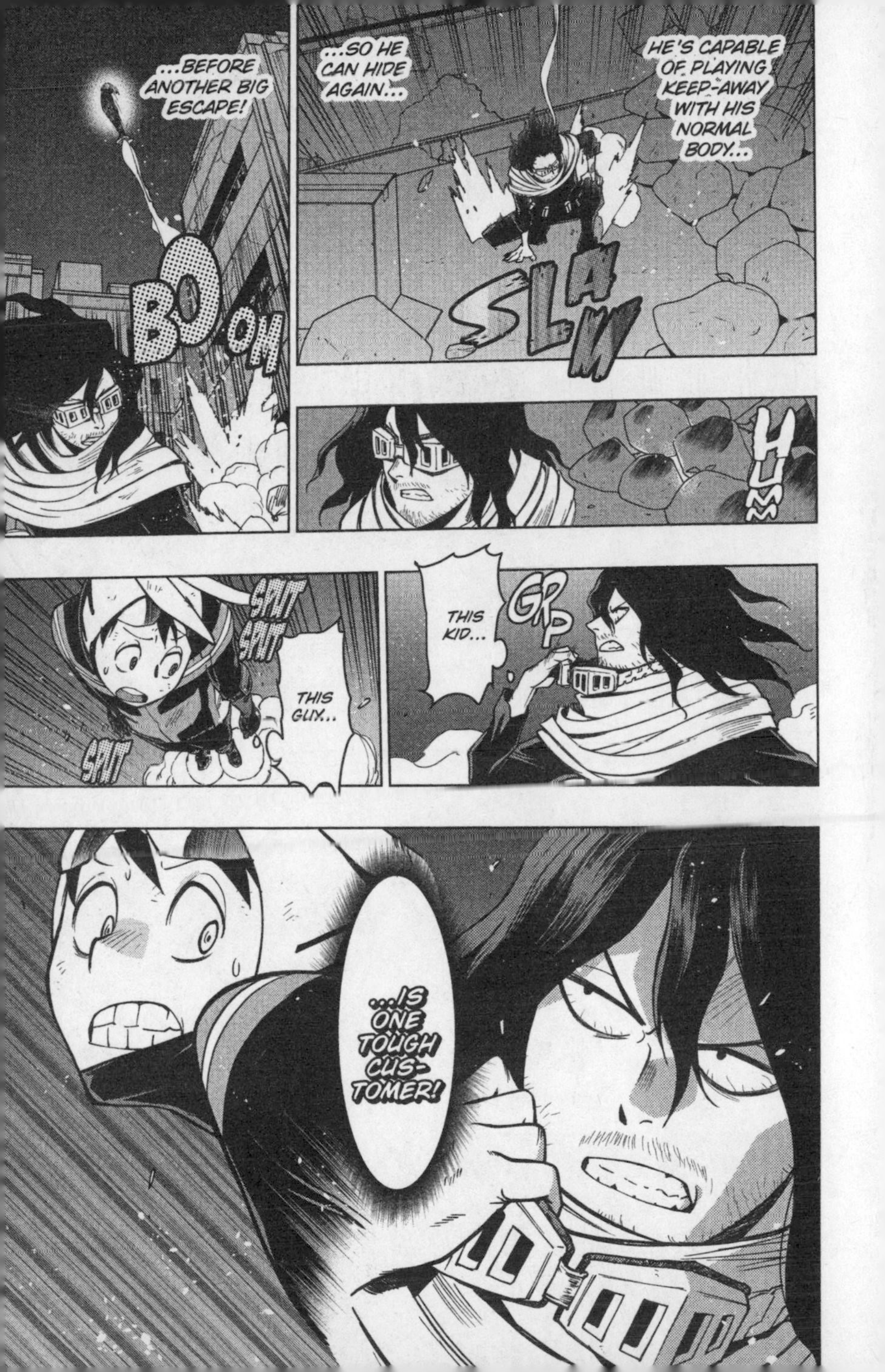
HE'S CAPABLE OF PLAYING KEEP-AWAY WITH HIS NORMAL BODY...
...SO HE CAN HIDE AGAIN...
SLAM
HUM
...BEFORE ANOTHER BIG ESCAPE!
BOOOM
GRP
THIS KID...
SPIT SPIT
THIS GUY...
SPIT
...IS ONE TOUGH CUS-TOMER!

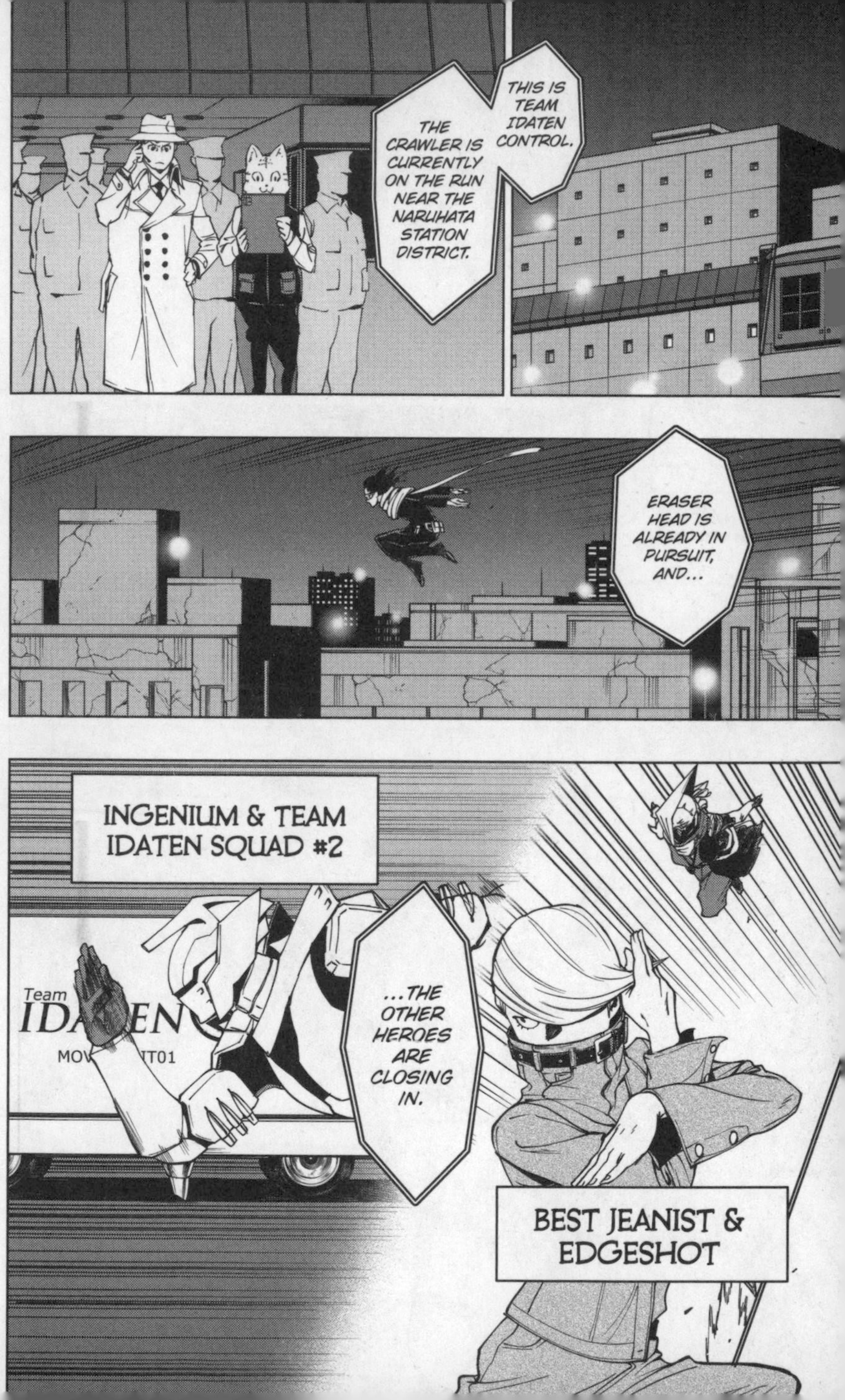
THIS IS TEAM IDATEN CONTROL.
THE CRAWLER IS CURRENTLY ON THE RUN NEAR THE NARUHATA STATION DISTRICT.
ERASER HEAD IS ALREADY IN PURSUIT, AND...
INGENIUM & TEAM IDATEN SQUAD #2
...THE OTHER HEROES ARE CLOSING IN.
BEST JEANIST & EDGESHOT

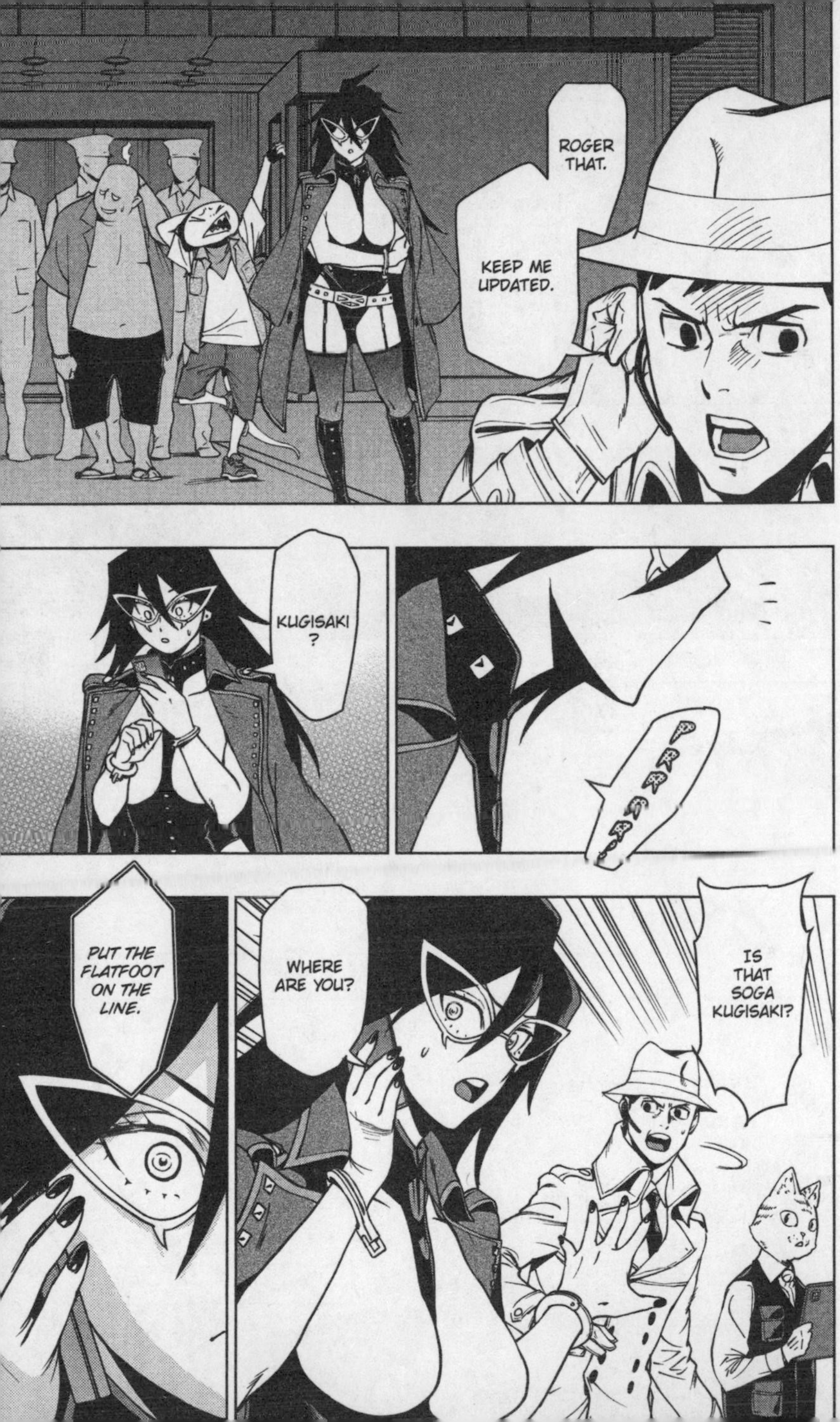
ROGER THAT.
KEEP ME UPDATED.
KUGISAKI ?
IS THAT SOGA KUGISAKI?
WHERE ARE YOU?
PUT THE FLATFOOT ON THE LINE.

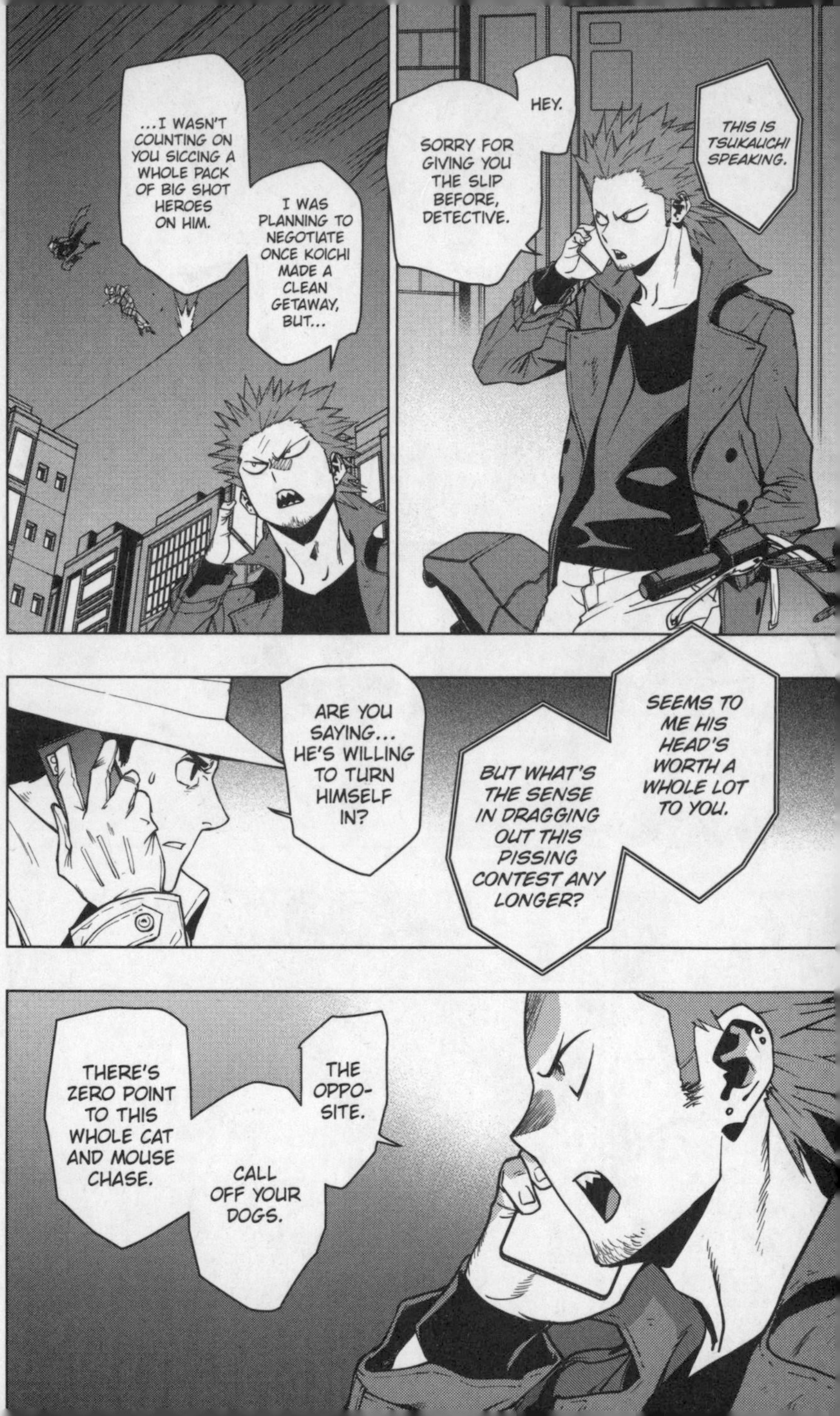
THIS IS TSUKAUCHI SPEAKING.
HEY.
SORRY FOR GIVING YOU THE SLIP BEFORE, DETECTIVE.
...I WASN'T COUNTING ON YOU SICCING A WHOLE PACK OF BIG SHOT HEROES ON HIM.
I WAS PLANNING TO NEGOTIATE ONCE KOICHI MADE A CLEAN GETAWAY, BUT...
SEEMS TO ME HIS HEAD'S WORTH A WHOLE LOT TO YOU.
BUT WHAT'S THE SENSE IN DRAGGING OUT THIS PISSING CONTEST ANY LONGER?
ARE YOU SAYING... HE'S WILLING TO TURN HIMSELF IN?
THE OPPO-SITE.
THERE'S ZERO POINT TO THIS WHOLE CAT AND MOUSE CHASE.
CALL OFF YOUR DOGS.

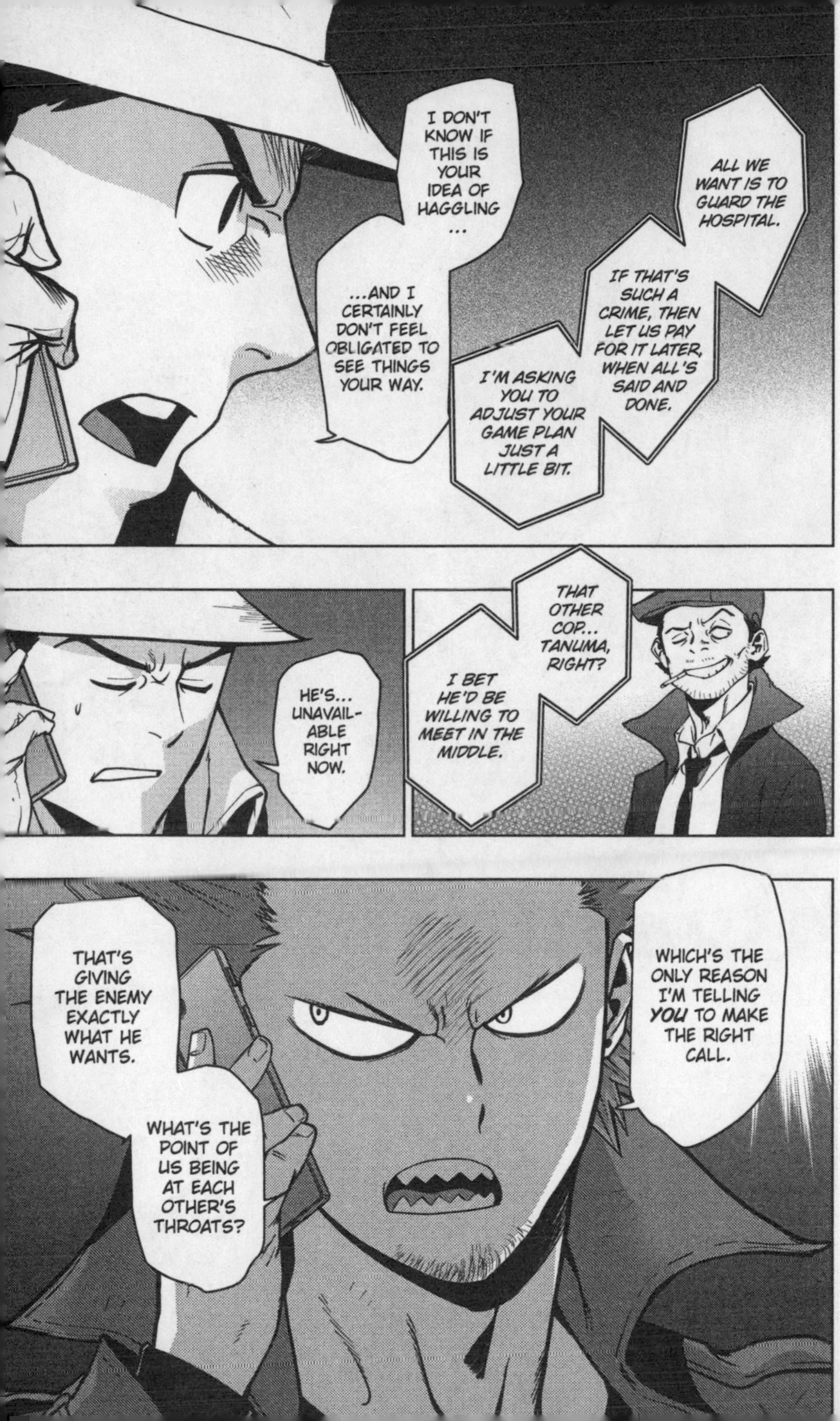
ALL WE WANT IS TO GUARD THE HOSPITAL.
IF THAT'S SUCH A CRIME, THEN LET US PAY FOR IT LATER, WHEN ALL'S SAID AND DONE.
I'M ASKING YOU TO ADJUST YOUR GAME PLAN JUST A LITTLE BIT.
I DON'T KNOW IF THIS IS YOUR IDEA OF HAGGLING...
...AND I CERTAINLY DON'T FEEL OBLIGATED TO SEE THINGS YOUR WAY.
THAT OTHER COP... TANUMA, RIGHT?
I BET HE'D BE WILLING TO MEET IN THE MIDDLE.
HE'S... UNAVAIL-ABLE RIGHT NOW.
WHICH'S THE ONLY REASON I'M TELLING YOU TO MAKE THE RIGHT CALL.
THAT'S GIVING THE ENEMY EXACTLY WHAT HE WANTS.
WHAT'S THE POINT OF US BEING AT EACH OTHER'S THROATS?

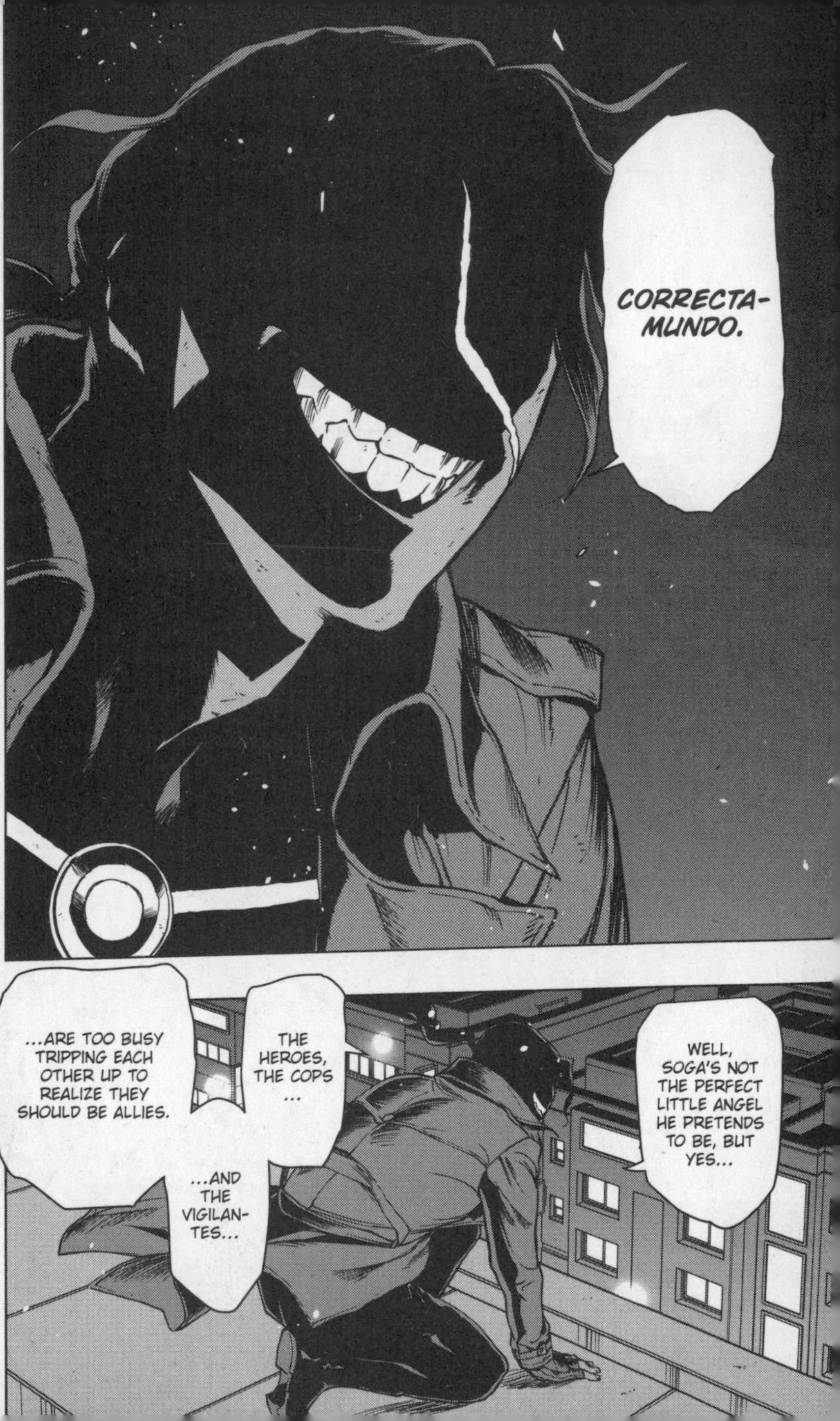
CORRECTA-MUNDO.
WELL, SOGA'S NOT THE PERFECT LITTLE ANGEL HE PRETENDS TO BE, BUT YES...
THE HEROES, THE COPS ...
...AND THE VIGILANTES...
...ARE TOO BUSY TRIPPING EACH OTHER UP TO REALIZE THEY SHOULD BE ALLIES.

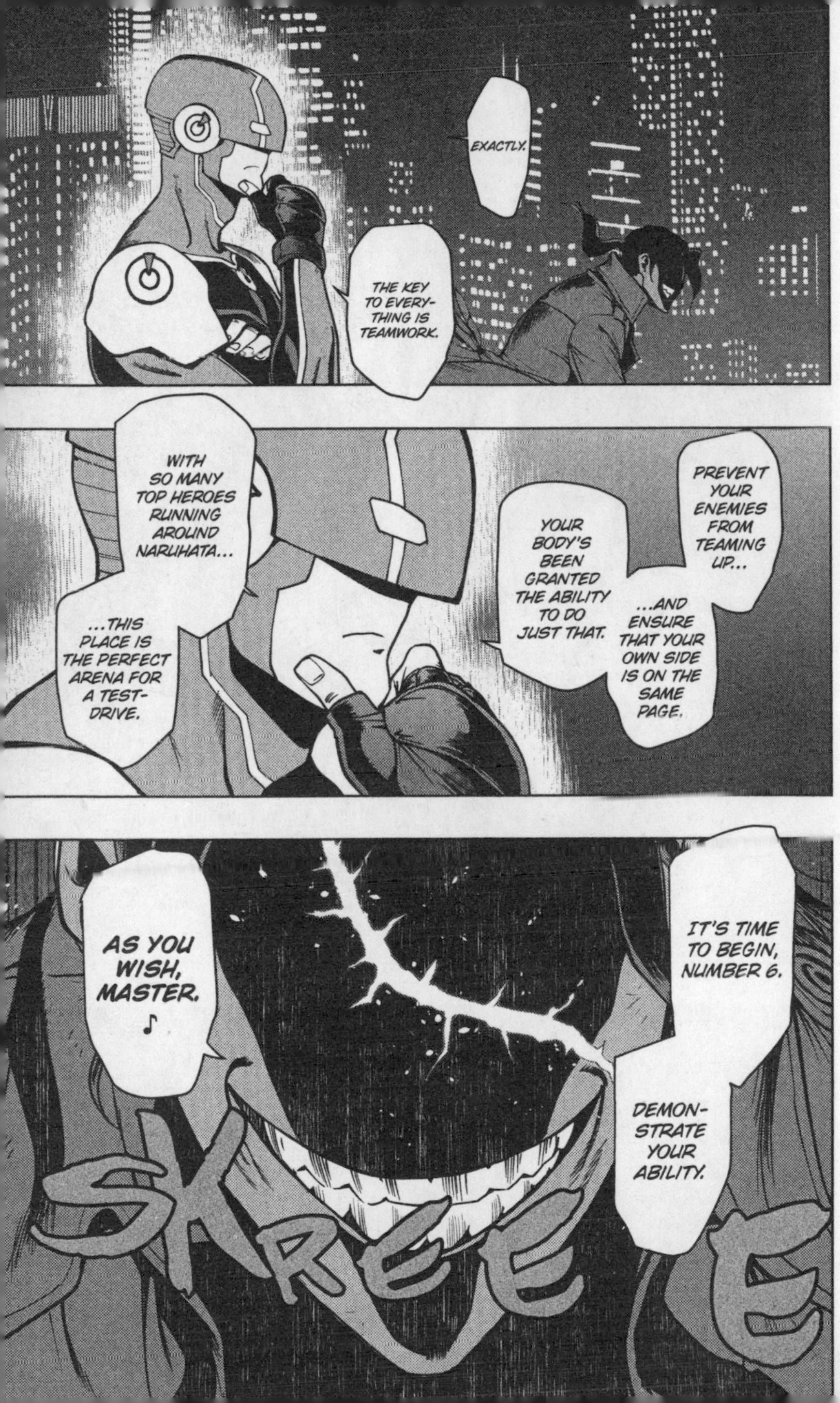
EXACTLY.
THE KEY TO EVERYTHING IS TEAMWORK.
PREVENT YOUR ENEMIES FROM TEAMING UP...
...AND ENSURE THAT YOUR OWN SIDE IS ON THE SAME PAGE.
YOUR BODY'S BEEN GRANTED THE ABILITY TO DO JUST THAT.
WITH SO MANY TOP HEROES RUNNING AROUND NARUHATA...
...THIS PLACE IS THE PERFECT ARENA FOR A TEST-DRIVE.
IT'S TIME TO BEGIN, NUMBER 6.
DEMONSTRATE YOUR ABILITY.
AS YOU WISH, MASTER. ♪
SKREEE

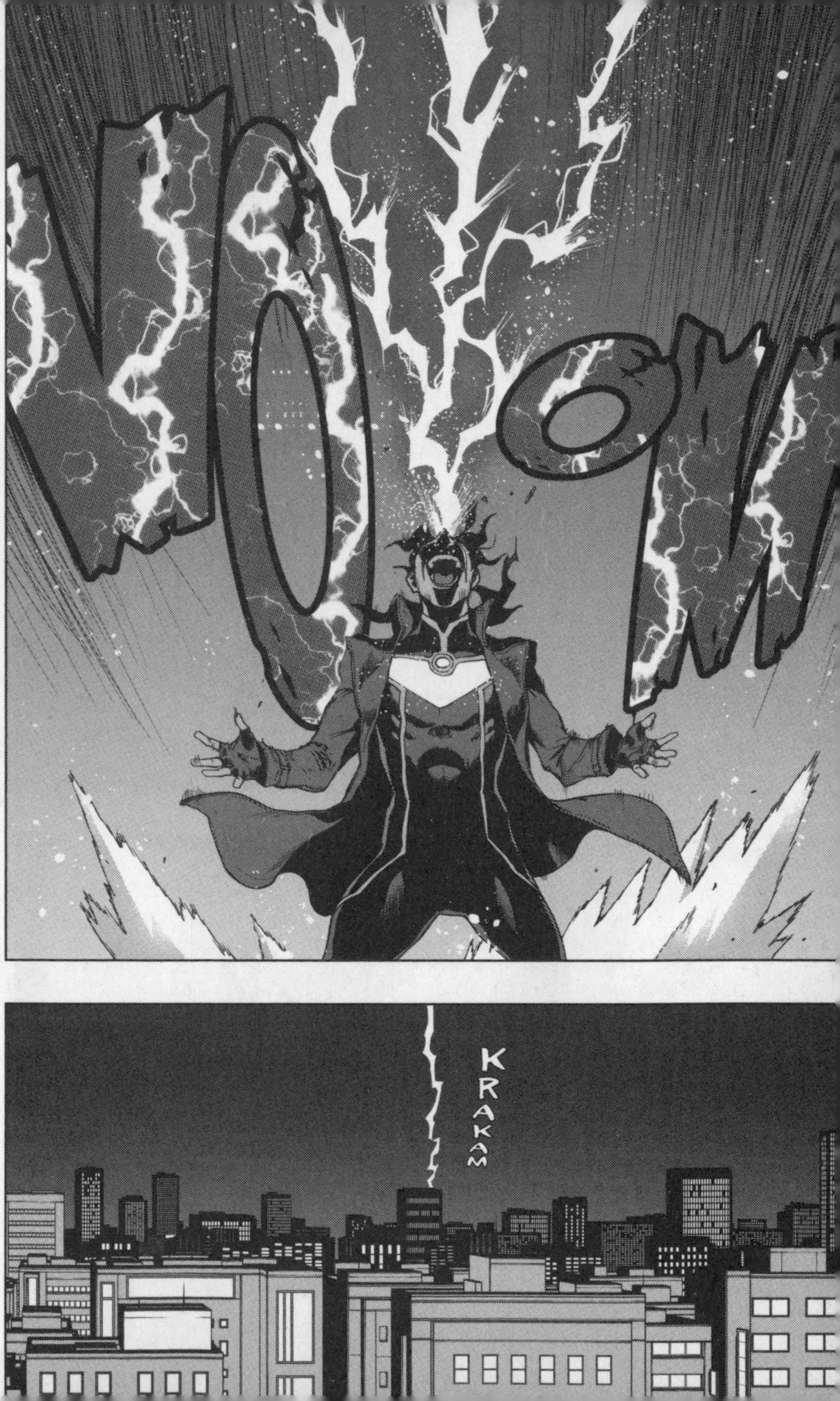
VOOM
KRAKAM

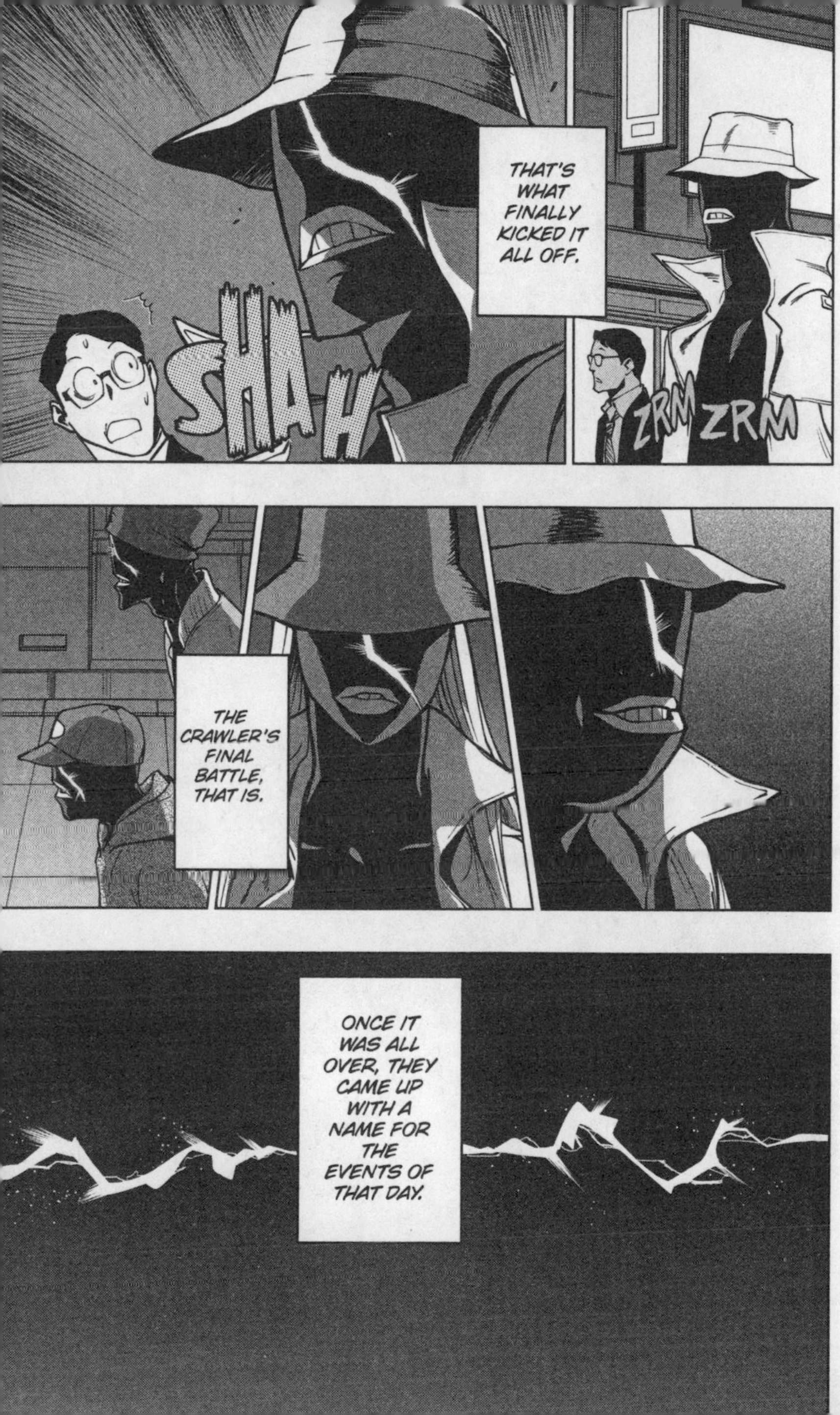
ZRM ZRM
THAT'S WHAT FINALLY KICKED IT ALL OFF.
SHAH
THE CRAWLER'S FINAL BATTLE, THAT IS.
ONCE IT WAS ALL OVER, THEY CAME UP WITH A NAME FOR THE EVENTS OF THAT DAY.

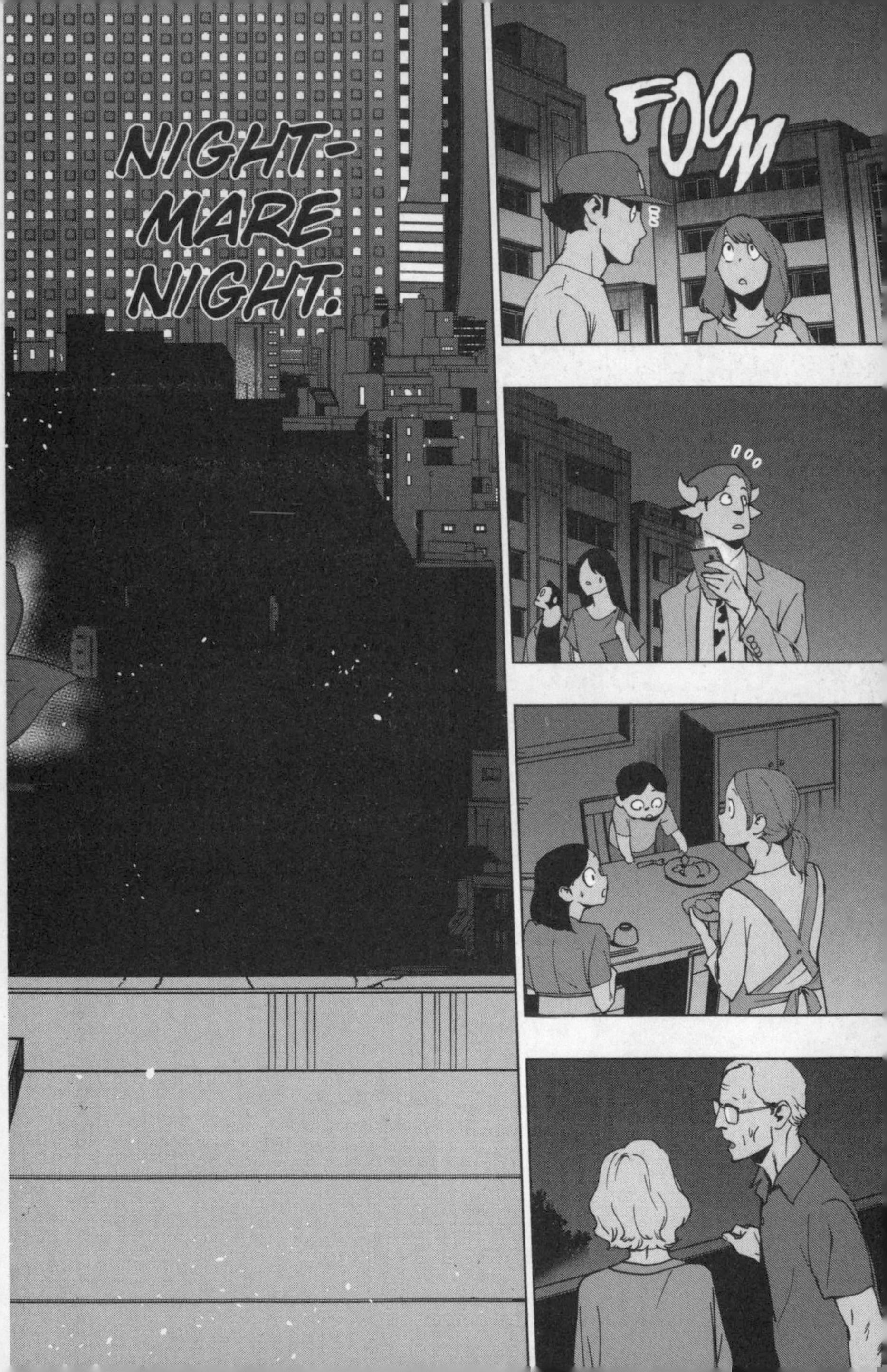
FOOM
NIGHT-MARE NIGHT.

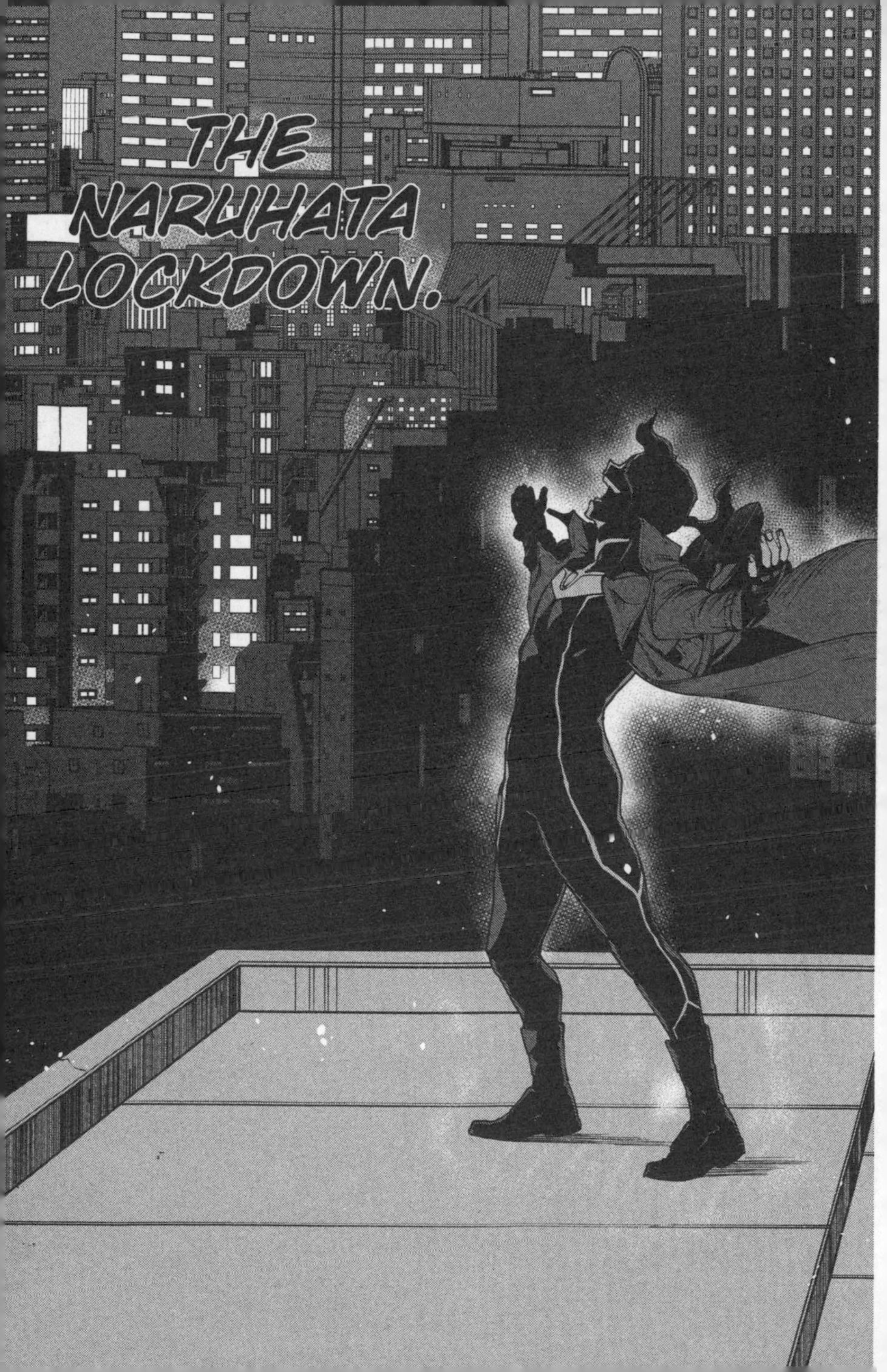
THE NARUHATA LOCKDOWN.

THE EXPLANATION

The subsequent Ep. 94.5 fills up the remaining pages in this book, and it felt like the perfect opportunity to consolidate and recap everything so far about the villainous plot and the vigilantes' heroics.

Everyone involved worked pretty hard on this.

For the good guys and bad guys alike, it's all coming to a head in this big battle. Study up before volume 13 drops!

—Furuhashi

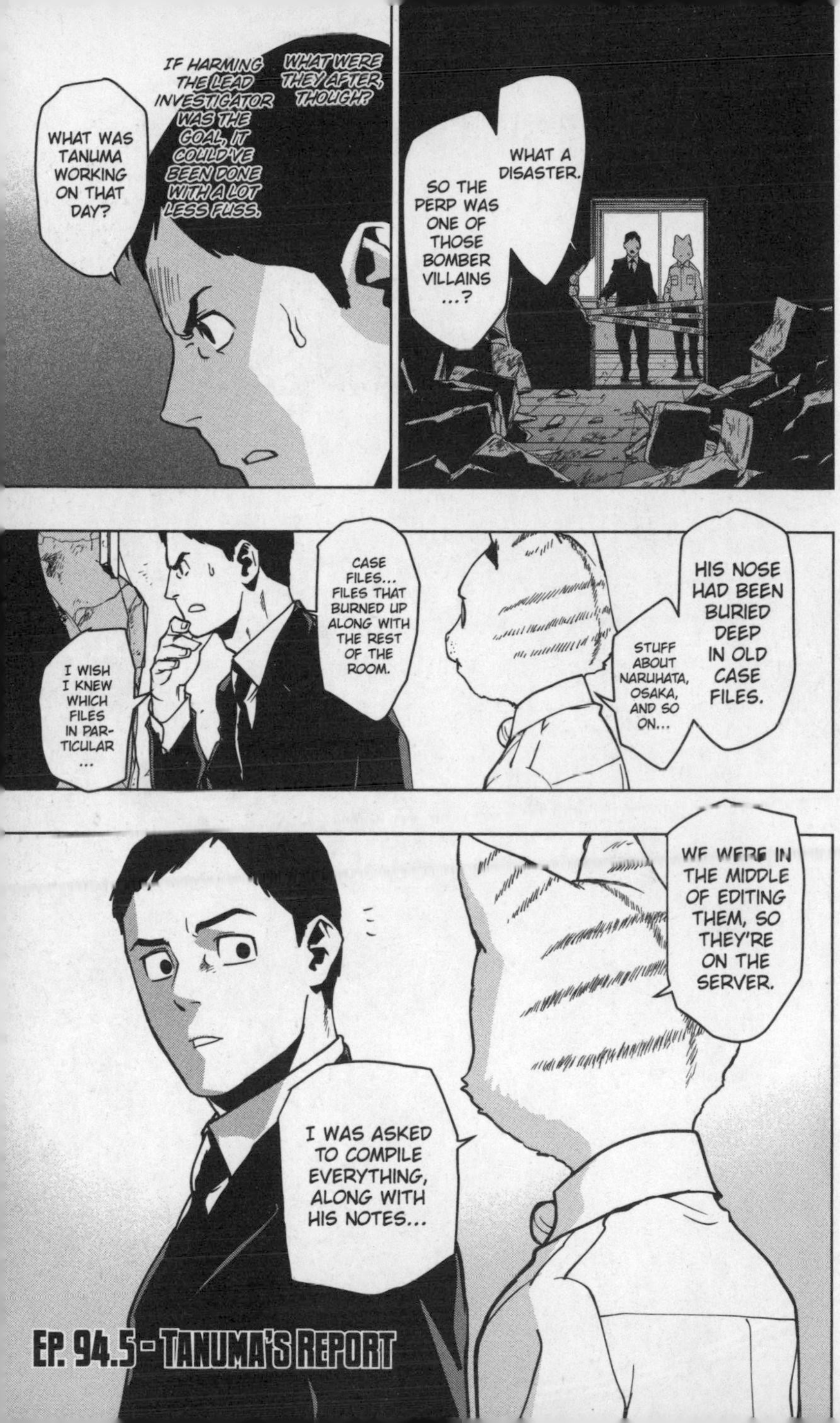
WHAT A DISASTER.
SO THE PERP WAS ONE OF THOSE BOMBER VILLAINS ...?
WHAT WERE THEY AFTER, THOUGH?
IF HARMING THE LEAD INVESTIGATOR WAS THE GOAL, IT COULD'VE BEEN DONE WITH A LOT LESS FUSS.
WHAT WAS TANUMA WORKING ON THAT DAY?
HIS NOSE HAD BEEN BURIED DEEP IN OLD CASE FILES.
STUFF ABOUT NARUHATA, OSAKA, AND SO ON...
CASE FILES... FILES THAT BURNED UP ALONG WITH THE REST OF THE ROOM.
I WISH I KNEW WHICH FILES IN PARTICULAR...
WE WERE IN THE MIDDLE OF EDITING THEM, SO THEY'RE ON THE SERVER.
I WAS ASKED TO COMPILE EVERYTHING, ALONG WITH HIS NOTES...
EP. 94.5 - TANUMA'S REPORT

EP. 94.5 - TANUMA'S REPORT

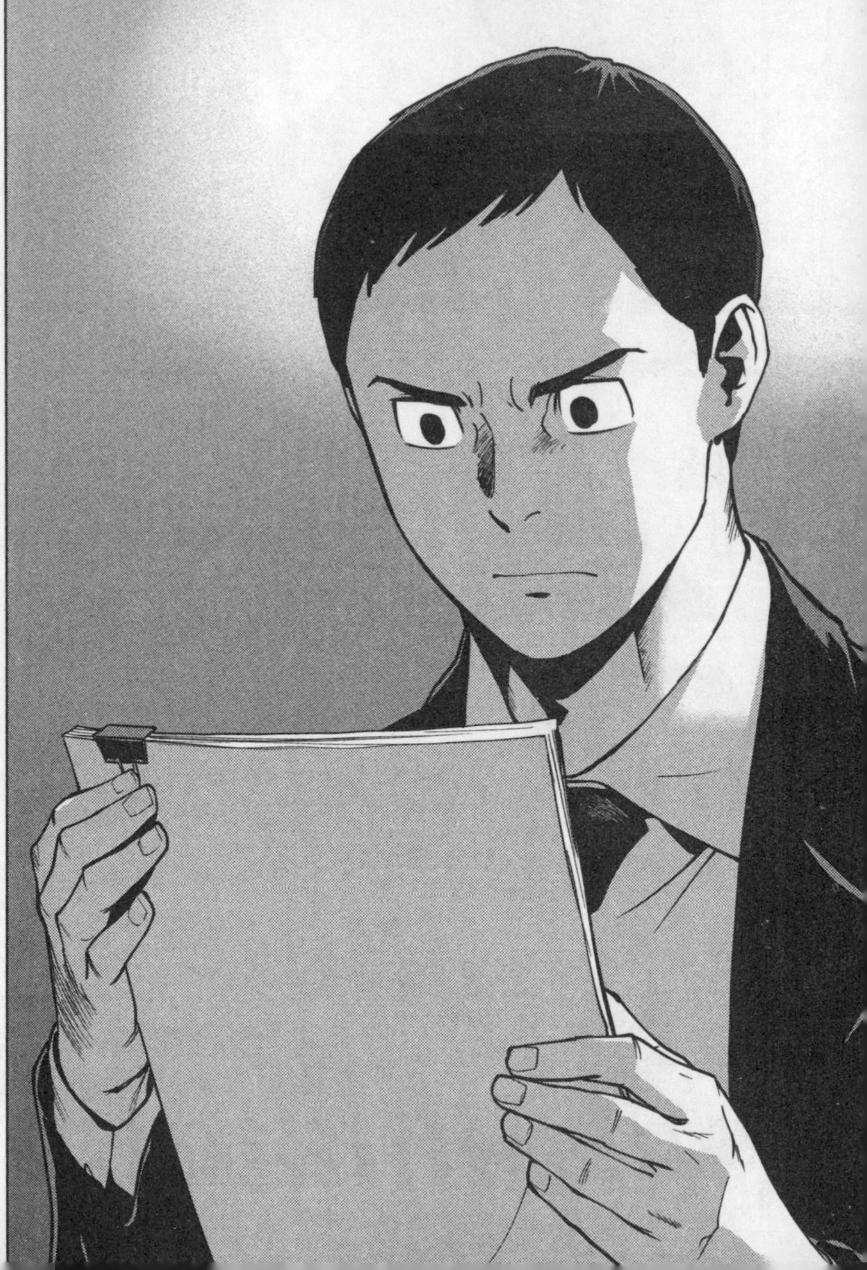

DRUG TRAFFICKING AND QUIRK RAMPAGE CASES

It all began with a new Quirk-enhancing drug called Trigger. The circulation of this drug was responsible for the rash of Quirk rampages that occurred in Naruhata between two and three years ago.

Previous investigations approached these events as localized, isolated incidents, but the investigation going forward will take a holistic approach and view them as links in a greater chain of scattered drug cases that plagued the nation in the past.

The following report compiles existing information on the villains connected to the events in Naruhata, in more or less chronological order.

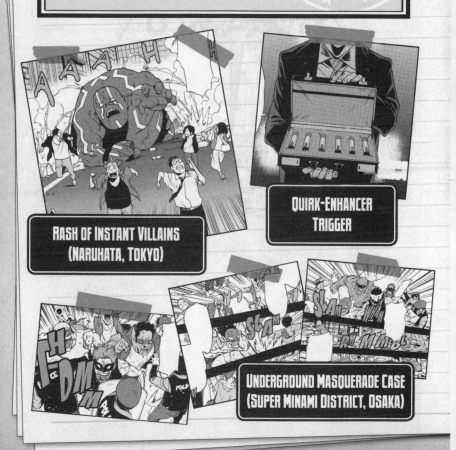

RASH OF INSTANT VILLAINS (NARUHATA, TOKYO)

QUIRK-ENHANCER TRIGGER

UNDERGROUND MASQUERADE CASE (SUPER MINAMI DISTRICT, OSAKA)

Instant Villains

"Instant villain" is the colloquial term for a person charged with Quirk-related crimes who has no previous offenses on record. These individuals do not meet the legal standards to be deemed typical villains.

Many exhibited abrupt and powerful manifestations of their Quirks via the Quirk-enhancing drug Trigger and were indistinguishable from law-abiding citizens beforehand. They also became agitated and confused when drugged. Few committed crimes that were in any way premeditated.

Charges were typically dropped in the aftermath, and these individuals were then regarded as victims within the greater drug case.

AKIRA IWAKO

QUIRK: HARDENING
CHARGES:
ASSAULT
PROPERTY DAMAGE
USE OF A CONTROLLED SUBSTANCE
QUIRK ABUSE
STATUS: DECEASED

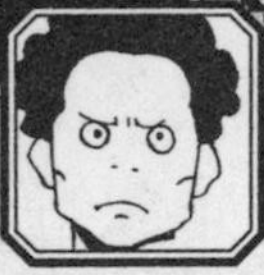

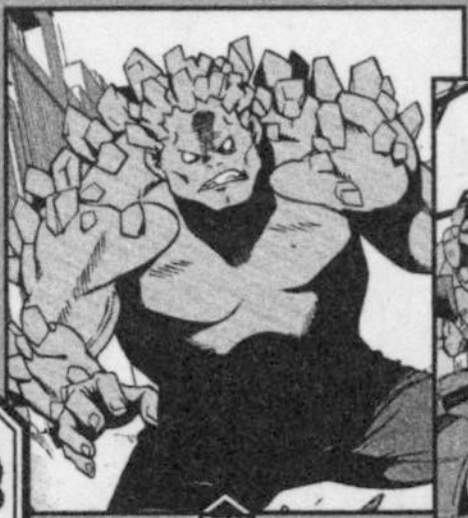

FIRST OFFENSE

REPEAT OFFENSE

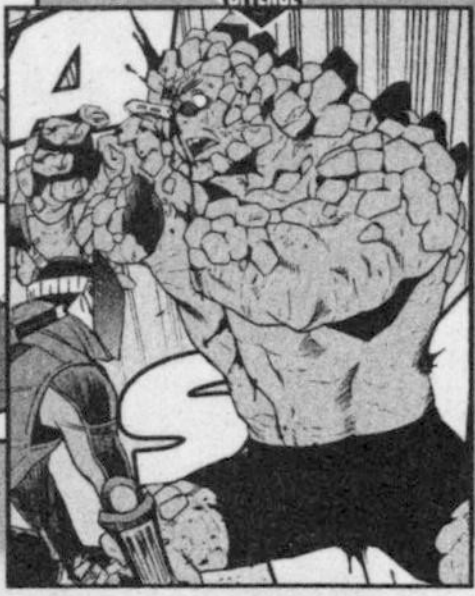

CHUMA YAKUMARU

QUIRK: BRUISER
CHARGES:
ASSAULT
PROPERTY DAMAGE
USE OF A CONTROLLED SUBSTANCE
QUIRK ABUSE
STATUS: INCARCERATED

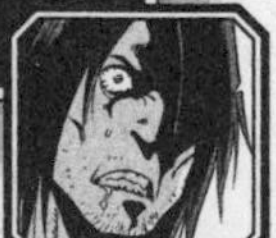

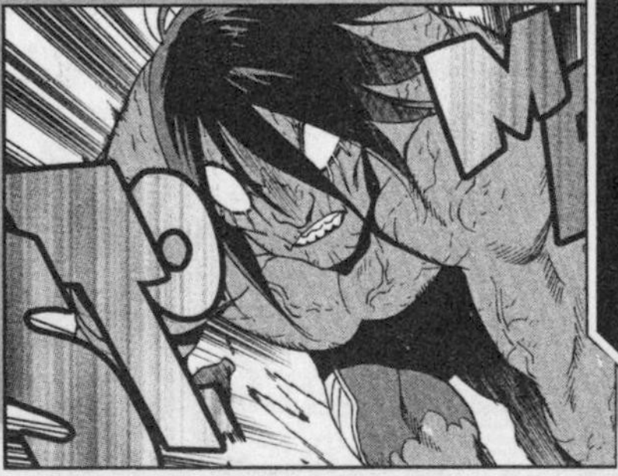

SOGA KUGISAKI

QUIRK: SPIKE
CHARGES:
ASSAULT
PROPERTY DAMAGE
USE OF A CONTROLLED SUBSTANCE
QUIRK ABUSE
STATUS: REINTEGRATED

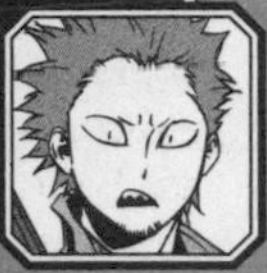

FIRST OFFENSE

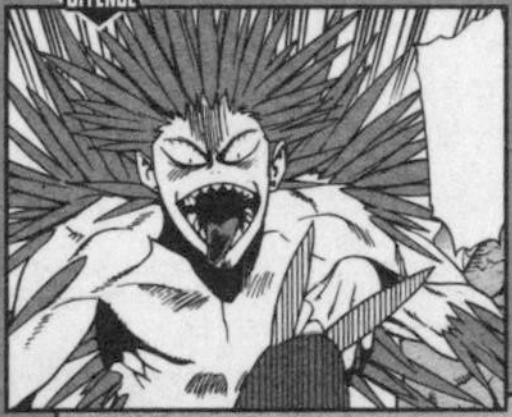

REPEAT OFFENSE

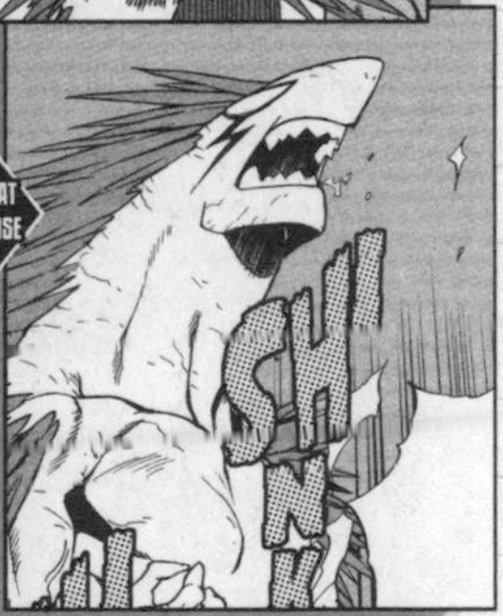
SHIN

RAPT TOKAGE

QUIRK: LIZARD
CHARGES:
ASSAULT
PROPERTY DAMAGE
USE OF A CONTROLLED SUBSTANCE
QUIRK ABUSE
STATUS: REINTEGRATED

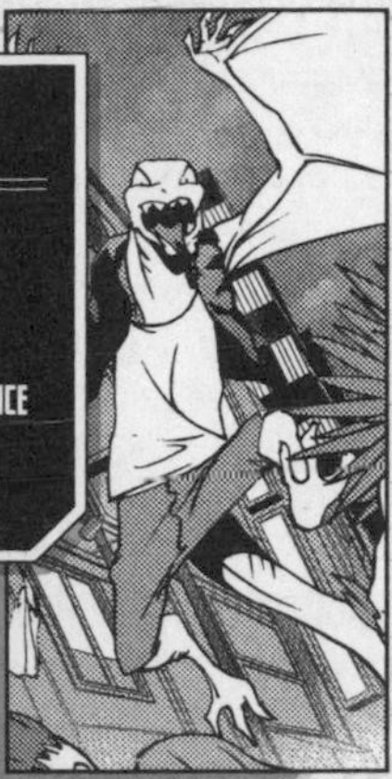

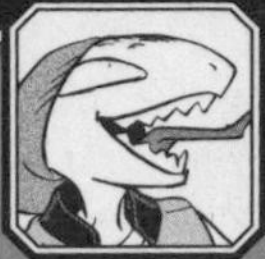

MOYURU TOCHI

QUIRK: IGNITION
CHARGES:
ASSAULT
PROPERTY DAMAGE
USE OF A CONTROLLED SUBSTANCE
QUIRK ABUSE
STATUS: REINTEGRATED

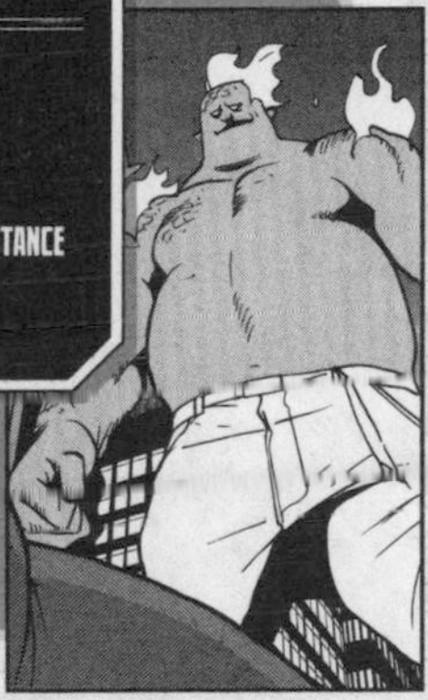

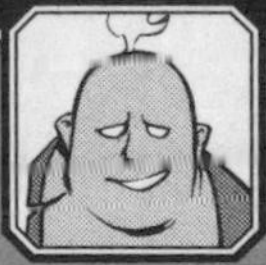

HOTTA BROTHERS

QUIRK: GRASSHOPPER (BOTH)
CHARGES:
TIES TO STOLEN PROPERTY
QUIRK ABUSE
STATUS: NEVER PROSECUTED

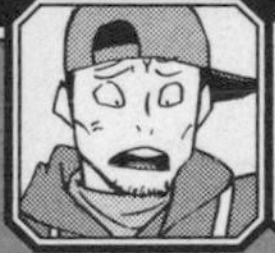

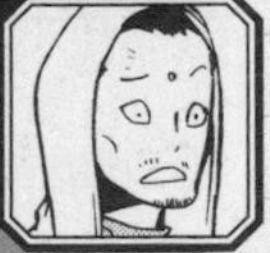

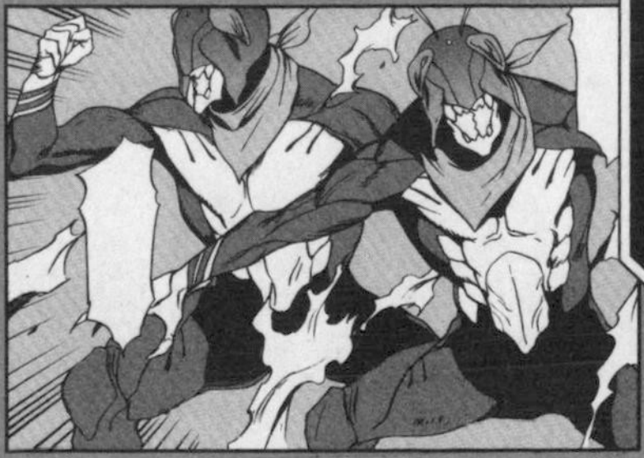

Supermassive Villains

Some among the instant villains manifested extreme versions of their gigantification Quirks and proceeded to rampage.

Taking into consideration the property damage caused in urban areas, these incidents rose beyond crimes to the level of bona fide disasters. Responses employing standard law enforcement tactics and ordinary heroes typically proved to be insufficient.

Several of the incidents that took place in Naruhata were resolved by pro hero Eraser Head (with his Quirk-nullifying Quirk) and the powerful American hero Captain Celebrity. Nevertheless, the neighborhood experienced significant damage to its infrastructure.

MARIO KUGUTSU

QUIRK: PLAYTIME
CHARGES:
PROPERTY DESTRUCTION, DISTRIBUTION OF A CONTROLLED SUBSTANCE, USE OF A CONTROLLED SUBSTANCE, QUIRK ABUSE
STATUS: INCARCERATED

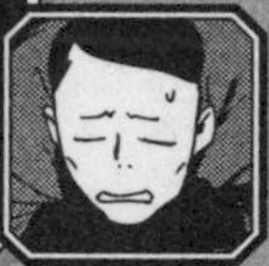

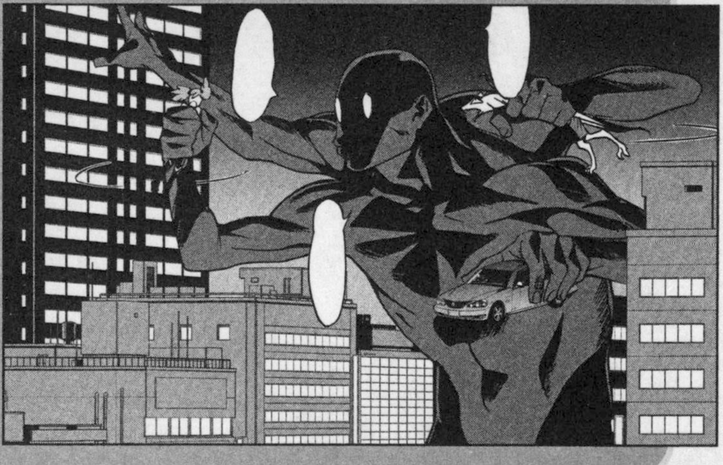

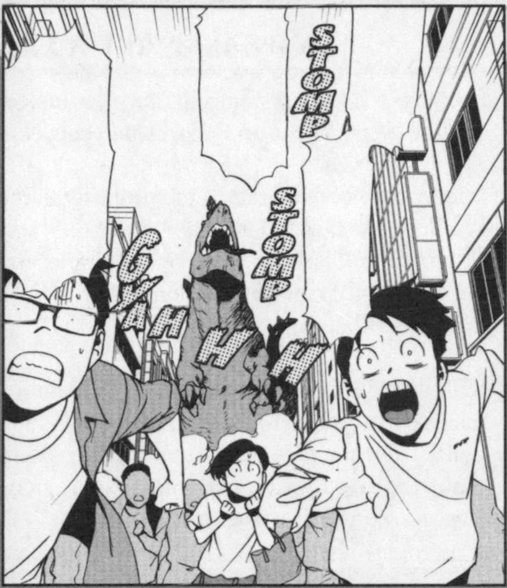
STOMP
STOMP
GYAHHHH

Ryuichi Gojiyama

Quirk: Kaiju
Charges:
Property destruction
Use of a controlled substance
Quirk abuse
Status: Reintegrated

NO IMAGE

Rikiya Eno

Quirk: Big Monkey
Charges:
Property destruction
Use of a controlled substance
Quirk abuse
Status: Reintegrated

NO IMAGE

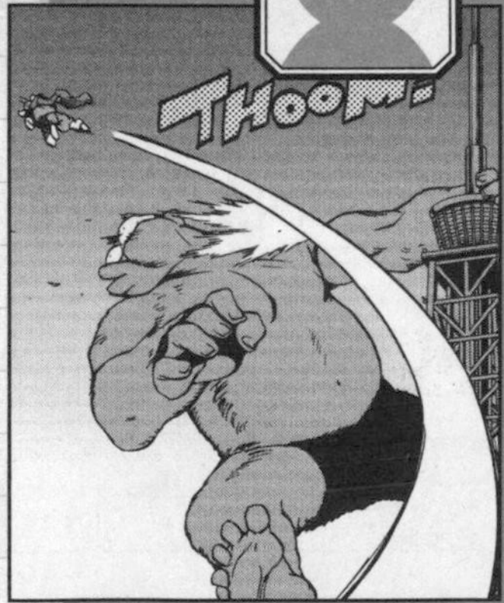
THOOM!

Eiji Okameda

Quirk: Gigantic Spinning Flying Turtle
Charges:
Property destruction
Use of a controlled substance
Quirk abuse
Status: Reintegrated

NO IMAGE

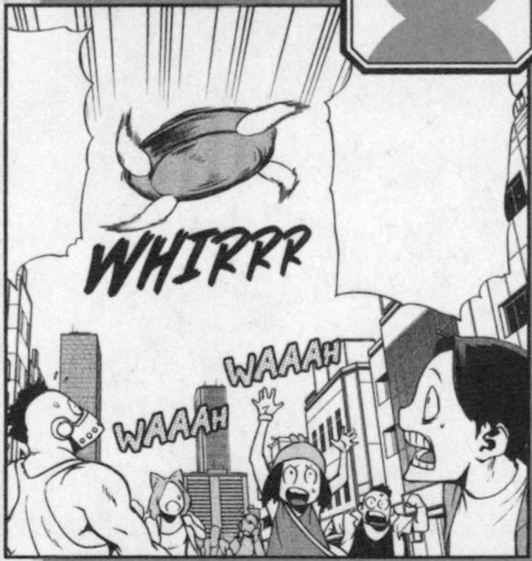
WHIRRR
WAAAH
WAAAH

Remodeled Villains

A more specialized breed of instant villain that began appearing when the initial rash of Quirk rampage cases in Naruhata began to abate.

These individuals exhibit large bodies and emphasized traits of their Quirks. These changes did not come about naturally, however, but were the result of a physical remodeling process performed on each subject over a period of several months (during which each was missing).

When the remodeled villains appeared, they had been given a large dose of the Quirk-enhancing drug, making them stronger and more violent than the average villain.

Individuals had no memories from the time of their remodeling up through their respective rampages, so most were treated as victims and rehabilitated in the aftermath. But the drastic and lasting physical transformations presented many with difficulties integrating back into society.

Teruo Unagisawa

QUIRK: EEL
CHARGES:
PROPERTY DAMAGE
USE OF A CONTROLLED SUBSTANCE
QUIRK ABUSE
STATUS: REHABILITATED

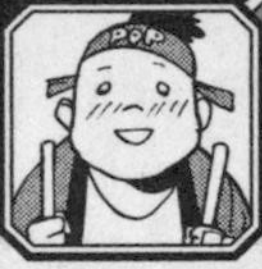

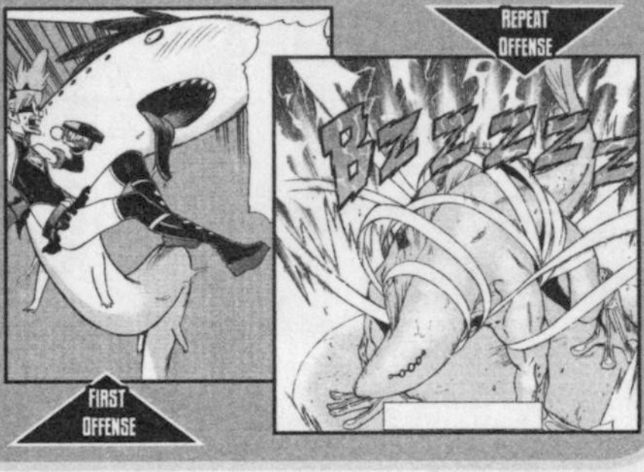
REPEAT OFFENSE
BZZZZZZ
FIRST OFFENSE

Batto Yobayakawa

QUIRK: BAT
CHARGES:
RECKLESS LOCOMOTION
USE OF A CONTROLLED SUBSTANCE
QUIRK ABUSE
STATUS: INCARCERATED

NO IMAGE

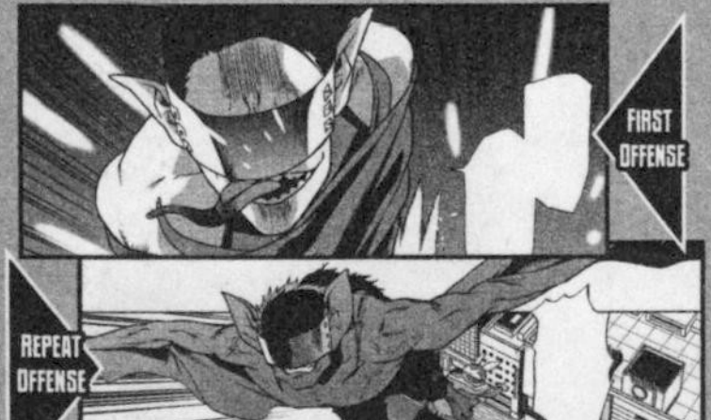
FIRST OFFENSE
REPEAT OFFENSE

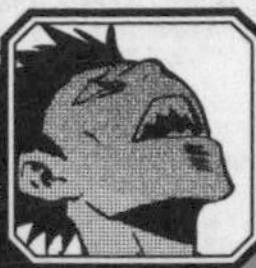

KIRIHITO KAMACHI

QUIRK: MANTIS
CHARGES:
ASSAULT
PROPERTY DAMAGE
USE OF A CONTROLLED SUBSTANCE
QUIRK ABUSE
STATUS: REHABILITATED

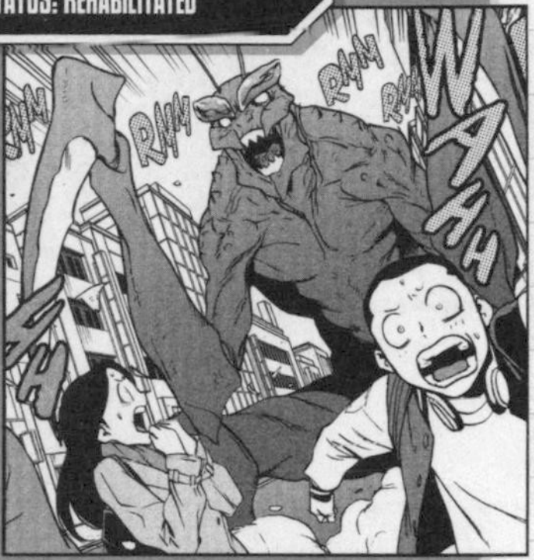
WAAHH
RMM
RMM
RMM
RMM

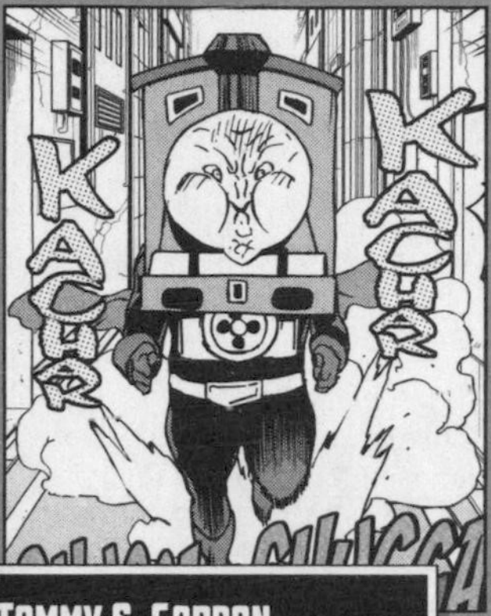
KACHR
KACHR

TOMMY S. GORDON

QUIRK: TANK ENGINE
CHARGES:
RECKLESS LOCOMOTION
USE OF A CONTROLLED SUBSTANCE
QUIRK ABUSE
STATUS: REHABILITATED

NO IMAGE

IKAJIRO TAKOBE

QUIRK: OCTOPUS (SQUID)
CHARGES:
ASSAULT
PROPERTY DAMAGE
USE OF A CONTROLLED SUBSTANCE
QUIRK ABUSE
STATUS: REHABILITATED

NO IMAGE

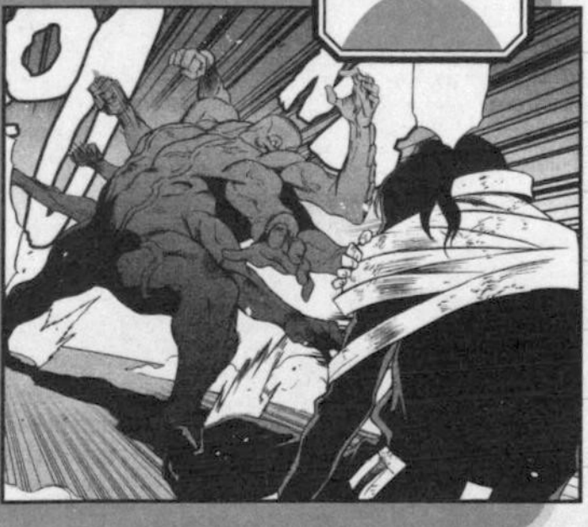

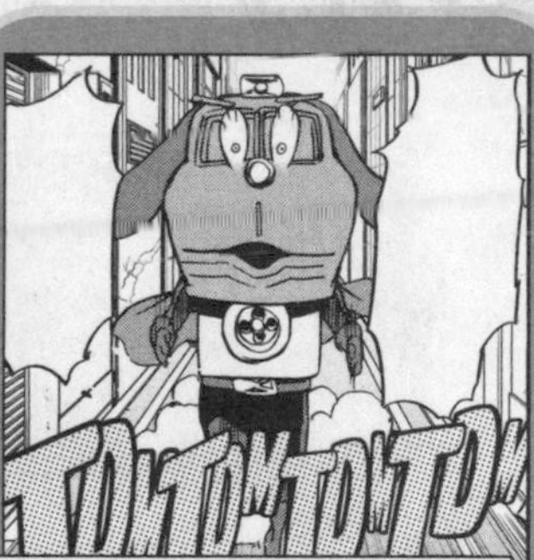

WILLY WANDA

QUIRK: DIESEL ENGINE
CHARGES:
RECKLESS LOCOMOTION
USE OF A CONTROLLED SUBSTANCE
QUIRK ABUSE
STATUS: REHABILITATED

NO IMAGE

Bomber Villains

Large villains with confirmed appearances in the Naruhata downtown area three years ago at the end of the year, and then again three months later, during the Sky Egg incident.

Dubbed "bomber villains" for convenience's sake, these entities possess Quirks enabling both flight and explosions. Individuals meeting these parameters do not exist in the official Quirk registry, so the bomber villains' identities are unknown.

These villains should be regarded as highly dangerous, as they exhibit zero sense of self-preservation and will not hesitate to perform suicide bomber attacks. Some are also capable of rapid cellular regeneration, which allows them to grow larger and perform fission.

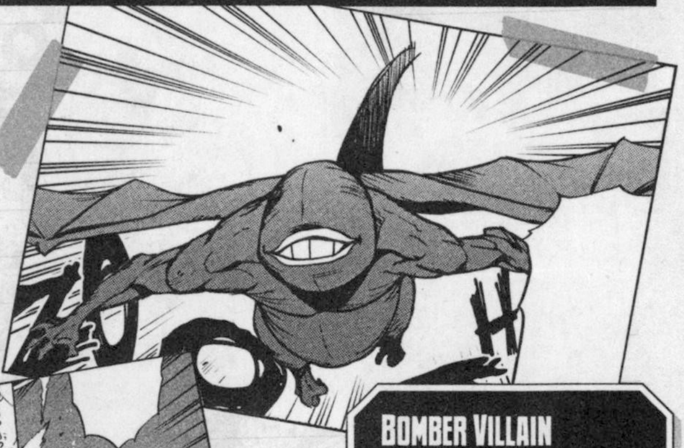

BOMBER VILLAIN

QUIRKS: FLIGHT, DETONATION
CHARACTERISTICS:
STANDARD BOMBER. FLIES TOWARD ITS TARGET AND BLOWS ITSELF UP.

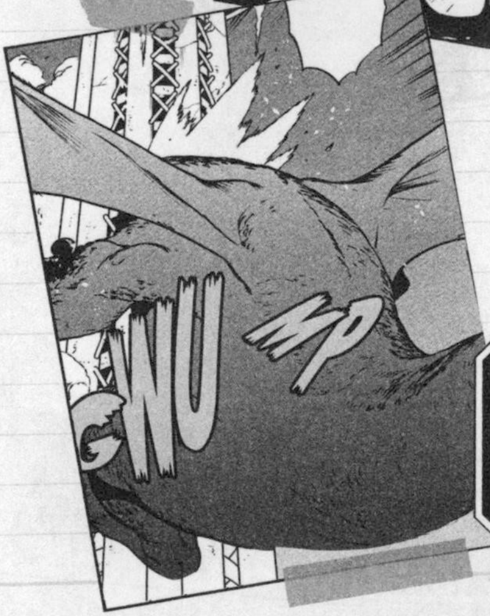
GWUMP

GIANT BOMBER

QUIRKS: FLIGHT, DETONATION
CHARACTERISTICS:
POSSESSES ASTOUNDING DESTRUCTIVE POWER, THANKS TO ITS OVERGROWN BODY.

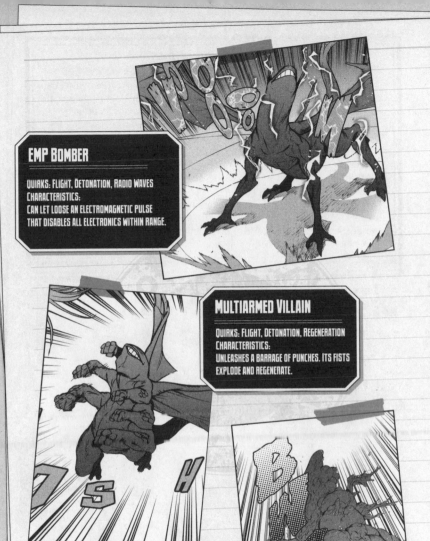

EMP BOMBER

QUIRKS: FLIGHT, DETONATION, RADIO WAVES
CHARACTERISTICS:
CAN LET LOOSE AN ELECTROMAGNETIC PULSE
THAT DISABLES ALL ELECTRONICS WITHIN RANGE.

MULTIARMED VILLAIN

QUIRKS: FLIGHT, DETONATION, REGENERATION
CHARACTERISTICS:
UNLEASHES A BARRAGE OF PUNCHES. ITS FISTS
EXPLODE AND REGENERATE.

CLUSTER BOMBER

QUIRKS: FLIGHT, DETONATION, PROPAGATION
RELEASES ABOUT 200 MINIATURE BOMBERS
FROM WITHIN ITS BODY ALL AT ONCE.

Coordinators

It is now reasonable to assume that some sort of organization is behind the continuous efforts to research and experiment with Quirk amplification, all of which led to the creation and deployment of the instant villains and supermassive villains (created via distribution of the Quirk-enhancing drug), as well as the remodeled villains and artificial villains.

Previous stages of the investigation treated the "Underground Masquerade," "Villain Factory," and others as separate cases, though it has become apparent that the full picture is not yet visible.

The inner workings of this organization are still relatively unknown, but at least two individuals are known to have had some degree of control over these ongoing, interconnected events.

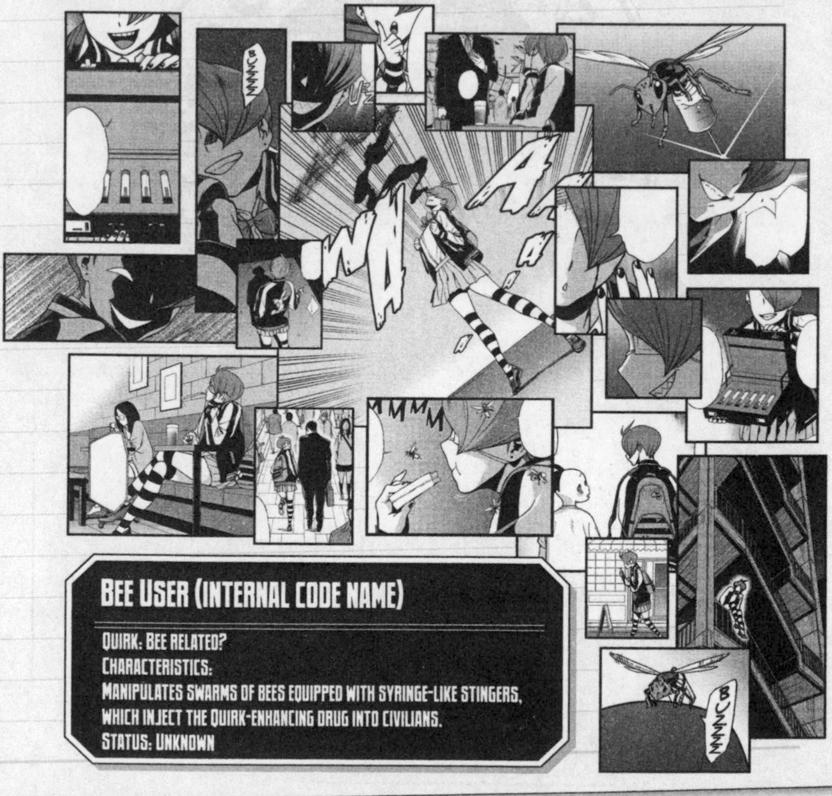
BUZZZ
BUZZZ

BEE USER (INTERNAL CODE NAME)

QUIRK: BEE RELATED?
CHARACTERISTICS:
MANIPULATES SWARMS OF BEES EQUIPPED WITH SYRINGE-LIKE STINGERS, WHICH INJECT THE QUIRK-ENHANCING DRUG INTO CIVILIANS.
STATUS: UNKNOWN

SCARRED MAN (INTERNAL CODE NAME)

QUIRK: ACCELERATION?

CHARACTERISTICS:

KNOWN TO HAVE INFILTRATED VARIOUS LOCATIONS WHILE IN DISGUISE, EITHER TO DEPLOY REMODELED VILLAINS OR TO DESTROY INCRIMINATING EVIDENCE.

STATUS: UNKNOWN

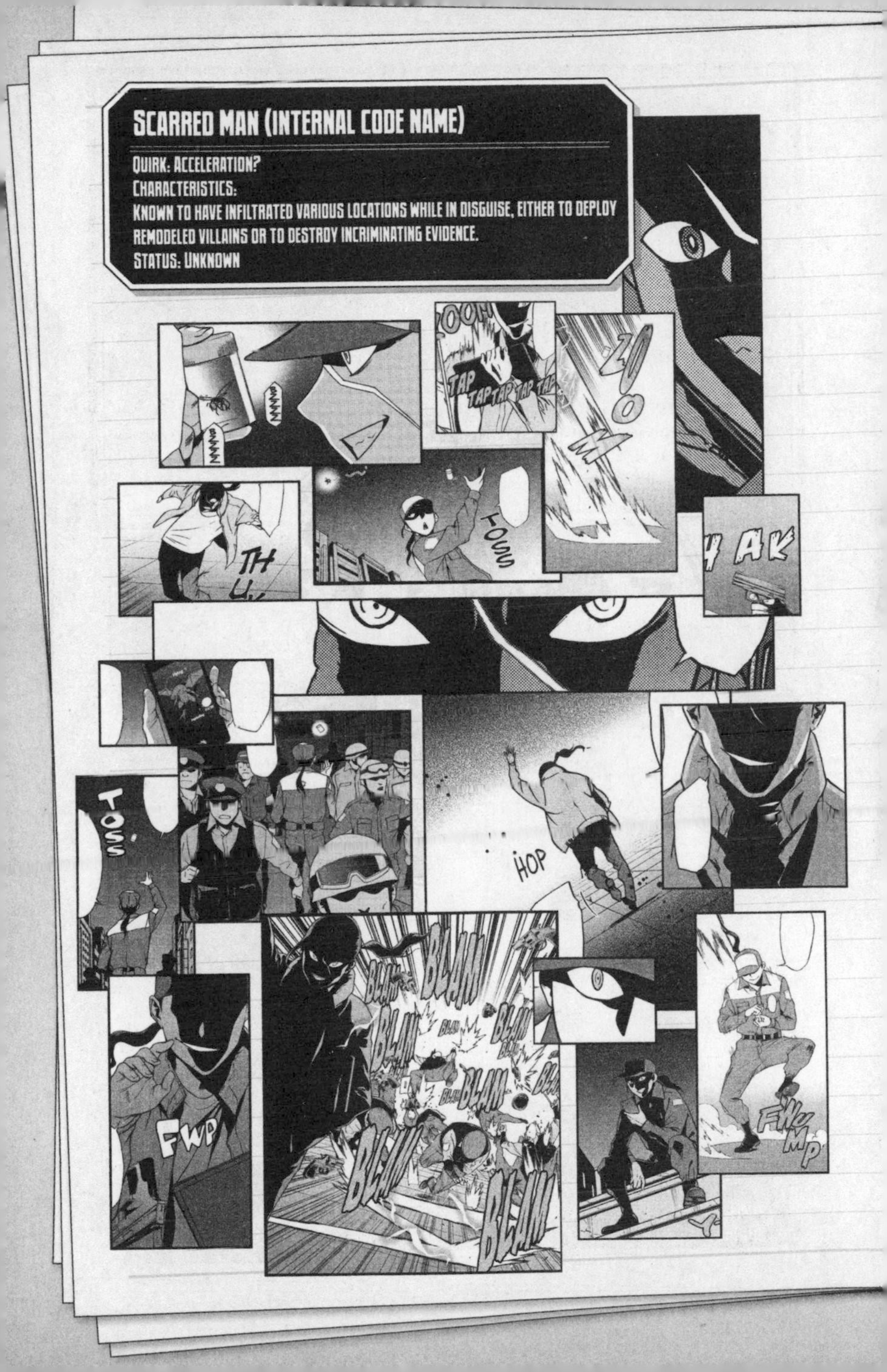
ZOOM
TAP TAP TAP TAP TAP
BZZZZ
BZZZZ
TOSS
TOSS
HOP
BLAM
BLAM
BLAM
BLAM
BLAM
BLAM
BLAM
FWUMP
FWP

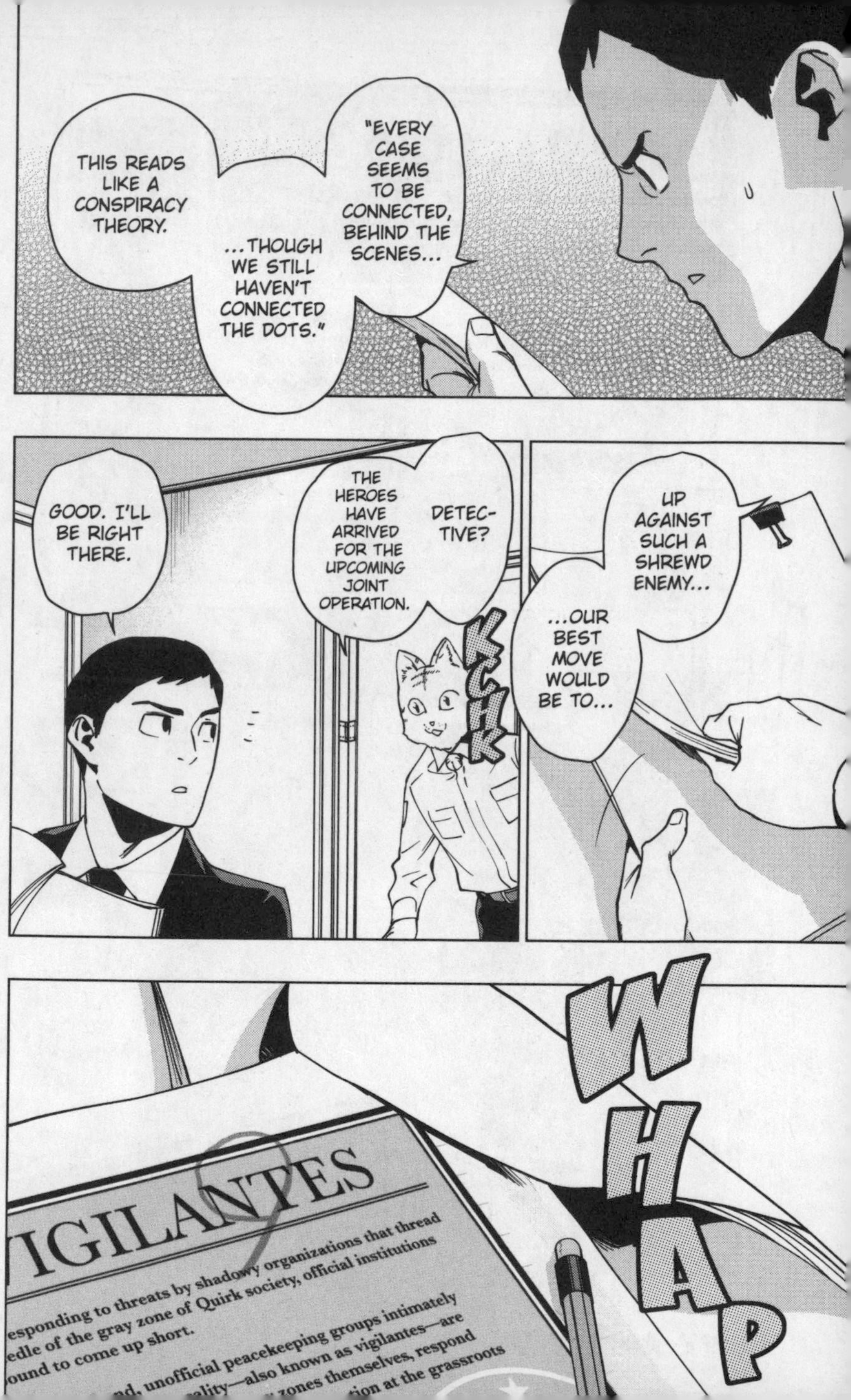
"EVERY CASE SEEMS TO BE CONNECTED, BEHIND THE SCENES...
...THOUGH WE STILL HAVEN'T CONNECTED THE DOTS."
THIS READS LIKE A CONSPIRACY THEORY.
UP AGAINST SUCH A SHREWD ENEMY...
...OUR BEST MOVE WOULD BE TO...
KCHK
DETEC-TIVE?
THE HEROES HAVE ARRIVED FOR THE UPCOMING JOINT OPERATION.
GOOD. I'LL BE RIGHT THERE.
WHAP
VIGILANTES
esponding to threats by shadowy organizations that thread
edle of the gray zone of Quirk society, official institutions
ound to come up short.
unofficial peacekeeping groups intimately
ality—also known as vigilantes—are
zones themselves, respond
tion at the grassroots

VIGILANTES

When responding to threats by shadowy organizations that thread the needle of the gray zone of Quirk society, official institutions are bound to come up short.

On the other hand, unofficial peacekeeping groups intimately familiar with a given locality—also known as vigilantes—are better able to navigate those gray zones themselves, respond quickly to incidents, and procure information at the grassroots level.

Naturally the efforts of vigilantes cannot be officially condoned, but I see their existence as a sort of necessary evil. I believe that keeping them on a generous leash while maintaining a cooperative relationship could be an effective measure against the villainous organization in question.

*"Fight fire with fire." — Note that this is not the department's official stance, of course.

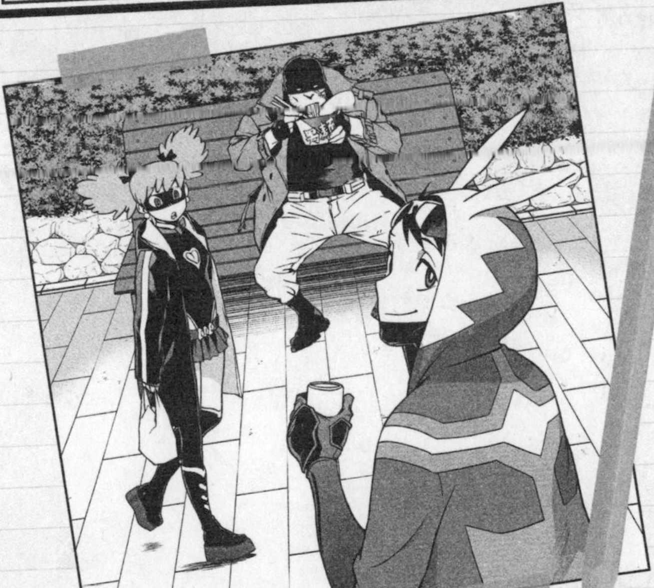

VOLUME 12 - MIGHT SIGNAL (END)

A HERO?

There are grander matters too, like what does it mean to be the ultimate hero in this particular world? What sort of person would that be? Those are questions and themes we'll leave to Deku, over in the main series. Meanwhile, one of the big themes in *Vigilantes* is what's the deal with plain-old Good Samaritans who aren't acting out of self-interest at all?

Plenty of people are motivated to act for the good of society, but the vast majority call it quits if that would involve breaking any rules or laws. Once in a while, you'll get someone who just goes for it anyway. I don't know if we should call that person a Good Samaritan or a criminal, but in any case, that's the story I've set out to tell.

Nevertheless, most rules exist for a reason, and breaking them arbitrarily is bound to lead to consequences. At this point, Pop and Koichi are currently facing the consequences of their actions.

How will they land, when it's all over? If you want to find out, please join me for the final few volumes.

—Hideyuki Furuhashi April 2021

Afterword

WHAT IS A HERO

A HERO is someone who helps people and battles evil. At least, that's the general image we have.

Strictly speaking, battling evil is usually for the good of society, so we could boil down the definition to "someone who fights for the good of people and society." Typically, we wouldn't call someone a hero if they're fighting for personal gain. However…

In the world of *MHA*, only professional heroes are recognized as heroes at all, so technically, every official hero performs heroics for personal gain. On the other hand, the series has introduced the notion that career heroes are not *true heroes*, and the public's faith in the pros is often shaken. As such, we once again have to ask ourselves how to define a hero. What is a hero's raison d'être?

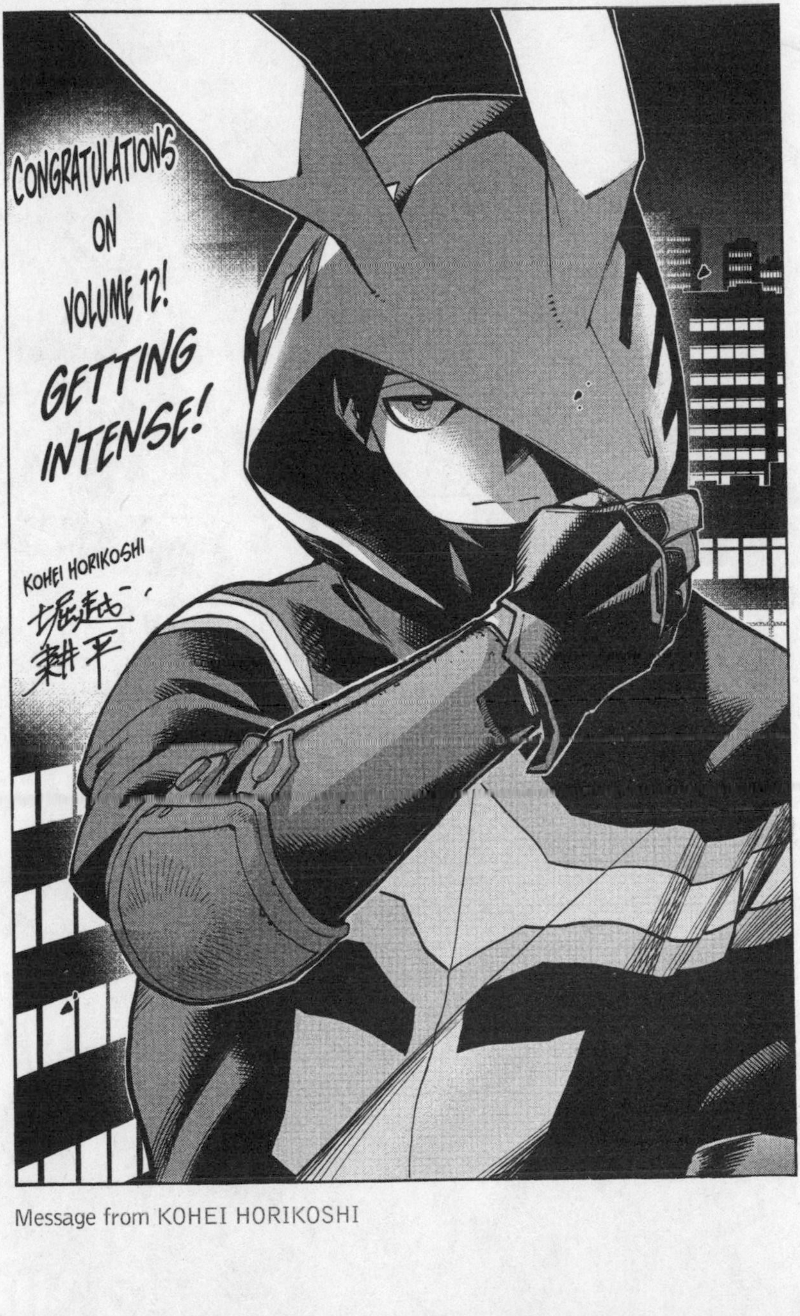
CONGRATULATIONS ON VOLUME 12! GETTING INTENSE!
KOHEI HORIKOSHI
堀越耕平

Message from KOHEI HORIKOSHI

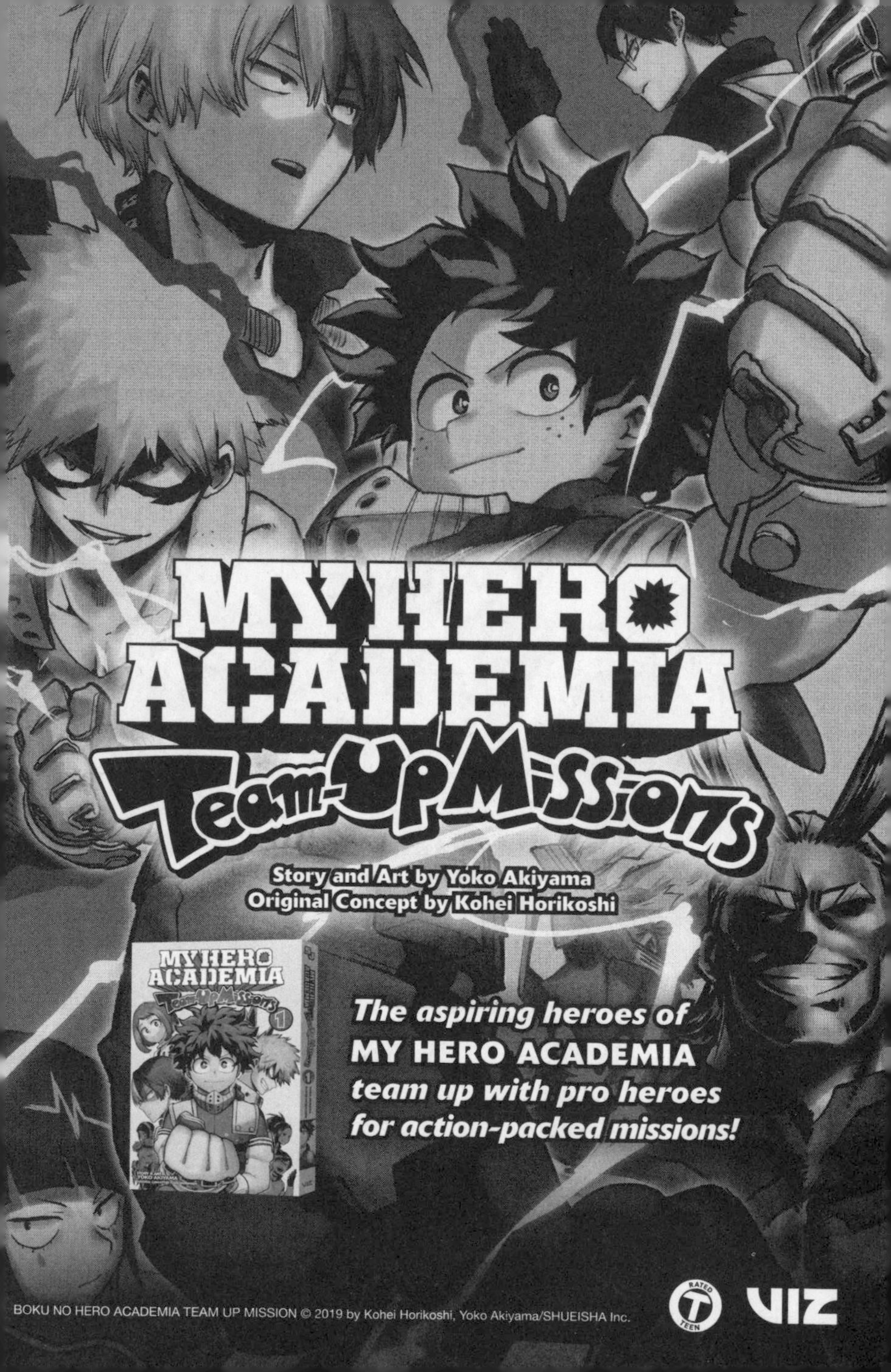
MY HERO ACADEMIA
Team-Up Missions
Story and Art by Yoko Akiyama
Original Concept by Kohei Horikoshi
MY HERO ACADEMIA
Team-Up Missions
1
The aspiring heroes of
MY HERO ACADEMIA
team up with pro heroes
for action-packed missions!
RATED T TEEN
VIZ
BOKU NO HERO ACADEMIA TEAM UP MISSION © 2019 by Kohei Horikoshi, Yoko Akiyama/SHUEISHA Inc.

MY HERO ACADEMIA

SCHOOL BRIEFS

ORIGINAL STORY BY KOHEI HORIKOSHI

WRITTEN BY ANRI YOSHI

Prose short stories featuring the everyday school lives of My Hero Academia's fan-favorite characters!

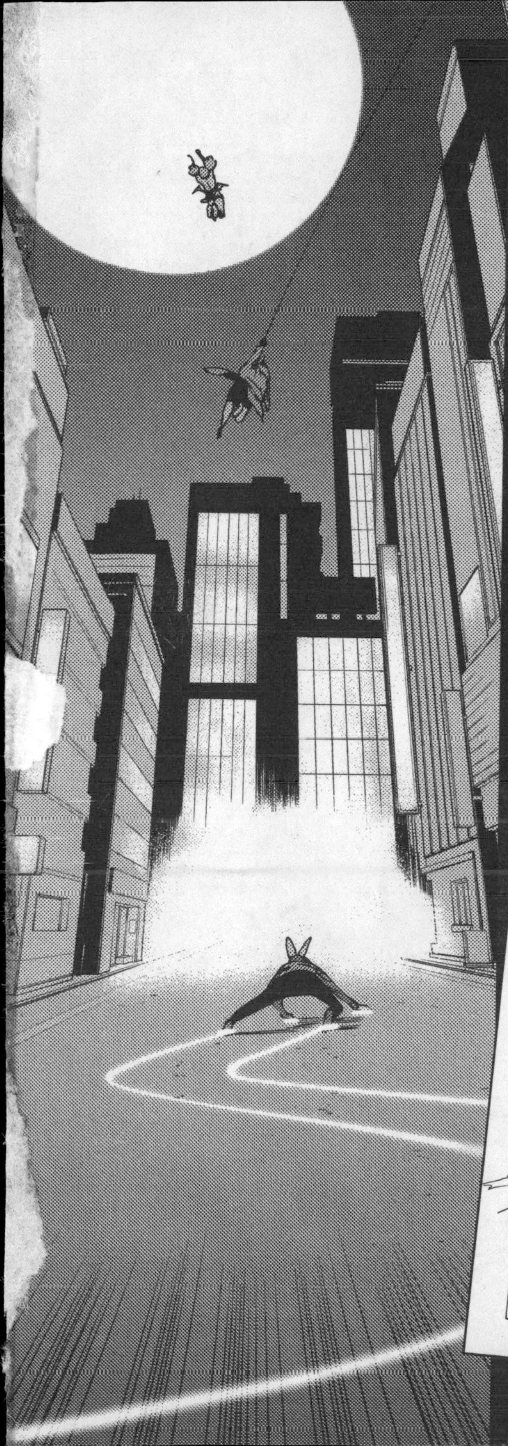

YOU'RE READING THE WRONG WAY!!

MY HERO ACADEMIA VIGILANTES

reads from right to left, starting in the upper-right corner. Japanese is read from right to left, meaning that action, sound effects, and word-balloon order are completely reversed from English order.

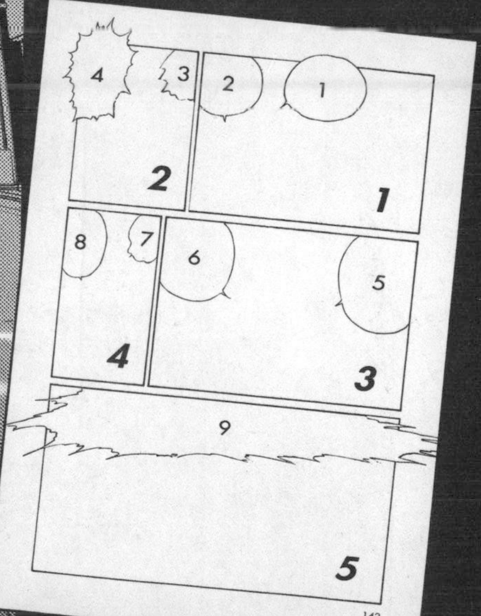

1
2
3
4
1
2
5
6
7
8
3
4
9
5
142

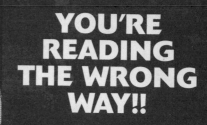

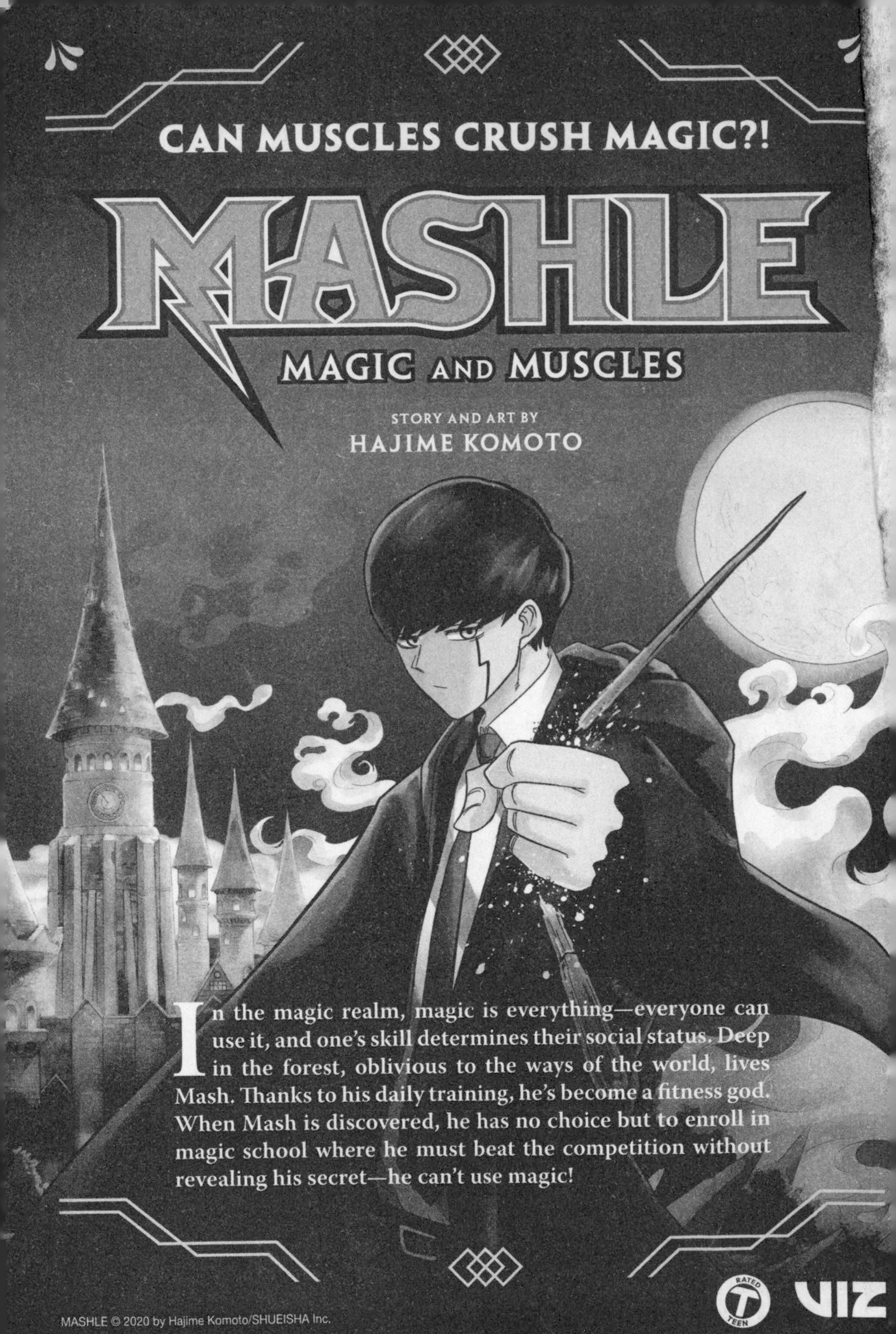
CAN MUSCLES CRUSH MAGIC?!
MASHLE
MAGIC AND MUSCLES
STORY AND ART BY
HAJIME KOMOTO
In the magic realm, magic is everything—everyone can use it, and one's skill determines their social status. Deep in the forest, oblivious to the ways of the world, lives Mash. Thanks to his daily training, he's become a fitness god. When Mash is discovered, he has no choice but to enroll in magic school where he must beat the competition without revealing his secret—he can't use magic!
RATED T TEEN
VIZ